Canon 1096 on Ignorance with Application to
Tribunal and Pastoral Practice

by
Girard M. Sherba

ISBN: 1-58112-134-2

DISSERTATION.COM

USA • 2001

Canon 1096 on Ignorance with Application to Tribunal and Pastoral Practice

Dissertation.com
USA • 2001

ISBN: 1-58112-134-2

www.dissertation.com/library/1121342a.htm

UNIVERSITE SAINT-PAUL

FACULTE DE DROIT CANONIQUE
CABINET DU DOYEN

SAINT PAUL UNIVERSITY

FACULTY OF CANON LAW
OFFICE OF THE DEAN

223 Main Ottawa ON Canada K1S 1C4
TEL. (613) 751-4035 FAX (613) 751-4036

Vidimus et approbavimus ad normam Statutorum Universitatis Sancti Pauli Ottaviensis.

Datum Ottavæ, August 8, 2001

(Msgr. Roch Pagé
Decanus

CANON 1096 ON IGNORANCE:
APPLICATION TO TRIBUNAL AND PASTORAL PRACTICE

by
Rev. Girard Michael SHERBA

A dissertation submitted to the Faculty of Canon Law, Saint Paul University, Ottawa, Canada, in partial fulfillment of the requirements for the degree of Doctor of Canon Law

Ottawa, Canada
Saint Paul University
2000

TABLE OF CONTENTS

4

ACKNOWLEDGEMENTS

I wish to express my sincere appreciation and heart-felt thanks to the following people in particular with whose support this dissertation has become a reality:

— the Most Reverend F. Joseph Gossman, Bishop of Raleigh, who allowed me to pursue this dream and who has supported me not only these past two years of doctoral studies, but throughout my priestly ministry;

— the Reverend Monsignor Roch Pagé, P.H., Dean of the Faculty of Canon Law, Saint Paul University, whose guidance and canonical insight have been a source of strength for me;

— the members of the Faculty of Canon Law, Saint Paul University: Reverend Augustine Mendonça, Vice Dean of the Faculty of Canon Law, who challenged me to focus my understanding of canon law by offering his insights, comments and emendations in order to help me fine tune this dissertation; Sister Marjory Gallagher, SC; Reverend John M. Huels, OSM; Reverend Wojciech Kowal, OMI; Dr. Lynda A. Robitaille, Reverend William H. Woestman, OMI, and the late Dr. Michel Thériault who have all been not only available to answer my many questions and concerns but also have been helpful above and beyond the call of duty;

— the Reverend Francis G. Morrisey, OMI, my Director, whose gentle yet challenging guidance, canonical insights, constant confidence in me and affirmation of my work over the past two years as well as his friendship and encouragement have brought this dissertation into existence;

— Mr. Larry Eshelman and the staff of the Allie Memorial Library for all their assistance.

There are also many people who have helped me "behind the scenes" which I would particularly wish to express my sincere appreciation:

— Sister Patricia M. Wilson, SC, Director of the Raleigh Diocesan Tribunal, who so graciously worked hard these past two years, along with Vikki Newell and Rosemary Dudash, so I was able to be here pursuing my doctorate;

— the Reverend Michael O'Reilly, OMI, whose scholarship and wisdom were invaluable to me in researching and writing Chapter Two;

— Cherry Heard, Secretary of the Faculty of Canon Law, Saint Paul University, whose constant affirmation of my work as well as her friendship helped me to keep a healthy perspective on life;

— the OMI community and fellow students of Deschâtelets, whose support and prayers over these past two years have been a source of joy and strength for me;

— my doctoral classmates and the JCL students of Saint Paul University, whose presence in my life I shall always cherish.

To all of these men and women of faith, as well as my many relatives, friends, and former parishioners who expressed their love and support in my endeavor to achieve my doctorate in canon law, I sincerely, and humbly, say thank you.

ABBREVIATIONS

AA   *Apostolicam actuositatem*, Vatican II
            Decree on the Apostolate of the Laity (18 November 1965)

AAS   *Acta Apostolicae Sedis*

ASS   *Acta Sanctae Sedis*

CCEO   *Codex canonum Ecclesiarum orientalium*

CIC   *Codex iuris canonici*

CLSA   Canon Law Society of America

GS   *Gaudium et spes*, Vatican II Pastoral Constitution on the Church in the Modern World (7 December 1965)

LG   *Lumen gentium*, Vatican II The Dogmatic Constitution on the Church (21 November 1964)

SRR Dec   *Sacrae Romanae Rotae. Decisiones seu sententiae* (1908-1980); *Apostolicum Rotae Romanae Tribunal. Decisiones seu sententiae* (1981-1992); *Rotae Romanae Tribunal. Decisiones seu sententiae* (1993-)

INTRODUCTION

Before Vatican II, marriage was often considered, or at least popularly expressed, as a union of bodies; that is to say, marriage was an exclusive contract by which a man and a woman mutually handed over their bodies for the purpose of acts which led to the procreation of children. Thus, matrimonial jurisprudence was focused on the primary end of marriage as stated in canon 1013, §1, of the 1917 *CIC*.[1] One definition of marriage found in a standard commentary defined it as:

> a lawful and exclusive contract by which a man and a woman mutually give and accept a right over their bodies for the purpose of acts which are in themselves suitable for the generation of children.[2]

In a footnote to this definition we read:

> This definition does not express the secondary end of marriage, which is nevertheless very important and may even be predominant in the minds of the parties, namely, mutual love and assistance, and the allaying of concupiscence.[3]

Three observations can be drawn from this simple definition: (1) marriage was understood in terms of a contract, with obligations to be fulfilled; (2) the focus was on the "union of bodies" with emphasis on the procreation of children; and (3) from a canonical perspective, what may have been important in the minds of the contractants, i.e., the secondary end of marriage, did not enter into the definition of marriage, although it was seen as "very important and may have even been predominant in the minds of the parties."

---

[1] Canon 1013, §1: "Matrimonii finis primarius est procreatio atque educatio prolis; secundarius mutuum adiutorium et remedium concupiscentiæ" ("The primary end of marriage is the procreation and education of children; its secondary end is mutual help and the allaying of concupiscence"), English translation as in T.L. BOUSCAREN, A.C. ELLIS, F.N. KORTH, eds., *Canon Law: A Text and Commentary*, 4th revised ed., Milwaukee, Bruce Publishing Company, 1966, p. 466.

[2] *Ibid.*

[3] *Ibid.*, footnote 6.

Furthermore, this seems to have had no direct juridical import in the development of jurisprudence.[4]

With the advent of Vatican II, its personalist understanding of marriage was most poignantly stated in *Gaudium et spes*, 48: marriage is an "intimate community of life and conjugal love". The concept, while not new in itself, broadened the Church's understanding of marriage which in turn helped lay the groundwork for the revision of the canon law regarding this sacrament. Marriage now becomes a union of "persons" which includes all the ramifications this simple yet complex term comprises. "Person" is more than a body; rather, a person is an individual consisting of wants, needs, desires, impulses, hopes and dreams, whose life experience has been shaped by the milieu — cultural, familial, religious — from which he or she comes. "Union" is still, to some extent, viewed as a contract, but it is nuanced by the theology of Vatican II and is also called a covenant, an on-going, loving relationship seen in Biblical terms rather than in merely Roman law or legal terms.

After extensive discussion and study, the Vatican II theology of marriage helped shape, as well as was sculpted into, the renewal of canon law as seen in the pertinent parts of the 1983 *Code of Canon Law* and the 1990 *Code of Canons of the Eastern Churches* (*CCEO*). The concepts of "person" and "covenant" converge into what in the Codes is called *consortium*, "partnership". The ramifications of this one term upon canon law have been the subject of much writing and discussion and continue to be so, the present work being one of the latest.

Prior to Vatican II, the concept of ignorance in regard to marriage (c. 1082 of the 1917 *CIC*) was simply measured in terms of how much the contractants knew about the sexual *copula*. The debates amongst canonists and commentators centered primarily on the degree of ignorance concerning sexual intercourse that was necessary before a marriage could be declared null on this ground. Even the question of ignorance of the "nature of marriage" was considered within the context of sexual intercourse, since the primary end of marriage was the procreation and education of children, as stated in canon 1013 of the 1917 *CIC*, and children were the result of the *copula*.

With Vatican II and the personalist perspective of marriage, the focus shifted to the partnership — as seen in terms of the *communio*, the *coniunctio*, the *consortium*, which were the various terms used at different times to express this partnership. How would this impact on the ground of nullity deriving from ignorance? Although there has been an ever-growing quantity of writing in the area of the psychological titles (canon 1095), little, however, has been written about ignorance, especially in English. There has been minimal discussion and development of canon 1096 in regard to its understanding, its jurisprudence and its possible application. This has led to my decision to study this topic. One of the purposes of this study is to trace the development of the concept to see not only where it has already led, but also to envision, using canonical tradition and jurisprudence, where it can possibly lead in the future. Under the 1917 *CIC*, jurisprudence on canon 1082 focused mainly on the minimal knowledge necessary regarding the sexual act. Ignorance, as a ground for nullity of marriage presented in canon 1096 of the 1983 *CIC*, has not been, as of this writing, developed in Rotal jurisprudence. This, in one sense is exciting and allows us to put forth our ideas and possible applications.

At this time we acknowledge that two doctoral dissertations (the first in English and the second in Latin) have been written on ignorance and matrimony pertaining to canon 1082 of the 1917 *CIC*. The first is by V.M. SMITH, *Ignorance Affecting Matrimonial Consent*.[5] Smith gives a detailed history of ignorance and a commentary on canon 1082. Part One concerns the development of law concerning contingent and

[4]A. MENDONÇA, "The Theological and Juridical Aspects of Marriage", in *Studia canonica*, 22 (1988), p. 284.

[5]V.M. SMITH, *Ignorance Affecting Matrimonial Consent*, Canon Law Studies, 245, Washington, DC, The Catholic University of America, 1950, viii, 118 p.

10

subsistent ignorance; Part Two discusses marriage and how it is vitiated by ignorance. The second is by F. LORENC, *De ignorantiae influxu in matrimoniali consenu.*[6] Lorenc discusses the use of reason and discretion needed for marriage, as well as ignorance and error. He further discusses defective consent under the title of "Ignorance of the nature of matrimony", citing commentators of the 1917 *CIC* and the jurisprudence of the Roman Rota. Both of these dissertations provide good historical background and explain the development of canon 1082 of the 1917 *CIC*.

In addition to these dissertations, however, one book which is to be mentioned concerning ignorance and marriage pertaining to the 1917 *CIC* is that by R. ZERA, *De ignorantia in re matrimoniali; eius natura iuridica et ambitus quoad consensus validitatem deque eiusdem probatione in iudicio.*[7] Zera begins with a study of the nature of marriage and shows how consent is the efficient cause of matrimony. Based upon various commentators and Rotal jurisprudence, he further discusses the knowledge necessary for marriage. He proceeds to incorporate the teachings of Vatican II, thus shedding new light on the use of ignorance as a ground for nullity. He then discusses proofs for the ground of ignorance. His fifth chapter deals with the relationship between ignorance and discretion of judgment and error. These three scholarly works are now somewhat limited due to the fact they were written before the 1983 *CIC*.

Since the 1983 *CIC*, one dissertation (in Portuguese) has been written by C.E. OLIVIERI, "A ignorância no matrimônio (c. 1096), Origem histôric, desenvolvimento doutrinal e jurisprudencial", in *Cuadernos doctorales*, 12 (1994), pp. 13-84. Olivieri's work concentrates on the presuppositions of canon 1082 of the 1917 *CIC* and its history. He discusses the relationship between ignorance and discretion of judgment, error and age; gives a detailed analysis of the Congregation of the Council's decisions of 19 May and 18 August 1888, *Ventimilien*, the proximate *fons* of canon 1082; then moves to the development of canon 1096. Chapter Eight is the author's interpretation of this canon. While this work is well documented, it is still rather limited in scope. It is our intention that the present dissertation will go forward, using the more recent works and jurisprudence which Olivieri did not have available at the time.

Given Vatican II's teaching on marriage, the changing focus of American tribunals from canon 1095 to the more "traditional" grounds for nullity, American society's stress on individuality, as well as a lack of understanding of permanence, and the renewed understanding of canon 1096 in its text and context as well as in relation to its predecessor canon 1082 of the 1917 *CIC*, it is our contention that ignorance can be approached anew and better utilized as a ground for nullity. The research shall address this possibility and test our hypotheses, showing how this newness could be applied.

In Chapter One, "The Concept of Ignorance in Canonical Tradition", we begin our study with the understanding of ignorance in the classical teachings and writings of Aristotle, Augustine, Thomas Aquinas and Alphonsus Liguori, leading to its understanding in both civil and canon law, specifically in relation to juridic acts. This sets the groundwork for a study of the influence of ignorance on matrimonial consent.

In Chapter Two, "Ignorance according to Canon 1082 of the 1917 *CIC* and Jurisprudence prior to Vatican II", we trace the development of ignorance through cases studied by the Congregation of the Council; these laid the foundation for the ground of ignorance codified in the 1917 *CIC* as canon 1082. The chapter continues with a commentary on the canon itself, referencing the various schools of thought concerning the amount of knowledge necessary for a valid marriage consent.

In Chapter Three, "Ignorance according to Canon 1096 of the 1983 *CIC*", our focus is on canon 1096 itself, beginning with the teachings of Vatican II on marriage. We then proceed with an examination of Rotal

---

[6]F. LORENC, *De ignorantiae influxu in matrimoniali consensu*, [Doctoral thesis], Romae, Pontificium Athenaeum Lateranense, 1955, 43 p.

[7]R. ZERA, *De ignorantia in re matrimoniali; eius natura iuridica et ambitus quoad consensus validitatem deque eiusdem probatione in iudicio*, Romae, Ancora, 1978, 108 p.

jurisprudence concerning ignorance, the revision process, a text and context commentary on canon 1096 and then complete this chapter by briefly tracing the development of the counterpart of canon 1096 in the *CCEO*, canon 819.

In Chapter Four, "Applicability of Canon 1096", we begin by making the distinction between ignorance and other grounds of nullity, with the hope that when these differences are better understood, ignorance as a ground for nullity may be further utilized. We then take a two-pronged practical approach to the applicability of canon 1096, showing how it can be better employed in the tribunal as a ground for nullity and, using the 1995 Creighton University Study, "Marriage Preparation in the Catholic Church: Getting it Right", how this canon and its contents can be integrated into pre-marital programs, thus possibly avoiding ignorance in the first place.

This is a broader treatment of the canon than we originally intended. Our study at first was concerned about what is new in canon 1096 in comparison to its predecessor canon 1082 of the 1917 *CIC* and what possibilities this newness would, if any, offer for tribunal ministry. However, in the process of our research, especially in light of a better understanding of the concept of the *consortium*, it was believed that more people could possibly benefit from our analysis, specifically those who actually prepare couples for marriage in the Catholic Church. Our study ends with general conclusions drawn from our research which, it is hoped, will lead not only to a more broadly based utilization of canon 1096 as a ground for nullity, but also to more discussion and study of its possible applications.

CHAPTER ONE

THE CONCEPT OF IGNORANCE IN CANONICAL TRADITION

INTRODUCTION

Ignorance, simply stated, is the lack of knowledge. However, within the theological and canonical tradition, ignorance is not simply the lack of knowledge, rather it is the lack of *due* knowledge.[8] To have an appreciation of the concept of ignorance, one needs to understand what knowledge is. With this basic grasp of knowledge, ignorance can then be better discerned in light of what it is not. Rather than present a theoretical discussion concerning the essence of knowledge, it may be more practical at this point simply to lay the foundation for a basic understanding of this concept.

One definition of knowledge is "the fact or condition of being cognizant, conscious or aware of something."[9] Knowledge could be *a posteriori*, i.e., cognition acquired through experience, thus called empirical knowledge.[10] Or, on the other hand, it could be *a priori*, i.e., cognition which embraces those principles inherent in human beings and is not the result of *a posteriori* exercises. This is referred to as pure or transcendental knowledge.[11] *A posteriori* knowledge is also called sense knowledge (since what is known is received through the senses), while *a priori* knowledge is called intellectual knowledge (since what is known is recognized within the context of the intellect).[12] Knowledge supposes three terms: a *being* (or subject) who knows, an *object* known and a *relation* determined between the being who knows and the object that is known. It is this relation which is "knowledge" properly understood,[13] for knowledge arises through

---

[8]See THOMAS AQUINAS, *Summa theologiae*, IaIIae, q. 76, 2. This point is discussed later in this chapter. A person who lacks knowledge is nescient, while a person who lacks knowledge of what ought to be known is ignorant. For more discussion on this topic, see R. CUNNINGHAM, "Marriage and the Nescient Catholic", in *Studia canonica*, 15 (1981), pp. 263-283. This distinction is also made by A.G. CICOGNANI, *Canon Law*, 2nd rev. ed., J. O'HARA and F. BRENNAN, trans., Philadelphia, Dolphin Press, 1935, p. 590.

[9]P.B. GOVE, editor in chief, *Webster's Third New International Dictionary of the English Language, Unabridged*, Springfield, Massachusetts, G&C Merriam Company, 1981, p. 1252. For further discussions concerning various philosophical understandings of knowledge, see W. BRUGGER, ed., *Philosophical Dictionary*, K. BAKER, trans. and ed. of the American edition, Spokane, Washington, Gonzaga University Press, 1974, pp. 212-217; H. CALDERWOOD, *Vocabulary of Philosophy*, New Delhi, Akashdeep Publishing House, 1992, pp. 220-222; A. FLEW, ed., *A Dictionary of Philosophy*, New York, St. Martin's Press, 1979, p. 180; F. MACHLUP, *Knowledge: Its Creation, Distribution, and Economic Significance*, vol. 1: *Knowledge and Knowledge Production*, Princeton, Princeton University Press, 1980, especially Part One, "Types of Knowledge", pp. 27-109, and Part Two, "Qualities of Knowledge", pp. 113-152; J.R. THOMSON, ed., *A Dictionary of Philosophy in the Words of Philosophers*, London, R.D. Dickinson, 1887, pp. 24-28, 83-127; J.O. URMSON, ed., *The Concise Encyclopaedia of Western Philosophy and Philosophers*, London, Hutchinson, 1960, pp. 28-50.

[10]W. HAMILTON, *Lectures on Metaphysics*, vol. II, H.L. MANSEL and J. VEITH, eds., Edinburgh, William Blackwood and Sons, 1859, p. 26.

[11]*Ibid.*, p. 26. Hamilton further points out, "our *a priori* [knowledge] is not antecedent to our *a posteriori* knowledge; for the internal conditions of experience can only operate when an object of experience has been presented. In the order of time our knowledge, therefore, may be said to commence with experience, but to have its principle antecedently in the mind" (pp. 26-27). In other words, the categories which allow us to make sense of our experience are already present within the mind.

[12]BRUGGER, *Philosophical Dictionary*, pp. 212-213.

[13]W. FLEMING, *The Vocabulary of Philosophy; Mental, Moral and Metaphysical*, London, R. Griffin, 1857, p. 281.

the activity of our human consciousness.[14]

This fundamental appreciation of knowledge enables us to discern ignorance. Nescience is the opposite of knowledge, while ignorance, for our purposes, is the opposite of due knowledge. In other words, borrowing from the definition of knowledge as stated above, ignorance is the fact or condition of *not* being cognizant, *not* being conscious, or *not* being aware of something that a person should be.[15] There is no relation, dynamic or otherwise, between the subject and the object because there is nothing to be known. Ignorance does not arise from an activity of the human consciousness, since there is nothing to engage one's awareness. Rather, there is a void, a "black hole" so to speak. It is important to note that this understanding of ignorance presupposes the subject is capable of knowledge. For example, an insane person is improperly said to be ignorant.[16] This will be further discussed in later chapters.

Through the ages, this basic definition of ignorance as the lack of due knowledge has been modified, enhanced, and clarified depending upon whether one was concerned with the subject who was ignorant or the object of ignorance. The explanation was further accommodated when the circumstances surrounding the object and the subject at a given point in time were considered.

In the first part of this chapter, we shall provide a brief analysis of the writings of some authors for the purpose of demonstrating the understanding of ignorance and how this awareness helped establish the canonical concept of ignorance, especially within the realm of marriage and consent. The number of writers selected had to be limited. Therefore, the authors chosen, in our opinion, have had a decisive influence upon canonists and have thus advanced the development of jurisprudence concerning the understanding of ignorance and its relation to marriage: Aristotle, Augustine of Hippo, Thomas Aquinas, and Alphonsus Liguori. In each case, we shall first present the writer's basic concept of knowledge followed by his theory of ignorance. Both notions are interrelated and, as stated above, it is important first to understand knowledge so ignorance can then be better understood.

In the second part, we shall relate the notion of ignorance to law in general, thus laying the foundation for the relation between ignorance and marriage. Looking briefly at Roman law and then civil law, we shall see how ignorance affects a person's responsibilities as a result of his or her actions.

In the third and final section of this chapter, we look at the juridic act, of which marriage consent is one, though *sui generis*, and how ignorance may or may not have bearing on it. Thus the basis will be set for presenting ignorance and its relation to marriage, the object of this study.

I. IGNORANCE IN CLASSICAL TEACHINGS

We begin our study with the theories of knowledge of Aristotle, Augustine, Thomas Aquinas and Alphonsus Liguori in order to understand more clearly the concept of ignorance.

---

[14]BRUGGER, *Philosophical Dictionary*, p. 212.

[15]L.R. SWOBODA, *Ignorance in Relation to the Imputability of Delicts; An Historical Synopsis and Commentary*, Canon Law Studies, 143,Washington, DC, The Catholic University of America Press, 1941, discusses this point on p. 115: "However, the 'should' must be understood in the sense of a natural perfection and not in the sense of a moral perfection or of a moral obligation. Consequently ignorance is defined as a privation of knowledge in a subject naturally capable of and constituted for knowledge. A great number of authors, in order to bring out the idea that ignorance is a privation and not a simple negation, define ignorance as the lack of knowledge which one can and should have." Swoboda further points out on p. 115 that this definition is based upon Thomas Aquinas. See THOMAS AQUINAS, *Summa theologiae*, IaIIae, q. 76, 2.

[16]SWOBODA, *Ignorance in Relation to the Imputability of Delicts*, p. 116.

a. Aristotle (384-322 BC)

Aristotle's thought has been called a major constitutive part of Western culture[17] since his extensive writings on logic, physics, natural history, psychology, politics, ethics and the arts have influenced countless authors and philosophers over the centuries. Aristotle considered knowledge under two general classifications: theoretical science and practical science.[18] Ignorance can result in either instance. In his many works, he refers to ignorance at least thirty-one times,[19] but it is in Book Six of his *Topica*, that he gives the basic definition of ignorance as the "privation of knowledge".[20]

In Book Three of his *Nicomachean Ethics*, Aristotle speaks of ignorance within the context of virtue, which is concerned with passions and actions.[21] Since voluntary actions are those to which praise or blame are bestowed and involuntary actions merit "pardon, and sometimes also pity",[22] a distinction must be made between the two types of actions, with respect to the actual moment of action.[23] Responsibility for one's actions can be disclaimed, according to Aristotle, by basically two conditions: duress (compulsion) and

---

[17]D. COLLINSON, *Fifty Major Philosophers: A Reference Guide*, London and New York, Routledge, 1987, p. 22.

[18]"All cases of knowledge exhibited in human claims to knowledge are considered by Aristotle under two classifications, dependent on whether or not the knowledge considered represents what is always true or what is merely true in many cases, yet of value for practical action. Knowledge which represents what is necessarily true independently of human desires and hopes is called theoretical science. True statements of theoretical science are always true, and hence the range of theoretical science is quite similar to the range of *knowledge* in Plato's defined sense. On the other hand, practical science is the result of studying what is quite often true (perhaps even true in every observed case), but which need not be true if human beings should desire to bring about some change" (R.J. ACKERMANN, *Theories of Knowledge: A Critical Introduction*, New York, McGraw-Hill, 1965, p. 57).

[19]T.W. ORGAN, *An Index to Aristotle in English Translation*, Princeton, Princeton University Press, 1949, p. 82. In contrast, T.P. KIERNAN, ed., *Aristotle Dictionary*, New York, Philosophical Library, 1962, pp. 295-296, lists ignorance only five times. It should be noted that the references made here are nothing more than a sentence that captures the sense of the discussion, since the actual discourse of the topic can continue for paragraphs if not pages. It is of interest to note these references, since they demonstrate the effects of ignorance: *Posterior Analytics*, 1.16 79b 23-24: "Ignorance, considered not according to negation but according to a disposition of mind, is deception produced through a syllogism"; *Nicomachean Ethics*, 3.2 1110b 28-30: "Ignorance is the error which makes people unjust and generally wicked"; *Eudemian Ethics*, 2.9. 12225b 5-7: "He who performs any action not knowing what the action is nor to what end it will lead nor about whom such action is conversant acts from ignorance essentially, and therefore acts involuntarily"; *Nicomachean Ethics*, 3.2 1110b 18-22: "An action which is due to ignorance is always non-voluntary; but it is not involuntary unless it is followed by pain and excites a feeling of regret"; *De longitudine et brevitate vitae*, 2.4 65a 22-23: "The corruption of ignorance is reminiscence and discipline."

[20]W.D. ROSS, ed., *The Works of Aristotle*, 12 vol., Oxford, Clarendon Press, 1908-1952, vol. I, *Topica*, 6.9 147b 30. This definition is given within the context of clarifying what is "privation" (6.9 147b 25-34): "Moreover, see if in rendering a term formed to denote privation, he has failed to render the term of which it is the privation, e.g. the state, or contrary, or whatever it may be whose privation it is: also if he has omitted to add either any term at all in which the privation is naturally formed, or else that in which it is naturally formed primarily, e.g. whether in defining 'ignorance' as a privation he has failed to say that it is the privation of 'knowledge'; or has failed to add in what it is naturally formed, or, though he has added this, has failed to render the thing in which it is primarily formed, placing it (e.g.) in 'man' or in 'the soul', and not in the 'reasoning faculty': for if in any of these respects he fails, he has made a mistake."

[21]ROSS, *The Works of Aristotle*, vol. IX, *Ethica Nicomachea*, 3.1 1109b 30-35.

[22]*Ibid.*, 3.1 1109b 31-32.

[23]*Ibid.*, 3.1 1110a 14. This reference to the time of the action is an important distinction to make. The time of the action involves the circumstances as well as the chronological aspect surrounding the action. Thus the time of the action can define it as voluntary or involuntary and, depending on the definition, can limit the responsibility of the person performing the action.

ignorance, which render an action as involuntary.[24] Once the involuntariness of the action is established, then responsibility can be disclaimed.[25] Aristotle points out that an action, done involuntarily and in ignorance, must be "painful and involve repentance"[26] in order truly to be deemed involuntary.

It is not ignorance of what is to one's advantage nor is it ignorance of the universal that deems a certain action as "involuntary", but rather ignorance of particulars.[27] Ignorance is confined to a given time and place, limited by what the person knows (or does not know) and the circumstances of the decision made. Thus, ignorance can be (1) of the thing done, (2) of the object of the act, (3) of the instrument, (4) of the result of the act, or (5) of the manner in which it was done.[28] A further distinction is made between an action done in ignorance, and thus involuntarily in the classic sense as discussed here, to which the person is not held responsible, and an action done ignorantly, i.e., performed without thinking, but for whose consequences the person is still held responsible.[29]

In Book Two of his *Eudemian Ethics*, Aristotle elaborates once again on voluntary and involuntary actions.[30] That which is performed as a result of ignorance on the part of the person, instrument or thing, is involuntary. If done involuntarily, the person is not held responsible. Here, Aristotle goes a step further and makes the distinction between the actual possession of knowledge and the use of knowledge.[31] If a person possesses knowledge but does not make use of what is known in performing a certain act, that person could technically be called "ignorant", but one must do further investigation to ascertain if that person acted without thinking (and thus was not held responsible for the action) or simply carelessly (not considering the consequences, but still nonetheless being held responsible).

Therefore, in Aristotle's thought, if a person does not possess knowledge, he or she is in a state of ignorance. A person acting in ignorance is not held responsible for the ramifications of that action. However, for Aristotle, a further distinction must be made: whether a person is indeed in ignorance (i.e., not having the necessary knowledge as to the act and its implications), or is acting out of ignorance (having knowledge but not using it, not thinking through the action and the effects it may have and thus merely acting rashly). In this

---

[24]*Ibid.*, 3.1 1109b 35.

[25]URMSON, ed., *The Concise Encyclopaedia of Western Philosophy and Philosophers*, p. 50.

[26]ROSS, *The Works of Aristotle*, vol. IX, *Ethica Nicomachea*, 3.1 1111a 20.

[27]*Ibid.*, 3.1 1110b 30-1111a 1: "... but the term 'involuntary' tends to be used not if a man is ignorant of what is to his advantage — for it is not mistaken purpose what causes involuntary action (it leads rather to wickedness), nor ignorance of the universal (for *that* men are *blamed*), but ignorance of particulars, i.e. of the circumstances of the action and the objects with which it is concerned. For it is on these that both pity and pardon depend, since the person who is ignorant of any of these acts involuntarily."

[28]J.A. STEWART, *Notes on the Nicomachean Ethics of Aristotle*, vol. 1, Oxford, Clarendon Press, 1892, p. 240.

[29]CALDERWOOD, *Vocabulary of Philosophy*, p. 190. Also ROSS, *The Works of Aristotle*, vol. IX, *Ethica Nicomachea*, 3.1 1110b 24-25: "Acting by reason of ignorance seems also to be different from acting *in* ignorance; for the man who is drunk or in a rage is thought to act as a result not of ignorance but of one of the causes mentioned, yet not knowingly but in ignorance." See also STEWART, *Notes on the Nichomachaen Ethics of Aristotle*, vol. 1, pp. 234-236.

[30]ROSS, *The Works of Aristotle*, vol. IX, *Ethica Eudemia*, 2.9 1225b 1-15.

[31]*Ibid.*, 2.9 1225b 11-15: "But since science or knowledge is of two sorts, one the possession, the other the use of knowledge, the man who has, but does not use knowledge may in a sense be justly called ignorant, but in another sense not justly, e.g. if he had not used his knowledge owing to carelessness. Similarly, one might be blamed for not having the knowledge, if it were something easy or necessary and he does not have it because of carelessness or pleasure or pain."

latter case, a person who acts out of ignorance is held responsible for the effects of his or her action.

b. Augustine of Hippo (354-430 AD)

Augustine is one of the key figures in the transition from classical antiquity to the Middle Ages.[32] We should recognize that his theory of knowledge was not a systematic exposition, but rather, for the most part, one developed within a context of religious ideas.[33] It is within this framework that we consider Augustine's view of reality. He was convinced that there were three distinct levels of beings to be known: the highest level was God; the second consisted in created spirits, angels and human souls; the third was that of bodies.[34] These three levels, respectively, correspond to the three visions of which the soul is capable: intellectual, imaginative and corporeal.[35] In turn, these three visions are also described as the three principal grades or forms of knowledge: sensible, rational and intellectual.[36]

While there were three forms of knowledge, Augustine held that there were two kinds of objects that can be known: objects of the senses and objects known independently of sensory experience, the latter being perceived through the mind itself. The objects perceived directly through the mind were also perceived more clearly, since they did not need to be "filtered" through the senses.[37] For Augustine, like Plato, the highest intellectual activity, i.e., the perception of objects on the intellectual level of knowledge, results in an illumination of the mind, a recognition of eternal truths.[38]

---

[32]P. EDWARDS, editor in chief, *The Encyclopedia of Philosophy*, vol. 1, New York, The Macmillan Company and the Free Press, 1967, p. 198. See also R.H. NASH, *The Light of the Mind: St. Augustine's Theory of Knowledge*, Lexington, University of Kentucky Press, 1969, p. vii.

[33]J.A. MOURANT, *Introduction to the Philosophy of Saint Augustine; Selected Readings and Commentaries*, University Park, Pennsylvania State University Press, 1964, p. 15. See also, NASH, *The Light of the Mind*, pp. 1-3.

[34]V.J. BOURKE, *Wisdom from St. Augustine*, Houston, Center for Thomistic Studies, University of St. Thomas, 1984, pp. 53-54. The author further distinguishes that God, on the first level, is absolutely Immutable; that on the second level, these beings are immutable in place but mutable in time; while beings on the third level are mutable in both place and time.

[35] "Augustine saw man as an immaterial soul, giving life and regulation to an organic body. This soul is capable of three kinds of vision: corporeal, imaginative and intellectual. The first way of seeing works through the eyes of the body; its objects are the sensible appearances (*species*) of material objects in man's environment.... The imaginative level of vision is cogitation, an act of thinking in terms of the images formed by the soul in the lowest kind of perception.... The third kind of seeing is purely mental and imageless: by it the human soul sees non-material objects (*rationes*) that have changeless meanings" (*ibid.*, pp. 106-107). See also NASH, *The Light of the Mind*, p. 9. Simply speaking, we could say that the corporeal is seen through the eyes of the body; the imaginative is seen through the eyes of the mind; the intellectual is seen through the eyes of the soul.

[36]For a more in-depth presentation, see S. CANDELA, *S. Agostino*, Napoli, Edizioni "Cenacolo Serafino", 1966, pp. 55-63. See also THOMAS AQUINAS, *Summa theologiae*, Ia, 85, 1.

[37]COLLINSON, *Fifty Major Philosophers*, p. 29.

[38]*Ibid.* The author further points out that with this illumination of the mind, there is "a recognition of certain and eternal truths which are latent in all human minds. These truths, he maintained, furnish us with standards against which we make our judgments of how things should be" (*ibid.*). For a more detailed discussion, see BOURKE, *Wisdom from St. Augustine*, pp. 53-62; E. PORTALIÉ, *A Guide to the Thought of Saint Augustine*, R.J. BASTIAN, trans., Chicago, Henry Regnery Company, 1960, pp.105-124; and J.M. RIST, *Augustine: Ancient Thought Baptized*, Cambridge, Cambridge University Press, 1994, pp. 41-48; 89-90. See also B. MONDIN, *Il pensiero di Agostino: filosofia, teologia, cultura*, Roma, Città nuova editrice, 1988, pp.120-124; and NASH, *The Light of the Mind*, pp. 1-11.

Augustine makes the distinction between wisdom (*sapientia*) and knowledge (*scientia*).[39] Wisdom is the highest form of knowledge since it is based upon superior reason (*ratio superior*) which gives one a knowledge of the eternal and incorporeal, while sense knowledge, based upon inferior reason (*ratio inferior*) gives knowledge only of the temporal and corporeal.[40] Since wisdom gives knowledge of the eternal and of God, and God is the highest tier of reality for Augustine, wisdom is thus the highest form of knowledge.[41] It is the highest truth after which one is to strive.[42] For Augustine, true knowledge is never far from faith,[43] as can be seen in *De Trinitate*.[44] Faith becomes a prerequisite for knowledge[45] but remains, nonetheless, inferior to it.[46]

Since knowledge is always understood within a context of faith, so too must ignorance be understood. In a sense, ignorance is not knowing where wisdom lies, resulting from the primal fall from divine favor.[47]

[39]MOURANT, *Introduction to the Philosophy of Augustine*, p. 20. See also BOURKE, *Wisdom from St. Augustine*, pp. 54-55. Augustine more thoroughly discusses this distinction in *De Trinitate*, Books XII through XIV.

[40]NASH, *The Light of the Mind*, pp. 7-9, offers various examples which clarify Augustine's understanding of the difference between wisdom and knowledge. For further elaboration, see MONDIN, *Il pensiero di Agostino*, pp. 132-133.

[41]MOURANT, *Introduction to the Philosophy of Augustine*, p. 20.

[42]A. WEBER, *Histoire de la philosophie européenne*, 7th ed., Paris, Fischbacher, 1905, p. 189: "La suprême vérité où nous devons tendre, c'est la sagesse."

[43]PORTALIÉ, *A Guide to the Thought of Saint Augustine*, p. 115.

[44] In *De Trinitate*, Book IX, Chapter 1: "For a certain faith is in some way the beginning of knowledge, but a certain knowledge will only be perfected after this life when we shall see face to face" (A. AUGUSTINUS, *The Trinity*, S. McKENNA, trans., Washington, DC, Catholic University of America Press, 1963, *The Fathers of the Church*, vol. 45, *The Writings of Saint Augustine*, p. 270).
"Certa enim fides utcumque inchoat cognitionem; cognitio vero certa non perficietur nisi post hanc vitam videbimus *facie ad faciem*" (A. AUGUSTINUS, *De Trinitate*, W.M. MOUNTAIN, ed., Turnholti, Typographi Brepols, 1968, *Corpus christianorum, Series latina*, vol. 50, pp. 292-293).

[45]As Augustine states in *De libero arbitrio*, Book I, Chapter 2, 4, 11: "For God will aid us and will make us understand what we believe. This is the course prescribed by the prophet who says, 'Unless you believe, you shall not understand,' and we are aware that we consider this course good for us' (A. AUGUSTINUS, *De libero arbitrio*, [= BENJAMIN, *On Free Choice*], A.S. BENJAMIN and L.H. HACKSTAFF, trans., Indianapolis, Bobbs-Merril, 1964, p. 5).
"Aderit enim deus et nos intelligere quod credidimus faciet. Praescriptum enim per prophetam gradum, qui ait: *Nisi credideritis, non intelligetis*, tenere nos bene nobis conscii sumus" (A. AUGUSTINUS, *De libero arbitrio*, [= GREEN, *De libero arbitrio*], W.M. GREEN, ed., Turnholti, Typographi Brepols, 1968, *Corpus christianorum, Series latina*, vol. 29, pp. 213).

[46]"Chronologiquement, la foi précède l'intelligence: pour comprendre une chose, il faut préalablement l'admettre — *credo ut intelligam*; mais la foi, pour être la condition du savoir, n'en est pas moins un état provisoire, un échelon inférieur à la science, dans laquelle elle finit par se résoudre" (WEBER, *Histoire de la philosophie européenne*, p. 189).

[47]J. WETZEL, *Augustine and the Limits of Virtue*, Cambridge, Cambridge University Press, 1992, pp. 79-80. This is clearly seen in *De libero arbitrio*, Book III, Chapter 20, 55, 186: "God, the highest Ruler of the universe, justly decreed that we, who are descended from that first union, should be born into ignorance and difficulty, and be subjected to death, because they sinned and were hurled headlong into the midst of error, difficulty, and death" (BENJAMIN, *On Free Choice*, p. 130).
"Ut autem de illo primo coniugio et cum ignorantia et cum difficultate et cum mortalitate nascamur, quoniam illi cum peccavissent et in errorem et in erumnam et in mortem praecipitati sunt" (GREEN, *De libero arbitrio*, p. 307).

Ignorance is understood within the context of sin.[48] It is not only a lacking of knowledge, but, given the ramifications of the fall, it can be understood as a deprivation of knowledge. Ignorance, as a deprivation, prevents a person from fully grasping what should be known in order to live a life in harmony with God, which is the highest good to be achieved. This can be seen in Augustine's discussion of ignorance in Book III of *De libero arbitrio*, when in Chapter 18 he writes: "We should not be amazed that, because of his ignorance, man has not free choice of will to choose what he should rightly do."[49]

Yet, for Augustine, ignorance has its merits. Even though ignorance and difficulty were the lot into which humanity is born, the soul, which for Augustine is on a higher level than the corporeal, seeks after God and God will help the soul not only to overcome ignorance and difficulty, but will use them as encouragement.[50] Because a person is born into ignorance, one is not condemned to remain in that state.[51] Rather, since each person is called to happiness and because ignorance prevents one from attaining happiness, ignorance can be overcome by the grace of God.

Therefore, for Augustine, as a result of the fall from divine favor, humanity is born into sin. It is within this imperfect world that one seeks knowledge. Ignorance, a result of sin, prevents a person from achieving knowledge while at the same time gives encouragement for the soul to seek God. Ignorance is not merely a lack of knowledge; rather, since Augustine sees the world within the context of faith, ignorance is a deprivation of knowledge. While ignorance (as well as difficulty) may prevent a person from doing what is honorable,[52] it is a condition into which one is born. This is not necessarily an eternal situation, since ignorance can be overcome through the grace of God[53] if one is willing to strive to do so. On the corporeal

---

[48]This is seen in *De libero arbitrio*, Book III, Chapter 20, 56, 189: "When the sinful soul comes upon ignorance and difficulty, it is right to say that this is a punishment, since before this punishment the soul was better" (BENJAMIN, *On Free Choice*, p. 131).
"Nam cum ad ignorantiam difficultatemque pervenerit illa peccatrix, ideo poena recte dicitur quia melior ante poenam fuit" (GREEN, *De libero arbitrio*, p. 307).

[49]BENJAMIN and HACKSTAFF, Book III, Chapter 18, 52, 177, p. 128. "Nec mirandum est quod vel ignorando non habet arbitrium liberum voluntatis ad eligendum quod recte faciat" (GREEN, *De libero arbitrio*, p. 305).

[50]In *De libero arbitrio*, Book III, Chapter 20, 56, 190-191: "The soul is not a mere intermediate good, not only because it is a soul and by its very nature surpasses every corporeal object, but also because it has means of educating itself with the help of its Creator and can, by pious zeal, acquire and possess all the virtues through which it can be freed of torturous difficulty and blinding ignorance. If this is the case, ignorance and difficulty will not be the punishment of sin for souls as they were born, but will be the encouragement for advancement and the beginning of perfection" (BENJAMIN, *On Free Choice*, p. 131).
"Non enim mediocria bona sunt non solum quod anima est, qua natura iam corpus omne praecedit, sed etiam quod facultatem habet ut adiuvante creatore se ipsam excolat et pio studio possit omnes adquirere et capere virtutes per quas et a difficultate cruciante et ab ignorantia caecante liberetur. Quod si ita est, non erit nascentibus animis ignorantia et difficultas supplicium peccati, sed proficiendi admonitio et perfectionis exordium" (GREEN, *De libero arbitrio*, p. 308).

[51]"For although it was born in ignorance and difficulty, nevertheless it is not compelled by necessity to remain in the state in which it was born" (BENJAMIN, *On Free Choice*, Book III, Chapter 20, 56, 192, pp. 131-132).
"Quamquam enim in ignorantia et difficultate nata sit, non tamen ad permanendum in eo quod nata est aliqua necessitate conprimitur" (GREEN, *De libero arbitrio*, p. 308).

[52]T.K. SCOTT, *Augustine: His Thought in Context*, New York, Paulist Press, 1995, p. 161.

[53]This is clearly seen in *De libero arbitrio*, Book III, Chapter 20, 58, 199: "He has arranged that, when those who are zealous and of good will overcome ignorance and difficulty, they merit a crown of glory. Yet when they are remiss and wish to defend their sins on the ground of weakness, He does not impose ignorance and difficulty as a penalty for crime. Instead, He justly punishes them because they desire to remain in ignorance and difficulty, and because they are unwilling to arrive at truth and peace through zealously seeking and learning, and humbly confessing and praying" (BENJAMIN, *On Free Choice*, p. 133).

or sensory level, simply stated, a person who knows something is no longer in the state of ignorance.

c. Thomas Aquinas (1225-1274)

Aristotle saw nature as existing apart from God. Augustine, however, repudiated this idea and emphasized that nature could not be nature apart from God. It was the Angelic Doctor, Thomas Aquinas, who brought the two positions together. His metaphysical exposition clarified existence as coming from God but not being defined by the fact. Thus, when this was acknowledged, the possibility for change became infinite. This gives humanity a dynamic existence in relation to the Absolute as well as an openness to knowledge.[54] It was by such a synthesis of Aristotle and Augustine that Thomas Aquinas was largely responsible for the incorporation of Aristotelian philosophy not only into Christian doctrine, but also into Western culture as well.[55]

Thomas Aquinas, like Augustine, does not present a definitive theory of knowledge,[56] although the topic is treated in depth in various works.[57] Since Thomas saw humanity as something dynamic, it is no surprise that he saw knowledge as a human activity.[58] Since there is activity, there is a relationship between the subject (the one who knows) and the object (the one or thing known). Thomas Aquinas tells us: "All cognition takes place through an assimilation of the knower to the known."[59] The subject (the "knower") is related to the object (the "known") through the act of knowing it.[60] Since the subject has a relationship with the object, the subject is affected by what he or she has come to understand through knowledge.[61] How a person acts or how one relates to another is based upon what that person knows about the object with which he or she interacts.

"Hanc enim ignorantiam et difficultatem studiosis et benevolis evincendam ad coronam gloriae valere praestaret, neglegentibus autem et peccata sua de infirmitate defendere volentibus non ipsam ignorantiam difficultatemque pro crimine obiceret, sed, quia in eis potius permanere quam studio quaerendi atque discendi et humilitate confitendi atque orandi ad veritatem ac facilitatem pervenire voluerunt, iusto supplicio vindicaret" (GREEN, De libero arbitrio, p. 309).

[54]M.T. CLARK, ed., An Aquinas Reader: Selections from the Writings of Thomas Aquinas, 5th ed., New York, Fordham University Press, 1996, p. 7.

[55]COLLINSON, Fifty Major Philosophers, p. 33.

[56]D.B. BURRELL, Aquinas: God and Action, Notre Dame, University of Notre Dame Press, 1979, p. 144. For further discussion concerning the various understandings of knowledge in Aquinas, see J. MARITAIN, Distinguer pour unir ou, Les degrés du savoir, 6th éd. rev. et augm., Paris, Desclée de Brouwer, 1959, especially pp. 215-248; L.-M. RÉGIS, Epistemology, I.C. BYRNE, trans., New York, Macmillan, 1959, especially pp. 109-144, "The Angelic Doctor's Method"; and F. VAN STEENBERGHEN, Épistémologie, 3rd ed., Louvain, Publications universitaires de Louvain, 1956, p. 56-59.

[57]For example, Summa contra Gentiles, Book 3; Summa theologiae, Ia, 84-89; and De veritate, especially q. 8, 5 and 6, which discuss human as well as angelic knowledge.

[58]VAN STEENBERGHEN, Épistémologie, p. 59: "La connaissance est une activité humaine."

[59]THOMAS AQUINAS, De veritate, vol. 1, 6th ed., Taurini, Marietti, 1931, p. 175: "Omnis enim cognitio est per assimilationem cognoscentis ad cognitum," q. 8, 5; English translation from THOMAS AQUINAS, De veritate, Truth, vol. 1, R.W. MULLIGAN, trans., Chicago, H. Regnery, 1952, p. 339.

[60]BURRELL, Aquinas: God and Action, p. 148.

[61]Ibid., pp.148-150.

For Thomas Aquinas, knowledge first depends upon sense experience.[62] However, it is not limited to sensory experience since such encounters do not give one intellectual knowledge of those things which have been encountered.[63] Rather, while knowledge takes its rise from the sensory level, the intellect comes to understand or think of things by extracting data and then assembling it into knowledge.[64] It is in the intellect that one comes to knowledge. Thomas Aquinas lists three levels of cognitive faculties through which objects are known: sense, human and angelic.[65] This hierarchy corresponds to the three levels of Augustine: sensible, rational and intellectual.

For Thomas Aquinas, it is the soul which gives the body life as well as giving the ultimate motive to understanding[66] and it is knowledge that leads the soul to understanding. Therefore, just as health is important for the body, so too knowledge is important for the soul.[67] This is significant because the whole world is

---

[62]B. DAVIES, *The Thought of Thomas Aquinas*, Oxford, Clarendon Press, 1993, p. 125; and M.C. D'ARCY, *Thomas Aquinas*, Westminster, Maryland, Newman Bookshop, 1944, p. 158.

[63]DAVIES, *The Thought of Thomas Aquinas*, p. 125. See also THOMAS AQUINAS, *De veritate*, vol. 1, 6th ed., Taurini, Marietti, 1931, p. 175

[64]DAVIES, *The Thought of Thomas Aquinas*, p. 125.

[65]*Summa theologiae* Ia, q. 85, 1: "Dicendum quod, sicut supra dictum est, objectum cognoscibile proportionatur virtuti cognoscitivae. Est autem triplex gradus cognoscitivae virtutis. Quaedam enim cognoscitiva virtus est actus organi corporalis, scilicet sensus.... Quaedam autem virtus cognoscitiva est quae neque est actus organi corporalis, neque est aliquo modo corporalis materiae conjuncta, sicut intellectus angelicus.... Intellectus autem humanus medio modo se habet: non enim est actus alicujus organi, sed tamen est quaedam virtus animae, quae est forma corporis, ut ex supra dictis patet" (THOMAS AQUINAS, *Summa theologiae*, vol. 12, *Human Intelligence* [= DURBIN, *Human Intelligence*], Latin text, English translation, P.T. DURBIN, Cambridge, Blackfriars in conjunction with Eyre & Spottiswoode, London, 1968, p. 50). All Latin and English texts are taken from this edition, with the volume and its title indicated.
   "As was said earlier, knowable objects are proportioned to knowing faculties, and there are three levels of such faculties. First, one kind of cognitive faculty is the form of a corporeal organ: such is sense.... A second kind of cognitive faculty is neither the form of a corporeal organ nor in any way joined to corporeal matter: such is an angel's intellect.... The human intellect stands in the middle. It is not the form of an organ, although it is a faculty of the soul which is the form of a body, as is clear from what was said earlier" (DURBIN, vol. 12, *Human Intelligence*, p. 51).

[66]*Summa theologiae*, Ia, q. 76, 1: "Manifestum est autem quod primum quo corpus vivit est anima. Et cum vita manifestetur secundum diversas operationes in diversis gradibus viventium, id quo primo operamur unumquodque operum vitae est anima; anima enim est primum quo nutrimur et sentimus et movemur secundum locum, et similiter quo primo intelligimus. Hoc ergo principium quo primo intelligimus, sive dicatur intellectus sive anima intellectiva, est forma corporis" (DURBIN, vol. 11, *Man*, p. 42).
   "Now it is obvious that the soul is the prime endowment by virtue of which a body has life. Life manifests its presence through different activities at different levels, but the soul is the ultimate principle by which we conduct every one of life's activities; the soul is the ultimate motive factor behind nutrition, sensation and movement from place to place, and the same holds true of the act of understanding. So that this prime factor in intellectual activity, whether we call it mind or intellectual soul, is the formative principle of the body" (*ibid.*, p. 43).

[67]*Summa theologiae*, Ia, q. 76, 1: "Dicendum quod necesse est dicere quod intellectus, qui est intellectualis operationis principium, sit humani corporis forma. Illud enim quo primo aliquid operatur est forma ejus cui operatio attribuitur, sicut quo primo sanatur corpus est sanitas, et quo primo scit anima est scientia — unde sanitas est forma corporis et scientia animae" (DURBIN, vol. 11, *Man*, p. 40).
   "The intellect, as the source of intellectual activity, is the form of the human body. For the prime endowment by virtue of which anything acts is the form of that to which the activity is attributed, as health is the prime endowment by virtue of which the body is made healthy, and knowledge is the prime endowment by which the soul knows, and health, therefore, is the form of the body and knowledge of the soul" (*ibid.*, p. 41).

potentially intelligible.[68] and as one grows in understanding, one becomes more aware of the potential for infinite change, which is an on-going, dynamic reality. What about ignorance? For Thomas Aquinas, ignorance is the privation of knowledge,[69] the definition most commonly accepted for ignorance and which one finds in the dictionary. He discusses the issue of ignorance in depth in Question 76 of the *Summa theologiae*.[70] Here he addresses four points of inquiry, all within the context of sin: (1) does ignorance cause sin; (2) is ignorance sinful; (3) does ignorance excuse us completely from sin; and (4) does ignorance lessen sin? Thomas Aquinas approaches these questions from two viewpoints, one which says "never" and one which says "always", and responds clearly and distinctly that there are no absolute answers to these questions, although within the framework of sin, his conclusions give us insight into the human intellect and a basis upon which to judge the ramifications of ignorance.

In article 1, "Does ignorance cause sin?", Thomas Aquinas addresses Augustine's contention that ignorance can cause some sin. He concludes by agreeing with Augustine that ignorance can cause some sin, but uses the Aristotelian distinctions of direct and indirect causes: he states that what is not cannot be the direct cause of what is, but it can be the indirect cause, e.g., as removing an impediment.[71] So, a person cannot willfully do something sinful if he or she does not know it,[72] but, by being ignorant, the person can indirectly do something sinful.[73]

In article 2, "Is ignorance sinful?", Thomas Aquinas first distinguishes between ignorance and nescience (not-knowing): anyone who lacks knowledge would be called nescient, but ignorance implies a lack of knowledge that one ought to have.[74] Without this necessary knowledge that one is to have, the person is unable to fulfill his or her duties. This is not a question of capacity or ability to know; rather, it is a question of opportunity: one is capable of knowing, but does not. This is different from not knowing because one is unable to comprehend.

Beginning with the premise that people are capable of knowing, Thomas Aquinas then states that all people are to know basic truths and the general principles of right and wrong as well as specific knowledge pertaining to one's station in life.[75] If a person does not have specific knowledge and fails to accomplish

---

[68]DAVIES, *The Thought of Thomas Aquinas*, p. 126.

[69]*Summa theologiae*, IaIIae, q. 76, 1: "Sed ignorantia est non ens, cum sit privatio quaedam scientiae" (DURBIN, vol. 25, *Sin*, p. 142).

[70]*Summa theologiae*, IaIIae, q. 76: *de causa peccati ex parte rationis*. Thomas Aquinas also discusses the effect of ignorance upon voluntary and involuntary acts in IaIIae, q. 6, 8.

[71]*Ibid.*, ad 1: "[Q]uod non ens non potest esse alicujus causa per se, potest tamen esse causa per accidens, sicut remotio prohibentis" (DURBIN, vol. 25, *Sin*, p. 144).

[72]*Summa theologiae*, IaIIae, q. 76, 1: "Sed voluntas non fertur nisi in aliquod cognitum: quia bonum apprehensum est objectum voluntatis." (DURBIN, vol. 25, *Sin*, p. 142). This axiom of Thomas Aquinas will be discussed at greater length in Chapter Two of this dissertation.

[73]See *Summa theologiae*, IaIIae, q. 76, 1 for the complete discussion.

[74]*Summa theologiae*, IaIIae, q. 76, 2: "Dicendum quod ignorantia in hoc a nescientia differt, quod nescientia dicit simplicem scientiae negationem, unde cuicumque deest aliquarum rerum scientia potest dici nescire illas... Ignorantia vero importat scientiae privationem, dum scilicet alicui deest scientia eorum quae aptus natus est scire." (DURBIN, vol. 25, *Sin*, p. 146).

[75]*Summa theologiae*, IaIIae, q. 76, 2: "Unde omnes tenentur scire communiter ea quae sunt fidei, et universalia juris praecepta: singuli autem ea quae ad eorum statum vel officium spectant," (DURBIN, vol. 25, *Sin*, p. 146).

22

something expected, then it is a sin of omission.[76] However, here he makes the distinction between invincible and vincible ignorance: a person who cannot possibly know something cannot be called negligent, since that person was never given the opportunity to learn. This is called "invincible" ignorance because it cannot be overcome "even with effort" and thus is not sinful.[77] "Vincible" ignorance, however, is that lack of knowledge which can be overcome with moral diligence and can be sinful, but only with reference to things that ought to be known.[78] So, even here, Thomas Aquinas is narrow in his assigning of blame due to ignorance and the blame is due to negligence rather than to ignorance itself.

In article 3, "Does ignorance excuse us completely from sin?", Thomas Aquinas follows logically from the above discussion and states that ignorance can be voluntary or involuntary. Voluntary ignorance can be directly or indirectly willed.[79] Voluntary ignorance is sinful because it is the result of negligence, which, as we have already seen, does not excuse from sin.[80] However, involuntary ignorance, that is, either invincible ignorance or ignorance of something which a person does not need to know, does excuse from sin.[81] Thus, he states that any type of ignorance does not excuse from sin, yet if ignorance precludes the use of reason, it entirely excuses from sin in those particular instances.[82]

In article 4, "Does ignorance lessen sin?", Thomas Aquinas replies that ignorance diminishes sin only as it infringes upon free will. Therefore, if ignorance does not lessen freedom, then it does not lessen sin.[83] He also states, once again, that if the ignorance is completely involuntary, then sin is not only lessened, but eliminated.[84]

---

[76]*Summa theologiae*, IaIIae, q. 76, 2: "Manifestum est autem quod quicumque negligit habere vel facere id quod tenetur habere vel facere peccat peccato omissionis. Unde propter negligentiam, ignorantia eorum quae aliquis scire tenetur, est peccatum." (DURBIN, vol. 25, *Sin*, p. 148).

[77]*Summa theologiae*, IaIIae, q. 76, 2: "Non autem imputatur homini ad negligentiam si nesciat ea quae scire non potest. Unde horum ignorantia invincibilis dicitur: quia scilicet studio superari non potest. Et propter hoc talis ignorantia, cum non sit voluntaria, eo quod non est in potestate nostra eam repellere, non est peccatum. Ex quo patet quod nulla ignorantia invincibilis est peccatum." (DURBIN, vol. 25, *Sin*, p. 148).

[78]*Summa theologiae*, IaIIae, q. 76, 2: "...ignorantia autem vincibilis est peccatum, si sit eorum quae aliquis scire tenetur; non autem si sit eorum quae quis scire non tenetur." (DURBIN, vol. 25, *Sin*, p. 148).

[79]*Summa theologiae*, IaIIae, q. 76, 3: "...quia scilicet ipsa ignorantia est voluntaria: vel directe, sicut cum aliquis studiose vult nescire aliqua, ut liberius peccet, vel indirecte, sicut cum aliquis propter laborem, vel propter alias occupationes, negligit addiscere id per quod a peccato retraheretur." (DURBIN, vol. 25, *Sin*, p. 152).

[80]*Summa theologiae*, IaIIae, q. 76, 3: "Talis enim negligentia facit ignorantiam ipsam esse voluntariam et peccatum, dummodo sit eorum quae quis scire tenetur et potest. Et ideo talis ignorantia non totaliter excusat a peccato." (DURBIN, vol. 25, *Sin*, p. 152).

[81]*Summa theologiae*, IaIIae, q. 76, 3: "Si vero sit talis ignorantia quae omnino sit involuntaria, sive quia est invincibilis, sive quia est ejus quod quis scire non tenetur, talis ignorantia omnino excusat a peccato." (DURBIN, vol. 25, *Sin*, p. 152).

[82]*Summa theologiae*, IaIIae, q. 76, 3: "...si esset talis ignorantia quae totaliter usum rationis excluderet, omnino a peccato excusaret: sicut patet in furiosis et amentibus." (DURBIN, vol. 25, *Sin*, p. 152).

[83]*Summa theologiae*, IaIIae, q. 76, 4: "Dicendum quod, quia omne peccatum est voluntarium, intantum ignorantia potest diminuere peccatum inquantum diminuit voluntarium: si autem voluntarium non diminuat, nullo modo diminuet peccatum." (DURBIN, vol. 25, *Sin*, p. 154).

[84]*Summa theologiae*, IaIIae, q. 76, 4: "Manifestum est autem quod ignorantia quae totaliter a peccato excusat, quia totaliter voluntarium tollit, peccatum non minuit, sed omnino aufert." (DURBIN, vol. 25, *Sin*, p. 154).

Therefore, Thomas Aquinas speaks of ignorance as a privation of knowledge, but the knowledge is specific: that is, it is of things which one ought to know. He makes the distinctions between invincible and vincible ignorance; between voluntary and involuntary ignorance; between direct and indirect voluntary ignorance. While these are categories which presuppose the fixing of human responsibility within the context of sin, and thus the discussion of their consequences centers upon determining whether one is sinning or not, they will form the basis from which later judgments can be made concerning responsibility for one's actions. We are able to move from a philosophical/theological/moral framework into a canonical one, a shift from "blame for" to "obligations resulting from" one's actions.

It is important to remember that this discussion of ignorance is situated within the framework of sin and, for Thomas Aquinas, sin presupposes that one has the ability to sin; otherwise an act would not be sinful.[85] Thus, when speaking of ignorance, it is presumed that one has the capacity to know. In other words, people have the intellect, that is, the power by which knowledge is attained,[86] but for some reason, were not given the opportunity or the experience to know what they were supposed to know, thus the differentiation of the various categories listed above. This is different from the situation of those who cannot know or are incapable of knowing due to some psychic abnormality or developmental handicap, as Thomas Aquinas himself lists as "imbecility and insanity."[87] It is within the context of capacity that the discussion of ignorance and marriage will take place.

d. Alphonsus Liguori (1696-1787)

The most noted and authoritative moral theologian in the Roman Catholic Church is probably Alphonsus de Liguori.[88] Alphonsus accepts that human activity is action proceeding from knowledge and free will. This is activity whereby people seek truth, practical truth, in order to act correctly.[89] He also agrees that the basic norm for judging human activity is the ultimate purpose intended by God,[90] that is, human destiny. Elevated by supernatural grace a person is destined, through knowledge and love of God, to be intimately united with God in an eternal union of knowledge and love. This destiny is what ultimately determines the morality of human activity.[91] The highest rule for humanity is the will of God, discovered through Revelation and Natural Law.[92] There are two norms by which one is able to discern what can lead to or what can deter a person from his or her ultimate destiny: law and conscience. Law is the external objective rule and

[85]A complete discussion of who is capable of sin is beyond the purview of this dissertation. For a better and more comprehensive understanding, see *Summa theologiae*, IaIIae, which deals with sin in qq. 71-80.

[86]COLLINSON, *Fifty Major Philosophers*, p. 36.

[87]*Summa theologiae*, IaIIae, q. 76, 3: "...furiosis et amentibus" (DURBIN, vol. 25, p. 152).

[88]F.J. CONNELL, "Liguori, St. Alphonsus and Catholic Moral Theology", in V. FERM, ed., *Encyclopedia of Morals*, New York, Greenwood Press, 1969, p. 294.

[89]T. REY-MERMET, *Moral Choices: The Moral Theology of Saint Alphonsus Liguori*, P. LAVERDURE, trans., Liguori, Missouri, Liguori Publications, 1998, p. 65.

[90]CONNELL, "Liguori, St. Alphonsus and Catholic Moral Theology", p. 296.

[91]*Ibid.*, p. 297.

[92]REY-MERMET, *Moral Choices*, p. 60.

24

conscience is the internal subjective one.[93] Our concern is for the external objective as envisioned in law. In regards to eternal law, Alphonsus accepts the definitions of Augustine and Thomas Aquinas, i.e., "the very reason or will of God ordering the natural order to be conserved."[94] He is also in agreement with Thomas Aquinas and defines natural law as the participation of the eternal law in the rational creature.[95] Alphonsus does not infer that the natural law is different from the eternal law. Rather, he asserts that the eternal law binds a person only insofar as this person knows the natural law, i.e., participates in the eternal law through the natural light of reason.[96] For Alphonsus, the natural law consists in that concept which communicates the obligation of acting correctly. It is the gift of natural reason that allows one to know the natural law.[97]

Alphonsus distinguishes three types of precepts pertaining to the natural law: (1) the most common precepts or certain first principles which are *per se* known, such as evil is to be avoided; (2) immediate or proximate conclusions which are closely connected with the first principles and easily deduced from them, such as the ten commandments; and (3) more mediate or remote conclusions which are deduced from the first principles only through a comparatively long discursive process, such as laws concerning interest and usury.[98] It is only in this third category, the more remote conclusions,[99] that Alphonsus allows for the possibility of invincible ignorance.[100]

Alphonsus addresses the effects of ignorance in his discussion of the human act,[101] where he states that

---

[93]CONNELL, "Liguori, St. Alphonsus and Catholic Moral Theology", p. 297.

[94]C. CURRAN, *Invincible Ignorance of the Natural Law according to St. Alphonsus*, Romae, Academia Alphonsiana, 1961, p. 25.

[95]*Ibid.*, p. 26.

[96]*Ibid.* See A. DE LIGUORI, *Apologia in cui si defende la dissertazione del medesimo prima data in luce circa l'uso moderato dell'opinione probabile dalle opposizioni da un molto Rev. P. Lettore che nomina Adelfo Dositeo*, Venezia, Remondini, 1764, pp. 47-49.

[97]CURRAN, *Invincible Ignorance*, p. 27.

[98]*Ibid.*, p. 28. "Ante omnia tria genera Praeceptorum naturalium considerata sunt. I. Alia sunt praecepta communissima, quae sunt quaedam prima principia per se nota, prout sunt illa: Malum est vitandum. Quod tibi non vis, alteri ne feceris; et similia. II. Alia sunt Conclusiones immediatae seu proximae, quae ex illis primis principiis clare inferuntur, prout sunt praecepta Decalogi. III. Alia vero sunt Praecepta, quae inferuntur difficiliori discursu, et dicuntur Conclusiones mediatae seu remotae, prout sunt Praecepta de vitandis usuris, odium in proximum, etc." (A. DE LIGUORI, *Theologia Moralis* II [1753], vol. 1, lib. 1, n. 169, p. 70).

[99]"Certum igitur est, quod *in primis iuris naturalis principiis*, aeque ac *in proximis conclusionibus*, et *certis obligationibus proprii status*, non datur invincibilis ignorantia, quia lumine ipso naturae, talia omnibus nota sunt, praeterquam illis qui oculos claudunt ne ea videant.... Contra vero, unanimis theologorum sententia est, tum probabilistarum, tum antiprobabilistarum, *in conclusionibus mediatis et obscuris*, seu remotis a principiis, utique dari et admitti debere ignorantiam invincibilem" (A. DE LIGUORI, *Theologia moralis* [all texts are taken from this edition], L. GAUDÉ, ed., Romae, ex Typographia Vaticana, 1905, vol. 1, lib. 1, nn. 170-171, p. 148).

[100]It must be noted, however, that in the second (1753), third (1757), fourth (1760) and fifth (1763) editions of *Theologia moralis*, Alphonsus was following the general opinion of the day that allowed, under certain circumstances, invincible ignorance in the second category. See CURRAN, *Invincible Ignorance*, pp. 28-29.

[101]*Liber quintus*, "De ratione cognoscendi et discernendi peccata", Tractatus praeambulus, "De actibus humanis in genere" (LIGUORI, *Theologia moralis*, vol. 2, pp. 689-703).

ignorance is multifaceted and is usually divided into a simple privation (of knowledge) which disrupts the order of things,[102] and can be divided into ignorance of law and ignorance of fact.[103] Alphonsus further divides ignorance, stating that it can be concomitant, consequent or antecedent.[104] Concomitant ignorance is that of a person who is actually unaware of what he or she is doing, but would still pursue the act if he or she were not ignorant. Here, Alphonsus gives the example of a hunter killing an animal and discovering that it is his enemy instead.[105]

Consequent ignorance follows from the determination of the will in so far as the ignorance is directly voluntary and proceeds from the will. Such ignorance is directly voluntary or affected ignorance if the person deliberately wills the lack of knowledge. It is indirectly voluntary or crass ignorance if the person neglects to know what one can and is obliged to know.[106] In both concomitant and consequent ignorance, a person can be, and often is, held responsible for the ramifications of his or her actions.

Antecedent ignorance, on the other hand, precedes the consent of the will and is not voluntary. However, it is the cause of willing that which otherwise would not be willed if the person were aware of the truth. This is what Alphonsus calls invincible ignorance. For a further discussion of this theme, he directs the reader to his tract on conscience.[107] It is invincible ignorance that Alphonsus also calls involuntary or inculpable ignorance, since the person who does not know the truth and cannot overcome this ignorance by

---

[102]"Ignorantia multiplex est. et dividi solet: 1°. Ignorantiam *simplicis privationis*, et ignorantiam *pravae dispositionis*" (*ibid.*, p. 695).

[103]"2°. Dividitur in ignorantiam *juris* et *facti*. — Ignorantia *juris* est cum quis legem seu aliquid esse praeceptum aut prohibitum ignorat; v. gr. si quis ignorat in vigilia Pentecostes esse praeceptum jejunium ex consuetudine. — Ignorantia facti est si quis nesciat factum ipsum esse prohibitum quod revera non licet; ut si quis ignoret esse carnem quam comedit die jejunii" (*ibid.*).

[104]For further discussion of the various notions of ignorance, see S. BERTKE, *The Possibility of Invincible Ignorance of the Natural Law*, Washington, DC, Catholic University of America Press, Studies in Sacred Theology, 58, 1941, pp. 48-52. These are the same distinctions made by Thomas Aquinas in the *Summa theologiae*, IaIIae, q. 6, 8.

[105]"Ignorantia *concomitans* est illa qua quis ignorat id quod agit, sed adhuc ageret si non ignoraret. Talis est ignorantia illius qui ignorans occidit hostem, putans occidere cervum; tamen si sciret, etiam occideret. — Haec ignorantia non est causa actionis; sed tantum per accidens actionem comitatur"(LIGUORI, *Theologia moralis*, vol. 2, lib. 5, n. 26, p. 695). See also CURRAN, *Invincible Ignorance*, p. 29.

[106]"Ignorantia *consequens* dicitur illa quae sequitur determinationem voluntatis, in quantum ipsa ignorantia est voluntaria et procedit a libera voluntate. Haec ignorantia consequens subdividitur in *voluntariam directe* seu *affectatam*, in voluntariam *indirecte* seu *crassam*, et ignoratiam *malae electionis*. — *Prima* est illa qua voluntas directe vult ipsam ignorantiam; ut cum aliquis vult ignorare, vel ut excusationem peccati jam commissi habeat, vel ut non retrahatur a peccato committendo... Hac ignorantia laborant ii qui data opera, nec consilium petunt in dubiis, nec conciones et catecheses adeunt, ne in malam fidem incidant et a suo proposito deterreantur. — Ignorantia *indirecte voluntaria* seu *crassa* est quando quis non affectat ignorare, sed negligit addiscere ea quae scire potest et debet. Et secundum hunc modum ignorantia universalium juris quae quis scire tenetur dicitur voluntaria, quasi proveniens a negligentia. — Tandem ignorantia *malae electionis* est illa quae actu non considerat quod hic et nunc considerare potest et debet, et provenit ex passione vel ex habitu" (LIGUORI, *Theologia moralis*, vol. 2, lib. 5, n. 26, pp. 695-696). See also CURRAN, *Invincible Ignorance*, p. 29.

[107]"Ignorantia *antecedens* est illa quae omnino antecedit consensum voluntatis, ita ut nullo modo sit voluntaria, et tamen est causa volendi id quod alias non vellet si sciret: puta cum aliquis adhibita diligentia interficit hominem, quem credit esse feram. Haec ignorantia appellatur etiam invincibilis. — De hac tamen ignorantia invincibili, sicut et de ignorantia vincibili, hic non loquimur; quia de iis sermonem fecimus in Tract. *de Consc., ex n. tres*" (LIGUORI, *Theologia moralis*, vol. 2, lib. 5, n. 26, p. 696). See also CURRAN, *Invincible Ignorance*, pp. 29-30.

ordinary diligence is not held responsible, and therefore is not sinning.[108] Diligence refers to moral diligence which is the effort a person is accustomed to use in acquiring knowledge. It will vary from person to person and from circumstance to circumstance.[109]

Not all ignorance is inculpable, as we have already seen. Following the teachings of Thomas Aquinas, Alphonsus teaches that ignorance could be voluntary and culpable in either of two ways: directly, when the person consciously attempts not to know, thus freeing himself or herself to sin; and indirectly, when that person neglects to employ the necessary means and diligence to overcome ignorance. This negligence renders the consequent ignorance voluntary and sinful if it pertains to those things which a person is obliged to know and is capable of knowing. However, involuntary ignorance, either because it is invincible or is concerned with things a person is not obliged to know, excuses the consequent act from guilt. Even if someone is obliged to know the law, that person's ignorance, according to Thomas Aquinas, can still be invincible.[110]

In summary, then, Alphonsus sees human activity as proceeding from knowledge and free will. This activity strives to follow the ultimate purpose of existence intended by God. This ultimate aim is to be united with God through knowledge and love. There are, however, impediments to attaining this aspiration which are called sins. Thus, ignorance, being the privation of due knowledge, is seen within the categories of sin and guilt, since it is a privation of a "good" that comes from God, so to speak.

Putting these categories of sin and guilt aside, Alphonsus gives us clearly delineated classes of ignorance — ignorance of law and of fact, as well as concomitant, consequent and antecedent ignorance. These classifications will allow us to differentiate more distinctively the relationship between ignorance and the intellect and between ignorance and the will, which will be important for our study since both the intellect and the will are intimately involved in consent, which forms the basis of marriage. How ignorance affects matrimonial consent will be discussed in detail in the subsequent chapters.

II. IGNORANCE AND THE LAW

As discussed in the previous section, ignorance is lack of specific, or due, knowledge; that which should be known by the subject. The lack of knowledge that a person is not required to have is nescience.[111] It is this qualifying definition of ignorance, i.e., lack of due knowledge, which determines whether a person

---

[108]"Quod ignorantia *antecedens* causat *simpliciter* involuntarium; quia nullo modo est volita, et vere invincibilis, quod nulla morali diligentia superari potest, ideoque est inculpabilis" (LIGUORI, *Theologia moralis*, vol. 2, lib. 5, n. 27, p. 696). See also CURRAN, *Invincible Ignorance*, p. 31.

[109]S. BERTKE, *The Possibility of Invincible Ignorance of the Natural Law*, p. 49.

[110]"Ita docet idem S. Thomas (Iallae, q. 76, 3), qui statuit dupliciter ignorantiam esse voluntariam et culpabilem: vel directe, sicut cum aliquis studiose vult nescire aliqua, ut liberius peccet; vel indirecte, sicut cum aliquis, propter laborem vel propter alias occupationes negligit addiscere id per quod a peccato retraheretur. Talis enim negligentia facit ignorantiam ipsam esse voluntariam et peccatum, dummodo sit eorum quae quis scire tenetur et potest; et ideo talis ignorantia non totaliter excusat a peccato. Si vero sit talis ignorantia, quae omnino sit involuntaria, sive quia est invincibilis, sive quia est ejus quod quis scire non tenetur, talis ignorantia omnino excusat a peccato.... Angelicus... sane ostendit, ignorantiam adhuc eorum quae scire tenemur, posito quod sit invincibilis, a peccato excusare" (LIGUORI, *Theologia moralis*, vol. 1, lib. 1, n. 171, p. 148). See also CURRAN, *Invincible Ignorance*, p. 32.

[111]CICOGNANI, *Canon Law*, p. 590. He also refers to this as *inscience*.

is held responsible for his or her actions in law.[112] It is also important to note that this definition of ignorance pertains to those people who are capable of having such knowledge in the first place.[113]

a. Ignorance and Roman Law

Generally, the law recognizes two types of ignorance: ignorance of law and ignorance of fact[114] which pertain to the object. These distinctions are also found in Roman law[115] but the context is different from that considered above in that ignorance was not confined to delicts. In Roman law, ignorance (and error which will be referred to briefly in this context) pertains to the law of obligations,[116] which includes both contracts and delicts. Contracts comprise the larger part of obligations, thus the general principles relating to their formation, subject matter and terms of performance are important to consider. These general principles which pertain to the many facets of a contract, in particular deal with the parties and their competence to enter into a contract as well as mitigating circumstances, of which ignorance was one.[117]

Ignorantia iuris (ignorance of law) was defined as ignorance (lack of knowledge) or an error (false

---

[112]The context of ignorance and law is that of crime and delict. While the focus of this dissertation is not concerned with crime or blame, it is concerned with the responsibility of one placing an act (marriage) while ignorant. Thus a brief discussion of this nature, i.e., the acceptance of responsibility for one's actions, is a propos and enlightening.

[113]Thus, those people who are incapable of knowledge, i.e., those who habitually lack the use of reason or suffer from psychological disorders, are not included. See U.C. BESTE, *Introductio in Codicem quam in usum et utilitatem scholae et cleri ad promptam expeditamque canonum interpretationem*, 4th ed., Neapoli (Italia), M. D'Auria, 1956, p.966; M. RAMSTEIN, *A Manual of Canon Law*, Hoboken, New Jersey, Terminal Printing and Publishing Co., 1947, pp. 671-672; F.X. WERNZ, *Ius canonicum*, vol. 1, Romae, apud Aedes Universitatis Gregorianae, 1938, pp. 254-256; S. WOYWOD, *A Practical Commentary on the Code of Canon Law*, vol. II, rev. and enlarged ed. by C. SMITH, New York, J.F. Wagner, Inc., 1957, p. 451.

[114] B.A. GARNER, ed., *Black's Law Dictionary*, 7th ed., St. Paul, Minnesota, West Group, 1999, p. 749. This latest edition, however, does not make the distinctions in law that the earlier, 1990 edition made. Thus, this earlier edition will be cited later in this study where pertinent.

[115]A. BERGER, *Encyclopedic Dictionary of Roman Law*, The American Philosophical Society, Philadelphia, 1953, p. 491. Although ignorance is listed in two categories, that of fact (*facti*) and that of law (*iuris*), Berger equates *ignorantia facti* with *error facti*. M.J. GARCIA GARRIDO, *Diccionario de jurisprudencia romana*, 3rd ed., Madrid, L'Auteur, 1988, p. 164, makes the same distinction.
A. WATSON, as English translator of *The Digest of Justinian*, T. MOMMSEN and P. KRUGER, eds., Philadelphia, University of Pennsylvania Press, 1985, translates *ignorantia* as "mistake" (see vol. 2, p. 653, which is Book XXII, VI of *The Digest of Justinian*). Mistake seems to be more aligned with modern law understanding. See W.L. BURDICK, *The Principles of Roman Law and Their Relation to Modern Law*, Rochester, Lawyers Co-operative Publishing Co., 1938, pp. 399-402, for a more in-depth treatment. In this section of the *Digest*, the translator interchanges *nesciat* and *ignoret* ("does not know"), while "mistake of law" and "mistake of fact" are the translations of *in iure errat* and *in facto errat*, respectively. See pp. 653-654. On the other hand, S.P. SCOTT, ed. and trans., *Corpus iuris civilis: The Civil Law*, vol. 3, New York, AMS Press, p. 237, presents a clearer translation. We have chosen to use Scott's translation for the purpose of this study.

[116]See BURDICK, *The Principles of Roman Law*, pp 386-402. Here, the author defines "obligation" as "a legal relation, a tie or bond, which holds two (or more) persons together, creating a duty and a right, the duty of the debtor to pay, and the right of a creditor to be paid."

[117]*Ibid.*, p. 392.

28

knowledge)[118] concerning the existence or meaning of a legal norm.[119]

    Ignorantia facti (ignorance of fact) was defined as ignorance or error of legally important circumstances surrounding an object.[120] The broad rule was ignorance of the law was not held excusable, while ignorance of fact was.[121] Ignorance of fact, in order to be excusable, was not to be of a peculiarly gross kind. There was to be a certain amount of diligence in seeking pertinent information.[122] Ignorance of law was excusable only in cases where the immediate purpose of the persons pleading it was to save themselves from loss and not to make some gain. Thus, the person who acted in ignorance, i.e., lack of knowledge of the law, had to bear the consequences which resulted from ignorance.[123] However, there were exceptions such as

---

[118]According to J.A.C. THOMAS, *Textbook of Roman Law*, Amsterdam, North-Holland Publishing Co., 1976, p. 228, "error", in Roman terms, "was a belief contrary to the truth, whether based on a false understanding of the facts or on ignorance of the truth, which prevented a person giving real consent to the agreement apparently concluded." Since error is beyond the scope of this study, for further reading and discussion concerning error in Roman law, see footnote 33 on p. 228.

    In many ways "error", "mistake" and "ignorance" were interchangeable terms, as is evidenced by the various translations of the terms by different authors (for example, see BESTE, *Introductio in Codicem*, pp. 76-77; G. MICHIELS, *Normae generales juris canonici: commentarius libri I Codicis juris canonici*, vol. 1, Tornaci, Desclée, 1949, p. 442; P. TOCANEL, *Compendium praelectionum de normis generalibus et de personis in genere*, Romae, Pontificium Institutum utriusque iuris, 1949-1950, pp. 73-74.) See J.A. ABBO and J.D. HANNON, *The Sacred Canons: A Concise Presentation of the Current Disciplinary Norms of the Church*, vol. 1, St. Louis, B. Herder Book Co., 1952, p. 30: "The juridical terms, ignorance, error, and inadvertence are practically interchangeable." For distinguishing between "ignorance" and "error", see F.M. CAPPELLO, *Summa iuris canonici in usum scholarum*, vol. 1, Romae, apud aedes Universitatis Gregorianae, 1945, p. 75; F. DELLA ROCCA, *Manual of Canon Law*, A. THATCHER, trans., Milwaukee, Bruce Publishing Co., 1959, pp. 62-63, footnote 121; L. CHIAPPETTA, *Il Codice di diritto canonico: commento giuridico-pastorale*, 2nd rev. ed.,vol. 1, Roma, Edizioni Dehoniane, 1996, p. 61; and T.I. JIMÉNEZ URRESTI, "De las normas generales" in *Código de derecho canónico: edición bilingüe comentada*, 4th ed., L. DE ECHEVERRIA, ed., Madrid, Biblioteca de Autores Cristianos, La Editorial Catolica, S.A., 1984, p. 26. Whether interchanging the terms or delicately pointing out the nuances between them, the result was the same: i.e., someone's judgment was impaired, which is the important point to keep in mind.

    It is important to note, however, that these terms are not interchangeable, which is clarified by H.C. BLACK, *Black's Law Dictionary*, 6th ed., St. Paul, West Publishing Co., 1990, p. 672: "'Ignorance' and 'error' or 'mistake' are not convertible terms. The former is a lack of information or absence of knowledge; the latter, a misapprehension or confusion of information, or a mistaken supposition of the possession of knowledge. Error as to a fact may imply ignorance of the truth; but ignorance does not necessarily imply error". The relation between the terms ignorance and error shall be discussed in later chapters. Suffice it to say at this point that various authors, especially European canonists, interchanged the concepts, as well as the terms, "error of substance" and "ignorance".

[119]BERGER, *Encyclopedic Dictionary of Roman Law*, p. 491.

[120]*Ibid.*, p. 456.

[121]S. AMOS, *The History and Principles of the Civil Law of Rome: An Aid to the Study of Scientific and Comparative Jurisprudence*, London, K. Paul, Trench and Co., 1883, p. 133.

[122]"Nec supina ignorantia ferenda est factum ignorantis, ut nec scrupulosa inquisitio exigenda: scientia enim hoc modo aestimada est, ut neque neglegentia crassa aut nimia securitas satis expedita sit neque delatoria curiositatis exigatur" (MOMMSEN and KRUEGER, *The Digest of Justinian*, vol. 2, p. 654).

    "Neither gross ignorance of the facts should be tolerated, nor scrupulous inquiry be exacted, but such knowledge should be demanded that neither excessive negligence, too great unconcern, nor the inquisitiveness that characterizes informers may be exhibited" (SCOTT, *Corpus iuris civilis: The Civil Law*, vol. 3, p. 238).

[123] AMOS, *The History and Principles of the Civil Law of Rome*, pp. 133-134. "Ignorantia vel facti vel iuris est. Nam si quis nesciat decessisse eum, cuius bonorum possessio defertur, non cedit ei tempus: sed si sciat quidem defunctum esse cognatum, nesciat autem proximitatis nomine bonorum possessionem sibi deferri, aut se sciat scriptum heredem, nesciat autem quod scriptis heredibus bonorum possessionem praetor promittit, cedit ei tempus, quia in iure errat" (MOMMSEN and KRUEGER, *The Digest*

women, minors, soldiers and inexperienced rustic persons (in Book XXII, Title VI of *The Digest of Justinian*).[124] These same exceptions are likewise listed in *The Code of Justinian*, in Book I, Title XVIII.[125]

b. Ignorance in the Civil Law and the Canon Law

The distinction between ignorance of law and ignorance of fact as seen in Roman law is also found in civil law and in canon law, where these two divisions pertain more to the object rather than to the subject.[126]

---

of Justinian, vol. 2, pp. 653-654).
"Ignorance is either of fact or law. For where anyone is not aware that he to the possession of whose property he is entitled is dead, time does not run against him. [This is ignorance of fact.] Where, indeed, he is aware that his relative is dead, but he does not know that his estate belongs to him on account of his being the next of kin, or, where he is aware that he has been appointed an heir, but does not know that the Praetor grants the possession of the property of a deceased person to those who have been appointed his heirs; time will run against him because he is mistaken with respect to the law [this is ignorance of law]" (SCOTT, *Corpus iuris civilis: The Civil Law*, vol. 3, p. 237).

[124]"Regula est iuris quidem ignorantiam cuique nocere, facti vero ignorantiam non nocere. Videamus igitur, in quibus speciebus locum habere possit, ante praemissao quod minoribus viginti quinque annis ius ignorare permissum est. Quod et in feminis in quibusdam causis propter sexus infirmitatem dicitur: et ideo sicubi non est delictum, sed iuris ignorantia, non laeduntur. Hac ratione si minor viginti quinque annis filio familias crediderit, subvenitur ei, ut non videatur filio familias credidisse. Si filius familias miles a commilitone heres institutus nesciat sibi etiam sine patre licere adire per constitutiones principales, ius ignorare potest et ideo ei dies aditionis cedit"(MOMMSEN and KRUEGER, *The Digest of Justinian*, vol. 2, p. 654).
"The ordinary rule is, that ignorance of law injures anyone, but ignorance of fact does not. Therefore, let us examine to what instances this rule is applicable, for it may be stated, in the first place, that minors under twenty-five years of age are permitted to be ignorant of the law; and this is also held with respect to women in certain cases, on account of the weakness of the sex; hence, so long as no crime has been committed, but only ignorance of the law is involved, their rights are not prejudiced. On the same principle, if a minor under the age of twenty-five lends money to a son under his father's control, relief is granted him, just as if he had not lent the money to a son subject to paternal authority. Where a son under paternal control, who is a soldier, is appointed heir by a comrade-in-arms, and does not know that he can enter upon the estate without permission of his father, he can ignore the law in accordance with the Imperial Constitution; and therefore the time prescribed for the acceptance of the estate does not run against him" (SCOTT, *Corpus iuris civilis: The Civil Law*, vol. 3, p. 239). Anyone who was not aware of the Imperial Constitution was seen as an "inexperienced rustic person"since inhabitants of the city would have been aware of the Constitution, as well as the other applicable laws.

[125]"Quamvis cum causam tuam ageres, ignorantia juris propter simplicitatem armatae militiae allegationes competentes omiseris, tamen si nondum satisfecisti, permitto tibi, si coeperis ex sententia conveniri, defensionibus tuis uti.... Cum ignorantia juris excusari facile non possis, si major annis vigintiquinque haereditati matris tuae renuntiasti: sera prece subveniri tibi desideras.... Quamvis in lucro nec foeminis jus ignorantibus subveniri soleat, attamen contra aetatem adhuc imperfectam locum haec non habere, retro principum statuta declarant.... Constitutiones principum nec ignorare quenquam, nec dissimulare permittimus" (P.-A. TISSOT, trans., *Corpus juris civilis*, vol. 8, *Les donze livres du Code de l'empereur Justinien*, Aalen. Allemagne, Scientia Verlag, 1979, pp.184-187).
"Although when you were conducting your case you may have omitted to make use of proper allegations through ignorance of the law, or because of your want of information as a soldier; still, if you have not yet satisfied the claim, I will permit you to avail yourself of all your means of defence, if proceedings have been begun to enforce the judgment.... You cannot readily be excused on account of your ignorance of the law, if, after having passed the age of twenty-five years, you rejected the estate of your mother; for your application for relief will be too late.... Although it is not customary to be granted to women who are ignorant of the law, in matters where they have been benefited, still, the constitutions of former Emperors stated that this rule does not apply to females who are minors.... We do not permit anyone to be, or pretend to be, ignorant of the Imperial Constitutions" (SCOTT, *Corpus iuris civilis: The Civil Law*, vol. 6, pp. 119-121).

[126]See CICOGNANI, *Canon Law*, pp. 590-591. In Canon law (as in moral theology) there is also the distinction of ignorance which pertains to the subject, which may be classified as invincible, vincible or affected. See also ABBO and HANNON, *The Sacred Canons*, vol. 1, p. 29; D.F. BLANCO NÁJERA, *El Código de derecho canónico, traducido y comentado*,

30

In the civil sphere, ignorance of law, according to *Black's Law Dictionary*, is the lack of knowledge or acquaintance with the laws of the land as they apply to the act, relation, duty or matter under consideration.[127] In other words, a person is unaware of the existence of the law itself. This same understanding of ignorance of law is seen in canon law,[128] but there is a caveat in relation to canonical jurisprudence as is discussed below. Ignorance of fact is the lack of knowledge of some fact or facts constituting or relating to the subject matter at hand.[129] In other words, a person is unaware of certain qualifying circumstances of an object or action. This same understanding of ignorance of fact is seen in canon law.[130]

As in Roman law, if a person is ignorant of a law, that person is still held responsible for his or her actions. This is a common legal axiom.[131] Ladislas Örsy, in his commentary on the General Norms of the

vol. 1, Cadiz, Establecimientos Cerón, 1942, pp. 34-35; A. BLAT, *Commentarium textus Codicis iuris canonici*, vol. 1, *Normae generales*, Romae, ex Typographia Pontificia in Instituto Pii IX (Iuvenum Opificum a S. Joseph), 1921, pp. 93-95; T.L. BOUSCAREN, A.C. ELLIS and F.N. KORTH, *Canon Law: A Text and Commentary*, 4th rev. ed., Milwaukee, Bruce Publishing Company, 1966, p. 31; CAPPELLO, *Summa iuris canonici*, vol. 1, p. 75; G. COCCHI, *Commentarium in Codicem iuris canonici ad usum scholarum*, vol. 1, 5th ed., Taurinorum Augustae, Marietti, 1938, pp. 186-188; MICHIELS, *Normae generales juris canonici*, vol. 1, pp. 442-447; E.F. REGATILLO, *Institutiones iuris canonici*, vol. 1, Santander, Sal Terrae, 1941, pp. 58-59; TOCANEL, *Compendium praelectionum*, pp. 73-74; A. VERMEERSCH, *Epitome iuris canonici*, vol. 1, Romae, H. Dessain, 1963, pp. 130-132. For the purposes of this section, where ignorance in civil law refers to the object, its parallel understanding in canon law is used to illustrate it.

[127]BLACK, *Black's Law Dictionary*, p. 672.

[128]CICOGNANI, *Canon Law*, p. 591. See also BLANCO NÁJERA, *El Código de derecho canónico*, p. 34; BLAT, *Commentarium textus*, vol. 1, *Normae generales*, p. 94; MICHIELS, *Normae generales juris canonici*, vol. 1, p. 448.

[129]BLACK, *Black's Law Dictionary*, p. 672.

[130]CICOGNANI, *Canon Law*, p. 591; TOCANEL, *Compendium praelectionum*, pp. 74-75. See also MICHIELS, *Normae generales juris canonici*, vol. 1, p. 443, for various categories of ignorance of fact.

[131]*Ignorantia legis neminem excusat* ("Ignorance of law excuses no one"). This is ordinarily held to be true in both civil and canon law. However, while generally accepting this axiom, canon law qualified it in canon 16, §1, of the 1917 *CIC* ("Nulla ignorantia legum irritantium aut inhabilitantium ab eisdem excusat, nisi aliud expresse dicatur"; "In the case of invalidating or incapacitating laws, no ignorance excuses from them, unless the law expressly so state", English translation based on BOUSCAREN, *Canon Law: A Text and Commentary*, p. 30) and in canon 15, §1, of the 1983 *CIC* ("Ignorantia vel error circa leges irritantes vel inhabilitantes earundem effectum non impediunt, nisi aliud expresse statuatur"; "Ignorance or error about invalidating or disqualifying laws does not impede their effect unless it is expressly established otherwise", English translation of the 1983 *CIC* in *Code of Canon Law: Latin-English Edition*, new English translation, Canon Law Society of America, Washington, DC, 1999, p. 9). Translations of the 1917 *CIC* are from BOUSCAREN until further noted. All translations of the 1983 *CIC* are from this edition.

In general, canon 16 was included so as not to minimize the effect of law. See C. A. BACHOFEN, *A Commentary on the New Code of Canon Law*, vol. 1, 6th rev. ed., St. Louis, B. Herder Book Co., 1931, p. 86. However, the legislator limited the effect of ignorance to invalidating and inhabilitating laws, allowing for ignorance (and error) in other explicitly noted cases. For more discussion concerning the difference between the civil and canonical understandings of ignorance, see P. LOMBARDÍA and J.I. ARRIETA, *Codice di diritto canonico: edizione bilingue commentata*, L. CASTIGLIONE, Italian ed., vol. 1, Roma, Edizioni Logos, 1986, pp. 64-65.

Both Codes thus stipulated that if cases were explicitly noted, ignorance was to be seen as a mitigating circumstance, which meant that a person would be excused. For a more detailed explanation, see the Commentary by P. LOMBARDÍA, updated by J. OTADUY, "De normis generalibus", in *Code of Canon Law Annotated*; Latin-English edition of the *Code of Canon Law* and English-language translation of the 5th Spanish-language edition of the commentary, E. CAPARROS, M. THÉRIAULT and J. THORN, eds., Montréal, Wilson & Lafleur Limitée, 1993, pp. 89-90. See also G. LOCASTRO, "Conoscenza e interpretazione del diritto", in *Il diritto della Chiesa: interpretazione e prassi*, Città del Vaticano, Libreria editrice Vaticana, Studi giuridici, 41, 1996, p. 19.

1983 *CIC*, states it well when he says that the reason for this rule is to "uphold and protect legal stability and security", since "laws operate independently from the state of mind of the persons." He goes on to say that if the efficacy of such laws depended upon the persons involved having knowledge of said laws, the entire community would suffer.[132]

However, if a person is ignorant of facts, it is not such a simple matter.[133] In canonical legislation, there was a gradation of imputability based upon the culpability of one's ignorance.[134] This imputability based upon ignorance is still evidenced in the 1983 *CIC*, in canon 1321, §1, although implicitly, since the word ignorance itself is not used in the canon.[135] However, according to the animadversions of the *Coetus studiorum de iure poenali* of 7 February 1976, *culpa* included culpable ignorance.[136] The distinction between invincible and vincible ignorance as clarified by Thomas Aquinas and Alphonsus Liguori is important. Where the violation of the law was the result of invincible ignorance, there was no imputability.[137] However, if the

---

Both canon 16 of the 1917 *CIC* and canon 15 of the 1983 *CIC* are in Book One, General Norms, of their respective Codes. This Book lays the foundation for the ecclesial legal system. They are principles which affect the entire Code, explaining the nature and extent of the laws. Thus, the understanding presented here in these first canons which deal with ignorance, sets the stage for how the canonist is (and, in the case of the 1917 *CIC*, was) to regard the impact of ignorance.

[132]L. ÖRSY, "General Norms: Canons 1-28", in *The Code of Canon Law: A Text and Commentary* (= *CLSA Commentary*), J.A. CORIDEN, T.J. GREEN and D.E. HEINTSCHEL, eds., commissioned by the Canon Law Society of America, New York, Paulist Press, 1985, p. 34. Here, Örsy's expertise as both a civil and canon lawyer, is invaluable for understanding the text and context of these canons. Claiming such ignorance, in general, could lead to chaos and the undermining of the community. Although discussing canon 15, §1, of the 1983 *CIC*, the understanding of this canon, since it is substantially the same in the 1917 *CIC*, sheds light on understanding its predecessor, canon 16, §1. As examples, see ABBO and HANNON, *The Sacred Canons*, p. 30; and S. WOYWOD, *A Practical Commentary*, p. 11.

[133]Here we have the axioms *Ignorantia facti excusat* ("Ignorance of fact excuses"), *Ignorantia facti excusat, ignorantia juris non excusat* ("Ignorance of fact excuses; ignorance of law excuses not"), *Ignorantia eorum quae quis scire tenetur non excusat* ("Ignorance of those things which one is bound to know excuses not"). While a person who is ignorant of specific facts may be excused (as is seen in the first two axioms), if that person should have known (or was in a position to have known better), then he or she is responsible for the action (as seen in the final axiom).

[134]In canon 2199 of the 1917 *CIC*, we read: "Imputabilitas delicti pendet ex dolo delinquentis vel ex eiusdem culpa in ignorantia legis violatae aut in omissione debitae diligentiae; quare omnes causae quae augent, minuunt, tollunt dolum aut culpam, eo ipso augent, minuunt, tollunt delicti imputabilitatem" ("The imputability of a crime depends on the malice (*dolus*) of the culprit or on his culpability (*culpa*) in being ignorant of the law or in failing to use due diligence was culpable; hence all causes which increase, diminish, or excuse from malice or culpability, automatically increase, diminish, or excuse from the imputability of the crime"). Canons 2199 through 2211 of the 1917 *CIC* pertain to the imputability of crimes. For further discussion, see SWOBODA, "Imputability of Crime", Chapter Five of his *Ignorance in Relation to the Imputability of Delicts*, pp. 82-113.

[135]Canon 1321, 1°: "Nemo punitur, nisi externa legis vel praecepti violatio, ab eo commissa, sit graviter imputabilis ex dolo vel ex culpa" ("No one is punished unless the external violation of a law or precept, committed by the person, is gravely imputable by reason of malice [*dolo*] or negligence").

[136]*Communicationes*, 8 (1976), p. 176. For further comment, see also T.J. GREEN, "Sanctions in the Church", in *CLSA Commentary*, p. 901; J. ARIAS, "De subiecto poenalibus sanctionibus obnoxio", in *Code of Canon Law Annotated*, pp.824-825; and P. LOMBARDÍA and J.I. ARRIETA, *Codice di diritto canonico*, vol. 2, p. 944.

[137]Canon 2202, §1, of the 1917 *CIC* reads: "Violatio legis ignoratae nullatenus imputatur, si ignorantia fuerit inculpabilis; secus imputabilitas minuitur plus minusve pro ignorantiae ipsius culpabilitate" ("The violation of a law of which one was ignorant is entirely non-imputable, if the ignorance was inculpable; if it was culpable, the liability varies in proportion to the culpability of the ignorance"), as taken from WOYWOD, *A Practical Commentary*, vol. II, p. 451. Unless otherwise noted, translations of the 1917 *CIC* for the rest of this chapter will be from either volume one or volume two of this edition. Here, the term used is

32

violation of the law was the result of vincible (culpable) ignorance, then the penalty was in proportion to the culpability of the ignorance,[138] which also took into consideration the importance of the law being violated, the gravity of the transgression, the person of the delinquent and all the actual circumstances of the case as they existed when the crime or delict was committed.[139]

Where canon law made the distinction between invincible and vincible ignorance and further delineated vincible ignorance into crass (or supine) and merely vincible,[140] civil law speaks of culpable, essential, involuntary, nonessential or accidental and voluntary ignorance.[141] There is no equivalent in civil law to what is known as affected ignorance in moral theology or canon law. .

Culpable ignorance results from a failure to exercise ordinary care to acquire knowledge. In this case, a person who had the opportunities of discovering what was needed to be known did not avail himself or herself of them. This is analogous to vincible ignorance in canon law.

Essential ignorance is ignorance of some essential circumstance so intimately connected with the matter in question and which influences the parties, that it induces them to act in the matter. In other words, if the party knew about a quality or a circumstance, the transaction would not have occurred. This is similar to antecedent ignorance.

Involuntary ignorance is ignorance which does not proceed from choice and which cannot be overcome by the use of any means of knowledge known to a person and within his or her power. This would be the civil law equivalent of invincible ignorance.

Nonessential or accidental ignorance is that which has not of itself any necessary connection with the business in question and which is not the true consideration for entering the contract. This is the case where something is not known, but had it been known, the result would remain the same. This is the civil law parallel to concomitant ignorance.

Voluntary ignorance exists when a party might, by taking reasonable efforts, have acquired the necessary knowledge.[142] This would be, according to Alphonsus Liguori, indirect culpable ignorance, i.e., the

"inculpable" (*inculpabilis*) but it is understood in the same manner as invincible ignorance, i.e., it could not be removed by the use of ordinary means or diligence. See DELLA ROCCA, *Manual of Canon Law*, p. 514. For another opinion, see BOUSCAREN, *Canon Law: A Text and Commentary*, p. 866, who states that inculpability can be either culpable ignorance of the law or culpable negligence.

The 1983 *CIC*, in canon 1323, 2°, which parallels this paragraph, does not differentiate or vary the liability: "Nulli poenae est obnoxius qui, cum legem vel praeceptum violavit:... 2° sine culpa ignoravit se legem vel praeceptum violare; ignorantiae autem inadvertentia et error aequiparantur" ("The following are not subject to a penalty when they have violated a law or precept:... 2° a person without negligence was ignorant that he or she violated a law or precept: inadvertence and error are equivalent to ignorance").

[138]"Since ignorance, inadvertence, error, excitement, depression and great mental or bodily sufferings disturb the mind and will, and frequently impede perfect deliberation in human acts, they may be pleaded as mitigating circumstances" (WOYWOD, *A Practical Commentary*, vol. II, p. 451).

[139]DELLA ROCCA, *Manual of Canon Law*, p. 514. This same distinction is made by BOUSCAREN, *Canon Law: A Text and Commentary*, p. 31.

[140]CICOGNANI, *Canon Law*, p. 591. Vincible ignorance is crass or supine when there is no effort made to dispel it. Merely vincible ignorance is when a person makes some effort to remove it but the effort is insufficient to do so.

[141]BLACK, *Black's Law Dictionary*, p. 672. The following definitions of the various kinds of ignorance that follow are taken from *Black's Law Dictionary*.

[142]J. McCLINTOCK and J. STRONG, *Cyclopedia of Biblical and Ecclesiastical Literature*, vol. 4, New York, Harper, 1872, p. 494, present a good description: "A sort of ignorance which is neither entirely willful nor entirely invincible."

person neglects to employ the necessary means and diligence to overcome ignorance.[143]

III. IGNORANCE IN RELATION TO JURIDIC ACTS

A simple definition of a juridic act which is used quite frequently is that of O. Robleda: "an externally manifested act of the will by which a certain juridic effect is intended."[144] While Robleda is succinct, G. Michiels, in his extensive treatment of the notion of juridic act,[145] gives both a broad and a strict definition of a juridic act.[146] In his strict definition, Michiels lists five major elements of the juridic act: 1) it is a human act; 2) it is a social act; (3) it is legitimately placed and declared; (4) the juridic effect of this act is determined by law and (5) the juridic effect is recognized by the law in so far as it is intended by the agent.

The fact that it is a human act means it is an act of the will, i.e. one in which the will is freely operating.[147] In other words, there is an interplay of the intellect and the will.[148] Simply stated, a truly human act must be based on sufficient knowledge to allow deliberation of the intellect as well as the inner freedom of the will.[149] Thus, on the part of the intellect, there is to be knowledge of the matter; and on the part of the will, there is to be a conscious and free determination in such a way that the agent can freely and deliberately act. This means that whenever knowledge on the part of the intellect or deliberation on the part of the will is substantially defective (or lacking), then by the natural law itself, consent is also defective (or lacking) and

---

[143]There is, in our opinion, a fine line between culpable and voluntary ignorance. The moral distinctions, defined by Thomas Aquinas and Alphonsus Liguori, are better and clearer.

[144]"...voluntatis actum externe manifestatum quo certus effectus iuridicus intenditur," in "Dissertationes et quaesita varia: de conceptu actus iuridici", in *Periodica*, 51 (1962), p. 419. For examples of the wide use of this definition, see K.A. HILL, "General Norms: Canons 124-203", in *CLSA Commentary*, p. 89; M. HUGHES, "A New Title in the Code: On Juridical Acts", in *Studia canonica*, 14 (1980), pp. 391-403; J.M. KUZIONA, *The Nature and Application of Juridical Acts according to Canon 124 of the Code of Canon Law*, [doctoral dissertation]. Ottawa, Saint Paul University, 1998, p. 15.

[145]G. MICHIELS, *Principia generalia de personis in Ecclesia: commentarius Libri II Codicis juris canonici, canones praeliminares 87-106*, editio altera penitus retractata et nobiliter aucta, Tornaci, Desclée, 1955, pp. 565-680.

[146]*Ibid.*, p. 572: "*Sensu lato*... actus juridicus dicitur quodcumque factum externum voluntarium, ab homine libere positum, cui qua tali lex de facto tribuit effectum juridicum determinatum, independenter tum ab intrinseco actus objecto, tum a fine ab agente directe intento.... *Sensu stricto* autem actus juridicus est 'actus humanus socialis legitime positus et declaratus, cui a lege ideo et eatenus effectus juridicus determinatus agnoscitur, quia et quatenus effectus ille ab agente intenditur.'"
"In a broad sense... a juridical act is any external fact, freely placed by the human person, to which the law attributes a determined juridical effect, independently from both the intrinsic object of the act, and from the purpose directly intended by the agent.... In a strict sense, on the other hand, a juridical act is a social human act which is legitimately placed and declared, and for which a determined juridical effect is recognized in law, because and in so far as it is intended by the agent", (KUZIONA, *The Nature and Application of Juridical Acts*, p. 15).

[147]MICHIELS, *Principia generalia de personis in Ecclesia*, p. 572.

[148]For a brief but clear explanation of this interplay, see D.E. FELLHAUER, "The Exclusion of Indissolubility: Old Principles and New Jurisprudence", in *Studia canonica*, 9 (1975), pp. 108-113. For a more in-depth study, see P.J. JUGIS, *A Canonical Analysis of the Meaning of Humano modo in Canon 1061.1*, Ann Arbor, Michigan, UMI, 1992, Canon Law Studies, 541, pp. 11-45. While the context of this part of his dissertation is Rotal jurisprudence concerning the human act, the discussion of intellect and will is worthy of reading.

[149]KUZIONA, *The Nature and Application of Juridical Acts*, p. 16.

34

one can no longer speak of a "human act".[150]

The act is performed by a person who is capable of doing so. As was discussed earlier in this chapter regarding having the capacity for knowledge, the person who performs a truly human act must have the capacity or ability to do so. From the canonical perspective, there are two types of capacity: natural and juridic.[151] Natural capacity pertains to the ability to think and reason as well as the ability to carry out the act; its basis is found in natural law. Juridic capacity, on the other hand, means that the person possesses those elements prescribed by law[152] as well as being free from impediments[153] which enable him or her to perform such an act.[154] Thus, it is grounded in ecclesiastical law. In canon law natural capacity is oftentimes denoted as *capacitas* and juridic capacity as *habilitas*. When pertaining to natural capacity, canon law presumes that a person is naturally capable of performing a juridic act.[155] This has been reiterated by our Holy Father in his allocution to the Roman Rota in 1982.[156]

---

[150]J.M. SHERBA, "Canon 1096: Ignorance as a Ground for Nullity", in *CLSA Proceedings*, 59 (1997), pp. 284-285.

[151]See F.J. URRUTIA, "Il libro I: le norme generali", in *Il nuovo Codice di diritto canonico: studi*, J. BEYER et al., eds., Torino, Editrice Elle Di Ci, 1985, p. 47. G. MAZZONI, "Le norme generali", in *La normativa del nuovo Codice*, E. CAPPELLINI et al., eds., 2nd ed., Brescia, Queriniana, 1985, p. 54, points out that the general conditions necessary for the validity of a juridic act are above all capacity (*capacità*) and the competence (*competenza*) of the person placing it, differentiating natural and juridic capacities.

[152]E.g., in canon 166 pertaining to elections, only members of the particular college or group can be convoked for the election within that aggregate. According to law, a person must have the status of being a member of a particular organization in order to have the right to vote in an election of that association.

[153]E.g., canon 1083 states that a man who has not completed his sixteenth year and a woman who has not completed her fourteenth year cannot enter a valid marriage. Thus, according to law, a man or a woman who are not of age are impeded from entering into a valid marriage.

[154]See A. McGRATH, "Title VII, Juridical Acts", in *The Canon Law; Letter & Spirit*, G. SHEEHY et al., eds., Collegeville, Minnesota, Liturgical Press, 1995, p. 72, where the author differentiates between general legal capacity and specific legal capacity (which would be similar to the freedom from impediments as discussed above). He also adds another category, i.e., competence, which he defines as having the required position or office to carry out the act. See also KUZIONA, *The Nature and Application of Juridical Acts*, p. 134-135, who lists four types of capacity, one of which is competence.

[155]Canon 124, concerning the validity of a juridic act, would be an example. The Latin term used is *habilis* and implies the fact that a person is legally qualified to perform the act. The English translation approved by conferences of bishops of Australia, Canada, England and Wales, India, Ireland, New Zealand, Scotland and Southern Africa points out this nuance by translating *habilis* as "legally capable" (see *The Code of Canon Law*, new revised English translation, prepared by the Canon Law Society of Great Britain and Ireland in association with The Canon Law Society of Australia and New Zealand and The Canadian Canon Law Society, HarperCollins Publishers, 1997, p. 24). In the first American English translation in 1983, the term "capable" was employed (see *Code of Canon Law; Latin-English Edition*, prepared under the auspices of the Canon Law Society of America, Washington, DC, Canon Law Society of America, 1983, p. 39). However, in the new English translation edition of 1999, the term "qualified" is used (p. 36).
The parallel canon in the *Code of Canons of the Eastern Churches*, canon 931, makes a further distinction by stating that the person must be *habilis et competens*, which is translated as "able and competent" (*Code of Canons of the Eastern Churches* (= *CCEO*), *Latin-English Edition*, translation prepared under the auspices of the Canon Law Society of America, Washington, DC, Canon Law Society of America, 1992, p. 453.) All *CCEO* canons in both Latin and English are from this edition.

[156]While referring to marriage specifically, the Holy Father's allocution verifies this point: "Indubbiamente, la natura umana in seguito al peccato è stata sconvolta, ferita; essa tuttavia non è stata pervertita; essa è stata risanata dall'intervento di Colui che è venuto a salvarla ed a elevarla fino alla partecipazione dalla vita divina. Ora, in verità, sarebbe demolirla, il ritenerla incapace d'un impegno vero, d'un consenso definitivo, d'un patto di amore che esprime quello che essa è, d'un sacramento istituito dal

Furthermore, a juridic act is a social act, which means it is externally manifested.[157] The act must take place because it is an action; it must be performed; it is not merely an intention or something which remains within the agent's mind. The act has ramifications upon other people.[158] It is the outward manifestation of a person's inner disposition and deliberation. When the act is performed, it is done so in a recognized and accepted manner according to the norms of the institution (e.g., Church, society, government, etc.) which gives legitimate status to the act.

Canonical legislation does not define juridic act either in the 1917 *CIC* or in the present 1983 *CIC*. The 1917 *CIC*, rather than speak of the juridic act, refers in canons 103, 104, and 1680[159] to how such an act can be null and void. In the 1983 *CIC*, however, there is Title VII in Book I: Juridic Acts. While the 1983 *CIC* still does not define a juridic act, it begins with canon 124 which addresses the validity of the act.[160]

Signore per guarirla, fortificarla, elevarla per mezzo della sua grazia" ("Undoubtedly, because of sin human nature has become disordered; wounded. Nevertheless it has not been corrupted; it has been restored by the intervention of him who came to save it and to raise it to the point of sharing in the divine life. Truly, to consider human nature incapable of assuming a real obligation; of giving definitive consent; of making a covenant of love expressing what it is; of receiving a sacrament instituted by the Lord to heal it, to strengthen it; and to elevate it by grace would be to destroy it" (JOHN PAUL II, Allocution to the Roman Rota, 28 January 1982, in *AAS*, 74 (1982), p. 452; English translation in W.H. WOESTMAN, ed., *Papal Allocutions to the Roman Rota 1939-1994*, Ottawa, Saint Paul University, 1994, p. 174).

[157]HUGHES, "A New Title in the Code: On Juridical Acts", p. 394.

[158]See McGRATH, "Title VII, Juridical Acts", in *The Canon Law; Letter & Spirit*, p. 72.

[159]Canon 103, §1: "Actus, quos persona sive physica sive moralis ponit ex vi extrinseca, cui resisti non possit, pro infectis habentur."
    §2: "Actus positi ex metu gravi et iniuste incusso vel ex dolo, valent, nisi aliud iure caveatur; sed possunt ad normam can. 1684-1689 per iudicis sententiam rescindi, sive ad petitionem partis laesae sive ex officio."
    Canon 103, §1: "Actions which are done by either a physical or a moral person through extrinsic compulsion ["force"] that could not be resisted, are considered as though they were not done."
    §2: "Actions based on great fear unjustly created or on deceit, are valid unless the law rules otherwise. They can, however, be declared null and void by the ecclesiastical judge, according to Canons 1684-1689, at the instance of the injured party, or even without such petition."
    Canon 104: "Error actum irritum reddit, si versetur circa id quod constituit substantiam actus vel recidat in conditionem *sine qua non*; secus actus valet, nisi aliud iure caveatur; sed in contractibus error locum dare potest actioni rescissoriae ad normam iuris" ("Error renders an act invalid if the error concerns the substance of the action or amounts to a *conditio sine qua non*; otherwise the act is valid, unless the law states the contrary; but in contracts, error may give the person contracting under such error the position for rescissory actions according to the norm of law"), translation based on BOUSCAREN, *Canon Law: A Text and Commentary*, p. 93.
    Canon 1680,§1: "Nullitas actus tunc tantum habetur, cum in eo deficiunt quae actum ipsum essentialiter constituunt, aut sollemnia seu conditiones desiderantur a sacris canonibus requisitae sub poena nullitatis" ("An act is null and void only when either the essential constituents of the act are wanting, or some formalities or conditions are lacking which the Sacred Canons require under pain of nullity").

[160]Canon 124, §1: "Ad validitatem actus iuridici requiritur ut a persona habili sit positus, atque in eodem adsint quae actum ipsum essentialiter constituunt, necnon sollemnia et requisita iure ad validitatem actus imposita."
    §2: "Actus iuridicus quoad sua elementa externa rite positus praesumitur validus."
    Canon 124, §1: "For the validity of a juridic act it is required that the act is placed by a qualified person and include those things which essentially constitute the act itself as well as the formalities and requirements imposed by law for the validity of the act."
    §2: "A juridic act placed correctly with respect to its external elements is presumed valid."
    This is almost identical to *CCEO* canon 931:
    Canon 931, §1: "Ad validitatem actus iuridici requiritur ut a persona habili et competenti sit positus atque in eodem assint, quae actum ipsum essentialiter constituunt, necnon sollemnia et requisita iure ad validitatem actus imposita."

which is a more positive approach than that of the 1917 *CIC* which spoke of the factors which could cause the nullity of the act.[161] This is also seen in the 1990 *CCEO* in canon 931. Thus, for a juridic act to be valid, the person must be capable (both naturally and juridically) of placing it; it must include all of its essential elements; and the formalities and requirements imposed by law for validity must be observed.[162]

After having delineated what is necessary for the validity of a juridic act, the subsequent two canons recognize the factors which could cause the invalidity of a juridic act: canon 125 (as does *CCEO* canon 932) speaks of extrinsic force and grave fear[163] while canon 126 speaks of ignorance and error (as does *CCEO* canon 933).[164] It is important to note that canon 126 (and *CCEO* canon 933) goes beyond the scope of its parallel in the 1917 *CIC*, canon 104. This earlier canon spoke only of error, not mentioning or referring to ignorance in any way. Likewise, canon 104 limited rescissory action to contracts, where canon 126 generalizes it to "juridic acts".[165] Since the 1917 canon referred to the cognitive aspect of the human act,[166] of which error is one deficiency, it made sense to add the category of ignorance, since it also is a traditional defect of knowledge.[167] Both ignorance and error are defects that affect the intellect directly and the will

---

§2: "Actus iuridicus circa sua elementa ad normam iuris positus praesumitur validus."

Canon 931, §1: "For the validity of a juridic act it is required that it be placed by a person able and competent to place it, and that it include those elements which essentially constitute it as well as the formalities and requisites imposed by law for the validity of the act."

§2: "A juridic act correctly placed with respect to its external elements is presumed to be valid."

[161]See HUGHES, "A New Title in the Code: On Juridical Acts", p. 400. The author points out that since the 1917 *CIC* did not propose a positive treatment of the topic, the commentators were satisfied simply to speak of the defects of juridic acts. See also MICHIELS, *Principia generalia de personis in Ecclesia*, p. 567.

[162]J.A. CORIDEN, *An Introduction to Canon Law*, New York, Paulist Press, 1991, pp. 151-152. See also F. BOLOGNINI, *Lineamenti di dirito canonico*, 4th ed., Torino, G. Giappichelli, 1993, pp. 132-133; E. MOLANO, "De actibus iuridicis", in *Code of Canon Law Annotated*, p. 141.

[163]It is beyond the scope of this dissertation to go into detail concerning the similarities and differences between this canon and its parallel canon 103 in the 1917 *CIC*.

[164]Canon 126: "Actus positus ex ignorantia aut ex errore, qui versetur circa id quod eius substantiam constituit, aut qui recidit in condicionem *sine qua non*, irritus est; secus valet, nisi aliud iure caveatur, sed actus ex ignorantia aut errore initus locum dare potest actioni rescissoriae ad normam iuris."

Canon 126: "An act placed out of ignorance or error concerning something which constitutes its substance or which amounts to a condition *sine qua non* is invalid. Otherwise it is valid, unless the law makes other provision. An act entered into out of ignorance or error, however, can give rise to a recissory action according to the norm of law."

Canon 933: "Actus iuridicus positus ex ignorantia aut ex errore, qui versetur circa id, quod eius substantiam constituit, aut qui recidit in condicionem sine qua non, nullus est; secus valet, nisi aliter iure cavetur, sed actus iuridicus ex ignorantia aut errore positus locum dare potest actioni rescissoriae ad normam iuris."

Canon 933: "A juridic act placed because of ignorance or error concerning an element which constitutes its substance or which amounts to a condition *sine qua non* is invalid; otherwise it is valid, unless the law makes some other provision. However, a juridic act placed out of ignorance or error can be the occasion for a recissory action in accordance with the norm of law."

[165]As can be seen in the above text, the parallel canon in the *CCEO* specifies the act as juridic (*actus juridicus*).

[166]R.A. HILL, "General Norms: Canons 124-203", in *CLSA Commentary*, p. 90.

[167]See *Communicationes*, 6 (1974), pp. 101-103, where ignorance is linked with error during the discussion of canons 103 and 104.

indirectly, thus they are intrinsic to the act itself.[168]

Furthermore, canon 126 stipulates that ignorance (or error) is to concern the substance of the act, i.e., its essential elements, or a condition *sine qua non*. While there is no exhaustive list of what constitutes "essential elements" of a given act, since there are different kinds of juridic acts, the law itself includes what is needed in order for the act to be valid.[169] The essential elements of matrimonial consent and marriage and the effect of ignorance upon each of them will be discussed in later chapters.

CONCLUSION

The purpose of this chapter has been to provide the basis for a better understanding and appreciation of the concept of ignorance and its effect in law. The word "appreciation" has been used here intentionally because we believe that ignorance is, at best, little understood and, at worst, misunderstood as it relates to the law concerning marriage, which is the basis of this thesis. Therefore, the knowledge and hopefully the appreciation of ignorance which this chapter has begun and will continue to develop throughout this dissertation, will provide the reader with another means of advancing the development of jurisprudence concerning the invalidity of marriage.

This chapter has looked at ignorance from the philosophical, moral, theological and canonical perspectives and how it affects a person's actions in relationship to law. Certain valuable conclusions and insights may still be made.

One such conclusion is that ignorance is not technically the absence of knowledge; rather, that is nescience. Ignorance is the absence of due knowledge, i.e., a certain degree of knowledge that a person within a given situation is expected to have. For instance, a microbiologist who has no knowledge of constellations would be nescient, since that is out of the purview of his or her expertise, while an astronomer who does not know the constellations would be ignorant, since it is presumed that an astronomer would know them. To understand that ignorance is the lack of due knowledge lays the basis, for later development in this thesis, for refining precisely what is the due knowledge that one must have concerning marriage in order to see how to apply this concept to marriage.

Another conclusion is that ignorance pertains to those people who are capable of having such knowledge but who do not because of various circumstances. Capability here refers to a person's natural ability to attain knowledge. This, by definition, precludes those who do not have such natural ability, e.g., those suffering from *amentia* or certain grave psychological disorders. Thus the foundation has been laid to develop the understanding of ignorance in this context and to demonstrate that it cannot be used as a ground for nullity when the validity of marriage is challenged, based upon whether one or both of the parties were incapable of knowledge at the time of consent. This distinction is important since in the past before the psychological conditions listed in canon 1095 of the 1983 *CIC* (and *CCEO* canon 818), ignorance was used by various canonists in this manner.

A related question, stemming from the above conclusion, is what are the various circumstances which could inhibit a person who is capable of knowledge from having it? Such a question needs to be answered, since it will have ramifications upon drawing the conclusion that a given person is ignorant. Thus, while

---

[168]E. MOLANO, "De actibus iuridicis", in *Code of Canon Law Annotated*, p. 143.

[169]For a fairly comprehensive list, see KUZIONA, *The Nature and Application of Juridical Acts*, pp. 147-148, especially footnote 108.

technically not a conclusion at this point of the study, it is important to keep in mind as the dissertation progresses.

Another conclusion which can be drawn is that since a juridic act is a truly human act, there must be sufficient knowledge to allow deliberation of the intellect, or it is not a juridic act. This lack of sufficient (or "due") knowledge is what we have concluded is ignorance. How does this definition affect our understanding of the specific juridic act we call marriage? This will be discussed in the following chapters.

Another way of looking at this same conclusion is that ignorance, in regard to a juridic act, can produce a juridic effect, i.e., invalidity, under certain circumstances. Those circumstances are delineated in the 1983 *CIC* in canon 126 and in the *CCEO* canon 933, i.e., "an element that constitutes its substance or which amounts to a condition *sine qua non.*" Since marriage is a juridic act, ignorance is listed as a defect in canon 1096 in the 1983 *CIC* and in *CCEO* canon 819. What insights can be drawn, in line with canonical tradition, so that canonists, given today's transient, live-for-today society as well as the impact of a person's particular culture, may more effectively utilize this canon in relation to marriage nullity cases? As this study continues, it is our hope that these questions will be answered.

CHAPTER TWO

IGNORANCE ACCORDING TO CANON 1082 OF THE 1917 *CIC* AND JURISPRUDENCE PRIOR TO VATICAN II

INTRODUCTION

In Chapter One we discussed the traditional doctrine of ignorance and its implications in law, concluding with a study of the influence of ignorance upon the juridic act. Since marriage is a juridic act,[170] we are now in the position to demonstrate, in canonical legislation, how ignorance specifically affects matrimonial consent. The subject cannot be attributed to any precise enactment or to any definite period of ecclesiastical legislation.[171] Although earlier canonical legislation[172] spoke of ignorance as it affected marriage, this chapter shall be concerned only with decisions prior to the 1917 *CIC*, and with canon 1082 which spoke of ignorance and its effect upon marriage.

Once the *fons* for canon 1082 is discussed, we shall then begin to focus on the canon itself, placing it in context within the norms on matrimonial consent. We shall then direct our attention to the elements of the canon. While examining the text, the doctrine and jurisprudence which developed from its application will also be discussed, with special care given to the various approaches adopted by authors. Finally, we shall point out certain deficiencies in the text of the canon which came to light before the Second Vatican Council. These inadequacies necessitated the changes that resulted in the formulation of canon 1096 of the 1983 *CIC*.

I. IGNORANCE IN THE PRE-1917 *CIC* DOCTRINE AND JURISPRUDENCE

Before the 1917 *CIC*, jurisprudence was drawn from various sources. The most prominent among them were the teachings of the popes who issued decrees on the validity or invalidity of marriages, the decretalists who commented upon these decisions, and the decisions of the Roman Rota and the Congregation of the Council. This latter Congregation was first established by Pius IV in 1564 as the official organ for the correct interpretation and practical application of the reforms enacted by the Council of Trent. Its field of competence was later broadened by Pope Gregory XIII and Pope Sixtus V assigned to it the charge of reviewing acts of provincial councils, while it still maintained its general designation to ensure the effectiveness of the decrees of the Council of Trent.[173]

In this section, three decisions of the Congregation of the Council are chosen to illustrate briefly the

---

[170]Specifically we are speaking about the act of matrimonial consent which brings about *matrimonium in fieri*. This will be discussed later in this Chapter.

[171]See V.M. SMITH, *Ignorance Affecting Matrimonial Consent*, Canon Law Studies, 245, Washington, DC, The Catholic University of America, 1950, p. 1.

[172]For an in-depth study and analysis of the earlier canonical legislation, see *ibid.*, Chapter One, "Legislation before the Council of Trent", pp. 1-10, and Chapter Two, "Juridic Doctrine from the Council of Trent to the Code of Canon Law". pp. 11-30. This historical study and elucidation of the various events and situations which gave rise to a canonical understanding of ignorance are invaluable.

[173]E.L. HESTON, *The Holy See at Work*, Milwaukee, Bruce Publishing Company, 1950, p. 75.

40

existing jurisprudence before the 1917 *CIC*. One is an infrequently cited case which concerns a *ratum et non consummatum* marriage, adjudicated 18 December 1869. A previous decision of the same Congregation (15 March 1856), which is referred to in the animadversions of the Defender of Marriage in the 1869 case, is briefly presented first because it is a part of this case. In the jurisprudential reasoning presented as part of the argument, there is reference to ignorance and marriage, as well as other interesting elements that will be discussed below. The second case is a more celebrated one, *Ventimilien*, from the diocese of Ventimiglia, and it is the direct *fons* for canon 1082 of the 1917 *CIC*. It is of interest to note that, although this case is often cited, only two other works were found that actually went into detail concerning this case,[174] other than stating the rudimentary facts of the case or referring to the resulting affirmative decision which pertains to ignorance.

a. Congregation of the Council Decision, 15 March 1856[175]

In this particular case the man, Joseph, had contracted marriage with the woman, Catherine. When he took her to his home, however, he was not able to induce her to exercise her conjugal rights. In this case, a judgment of nullity was first sought on the ground of defective consent because of error or ignorance pertaining to marriage. However, the case was dismissed with negative decisions at first, second and third instance. In time, however, the man petitioned the Holy See, asking that his marriage be declared null or at least dissolved due to non consummation. Both the theologian and the canonist[176] agreed that the marriage was *ratum et non consummatum*, yet they both later abandoned the cause when the woman herself, in her deposition, showed that it had indeed been consummated quite often at a later time in the marriage. The negative judgments previously rendered prevailed.

b. Congregation of the Council Decision, 18 December 1869[177]

The decision in question concerns a marriage that took place between Antonio, twenty-five years of age, and Rosa, nineteen. For six days and nights, Antonio tried to perform the conjugal act with Rosa, who adamantly refused. There arose such great hostility between them that he returned her to her parents' home. The local pastor, the parents of the woman and even the archdeacon intervened in order to get the couple to reconcile, but to no avail. They lived apart for three years, with hatred and scandal increasing. Finally, the bishop asked the Holy Father to adjudicate the case, and it was sent to the Congregation of the Council, to be dealt with as a *ratum et non consummatum* case.

---

[174]P. GASPARRI, *Tractatus canonicus de matrimonio*, vol. 2, Romae, Typis polyglottis Vaticanis, 1932, pp. 12-13, and C.E. OLIVIERI, "A ignorância no matrimônio (c. 1096). Origem histórica, desenvolvimento doutrinal e jurisprudencial", in *Cuadernos doctorales*, 12 (1994), pp. 13-84. While Olivieri gives a rather detailed presentation of the *vota* of both the canonist and the theologian as well as the animadversions of the Defender of Marriage, a more in-depth examination of the case will be carried out in this study.

[175]Bamberg, found in S. PALLOTTINI, *Collectio omnium conclusionum et resolutionum que in causis propositis apud Sacram Congregationem Cardinalium S. Concilii Tridentini interpretum prodierunt ab eius institutione anno MDLXII ad annum MDCCCLX, distinctis titulis alphabetico ordine per materias digesta* (= PALLOTTINI), Romae, Typis S. Congregationis de Propaganda Fide, 1868-1895, see vol. 12, 1886, *Matrimonium*, III, *Quoad consensum eiusque renovationem*, nn. 25-29, pp. 475-477. See also SMITH, *Ignorance Affecting Matrimonial Consent*, p. 27.

[176]In cases that were presented to the Congregation of the Council, both a theologian and a canonist reviewed the *acta* and gave their animadversions.

[177]*Acta Sanctae Sedis* (= *ASS*), 5 (1869), Romae, Typographia Polyglotta, pp. 551-554.

According to the *acta*, Rosa stated that she was never willing to consummate the marriage, since she did not know that marriage entailed such moral baseness (performing the conjugal act). She thought that she could live with a man as she was accustomed to live with her parents, without the "use of the body".[178] Both the theologian and the canonist who reviewed the case agreed that the Holy Father should grant the dissolution, pointing out that the marriage would not be consummated by the woman since she probably suffered from frigidity.[179]

The Defender of Marriage, as was his function, did not agree with the theologian and the canonist and he opposed the dispensation. In his animadversions, he cited a previous case handled by the Congregation of the Council, Bamberg, 15 March 1856,[180] which also concerned non consummation.[181]

However, in the 1869 case, the Congregation issued an affirmative decision to forward it to the Holy Father as a *ratum et non consummatum* case, given the testimony of the Respondent and verified by the witnesses that she (the Respondent) did not nor did she ever intend to consummate the marriage. The decision carried with it a *vetitum*: the woman must contact the Congregation should she wish to attempt another marriage.[182]

This case presents a few important points for our consideration. First of all, in the animadversions presented by the Defender of Marriage, he writes that the woman should fulfill the conjugal debt, even under the threat of an ecclesiastical censure, since the power over the body belongs to the man because the couple entered marriage, which is a "*consortium omnis vitae*".[183] Furthermore, in the four conclusions cited at the

---

[178]*Ibid.*, p. 552: "... quod ipsa nesciret talem turpitudinem matrimonio iunctam esse; ac pro certo haberet, eam posse cum viro degere vitam, quam antea cum parentibus degere consueverat; simulque affirmavit, se usum corporis neque huic, neque ulli alteri viro umquam esse praebituram."

[179]*Ibid.*: "Tum Theologus tum Canonista ostenderunt matrimonium non fuisse consummatum; quod quidem ex ipsis processus actis scatebat. Ostenderunt pariter causas plures concurrere, quae idoneae essent ad consulendum SSmum Patrem pro concedenda dispensatione, inter quas Canonista et illam innuebat, quod improbabile non esset mulierem morbo aliquo frigiditatis laborare, quod et in mulieribus dari posset."

[180]*Ibid.*, p. 553.

[181]*Ibid.* The similarity between this case and the case at hand lies not only in the fact that both were presented as *ratum et non consummatum* cases. In both cases, the women involved stated that they had no idea that sexual intercourse was part of marriage. In the 1856 case, the Congregation stated that such ignorance had no bearing on the validity of the marital contract, since the ignorance did not pertain to the essence of marriage. In the end, the Congregation declared that it sufficed for the validity of the marriage that the contractants knew that marriage consisted in a mutual concession of the corporal rights of the married and in a non-repudiation of the indissoluble marriage bond. See SMITH, *Ignorance Affecting Matrimonial Consent*, p. 27 and PALLOTTINI, pp. 475-477.

Thus both cases dealt with women who were ignorant of sexual intercourse and both were directed to the Holy See as *ratum et non consummatum cases*. That is where the similarity ends, for in the Bamberg case while the couple did not consummate the marriage at the beginning, later on (and no indication is noted of how much later) the marriage was indeed consummated.

This is different from the case at hand because while the Bamberg case is cited primarily for its jurisprudential precedence, it is very clearly demonstrated that Rosa absolutely refused ever to consummate marriage with any man, as indicated above. Thus the circumstances as well as the outcome in both cases were different.

[182]*ASS*, 5 (1869), p. 553: "Affirmative, vetito mulieri transitu ad alias nuptias inconsulta S. Congregatione; idque notificetur eidem mulieri ante novam propositionem."

[183]*Ibid.*, p. 554: "... cogendam mulierem esse per ecclesiasticas censuras, ut debito coniugali satisfaceret, quum ipsa, contracto matrimonio, potestatem sui corporis non habeat, sed eius vir; matrimonium esse consortium omnis vitae."

The concept of *consortium* (based upon the Latin word *consors* which means having an equal share, sharing in or partaking of) finds its origin in Roman law, used within the context of the law of obligations resulting from contracts. See W.W.

end of the decision, two are of particular interest.

In the first conclusion, the Congregation states that a marriage is valid even though afterwards one of the spouses is found to be ignorant of the matrimonial debt and would not have entered into marriage had that fact been previously known.[184] This statement would have had direct bearing upon the outcome of the case, had it not been adjudicated as a *ratum et non consummatum* case. But, since there was direct evidence (by the woman herself, by the man and substantiated by midwives) that she did not and would not have sexual relations with the man, the marriage was dissolved since it was non-consummated. However, in the testimony, the woman stated that she did not know (*nesciret*) that marriage involved having sexual relations with the husband. Furthermore, she abhorred the very idea of having sexual intercourse. Thus, she was ignorant of the obligation of the *matrimoniale debitum* which was to be rendered. It was clearly demonstrated that the woman was ignorant of the very nature of marriage. Yet, the Congregation stated that such ignorance does not nullify a marriage. This, in fact, was the general practice of the Holy See, since the *copula* was not considered part of the essence of marriage.[185]

In the second conclusion, it is stated that in order for the marriage contract to be valid, most importantly if there is not just one obligation to be undertaken, it is not necessary that all the obligations be known by the parties. Rather, it is sufficient that the will of the contractants embrace what is universally or generally assumed, as well as what has become customary and repeated by others.[186]

Here, the Congregation taught that a person who enters into marriage need not know all the obligations and responsibilities that marriage entails. This is in light of the facts of the case at hand, where the evidence

---

BUCKLAND and A.D. McNAIR, *Roman Law and Common Law: A Comparison in Outline*, 2nd ed. rev. by F.H. LAWSON, Cambridge, University Press, 1952, pp. 304-305. *Consortium*, or partnership, was the basis for the *societas omnium bonorum* whereby heirs kept their inheritance in common rather than dividing it. See H.F. JOLOWICZ, *Historical Introduction to the Study of Roman Law*, Cambridge, University Press, 1932, p. 306. Thus, there existed a partnership whereby those involved shared responsibilities and obligations while, at the same time, the relationship proved profitable for them to be in such a partnership.

In Roman law, marriage was seen as a social fact which had almost no effect on the legal condition of the parties involved. See B. NICHOLAS, *An Introduction to Roman Law*, Oxford, Clarendon Press, 1962, p. 80. The Romans did not regard marriage as a contract in the juridic sense. Instead, marriage was a way of life, a domestic union. It was a status realized by the agreement of the parties and regulated by law. See W.A. VAN OMMEREN, *Mental Illness Affecting Matrimonial Consent*, Canon Law Studies, 415, Washington, DC, The Catholic University of America, 1961, p. 7.

Although marriage was not seen within the context of the law of contracts, one of the definitions provided by Roman law, that attributed to Modestinus, found in the *Digest*, is, "Marriage is the union of a man and a woman, and a lifelong fellowship, a sharing of sacred and human law" ("Nuptiae sunt coniunctio maris et feminae, consortium omnis vitae, divini et humani iuris communicatio"), D. 23, 2, 1. See A. GAUTHIER, *Roman Law and Its Contribution to the Development of Canon Law*, 2nd ed., Ottawa, Saint Paul University, 1996, p. 36. The idea of partnership of the whole of life (*consortium omnis vitae*) pertaining to marriage seems to be understandable: two people entered into a lifelong union which established obligations and responsibilities for each of them. However, we must remember the context of marriage in Roman law, i.e., a social fact that had almost no effect on the legal condition of the parties. Thus, there was no automatic right of the man over the woman; rather, there was the mutual *ius in corpus*, which became so prevalent in Church teaching and is evidenced in the animadversions of the Defender of Marriage cited above.

By reading the Defender's statement, it can be assumed that by the mid 19th Century marriage was seen as a partnership, but one in which both parties did not share equally.

[184] *ASS*, 5 (1869), p. 554: "Matrimonium validum esse, quamquam aliquis ex coniugibus postea ignorasse se dicat matrimoniale debitum, eoque cognito non fuisse matrimonium initurum affirmet."

[185] *Ibid*. See also SMITH, *Ignorance Affecting Matrimonial Consent*, p. 28.

[186] *ASS*, 5 (1869), p. 554: "Ut enim contractus quivis validus sit (maxime si non unam tantum obligationem secumferat), non exigitur, ut singula officia et obligationes cognoscant contrahentes, quae ex ipso contractu derivent: sed satis est, ut voluntas contrahentium feratur in contractum universim sumptum prout ab aliis frequentari consueverit."

demonstrated that the woman had no idea that marriage involved having sexual intercourse which she considered to be disgusting. The Congregation further added that it is sufficient that the parties merely have a general understanding of marriage. Such a statement sets the stage for the later development of canon 1082 in the 1917 *CIC*, where the law lists those things of which a person should not be ignorant. Also, this conclusion affirms that it suffices for the will of the parties to embrace what is universally or generally accepted as marriage. This is a presumption which is found in the writings of Benedict XIV in *De synodo diocesana*.[187] Although within this context Benedict was addressing error, reference to the general intention of contracting marriage according to the institution of Christ was used by both the Congregation and the Roman Rota.[188] This presumption came from a time when most of the known world was Christian or at least had heard the preaching of the Gospel. However, it was not seen as a specifically Christian norm, but rather one that was founded in natural law. Thus missionaries applied it to non-Christian cultures as well, holding pagans and those who were unbaptized to the understanding of marriage as held by the Church.[189] As can be seen in this second conclusion, nothing specific concerning what is universally or generally assumed about marriage is mentioned. This allowed for broad interpretations of what is generally accepted and repeated by others in cases processed by the Congregation of the Council and by the Roman Rota.

c. Congregation of the Council Decisions, Ventimiglia, 13 June 1885 and 19 May 1888[190]

This case concerns the marriage between Antonio, age 25, and Catherina, age 12 years and nine months.

1. The facts of the case

Antonio was four months out of the military and living with Catherina's family. When he first proposed, the pastor was unwilling to perform the marriage due to the age of the girl and her low intelligence. Nonetheless, her mother insisted that the marriage take place, perhaps for personal motives (it was suspected that she herself was having an affair with Antonio, which was to be confirmed later) and solicited the help

---

[187]BENEDICT XIV, *De synodo dioecesana*, Romae, ex Typographia Sacrae Congregationis de Propaganda Fide, 1806, vol. II, l. XIII, c. XXII, nn. 3 and 7, pp. 293-294: "Privatus enim error nec anteponi debet, nec praejudicium afferre potest generali, quam diximus, voluntati, ex qua contracti matrimonii validitas, et perpetuitas pendet, ... dum matrimonium, prout a Christo institutum fuit, inire voluerunt, ... praevalente nimirum generali, quam diximus, voluntate de matrimonio juxta Christi institutionem ineundo..." Benedict is stating that a private error should not be given preference over what is called the general intention on which the validity and perpetuity of the marriage contract depend, nor can it prejudice it because then the general intention of the contracting parties according to the institution of Christ prevails; this general influence is the desire to undertake marriage according to the institution of Christ.

[188]It was not until the 1970s that this presumption began to be questioned in the decisions of the Roman Rota. For particular examples, see *coram* POMPEDDA, 23 January 1971, TRIBUNAL APOSTOLICUM SACRAE ROMANAE ROTAE, *Decisiones seu sententiae selectae inter eas quae anno [...] prodierunt cura eiusdem Apostolici Tribunalis editae* (= *SRR Dec*), Vatican City, Libreria editrice Vaticana, 63 (1971), pp. 53-59, specifically p. 54; and *coram* PINTO, 6 November 1972, *ibid.*, 64 (1972), pp. 672-680, specifically p. 673.

[189]D.M. CAMPBELL, "Canon 1099: The Emergence of a New Juridic Figure?", in *Quaderni Studio Rotale*, 5 (1990), p. 50.

[190]*ASS*, 21 (1888), pp. 162-181.

44

of the Vicar General who ordered the pastor to celebrate the marriage.[191]

For eight months the couple lived together, partly at the home of her parents and partly at the home of his parents. During the first two months, the couple had frequent intercourse. However, as time went on, quarreling and disagreements occurred and the woman finally returned to the home of her parents. She then contracted marriage civilly with another man. Finally, perhaps because of her conscience, Catherina began proceedings to have her marriage to Antonio either declared null on the grounds of force and fear of her mother on her part, or that a dispensation from a *ratum et non consummatum* marriage be granted, since she affirmed under oath that the man was unable to penetrate her fully.[192]

2. The *votum* of the canonist

The canonist, in his *votum*,[193] contended that there were two grounds for the marriage to be declared null: that sufficient knowledge of consent was lacking on the part of the woman, and that an impediment of affinity arose from Antonio's illicit intercourse with Catherina's mother.[194] Concerning the lack of consent, the canonist stated that the consent needed to establish an indissoluble bond is more than is required for other contracts. Furthermore, he stated that the woman's consent was not free principally because of the fact that her critical judgment was not fully developed.[195] In other words, she lacked sufficient critical understanding that is necessary to establish the indissoluble bond of marriage.

The canonist further stated that this defect in Catherina, who was not yet thirteen years of age at the time of the marriage — even though there are those who believe that physical and intellectual development is complete after age twelve[196] — was due to the tardiness of her understanding derived from only a moderate change in bodily appearance and from the lack of instruction. In such circumstances, one would expect that moral puberty would exist. There was concern that Catherina was not as mature as would be expected of a girl who was over twelve years of age.

The fact that she was not mature was attested to by the pastor who at first refused to perform the marriage, by the testimony of her parents, and by the depositions of many witnesses who participated in the investigation. It was unanimously stated that Catherina did not possess the discretion needed to contract marriage and therefore she did not have true freedom. Some witnesses even stated that she was a fool. In spite of what appears to be obvious today, the Vicar General was not held in bad light by the canonist for forcing the pastor to perform the marriage. Rather, it was seen that he was simply considering the age of the

[191]*Ibid.*, p. 162.

[192]*Ibid.*, p. 163.

[193]For the complete text of the *votum* of the canonist, see *Thesaurus resolutionum Sacrae Congregationis Concilii* (= *Thesaurus*), 144 (1885), Romae, ex Typographia Vaticana, pp. 315-325. For another presentation of the *vota* of both the canonist and the theologian and the animadversions of the Defender of Marriage, see OLIVIERI, "A ignorância no matrimônio (c. 1096)", pp. 27-32.

[194]*ASS*, 21 (1888), p. 163.

[195]*Ibid.*, pp. 163-164.

[196]*Ibid.*, p. 164.

girl objectively, instead of taking into consideration the circumstances of the girl in this particular case.[197] Further evidence of the lack of freedom was presented by the witnesses who stated that the consent was extorted by moral pressure: Catherina's mother, by incredible efforts, desired her daughter's wedding. In her deposition, Catherina herself confirmed the moral coercion by breaking into tears before the altar at the wedding. She further stated that if she were able, she would have withdrawn and not continued with the wedding. The canonist concluded that there was negative proof: her tears and aversion, her lament concerning the marriage to be contracted or already contracted, and the fact she was forced into a marriage which she did not want.[198]

Concerning the impediment of affinity that arose from illicit prior intercourse between Antonio and Catherina's mother (which, at the time was viewed as an invalidating impediment)[199] the canonist concluded that such an impediment truly existed. His moral certitude was derived from the spontaneous confessions of both Catherina's mother and Antonio. Further proof was received from several witnesses who verified the circumstances of the illicit intercourse. This validated his certitude, because such proof was often very difficult to acquire since such behavior caused shame.[200]

3. The *votum* of the theologian

In his *votum*,[201] the theologian expressed several concerns about the imperfect process[202] and did not agree with the canonist concerning both force and fear and the non consummation of the marriage. He also rejected the argument that Catherina lacked sufficient discretion. His reasoning was based on the fact that the matter was referred to the diocesan curia (the Vicar General) and, after she was seen and questioned, it was decided that the marriage should, in fact, take place.[203] Furthermore, he did not accept the ground of the impediment of affinity, fearing collusion, and thus he discounted the testimony of both Catherina's mother

---

[197]*Ibid.* This justification of the Vicar General's action reflected the then current understanding that once a person had reached puberty, which at the time was twelve years of age for a woman, that person was presumed to have enough knowledge to enter marriage.

[198]*Ibid.*, pp. 164-165: "Hisce in vado positis, unanimem canonistarum sententiam esse asserit, quod lacrymae, aversio, lamentatio mulierum circa matrimonium vel contrahendum vel contractum, signa esse negativa consensus."

[199]*Ibid.*, p. 165. This impediment was declared by the Council of Trent (Cap. 4, Sess. 24 de Reform. matrim.): "Praeterea sancta synodus, eisdem et aliis gravissimis de causis adducta, impedimentum, quod propter affinitatem ex fornicatione contractam inducitur et matrimonium postea factum dirimit, ad eos tantum, qui in primo et secundo gradu coniunguntur, restringit. In ulterioribus vero gradibus statuit, huiusmodi affinitatem matrimonium postea contractum non dirimere" ("Moreover, the holy council, moved by the same and other very grave reasons, restricts the impediment which arises on account of the affinity contracted from fornication, and which dissolves the marriage afterward contracted, to those only who are united in the first and second degree; in more remote degrees it ordains that affinity of this kind does not dissolve the marriage afterward contracted") CONSILIUM [sic] TRIDENTINUM, 1545-1563, *Diariorum, actorum, epistolarum, tractatuum nova collectio*, vol. 9, Edidit Societas Goerresiana, Friburgi Brisgoviae, Herder, 1924, p. 970; English translation from H.J. SCHROEDER, *Canons and Decrees of the Council of Trent; Original Text with English Translation*, St. Louis, B. Herder Book Co., 1941, p. 186.

[200]*ASS*, 21 (1888), p. 165.

[201]For the complete text of the *votum* of the theologian, see *Thesaurus*, 144 (1885), pp. 298-315.

[202]*ASS*, 21 (1888), p. 166: "circa processus imperfectionem".

[203]*Ibid.*, p. 168.

and Antonio as well as that of the various witnesses.[204] In his animadversions, the Defender of Marriage[205] agreed with the theologian, stating that force and fear, defect of consent and non consummation were not proved.[206]

At this point, the marriage was not proved to be invalid. However, concerning the dissolution of the marriage, the Congregation resolved that more proofs were to be presented.[207]

4. The new presentation of the case; the new *votum* of the theologian

It took a long time for the new evidence to be gathered, since the village was nearly impossible to reach; however, nine new witnesses were interrogated and the case was once again presented to the theologian and the Defender of Marriage. This time, the theologian stated that, in his opinion, the marriage would be null due to the lack of sufficient discretion on the part of the woman or be declared non consummated.[208]

In his new *votum*,[209] the theologian stated that it is the unanimous opinion of the doctors[210] that in contracting marriage, there are two requirements: one must have knowledge, or discretion of judgment in order to act; and that the party have the legitimate age of puberty, which is fourteen for men and twelve for women, unless precocity (*malitia*) or intellectual keenness (*sagacitas*) supplies for age.[211] Furthermore, he stated that for marriage a little discretion is not enough; the greatest (*maxima*) discretion is required.

After having reviewed the new testimony, the theologian[212] stated that in this case, even though the woman was twelve years, nine months of age, and consequently reached puberty according to law, sufficient discretion had not been attained. All the witnesses testified that the woman, at the time of the marriage, was

---

[204]*Ibid.*, pp. 170-171.

[205]For the complete text of the animadversions of the Defender of Marriage, see *Thesaurus*, 144 (1885), pp. 326-331. It is interesting to note that the title, Defender of Marriage, is interchanged with Defender of the Bond throughout this decision, since this was not done in the other cases of the Congregation of the Council referred to earlier.

[206]*ASS*, 21 (1888), pp. 172-174.

[207]*Ibid.*, pp. 174-175.

[208]*Ibid.*, p. 175. It is interesting to note that in his first *votum*, the theologian referred to the Petitioner as "Catherina" or as *actrix* (plaintiff), which would seem to indicate that she was an adult, whereas in this *votum* he referred to her only as *puella* (girl), and only once as *actrix*, in the formal wording of the reasons for nullity. It appears, in our opinion, that once the theologian read the new testimony, he was of the opinion that Catherina, although chronologically of age to enter marriage, was not so mentally, and thus refers to her as a girl and lacking the sufficient discretion for marriage.

[209]For the complete text of the new *votum* of the theologian, see *Thesaurus*, 147 (1888), pp. 294-309.

[210]*ASS*, 21 (1888), pp. 175-176. The theologian is citing doctors of canon law: Pirhing, Barbosa, Cuvarruvias, Gonzalez, Saint Thomas Aquinas and Sanchez.

[211]*Malitia* would refer to the premature development of one's capacity for reproduction, i.e., having carnal knowledge beyond what is usually expected at one's chronological age. If a child had had sexual relations, he or she had, in effect, reached puberty. It was usually denoted as ill will or malice or precocity. *Sagacitas*, on the other hand, would refer to an acuteness of mental discernment or soundness of judgment, i.e., the ability to use this knowledge in ways that would be expected of someone at a more advanced chronological age.

[212]Another presentation of the second *votum* of the theologian, although brief, may be found in OLIVIERI, "A ignorância no matrimônio (c. 1096)", pp. 32-33.

totally ignorant of the mundane, but without *malitia*.[213] She simply was intent on childish games and was not yet gifted with the capacity of discerning what she did. So much so, wrote the theologian, that a founded doubt was raised:[214] she was ignorant of distinguishing "yes" from "no" at the marriage ceremony. This girl seemed to be led by the hand of her mother, with promises of gifts and other such promises, as happens with children who have not yet been gifted with sufficient discretion, so that she would say whatever her mother wanted her to say. The witnesses unanimously affirmed that the marriage was not the will of the daughter, but of the mother. This opinion was shared by the entire town which was convinced that this marriage will have to be declared null.[215]

The theologian further stated that this approach is not harmful since the law presumes that there is sufficient discretion in a girl who has reached puberty. Indeed, her marriage would be recognized as valid by the Church. This teaching is found in Gonzalez who states that even though, as a general rule, it would be admitted that the lawful age is twelve (in girls) and fourteen (in boys), nevertheless if one is found to be deficient (*inhabilis*), the marriage is not to be sustained. Rather, it is the truth of the matter which counts, not the presumption or the precept.[216] Concerning the non consummation of the marriage, given all the testimony, the theologian concurs that the marriage was not consummated.[217]

He concludes, then, that from the newly attained testimony read in conjunction with that from the first process, it is evident that the girl, at the time of the marriage, did not possess sufficient discretion binding her to the marriage bond. The reason he gives is that she was deficient (*inhabilis*) to fulfill the consent necessary to undertake marriage, for without sufficient discretion, according to Sanchez, one is unable (*nequit*) to give consent for marriage. Therefore, he concludes, the marriage was null from the beginning.[218]

5. The new animadversions of the Defender of Marriage

In his new animadversions,[219] the Defender of Marriage stated that nothing has been brought forth that would change his position concerning the impediments of force and fear and affinity. In regard to the lack of sufficient discretion, however, he stated that Catherina had reached puberty and, therefore, the presumption arose that she did, in fact, possess the discretion necessary for marriage.[220] He cites Sanchez who wrote that the nearness of puberty creates the presumption of sufficient discretion about the most grave and perpetual bond of marriage. Little weight should be given to the witnesses who insisted on Catherina's simplicity. He stated that not only did she exhibit much more discretion, but also a superabundance of *malitia*. He concluded

---

[213]*ASS*, 21 (1888), p. 176: "... puellam de rebus mundanis omnino ignaram, sine ulla malitia..."

[214]*Ibid.*, "... nondum praeditam capacitate discernendi quid ageret, adeo ut fundatum praeberet dubium..."

[215]*Ibid.*, "... hinc communem in illis oppidanis persuasionem, quod matrimonium fuerit nullum."

[216]*Ibid.*, p. 176.

[217]*Ibid.*, pp. 176-177.

[218]*Ibid.*, p. 177.

[219]For the complete text of the revised animadversions of the Defender of Marriage, see *Thesaurus*, 147 (1888), pp. 309-314.

[220]*ASS*, 21 (1888), p. 178: "... propinquitas pubertatis facit praesumere discretionem sufficientem ad gravissimum ac perpetuum matrimonii vinculum."

48

by asking the Congregation to respond negatively to all grounds.[221] However, on 19 May 1888, the Congregation replied in the affirmative and the marriage was declared null on the ground of defect of sufficient discretion on the part of the plaintiff. The second ground, that of non consummation, was not addressed since it was provided for in the first one.

6. The conclusions of the 1888 decision

There are eighteen conclusions at the end of the decision, five of which (VIII, IX, XI, XII and XVIII) have important bearing on our study. Conclusion VIII states that in contracting marriage, two things are required: one is knowledge, or discretion of judgment, by which one knows what one does; the other is that the parties be of legal age, which is understood as the age of puberty, which for men begins after fourteen years of age and for women after twelve years of age, unless precocity (*malitia*) or intellectual keenness of nature (*sagacitas*) supplies for age.[222] Concerning the first requirement, that of knowledge, it is presented as synonymous with discretion of judgment. Both refer to the ability to know and understand what one is undertaking in order to carry out the act. Discretion, therefore, is equivalent to due knowledge, which was discussed at length in Chapter One. This follows the reasoning of Aristotle who wrote that nothing could be considered as flowing from the will unless it was first presented to the will by the intellect.[223] One could not will what one did not know. Sanchez taught that such ignorance vitiates marriage.[224] In the case at hand, it was demonstrated that Catherina's mental capacity was such that she did not understand what she was consenting to do. With regard to the second requirement, that of legal age, we see here the statement of the presumption that legal age corresponds to puberty, which was taught by many commentators, including Sanchez, Gonzalez-Tellez and Pirhing.[225] This was the basis upon which the marriage was presumed to be valid, since Catherina was of legitimate age to enter into marriage.

Conclusion IX states that sufficient discretion is presumed in those who attain the legitimate age of puberty and a valid marriage is contracted at that age except where a person is found to be deficient because, in this matter, the truth is always to be favored, not the presumption of law or the precept.[226] This is a logical progression from the previous conclusion: since the parties who contract marriage must be of legal age, then those of such age are presumed to have the sufficient discretion of judgment necessary to understand what

---

[221] *Ibid.*, pp. 178-179.

[222] *Ibid.*, p. 180: "In contractibus matrimonii duo necessario requiri, scilicet scientiam, sive iudicium discretionis, quo quis intelligat, quid agat; et aetatem legitimam, nempe pubertatis, et hanc in masculo post 14 annum, in femina post 12 incipere, nisi malitia, sive sagacitas naturae suppleat aetatem."

[223] SMITH, *Ignorance Affecting Matrimonial Consent*, p. 22.

[224] "Ignorantia instar erroris impedit consensum efficitque ne actus sit voluntarius: nihil enim volitum quin praecognitum, teste Philosopho. Ignorantia cognitionem tollit, sicut error veram; unde quoad dirimendum matrimonium non differt an dicatur ignorantiam an errorem impedire" (SANCHEZ, *De sancto matrimonii sacramento*, lib. VII, disp. XVIII, n. 1).

[225] For an in-depth presentation on this particular topic, see SMITH, *Ignorance Affecting Matrimonial Consent*, pp. 22-26.

[226] *ASS*, 21 (1888), p. 180: "A iure praesumi sufficientem discretionem in illis, qui ad aetatem pubertatis pervenerunt, et validum matrimonium in illa aetate contractum, excepto tamen casu, quo inhabiles ad contrahendum reperiantur, quia ea in re semper veritas attenta est, non iuris praesumptio aut praescriptio."

marriage entails.[227] This presumption was held by both the Congregation of the Council and the Roman Rota when adjudicating matrimonial nullity cases.[228] In this case, Catherina, was found to be deficient in discretion of judgment. In fact, she was seen to be much less mature than others presumably of her age. Thus, the truth of the matter overturned the presumption of law.

Conclusion XI states that in a marriage contract, because of the indissoluble bond, a level of consent would be required which is more unimpeded than that which is needed to enter into other contracts.[229] In other words, the contracting parties must have that degree of knowledge which enables them to comprehend that marriage has life-long consequences of utmost importance. The significance of this conclusion is that marriage is considered more than merely a contract. It changes the status of the parties involved (borrowing this idea from Roman law) and at the same time is a sacrament (enabling them to live a life specially graced by God). Thus, the consent to marry must be made freely and without any reservation, much more so than the consent given to any other contract. In the case at hand, Catherina, given her age and lack of experience, did not fully understand the consequences of marriage and thus could not give the full consent which was needed to enter marriage. In other words, she lacked the discretion of judgment which is seen as vital in order to give full consent to marriage.

Conclusion XII states that free consent is lacking not only where force or fear have intervened, but also when the development of the capacity for judgment is defective.[230] A person must be free to enter into marriage and such freedom is precluded when one is coerced into giving consent by force or fear.[231] The Congregation goes further, however, by stating that there is also a lack of freedom when there is a lack of understanding. In other words, a person who is not able to comprehend the ramifications of his or her actions is unable to give full consent of the will. In the case at hand, Catherina was so deficient in understanding that she simply followed the judgment of her mother in marrying Antonio. Thus her lack of freedom was not the result of force or fear but, rather, it arose from her inability to make her own decision.

Finally, conclusion XVIII states that, in this case, it would seem that the marriage was declared null particularly because of a defect of sufficient discretion in the plaintiff or because of a defect of consent to oblige herself to marital obligations.[232] Having already presented the reasons for the final decision, this

---

[227]The discussion of puberty and the presumption of the necessary knowledge concerning marriage will be considered later in this chapter when canon 1082, §2, is addressed.

[228]See SMITH, *Ignorance Affecting Matrimonial Consent*, p. 25.

[229]*Ibid.*, p. 180: "Matrimonii contractum, propter vinculi indissolubilitatem, talem consensum requiri, qui liberior sit illo, quo alia pacta aliique contractus firmantur."

[230]*Ibid.*, p. 181: "Liberum consensum deesse, nedum ubi metus vel coactio intercedit, sed etiam ex defectu plenae evolutionis criterii."

[231]Discussion of force and fear (*vis et metus*) is outside the scope of this study.

[232]*ASS*, 21 (1888), p. 181: "In themate matrimonium nullum declaratum fuisse videri, praesertim ex defectu sufficientis discretionis in actrice, seu ex defectu consensus ad sese vinculo maritali obligandum."
We must always be aware of reading too much into statements written from another era. However, we are able to note that the terms used in this conclusion, "defect of sufficient discretion" and "defect of consent to oblige herself to marital obligations", are consonant with terms used in our present canon 1095, 2° and 3°. It should also be noted that the *fontes* for these two numbers are Rotal decisions which do not specifically refer to ignorance. Yet, from the discussion already presented, there is no doubt that other cases which dealt with "defect of sufficient discretion" and "defect of consent" were adjudicated under the ground of ignorance.
OLIVIERI, "A ignorância no matrimônio (c. 1096)", pp. 49-53, discusses this topic at length.

50

statement is simply a summation of the case. While only a summation, it is important to note that it states that the plaintiff did indeed lack the sufficient discretion of judgment for marriage: she did not have the necessary knowledge required for marriage and could not oblige herself to the obligations of marriage. The Congregation, therefore, helped to establish the jurisprudence pertaining to ignorance in regards to marriage consent.

II. IGNORANCE ACCORDING TO CANON 1082 OF THE 1917 *CIC*

As has been seen in the previous section, the Congregation for the Council, through its decision, *Ventimiglia* of 19 May and 18 August 1888, laid the foundation for canon 1082 of the 1917 *CIC* and is the sole *fons* listed for this canon. While one can see its direct influence on paragraph two of canon 1082,[233] paragraph one is more of an inference from the facts of the case (that Catherina was ignorant of the nature of marriage) and a compilation of those aspects of marriage of which one should not be ignorant. The 1917 canon was identical to the one presented by Gasparri in the *sub secreto* Schema of 1916.[234]

a. Context of canon 1082

To understand the text of canon 1082, we must have a sense of its context within the 1917 *CIC*. Working in reverse, we can note that canon 1082 is the second canon in Chapter V (*De consensu matrimoniali*) of Title VII (*De matrimonio*) of Part I (*De sacramentis*) of Book III (*De rebus*). The Code presents what is necessary for a couple to enter marriage and then proceeds to list those causes which may prevent a person from giving full consent. Thus the 1917 *CIC* begins with a general introduction to the sacrament of marriage, proceeds with what is necessary for its preparation, outlines the impediments which may prohibit persons from entering into marriage, and then considers what brings it into existence as understood by the Church.

b. Canon 1082 in relation to canon 1081

Since canon 1082 concerned matrimonial consent and the effects of ignorance upon it, we must see it in relation to canon 1081,[235] where consent was defined.

---

[233]Although it would seem to have bearing on this paragraph, it is not listed as a *fons* for it.

[234]P. GASPARRI, *Codex iuris canonici, (Schema Codicis iuris canonici; sub secreto pontificio)*, Romae, Typis polyglottis Vaticanis, 1916, p. 455. Here, the canon pertaining to ignorance is numbered canon 1085. Both the wording and the *fons*, however, are identical to those found in the official 1917 *CIC* promulgated the following year.

[235]For a very thorough discussion of this subject, see O. FUMAGALLI CARULLI, "La relazione dinamica tra il can. 1082 e il can. 1081 *Cod. Iur. Can.*", in *Ephemerides iuris canonici*, 33 (1977), pp. 247-279 (also found in *Il matrimonio canonico dopo il Concilio: capacità e consenso*, Milano, A. Giuffrè Editore, 1978, pp. 97-131); and F. GONZALEZ Y GONZALEZ, "Los cánones 1081 y 1082 y la relación entre actividad intelectual y volición", in *Ignorancia y consentimiento matrimonial*, León, Colegio Universitario de León, 1982, pp. 57-102. For other works relating canons 1081 and 1082, see M. CONTE A CORONATA, *De sacramentis: tractatus canonicus*, vol. 3, Taurini, Marietti, 1946, pp. 573-599; P. FEDELE, *L'"ordinatio ad prolem" nel matrimonio in diritto canonico*, Milano, A. Giuffrè Editore, 1962, pp. 215-268; J.M. MANS PUIGARNAU, *Derecho matrimonial canónico*, vol. 1, Barcelona, Bosch, pp. 298-338; P. PELLEGRINO, "L'errore di diritto nel matrimonio canonico (cann. 1096-1099)", in *Il diritto ecclesiastico*, 108 (1997), pp. 363-404, specifically pp. 367-375.

I. Matrimonial consent

In canon 1081 we read:

§1: Matrimonium facit partium consensus inter personas iure habiles legitime manifestatus; qui nulla humana potestate suppleri valet.

§2: Consensus matrimonialis est actus voluntatis quo utraque pars tradit et acceptat ius in corpus, perpetuum et exclusivum, in ordine ad actus per se aptos ad prolis generationem.[236]

Since marriage was seen as a contract as defined in the very first canon on marriage (1012, §1),[237] that which brought a contract into existence was the consent of the parties involved.[238] This was known as marriage *in fieri*.[239] Since consent is the very essence of contracts and marriage is a contract, without consent no marriage can exist.[240] The result of the contract brought into existence by the consent of the two parties was called marriage *in facto esse*,[241] the actual society itself, the perpetual union, the indissoluble bond.[242]

---

[236] §1: "Marriage is effected by the consent of the parties lawfully manifested between persons who are capable according to law; and this consent no human power can supply."
§2: "Matrimonial consent is an act of the will by which each party gives and accepts a perpetual and exclusive right over the body, for acts which are of themselves suitable for the generation of children", translation as in T.L. BOUSCAREN, A.C. ELLIS, F.N. KORTH, eds., *Canon Law: A Text and Commentary*, 4th revised ed., Milwaukee, Bruce Publishing Company, 1966, p. 565. Translations of the 1917 *CIC* will be based on this edition of BOUSCAREN et al.

[237] §1: "Christus Dominus ad sacramenti dignitatem evexit ipsum contractum matrimonialem inter baptizatos" ("Christ our Lord elevated the very contract of marriage between baptized persons to the dignity of a sacrament"). For more discussion on the nature of marriage as a contract, see BOUSCAREN, *Canon Law: A Text and Commentary*, pp. 464-466; F.M. CAPPELLO, *De matrimonio*, in *Tractatus canonico-moralis de sacramentis*, 7th ed., vol. 5, Romae, Marietti, 1961, pp. 20-23; F.X. WERNZ and P. VIDAL, *Ius canonicum*, vol. 5, *Ius matrimoniale*, Romae, Apud aedes Universitatis Gregorianae, 1946, pp. 44-49.

[238] See BOUSCAREN, *Canon Law: A Text and Commentary*, p. 565. See also U. NAVARRETE, *Quaedam problemata actualia de matrimonio*, 3rd ed., Romae, Pontificia Universitas Gregoriana, 1979, pp. 87-89.

[239] For a very well annotated study on this topic, see C.J. SCICLUNA, "The Essence and Definition of the *Matrimonium in fieri*", in his book *The Essential Definition of Marriage according to the 1917 and 1983 Code of Canon Law: An Exegetical and Comparative Study*, Lanham, Maryland, University Press of America, 1995, pp. 122-138. The author presents a discussion of and documentation for various themes and definitions concerning *matrimonium in fieri* given by various commentators.

[240] M. RAMSTEIN, *A Manual of Canon Law*, Hoboken, New Jersey, Terminal Printing and Publishing, 1947, p. 485. This has been reaffirmed in the *Catechism of the Catholic Church*, Ottawa, Publications Service, Canadian Conference of Catholic Bishops, 1994, n. 1626: "The Church holds the exchange of consent between the spouses to be the indispensable element that 'makes the marriage.' If consent is lacking there is no marriage."

[241] For a very well annotated and documented presentation on this topic, see SCICLUNA, "The Essence and Definition of the *Matrimonium in facto esse*", in *The Essential Definition of Marriage*, pp. 138-153.

[242] F. DELLA ROCCA, *Manual of Canon Law*, trans. by A. THATCHER, Milwaukee, the Bruce Publishing Company, 1959, p. 249. See also A.C. JEMOLO, *Il matrimonio nel diritto canonico*, Bologna, Società Editrice il Mulino, 1993, pp. 107-122; P. GASPARRI, *Tractatus canonicus de matrimonio*, vol. 1, Romae, Typis polyglottis Vaticanis, 1932, p. 12; and D.E. FELLHAUER, "The *consortium omnis vitae* as a Juridic Element of Marriage", in *Studia canonica*, 13 (1979), pp. 7-171, specifically pp. 55-72, "The Classical Formulation of the Nature of Christian Marriage: The Object of Matrimonial Consent". Going into detail concerning the evolution of canonical understanding about consent and marriage is outside the scope of this study. Suffice to say that Peter Lombard and the School of Paris held that consent effected a true marriage. The School of Bologna, following the teaching of Hincmar of Rheims, held that the act of copulation was an essential element in a true marriage. It was

52

The personal consent of the parties is not only the efficient cause of marriage *in facto esse*, but is the very essence of marriage *in fieri*.[243]
 In canon 1081, §2, we find the definition of matrimonial consent.[244] First of all, it is "an act of the will", which means that the parties who are entering marriage know and understand what they are doing. Consent involves both intellect and will.[245] It was Thomas Aquinas who defined consent as an internal act of one of the spiritual faculties of the soul, namely the will, under the guidance of another faculty, the intelligence. Both mutually supported and completed the other.[246] In other words, consent is a human act and, as such from Thomas Aquinas' perspective, it is thus founded in the natural law. Commenting on Peter Lombard, Thomas Aquinas further stated that consent brings about marriage.[247] Since it was the parties who

Pope Alexander III who settled the question by decreeing that consent in itself brought about marriage, but he denied absolute indissolubility to a non-consummated marriage.
 For brief but enlightening presentations of the debate between the School of Paris and the School of Bologna, see CAPPELLO, *De matrimonio*, pp. 502-505; E. MONTERO Y GUTIÉRREZ, *El matrimonio y las causas matrimoniales; disciplina de la Iglesia y de los principales estados, especialmente de España y jurisprudencia de la S. Rota Romana, con las normas de la S. Congregación de sacramentos regulando la dispensa 'super matrimonio rato et non consummato', y el procedimiento en las causas de nulidad de matrimonio*, 5th rev. ed., Madrid, Sáez, 1950, pp. 203-204; L. ÖRSY, *Marriage in Canon Law: Texts and Comments, Reflections and Questions*, Wilmington, M. Glazier, 1986, pp. 24-26; and SMITH, *Ignorance Affecting Matrimonial Consent*, pp. 32-35.

[243]L. CHIAPPETTA, *Il matrimonio: nella nuova legislazione canonica e concordataria: manuale giuridico-pastorale*, Roma, Dehoniane, 1990, p. 196.

[244]Pius XI commented on the nature of matrimonial consent in his encyclical *Casti connubii*, in *Acta Apostolicae Sedis*, (= *AAS*), Civitate Vaticana, Typis polyglottis Vaticanis, 22 (1930), pp. 539-592, giving special attention to what is meant by consent of the contractants, pp. 541-542: "At, quamquam matrimonium suapte natura divinitus est institutum, tamen humana quoque voluntas suas in eo partes habet easque nobilissimas; nam singulare quodque matrimonium, prout est coniugalis coniunctio inter hunc virum et hanc mulierem, non oritur nisi ex libero utriusque sponsi consensu: qui quidem liber voluntatis actus, quo utraque pars tradit et acceptat ius coniugii proprium, ad verum matrimonium constituendum tam necessarius est ut nulla humana potestate suppleri valeat. Haec tamen libertas eo tantum spectat ut constet, utrum contrahentes re vera matrimonium inire et cum hac persona inire velint an non; libertati vero hominis matrimonii natura penitus subducitur, ita, ut, si quis semel matrimonium contraxerit, divinis eius legibus et essentialibus proprietatibus subiciatur. Nam Angelicus Doctor de fide et prole disserens, 'haec, inquit, in matrimonio ex ipsa pactione coniugali causantur, ita quod si aliquid contrarium his exprimeretur in consensu qui matrimonium facit, non esset verum matrimonium.'" ("Yet, although matrimony is of its very nature of divine institution, the human will, too, enters into it and performs a most noble part. For each individual marriage, inasmuch as it is a conjugal union of a particular man and woman, arises only from the free consent of each of the spouses; and this free act of the will, by which each party hands over and accepts those rights proper to the state of marriage, is so necessary to constitute true marriage that it cannot be supplied by any human power. This freedom, however, regards only the question whether the contracting parties really wish to enter upon matrimony or to marry this particular person; but the nature of matrimony is entirely independent of the free will of man, so that if one has once contracted matrimony he is thereby subject to its divinely made laws and its essential properties. For the Angelic Doctor, writing on conjugal honor and on the offspring which is the fruit of marriage, says: 'These things are so contained in matrimony by the marriage pact itself that, if anything to the contrary were expressed in the consent which makes the marriage, it would not be a true marriage'"). English translation in *Five Great Encyclicals: Labor, Education, Marriage, Restructuring the Social Order, Atheistic Communism*, New York, Paulist Press, 1959, pp. 78-79.

[245]R. ZERA, *De ignorantia in re matrimoniali; eius natura iuridica et ambitus quoad consensus validitatem deque eiusque probatione in iudicio*, Romae, Ancora, 1978, p. 26.

[246]ÖRSY, *Marriage in Canon Law*, p. 30. See also THOMAS AQUINAS, *Summa theologica*, IaIIae, q. 15 (*de consensu*).

[247]THOMAS AQUINAS, *Commentum in quattuor libros Sententiarum Petri Lombardi*, q. 1, 3, from S.E. FRETTÉ and P. MARÉ, eds., *Opera omnia Thomae Aquinatis* (= FRETTÉ, *Opera omnia*), vol. 11, Parisiis, L. Vivès, 1874, p. 99: "Sed causa efficiens matrimonii est consensus per verba de praesenti expressus." All Latin citations will be from this source.

manifested consent and thus brought the contract into existence, this consent could not be supplied by any other human power (canon 1081, §1) except the parties themselves.[248] Consent presupposed, on the part of the persons concerned, a natural capacity of intention and will,[249] i.e., the law presumed that those who entered marriage were not only qualified in law[250] (canon 1081, §1) but were also able to manifest consent for themselves, having the capacity both *ex parte voluntatis* and *ex parte intellectus*. This consent was to be internal, deliberate, true and free as well as externally manifested and legitimate.[251] Furthermore, the consent was to be given at the same time and the parties were to be present, either in person or by proxy, since it was a bilateral action, as stated in canon 1088, §1.[252]

2. Object of matrimonial consent

When a person consented to marriage, he or she intended to form, by mutual consent, a union, an intimate relationship,[253] by accepting and receiving the right over each other's body. This *ius in corpus* was called by many commentators the essential object of marriage.[254] A distinction should be made between the *right* over the body, which is the essential object of matrimonial consent, and the *use or exercise* of that right.

---

[248]See C.A. BACHOFEN, *A Commentary on the New Code of Canon Law*, vol. 5, 6th rev. ed., St. Louis, B. Herder Book Co., 1935, p. 227. Reference is made to THOMAS AQUINAS, *Suppl.*, III, q. 45, 1. It is here in the third supplement that Thomas Aquinas speaks of matrimonial consent and states: "Praeterea, unus non accipit potestatem in eo quod est libere alterius, nisi per ejus consensum. Sed per matrimonium accipit uterque conjugum potestatem in corpus alterius, ut patet I Corinth., VII, cum prius uterque liberam potestatem sui corporis haberet. Ergo consensus facit matrimonium." ("Further, one person does not receive power over that which is at the free disposal of another, without the latter's consent. Now by marriage each of the married parties receives power over the other's body (I Cor. vii. 4), whereas hitherto each had free power over his own body. Therefore consent makes a marriage"). Latin text from FRETTÉ, *Opera omnia*, vol. 6, p. 69; English translation from *The "Summa Theologica" of St. Thomas Aquinas*, *Supplementum tertiae partis* (= *Supplement*) vol. 19, literally translated by the Fathers of the English Dominican Province, London, Burns Oates & Washbourne Ltd, 1932, p. 114. All English translations will be from this source. Since one is giving consent over one's body (and, therefore, giving one's life to another by entering into the life-long commitment of marriage), only the person consenting has the power to do this.

[249]DELLA ROCCA, *Manual of Canon Law*, p. 286. There was one exception, marriage by proxy (*procurator*), noted in canon 1089. Since this was an exception, the conditions stated in the this canon had to be followed for validity.

[250]The parties were free from any impediments and thus able to marry.

[251]A. VERMEERSCH and I. CREUSEN, *Epitome iuris canonici cum commentariis*, 7th ed., vol. 2, Mechliniae, H. Dessain, 1954, p. 262. See also CAPPELLO, *De matrimonio*, pp. 501-502; CHIAPPETTA, *Il matrimonio*, pp. 30-31; P. CHRÉTIEN, *De matrimonio*, 2nd ed., Metis, Journal "Le Lorrain", 1937, pp. 302-303; J.M. MANS PUIGARNAU, *El consentimiento matrimonial: defecto y vicios del mismo como causas de nulidad de las nupcias*, Barcelona, Bosch, 1956, pp. 61-73; H. NOLDIN, *De iure matrimoniali iuxta Codicem iuris canonici*, Lincii, Typis Associationis Catholicae, 1919, pp. 7-9. Furthermore, D.G. OESTERLE, "Nullitas matrimonii ex capite ignorantiae (Can. 1082)", in *Ephemerides theologicae lovanienses*, 15 (1938), p. 650, lists the five qualities which are necessary for consent: true (*verus*), deliberate (*deliberatus*), mutual (*mutuus*), manifested in sensible signs (*signo sensibili manifestatus*), between persons qualified to do so (*inter persons habiles elicitus*).

[252]§1: "Ad matrimonium valide contrahendum necesse est ut contrahentes sint praesentes sive per se ipsi sive per procuratorem" ("In order that marriage be contracted validly it is necessary that the contracting parties be present either in person or by proxy").

[253]G. PAYEN, *De matrimonio in missionibus ac potissimum in Sinis*, vol. 1, Zi-Ka-Wei, 1935, p. 53.

[254]SCICLUNA, *The Essential Definition of Marriage*, p. 135. See also footnote 151 on that page, which lists the great number of authors who referred to the *ius in corpus* as the object, formal object, or essential formal object of matrimonial consent.

54

The use or exercise does not belong to the essence of marriage, and could, by mutual agreement, be excluded without rendering the marriage invalid as long as the *right* itself was exchanged.[255] The *ius in corpus* was seen as a narrow and unilateral definition as well as one that was essentially physiological.[256] Nevertheless, this right was perpetual and exclusive and was to be used for acts which in themselves were open to the generation of children.[257] In addition to consenting to the right over the body, it was also required that this right be exchanged, i.e., given and accepted on the part of each toward the other.[258] Each person was not only to give the other the right over his or her body, but also was to accept the other's right at the same time. Since the object of consent included the essential properties as well as the primary and secondary ends of marriage, it could be said that the object of consent was the essence of marriage.[259]

It was, however, in canon 1082, §1, that marriage was described as a permanent society between a man and a woman for the procreation of children. Canon 1081 articulated the substance of marriage; canon 1082 enunciated its identity.[260] Canon 1081 spoke of the object of matrimonial consent from the viewpoint of the contract, while canon 1082 spoke of it from the perspective of the contractants.[261] The difference was the fact that canon 1081 spoke of the act of the will required for matrimonial consent to be valid, while canon 1082 established the knowledge, which was quantitatively and qualitatively distinct from the will, that was to be present in order to give consent.[262]

Although great emphasis was placed upon the *ius in corpus* by commentators, it must be remembered

---

[255]See S. WOYWOD, *A Practical Commentary on the Code of Canon Law*, vol. I, rev. and enlarged ed. by C. SMITH, New York, Joseph F. Wagner, Inc., 1957, pp. 740-741; L.J. NAU, *Manual on the Marriage Laws of the Code of Canon Law*, 2nd rev. ed., New York, Frederick Pustet Co., Inc., 1934, p. 122.

Cappello makes the distinction that the right over the body is not absolute or unlimited. Rather, it is limited *ad corpus*, i.e., when the body is used for acts that are for the generation of children, not for acts that are contrary to it. He further states that the use of the body for the generation of children can be either positive or negative: positive when the acts are apt for generation; negative when the acts exclude or destroy the possibility of generation. See CAPPELLO, *De matrimonio*, pp. 500-501. Payen states that *in ordine ad actus per se aptos ad prolis generationem* defines the essential object of marriage. See PAYEN, *De matrimonio in missionibus*, vol. 1, p. 56.

[256]CHIAPPETTA, *Il matrimonio*, p. 32.

[257]Here the canon is referring back to canon 1013. "Perpetual and exclusive" used in canon 1081, §1, are adjectives which refer to the essential properties of marriage which have already been listed in canon 1013, §2, "unity and indissolubility" although in reverse order. Concerning the acts for the generation of children, this refers to the then primary end of marriage listed in canon 1013, §1, which is two-fold, i.e., "the procreation and education of children". Since the acts for the generation of children are, in reality, the act of sexual intercourse, it can be implied that these acts would also include the secondary end of marriage, i.e., "to furnish mutual aid and a remedy for concupiscence."

[258]CAPPELLO, *De matrimonio*, p. 499.

[259]E. MOLANO, *Contribución al estudio sobre le esencia del matrimonio*, Pamplona, Ediciones Universidad de Navarra, 1977, p. 113.

[260]FUMAGALLI CARULLI, "La relazione dinamica tra il can. 1082 e il can. 1081", p. 251.

[261]FEDELE, *L' "ordinatio ad prolem" nel matrimonio in diritto canonico*, p. 218. Fedele is citing the 17 May 1957 Rotal case *coram* STAFFA, the complete text of which is found in *SRR Dec*, 49 (1957), pp. 426-430.

[262]GONZALEZ Y GONZALEZ, *Ignorancia y consentimiento matrimonial*, p. 63.

that the spiritual value of marriage, at the same time, had also been affirmed.[263] Nevertheless, it was the *ius in corpus* — the perpetual and exclusive right over the body, mutually given and accepted, to be used for acts that are apt for the generation of children — to which a great deal of attention was given by the commentators. The importance of the *ius in corpus* cannot be understated: as understood, it was the concretization of the primary and secondary ends of marriage and embodied the essential characteristics (properties) of marriage as found in canon 1013, §2. These were reiterated in canon 1081, §2, and formulated in the term *ius in corpus*. It was also inferred in canon 1082, §1, where marriage was described as that state of life in which the right over the body was exercised.

c. Canon 1082

Whereas canon 1081 presented and defined the canonical concept of matrimonial consent, canon 1082,[264] in addition to its description of marriage, began the list of defects of intellect and will which affected the validity of marriage: canons 1082, ignorance; 1083, §1, error regarding the person; 1083, §2, error regarding quality of the person; 1084, simple error regarding the unity, indissolubility or sacramental dignity of marriage; 1086, §2, simulation; 1087, §1, force or grave fear; 1092, condition. In many ways, canon 1082 is very simply worded. However, possibly due to the economy of words used, the exact meaning of those words has led to diverse opinions and oftentimes conflicting understandings of the concepts contained in the canon.

---

[263]Two such examples are the encyclicals *Arcanum divinae sapientiae* of 10 February 1880 by Leo XIII, in *ASS*, 12 (1878-1880), pp. 385-402, written prior to the 1917 Code; and *Casti connubii* of 31 December 1930 by Pius XI, in *AAS*, 22 (1930), pp. 539-592, written after the Code's promulgation. While both of these encyclicals are pastoral in nature, they speak, at times, in juridic language.
Leo XIII, for example, lists the two most eminent properties of marriage, i.e., unity and perpetuity (p. 386). He also speaks of the perpetual bond of marriage (p. 388). He later quotes the Council of Trent and addresses the sanctity of the married state. Pius XI, issuing his encyclical fifty years after that of Leo XIII, addresses the mutual love found in marriage, p. 548: "Hoc autem opus in domestica societate non modo mutuum auxilium complectitur, verum etiam ad hoc extendatur oportet, immo hoc in primis intendat, ut coniuges inter se iuventur ad interiorem hominem plenius in dies conformandum perficiendumque; ita ut per mutuam vitae consortionem in virtutibus magis magisque in dies proficiant, et praecipue in vera erga Deum proximosque caritate crescant, in quia denique 'universa Lex pendet et Prophetae'" ("This outward expression of love in the home demands not only mutual help but must go further; must have as its primary purpose that man and wife help each other day by day in forming and perfecting themselves in the interior life, so that through their partnership in life they may advance ever more and more in virtue, and above all that they may grow in true love toward God and their neighbor, on which indeed 'dependeth the whole Law and the Prophets'"). English translation in *Five Great Encyclicals*, pp. 83-84.

[264]For important works specifically on canon 1082, apart from the commentaries on the 1917 *CIC*, some of which treat this canon in depth, see A. ALVAREZ FERNANDEZ, "El tema de la ignorancia en el consentimiento matrimonial", in *El consentimiento matrimonial hoy, trabajos de la XV Semana de derecho canónico*, Barcelona, Banchs, 1976, pp. 31-61; R. BIDAGOR, "Circa ignorantiam naturae matrimonii", in *Periodica*, 29 (1940), pp. 269-289 (also in W. BERTRAMS et al., eds., *De matrimonio coniectanea*, Roma, Università Gregoriana Editrice, 1970, pp. 161-175); A. DE LA HERA, "El supuesto de hecho del c. 1082 §1: 'ignorata natura matrimonii'", in *Ius canonicum*, 4 (1964), pp. 533-556; F. LORENC, *De ignorantiae influxu in matrimonialii consensu*, Romae, Pontificium Athenaeum Lateranense, 1955; H.G. MARTINEZ, *De scientia debita in matrimonio ineundo; doctrina auctorum et iurisprudentia Sacrae Romanae Rotae*, Roma, Desclée, 1966; J.M. SERRANO, "Sobre el conocimiento que se requiere para la validez del matrimonio (can. 1082)", in *Angelicum*, 50 (1973), pp. 357-375. See also the works cited earlier in this chapter, namely, OESTERLE, "Nullitas matrimonii ex capite ignorantiae", pp. 647-673; SMITH, *Ignorance Affecting Matrimonial Consent*; and ZERA, *De ignorantia in re matrimoniali*.

56

Since the will is informed and moved by the intellect,[265] it is logical that the defects of cognition (ignorance and error[266]) be listed first. Since error is based on ignorance,[267] i.e., if something is not known, it follows that incorrect assumptions are made or wrong conclusions are drawn, then the person makes an error in judgment; it stands to reason that the discussion of the defects of cognition would commence with ignorance. Ignorance does not, of its very nature, imply an act of knowledge.[268] In other words, if someone knows nothing, nothing is willed.[269] If nothing is willed, no action is taken. There is no human act and, therefore, no marriage. Thus, many authors combined ignorance and error or, when referring to ignorance, called it "error of substance" or "substantial error", or "error of law".[270]

---

[265]THOMAS AQUINAS, *Summa theologica, Supplementum,* q. 51, 1: "Consensus autem voluntatis est actus, qui praesupponit actum intellectus" ("...consent is an act of the will presupposing an act of the intellect..."). FRETTÉ, *Opera omnia,* vol. 6, p. 91; *Supplement,* vol. 19, p. 166. This concept is also seen in the philosophical axiom, "Nihil enim (also sometimes quoted simply as "nil") volitum quin praecognitum" ("Nothing is willed unless it is known beforehand").

Concerning the concepts of will and intellect, C. ALUEDE OJEMEN, *Psychological Factors in Matrimonial Consent in the Light of Canonical Legislation,* Roma, Pontificia Universitas Urbaniana, 1986, pp. 139-140, points out "that the cognitive and volitive faculties we are referring to here do not in any way constitute autonomous factors within the complex reality of the human organism. These faculties are mere spiritual principles. The names they are given represent mere functional names for some of the ways the human person manifests his rational spiritual qualities.... It means that anything that affects the human personality could also affect in some way the cognitive and volitive activities of the person."

[266]Some authors would add deceit (or fraud) to this list, since it is a form of error. However, there is no canon in the 1917 *CIC* specifically pertaining to deceit in regard to marriage.

[267]See THOMAS AQUINAS, *Summa theologica, Supplementum,* q. 51, for a discussion of error as an impediment to marriage.

[268]*Ibid.,* q. 51, 1: "Ignorantia de sui ratione non importat cognitionis actum." See also ZERA, *De ignorantia in re matrimoniali,* p. 29.

[269]For further discussion, see GONZALEZ Y GONZALEZ, *Ignorancia y consentimiento matrimonial,* pp. 62-102. In this section the author discusses, in detail, the axiom "Nil volitum quin praecognitum." He gives a comprehensive list of Rotal decisions showing that there was not a consensus how the axiom was utilized in jurisprudence, pp. 62-63.

[270]This is clearly seen in many of the European canonists. See O. GIACCHI, *Il consenso nel matrimonio canonico,* 3rd ed., Milano, A. Giuffrè Editore, 1968, pp. 79-84. See also WERNZ-VIDAL, *Ius canonicum,* vol. 5, *Ius matrimoniale,* pp. 596-623. Here, the author lists canon 1082 under error. Also G. CARNERO, "Nullidad por error acerca de persona o de sus cualidades", in *Las causas matrimoniales: trabajos de la cuarta semana de derecho canónico celebrada en el monasterio Na. Sa. De Montserrat,* Salamanca, Tipografía FLO-REZ, 1953, p. 205. The author further states, on this same page, that the effects of error are identical to the effect of ignorance, and "Todo cuanto hemos de decir, por tanto, acerca error, se debe aplicar igualmente a la ignorancia." Likewise, E. GRAZIANI, *Volontà attuale e volontà precettiva nel negotio matrimoniale canonico,* Pubblicazioni dell'Istituto di scienze giuridiche, economiche, politiche e sociali della Università di Messina, 34, Milano, A. Giuffrè Editore, 1956, p. 98, calls error "a subspecies of ignorance" ("una sottospecie dell'ignoranza"). See MANS PUIGARNAU, *El consentimiento matrimonial,* pp. 21, 108-115.

Joining ignorance and error can be seen in the writings of Aquinas, who states in the *Summa theologica, Supplementum,* q. 51, 1: "Tamen quantum ad hoc quod est impedire voluntarium, non differt utrum dicatur ignorantia vel error, quia nulla ignorantia potest impedire voluntarium, nisi quae habet errorem adjunctum, eo quod actus voluntatis praesupponit aestimationem sive judicium de aliquo, in quod fertur: unde si est ibi ignorantia, oportet ibi esse errorem. Et ideo etiam ponitur error quasi causa proxima" ("However, as regards being an impediment to the voluntary, it differs not whether we call it ignorance or error, since no ignorance can be an impediment to the voluntary, unless it have error in conjunction with it, because the will's act presupposes an estimate or judgment about something which is the object of the will. Wherefore if there be ignorance there must needs be error; and for this reason error is set down as being the proximate cause"), FRETTÉ, *Opera omnia,* vol. 6, p. 91; *Supplement,* vol. 19, p. 166-167.

In canon 1082 we read:

§1: Ut matrimonialis consensus haberi possit, necesse est ut contrahentes saltem non ignorent matrimonium esse societatem permanentem inter virum et mulierem ad filios procreandos.

§2: Haec ignorantia post pubertatem non praesumitur.[271]

In canon 1081, §1, we are told that marriage comes into existence through the consent of the parties and, in §2, matrimonial consent is defined. Canon 1082, §1, expresses the minimum of knowledge which is necessary in order to give consent. Since the act of the will which constitutes consent must have the interaction of the intellect in order to make such assent, if knowledge is lacking there can be no human act and, therefore, no consent. Thus, canon 1082, seen in relationship to canon 1081, clearly derives from the nature of marriage itself: without the minimum knowledge needed, there can be no act of the will; without the act of the will, there can be no consent; without consent, there can be no marriage.[272] It is common sense that a person cannot rationally will something of which he or she has no knowledge.[273]

Here in canon 1082, §1, we are given the description of marriage: a permanent society[274] between a man and a woman for the procreation of children. This description of marriage established the basic knowledge to be found in those parties who intended to enter into marriage. "They were not to be ignorant", which was a negative way of stating that they were to have some knowledge of these facts for matrimonial consent to be possible. Although the "what" of the necessary knowledge was given, the "how much" was not. The degree of this specific knowledge was not explicit, thus leading to much discussion and debate.

In §2, it was stated that this basic knowledge of marriage was to be presumed after puberty. This was a presumption of law,[275] which could be overturned by contrary proof. We shall now proceed with an analysis of the text of the canon.

1. *Ut matrimonialis consensus haberi possit...*

Canon 1082 begins with a conditionally stated presupposition: if the conditions which follow are fulfilled, the matrimonial consent, as defined in canon 1081, §2, will be valid. Since consent makes marriage,

---

[271]§1: "In order that matrimonial consent may be possible it is necessary that the contracting parties at least not be ignorant that marriage is a permanent society between a man and a woman for the procreation of children."
§2: "This ignorance is not to be presumed after puberty."

[272]See BOUSCAREN, *Canon Law: A Text and Commentary*, p. 567. See also CAPPELLO, *De matrimonio*, pp. 505.

[273]WOYWOD, *A Practical Commentary*, vol. I, p. 742.

[274]Depending upon the commentator(s), the word *societas*, which is used in the canon, is translated as "association" or "society" or "union". Less frequently, it is translated as "partnership". Since no official translation of the 1917 *CIC* was authorized, the word was left to the discretion of the commentator(s).

[275]A presumption was defined in canon 1825, §1, as "a probable conjecture of something which is uncertain". It may take the place of proof when the proof is wanting. There were two kinds of presumptions, those established by the law itself (*praesumptio iuris*) and those established by the judge (*praesumptio hominis*). There were also two types of *praesumptio iuris*: the *iuris simpliciter*, a simple presumption which yields to contrary proof and the *iuris et de iure*, an absolute presumption which excludes contrary proof (see canon 1826). Here, in canon 1082, §2, we have a simple presumption of law. See BOUSCAREN, *Canon Law: A Text and Commentary*, p. 568; WOYWOD, *A Practical Commentary*, vol. II, p. 316.

once it is exchanged, the marriage is presumed to be valid.[276] This is the basic starting point for canonical legislation in regard to the validity of marriage: all things being equal, once a couple exchanges consent, it is presumed valid. However, the verb in this portion of the canon was written in the subjunctive, which indicated that certain conditions were necessary in order for the matrimonial consent, which was presumed valid, to be possible.

2. ...Necesse est ut contrahentes saltem non ignorent matrimonium esse societatem permanentem inter virum et mulierem ad filios procreandos

The canon continues with the equivalent of a double negative proposition: that the contracting parties "at least not be ignorant".[277] Knowledge is necessary for the act of instituting a valid marriage.[278] This is a requirement of natural law itself.[279] What is important to note is that the wording of the canon is such that there is no distinction as to whether a person who is entering marriage is capable of such knowledge or not. The canon speaks only of a defect in cognition, i.e., the contractants do not know something. This "not knowing" can result from many possible causes, e.g., from a defect in the use of reason, a defect in discretion of judgment, a defect in a person's psychological or physiological makeup, a defect in one's upbringing. What is important to note is that the canon gave no indication as to the cause of this lack of knowledge, this defect of cognition. Thus, psychological (mental) defects, such as insanity (amentia), dementia, chronic alcoholism, sleepwalking and other defects of the intellect such as mental retardation were listed under the heading of this canon.[280] Also included were physical defects which rendered the acquisition of intellectual knowledge either impossible or difficult, such as being blind or deaf or mute.[281]

There was much debate among canonists as to the precise meaning of the word saltem. What did the word, translated as "at least", actually mean within the context of knowledge? In other words, what degree of knowledge was sufficient for a valid exchange of consent? This gave rise to diverse opinions which were grouped into three categories, emerging from doctrine and jurisprudence, which addressed the amount of

---

[276]Canon 1014: "Matrimonium gaudet favore iuris; quare in dubio standum est pro valore matrimonii, donec contrarium probetur, salvo praescripto can. 1127" ("Marriage enjoys the favor of the law; hence, in doubt, the validity of marriage is to be upheld until the contrary is proved, except as provided in canon 1127"). This canon established the presumption of the validity of marriage. Originally based upon the Holy Office decisions of 18 December 1872 and 24 January 1877 which declared marriages among pagans to be valid, the principle was broadened to apply to all marriages. See BOUSCAREN, Canon Law: A Text and Commentary, p. 469.

[277]For a thorough discussion of this topic, see GONZALEZ Y GONZALEZ, "Caracteres del conocimiento exigido por el canon 1082; la clausula 'saltem non ignorent'", in Ignorancia y consentimiento matrimonial, pp. 143-180.

[278]SMITH, Ignorance Affecting Matrimonial Consent, p. 45.

[279]M.F. POMPEDDA, Studi di diritto matrimoniale canonico, Milano, Giuffrè Editore, 1993, p. 208.

[280]See SMITH, Ignorance Affecting Matrimonial Consent, pp. 46-57; LORENC, De ignorantiae influxu in matrimoniali consensu, pp. 16-18; CAPPELLO, De matrimonio, pp. 505-507. CONTE A CORONATA, De sacramentis, vol. 3, pp. 582-599, also lists hypnosis as such a condition, pp. 597-598. WERNZ-VIDAL, Ius canonicum, vol. 5, Ius matrimoniale, p. 589, went so far as to state that those who lacked discretion of judgment or who were ignorant were incapable of contracting marriage.

[281]SMITH, Ignorance Affecting Matrimonial Consent, pp. 57-62. He lists those defects which rendered a person deaf, dumb or blind among the most pre-eminent. A more extensive list is given by CONTE A CORONATA, De sacramentis, pp. 598-599, where he includes hysteria, epilepsy, chronic alcoholism, phobias and nervous exhaustion as other possible causes. CAPPELLO, De matrimonio, p. 507, lists grave and long-lasting melancholy as well as many other illnesses that affect the brain or the nervous system.

knowledge necessary to enter marriage: minimalist, maximalist and traditional or moderate.

The knowledge, as stated in the canon, is the fact that marriage is a permanent society between a man and a woman for the procreation of children. To know that marriage is a society is to know that (1) it involves rights and obligations and (2) its end is to be attained through the corporal activity of the parties.[282] The natural bodily union is the basis of marriage.[283] From this union of bodies comes the generation of offspring. The three schools of thought which emerged revolved around the amount of knowledge required regarding the procreation of children.

a. "Minimalist school"

Some commentators wrote that the minimal knowledge that the couple must have in order for the marriage to be valid was that they intend to do what others do when contracting marriage. There need not be knowledge of actual sexual copulation. Since carnal copulation did not pertain to the essence of the matrimonial contract, ignorance of the *copula* did not affect the validity of consent. Both the Congregation of the Council and the Roman Rota maintained this viewpoint and upheld the validity of marriages presented to them when the unions were challenged on the ground of ignorance concerning the carnal act of copulation.[284]

The major proponent of this teaching was P. Gasparri. According to him, if a girl who is marrying knows that matrimony is a union with a man who, with his wife, procreates children, and consents to this union, but does not know that having children comes from carnal copulation, indeed is absolutely ignorant of this carnal copulation, this ignorance does not exclude matrimonial consent.[285] There was to be some knowledge, even if it were confused, of what constitutes the essential object of marriage, i.e., the establishing of a society which led to the generation of children. No clear or explicit knowledge of the conjugal act was needed.[286] Furthermore, the right need not be explicitly intended to be exchanged. Rather, as long as the

---

[282]SMITH, *Ignorance Affecting Matrimonial Consent*, p. 77. See also L. RULAND, *Morality and the Social Order*, vol. 3, T.A. RATTLER, trans., St. Louis. Herder. 1942, pp. 149-155.

[283]RULAND, *Morality and the Social Order*, p. 149.

[284]SMITH, *Ignorance Affecting Matrimonial Consent*, p. 83. For examples of Rotal decisions, see *coram* PARRILLO, 16 February 1928, *SRR Dec*, 20 (1928), pp. 57-81; *coram* PARRILLO, 20 July 1929, *SRR Dec*, 21 (1929), pp. 306-312; *coram* QUATTROCOLO, 7 August 1929, *ibid.*, pp. 392-405; *coram* WYNEN, 14 March 1935, in *SRR Dec*, 27 (1935), pp. 128-150; *coram* GRAZIOLI, 7 August 1936, in *SRR Dec*, 28 (1936), pp. 570-582; *coram* GRAZIOLI, 12 January 1942, in *SRR Dec*, 34 (1942), pp. 31-41; *coram* CANESTRI, 16 July 1943, in *SRR Dec*, 35 (1943), pp. 594-612; *coram* WYNEN, 27 February 1947, in *SRR Dec*, 39 (1947), pp. 119-128; and *coram* STAFFA, 17 May 1957, in *SRR Dec*, 49 (1957), pp. 426-430.

[285]GASPARRI, *Tractatus canonicus de matrimonio*, vol. 2, pp. 12-16.

[286]H.A. AYRINHAC and P.J. LYDON, *Marriage Legislation in the New Code of Canon Law*, new rev. ed., New York, Benziger, 1939, p. 194. The authors go on to say: "If one, knowing that the purpose of marriage is the procreation of children, would enter the contract with that in view and would consent to all it implies, although having no distinct idea what is required for generation, there would be confused knowledge of, and consent to, what constitutes the essential object of the contract, and the marriage would be valid; even if the party was so disposed that if he knew what the act of generation really is, he would not give his consent. But at least that confused knowledge of the substantial object of the contract is necessary."

This is also reflected in the 30 July 1927 Rotal decision *coram* MANNUCCI, which stated, after citing canon 1082, "... nec alia requiritur distincta et explicita notitia sive actuum ipsorum, sive modi vel organi quibus ponantur, sive momenti iuridici eorumdem actuum in ordine ad matrimonialem contractum" ("Distinct and explicit knowledge, either of the acts themselves, or of the way in which, or the organs by which they are exercised, or of their juridical importance for the marriage contract, is not required"), in *SRR Dec*, 19 (1927), p. 352; English translation from BOUSCAREN, *Canon Law: A Text and Commentary*, p. 568.

couple knew that marriage was described as a society for the procreation of children, this knowledge was sufficient for the marriage to be valid since the contractants were thus intending a union which in itself was the means of procreation.[287] However, the couple had to know that the society which they were forming was a sexual one, i.e., it was more than a living together in friendship or to help the other spouse. It was, primarily, a union from which children were born.[288] Other authors who held this opinion were T. Sanchez,[289] P. Chretien,[290] G. Payen,[291] J.M. Mans Puigarnau,[292] F. Wernz- P. Vidal,[293] R. Bidagor,[294] and C. Viglino.[295]

b. "Maximalist school"

Whereas the minimalist tradition spoke of at least some kind of knowledge concerning the sexual act, albeit indistinct or confused, on the part of the contractants, the commentators who held the maximalist view maintained that there was to be the knowledge that the act of procreation was indeed a sexual one. In other words, it was necessary that the parties possessed the knowledge that the process of procreation involved the sexual cooperation of bodies.[296] In fact, if one or the other contractant truly believed that children came into being not through the bodily sexual union, as the Creator ordained, but rather through some other means (such as holding hands or kissing),[297] that marriage would be null.[298] By virtue of the natural law, one author argues,

---

[287]L. DE SMET, *Tractatus theologico-canonicus de sponsalibus et matrimonio*, Brugis, Car. Beyaert, 4th ed., 1927, p. 83. This was known as consenting implicitly to the conjugal society. This view was held by Gasparri, Wernz and Vidal. See the 10 November 1930 Rotal decision *coram* MANNUCCI, in *SRR Dec*, 22 (1930), pp. 605-612, especially p. 607.

[288]P. CHRÉTIEN, *De matrimonio: praelectiones*, 2nd ed., Metis, Journal "Le Lorrain", 1937, pp. 307-308.

[289]T. SANCHEZ, *De sancto matrimonii sacramento disputationum tomi tres*, Norimbergae, sumptibus Jo. C. Lochneri, 1706, lib. II, d. 28.

[290]CHRÉTIEN, *De matrimonio: praelectiones*, pp. 307-308.

[291]PAYEN, *De matrimonio in missionibus*, vol. 3, pp. 271-272.

[292] MANS PUIGARNAU, *El consentimiento matrimonial*, p. 113.

[293]WERNZ-VIDAL, *Ius canonicum*, vol. 5, *Ius matrimoniale*, p. 547, in which the authors cite GASPARRI, *Tractatus canonicus de matrimonio*, vol. 2, pp. 12-16; I. CHELODI, *Ius canonicum de matrimonio et de iudiciis matrimonialibus*, 5th ed., Vicenza, Società Anonima Tipographica Editrice, 1947, pp.132-134; DE SMET, *Tractatus theologico-canonicus*, p. 83; and VLAMING, *Praelectiones iuris matrimonii*, pp. 381-382.

[294]BIDAGOR, "Circa ignorantiam naturae matrimonii", pp. 284-288.

[295]C. VIGLINO, "Oggetto e fine primario del matrimonio", in *Diritto ecclesiastico italiano*, 35 (1929), p. 148.

[296]ZERA, *De ignorantia in re matrimoniali*, p. 39.

[297]G. OESTERLÉ, "Consentement matrimonial", in *Dictionnaire de droit canonique*, vol. 4, R. NAZ, ed., Paris, Letouzey et Ané, 1949, col. 308. While researching this particular topic, it appeared that the author of this entry in the *Dictionnaire* was incorrectly identified as E. JOMBART twice: MARTINEZ, *De scientia debita in matrimonio ineundo*, p. 131, footnote 67; and ZERA, *De ignorantia in re matrimoniali*, p. 39, footnote 45.

[298]ZERA, *De ignorantia in re matrimoniali*, p. 39. For examples, see the Rotal decisions *coram* MASSIMI, 2 August 1929, in *SRR Dec*, 21 (1929), pp. 363-369; *coram* CANESTRI, 16 July 1943, in *SRR Dec*, 35 (1943) pp. 594-612; and *coram* TEODORI, 8 July 1949, in *SRR Dec*, 41 (1949), pp. 368-373.

the contractants were able to know that marriage was essentially a union of bodies, specifically a joining of the genital organs.[299] Another author simply states that the couple, when giving consent, must know that the matrimonial society they are forming is for the procreation of children which is brought about through physical, sexual contact between a man and a woman. They are to know, at least in general terms, and not necessarily with medical precision, the mode with which they join for the actual procreation of children.[300] Probably the most famous proponent of this position was F.M. Cappello who stated that even if a most honest girl knows that marriage is a society instituted for the procreation of children, but is entirely (*omnino*) ignorant that it happens through the mutual joining of bodies, then that marriage would not prevail because what is necessary for consent is the knowledge of the essential object which is the right of the body (*ius in corpus*) for the procreation of children.[301] His emphasis was on the word *omnino*: if one entirely or completely does not know, then there is no marriage. He does, however, concede that if a person knows in some way, even in a confused or implicit way, that there needs to be a joining together, then there would be a marriage.[302] Other commentators who held this position were O. Giacchi[303] and G. Oesterlé.

c. "Traditionalist school"

The commentators who wrote concerning the traditional knowledge that was needed for marriage constituted the middle ground between the minimalists and the maximalists.[304] They held that the contractants were to have some knowledge, although perhaps indistinct or even confused about the actual act, but nonetheless accepted the fact that there was some kind of physical joining necessary for the procreation of children.[305] But if the parties were entirely ignorant of the physical joining, this would not invalidate the matrimonial consent, for as long as they intended and accepted the end of marriage, i.e., the procreation of children, then the *copula* was implicit and thus intended since that was the means by which children were procreated.[306] No maximum knowledge, i.e., the actual way of copulation, therefore was required. All that was necessary was that the contractants knew of a physical relationship between themselves that pertained

---

[299]G. OESTERLÉ, *Consultationes de jure matrimoniali*, Romae, Officium Libri Catholici, 1942, p. 312. He goes on to state that exact physiological knowledge is not necessary for the copulation ("Exacta physiologica cognitio de processu copulae carnalis non requiritur"). A couple would simply know what to do by instinct.

[300]GIACCHI, *Il consenso nel matrimonio canonico*, p. 81. The author cites the 14 March 1935 Rotal decision *coram* WYNEN, in *SRR Dec*, 27 (1935), pp. 128-150, as proof of the changing jurisprudence of the Roman Rota regarding ignorance pertaining to the sexual act. As we have seen earlier, the jurisprudence of both the Congregation of the Council and the Rota was to render negative decisions if a party impugned a marriage based upon ignorance of the act of copulation.
However, it should be noted that the decision *coram* MASSIMI, 2 August 1929, cited above, would be an earlier indication of a shift from the very narrow interpretation of canon 1082: "Necesse scilicet ante omnia est, ut contrahens uterque sciat filios procreari mutua opera coniugum, idest utriusque concursu" (*SRR Dec*, 21 [1929], p. 364).

[301]CAPPELLO, *De matrimonio*, p. 509.

[302]*Ibid*.

[303]GIACCHI, *Il consenso nel matrimonio canonico*, footnote 31, pp. 81-82

[304]ZERA, *De ignorantia in re matrimoniali*, p. 40.

[305]MARTINEZ, *De scientia debita in matrimonio ineundo*, pp. 125-131. See also LORENC, *De ignorantiae influxu in matrimoniali consensu*, pp. 21-22.

[306]See LORENC, *De ignorantiae influxu in matrimoniali consensu*, p. 21.

62

to marriage, the end of which was procreation of children.[307] Authors who promoted this position were, among others, E. Graziani,[308] F. Lorenc, H.G. Martinez and A. Vermeersch.[309] The generally accepted definitive statement on this issue is the Rotal decision *coram* MATTOLI of 25 November 1964,[310] where it is stated that this cooperation must be known to be a physically sexual one.[311]

d. "A new way"

Some authors refer to a new way of thinking[312] which arose from the milestone decision of 22 March 1963 *coram* SABATTANI[313] where he stated that rather than ignorance there is error on the part of the contractants, since ignorance is static while error is dynamic and thus influences the will.[314] For the most part, jurisprudence concerning ignorance came to a virtual standstill.[315] However, the changes begun by Vatican II and the renewal of canon law were just beginning, which will be discussed in the next chapter.

3. ...*Societatem permanentem inter virum et mulierem*...

As can be witnessed from the above discussion, the greatest amount of debate and deliberation concerned the *ius in corpus*, or more specifically, the knowledge of how to utilize the right of the body for the procreation of children. This is understandable from the viewpoint that the procreation of children (along

---

[307]ZERA, *De ignorantia in re matrimoniali*, p. 41. For examples of Rotal decisions, see *coram* JULLIEN, 21 December 1938, in *SRR Dec*, 30 (1938), pp.715-726; *coram* HEARD, 13 July 1946, in *SRR Dec*, 38 (1946), pp. 360-368; *coram* JULLIEN, 16 April 1948, in *SRR Dec*, 40 (1948), pp.119-128; *coram* TEODORI, 26 May 1948, *ibid.*, pp. 203-208; *coram* PINNA, 30 October 1958, in *SRR Dec*, 50 (1958), pp. 556-564; and *coram* HEARD, 30 July 1959, in *SRR Dec*, 51 (1959), pp. 420-424.

[308]E. GRAZIANI, "Osservazioni sulla fattispecie dell'̔ignorata natura matrimonii̓'", in *Il diritto ecclesiastico*, 68 (1957), II, pp. 31-39, especially pp. 33-34.

[309]A. VERMEERSCH, *Theologia moralis principia, responsa, consilia*, 4th ed., v. 3, *De personis, de sacramentis, de legibus Ecclesiae et censuris*, Roma, Pontificia Università Gregoriana, 1948, pp. 478-479.

[310]*SRR Dec*, 56 (1964), pp. 867-883. OLIVIERI, "A ignorância no matrimònio (c. 1096)", pp. 56-59, discusses this decision and its ramifications at length.

[311]D. KELLY, "Canon 1096", in G. SHEEHY et al., eds., *The Canon Law, Letter and Spirit: a Practical Guide to the Code of Canon Law*, prepared by the Canon Law Society of Great Britain and Ireland in association with the Canadian Canon Law Society, Collegeville, The Liturgical Press, 1995, p. 613. See also T.L. BOUSCAREN and J.I. O'CONNOR, eds., *The Canon Law Digest*, 6 (1963-1967), Milwaukee, Bruce Publishing Com., 1969, p. 624.
It is interesting to note that in his decision, Mattioli cites only *coram* SABATTANI, 22 March 1963, in *SRR Dec*, 55 (1963), p. 205, where Sabattani declares if a couple marries thinking that marriage is something other than a sexual union, they marry invalidly. However, he does not cite p. 207, where Sabattani states that the contractants had to be aware of the mutual physical joining of the sex organs.

[312]See ZERA, *De ignorantia in re matrimoniali*, pp. 47-48.

[313]*SRR Dec*, 55 (1963), pp. 196-221. This decision is quoted in Chapter Three.

[314]*Ibid.*, p. 199.

[315]ZERA, *De ignorantia in re matrimoniali*, p. 48. It was Sabattani, with the statement that the contractants were to know of the sexual cooperation, who influenced subsequent Rotal decisions (e.g., *coram* MATTIOLI of 25 November 1964) and led to the development of the new canon 1096, §1. See PELLEGRINO, "L'errore di diritto nel matrimonio canonico", pp. 398-399.

with their education) was the primary end of marriage as stated in canon 1013, §1. There was little discussion during this period of two other elements mentioned in this part of paragraph one, namely, that marriage was a *permanent* society *between a man and a woman* (for the procreation of children). With regard to the concept of society, this was the context within which the debate concerning the *ius in corpus* took place, so its essence was described within that framework which, according to the wording of the canon, was *ad filios procreandos*. Suffice to say that marriage was, above all else, an institution; the basis of society in general. It was a stable union.[316] In order to survive, a society must look to the future, i.e., the next generation. Thus, it is easy to understand the importance placed upon having children, since society's prime concerns were the preservation and propagation of the human species.[317]

Society, in general, was characterized as a union in which the parties had rights and obligations.[318] It was seen as a highly structured system of human organization for large-scale community living that normally furnished protection, continuity and security.[319] As it pertained to marriage, both the rights and the obligations fundamentally concerned the procreation of children. Thus, marriage was the society which a man and a woman primarily formed in order to generate children and rear them. From a canonical point of view, anything else that related to marriage was secondary, as seen in canon 1013, §1, which literally lists the secondary ends of marriage.

Canon 1081, §2, describes marriage as *perpetuum et exclusivum*, while canon 1082, §1, describes it as *permanentem inter virum et mulierem*. As was stated earlier, canon 1081 referred to the will and canon 1082 referred to the intellect. However, while each of these canons pertained to a different aspect of the human person, these descriptions of marriage were simply different ways of stating the same entity. In other words, perpetuity, i.e., indissolubility, is substituted with *societas permanens* and exclusivity, i.e., unity, is substituted with *societas inter virum et mulierem*.[320] In effect, the legislative formula, in both these canons were to be considered "perfectly identical".[321] They both referred to the requirements and characterization of the marriage bond which the Legislator required the contractants to be capable of recognizing intellectually as well as to be able to elect volitively. If they were able to do so, then the parties were truly *habiles ad contrahendum*.[322] Another way to see the difference in the terms used was put forward by P. Fedele who stated that it was not necessary that the terms be identical because in order to have matrimonial consent, the contractants are not to be ignorant of the essential properties of marriage, namely, indissolubility and unity,

---

[316]CAPPELLO, *De matrimonio*, p. 508. See also ZERA, *De ignorantia in re matrimoniali*, pp. 58-59, where he states that permanence refers to stability; and GIACCHI, *Il consenso nel matrimonio canonico*, p. 86.

[317]CAPPELLO, *De matrimonio*, p. 16.

[318]RULAND, *Morality and the Social Order*, p. 149.

[319]*The Random House College Dictionary*, rev. ed., J. STEIN, ed., New York, Random House, Inc., 1975, p. 1247.

[320]FEDELE, *L."ordinatio ad prolem" nel matrimonio in diritto canonico*, pp. 215-216.

[321]P.A. BONNET, "L'errore di diritto giuridicamente rilevante nel consenso matrimoniale canonico", in *Scritti in memoria di Pietro Gismondi*, vol. 1, Milano, A. Giuffrè Editore, 1987, p. 143. See also PELLEGRINO, "L'errore di diritto nel matrimonio canonico", p. 367. Also see MARTINEZ, *De scientia debita in matrimonio ineundo*, p. 161, where he also equates the terms from both canons.

[322]P.A. D'AVACK, *Cause di nullità e di divorzio nel diritto matrimoniale canonico*, vol. 1, Firenze, Casa Editrice del Dott. Carlo Cya, 1952, pp. 137-138.

64

which were mentioned in the preceding canon.[323] The contractants were required to know that marriage was between a man and a woman, since the marriage was ordered for the procreation of children.[324]

4. *Haec ignorantia post pubertatem non praesumitur*

It was the determination of the legitimate age for the establishment of marriage which gave rise to the presumption of law that a person who reached a certain age also had sufficient knowledge to enter marriage. This can be found in the writings of Thomas Sanchez.[325] The age of puberty was seen as the time appropriate for marriage, since it is the time of a person's life when the body changes and ability to reproduce is realized. Along with this ability, the presumption was that the parties also knew how to reproduce. Thus, before the 1917 *CIC*, puberty was the acceptable age, yet exceptions were made if a boy or girl had physically matured at a faster rate.[326] With canon 1067, §1, of the 1917 *CIC*, however, the age for marriage was set at a higher age.[327] While there was no direct requirement by natural law as to age, what was required was the mental capacity for matrimonial consent, which was established by positive Church law in canons 1081 and 1082.[328] According to Church law, a person could not validly marry before a certain age, which was higher than that which the *CIC* set for the age of puberty (cf. canon 88, §2). Thus the *CIC* fortified the presumption that the knowledge about marriage had occurred with puberty and was strengthened by at least a few years of life experience.

This paragraph distinguishes between before puberty and after it. Before puberty, the sufficient knowledge to enter marriage must be proved; after puberty such knowledge is presumed and therefore ignorance must be proved.[329]

CONCLUSION

Ignorance in canonical tradition has a long history, but we have focused on the period immediately before and during the era of the 1917 *CIC*. We saw a development in understanding of ignorance as it related to marriage. In 1856, the Congregation of the Council did not recognize the invalidity of a marriage (Bamberg), stating that the conjugal act was not essential to the marriage contract even though the woman

---

[323]FEDELE, *L'"ordinatio ad prolem" nel matrimonio in diritto canonico*, p. 220-221.

[324]See *coram* Di FELICE, 25 July 1973, in *SRR Dec*, 65 (1973), pp. 619-625, especially p. 620.

[325]T. SANCHEZ, *De sancto matrimonii sacramento disputationum tomi tres*, lib. VII. See SMITH, *Ignorance Affecting Matrimonial Consent*, pp. 24-25. Smith further elaborates that such a presumption was held by both the Congregation of the Council and the Roman Rota through the demands each made for proof of ignorance.

[326]See WOYWOD, *A Practical Commentary*, vol. I, p. 708.

[327]"Vir ante decimum sextum aetatis annum completum, mulier ante decimum quartum item completum, matrimonium validum inire non possunt" ("A man before completing his sixteenth year, and a woman before completing her fourteenth, cannot contract a valid marriage").

[328]BOUSCAREN, *Canon Law: A Text and Commentary*, p. 533.

[329]C. LEFEBVRE, "De defectu discretionis iudicii in rotali iurisprudentia", in *Periodica*, 69 (1980). p. 565.

stated she had no idea of the physical aspects of marriage at the time of consent. In 1869, however, the same Congregation declared a marriage invalid for the same reason, but under different circumstances. Three points in the 1869 case which are relevant to our discussion are: (1) the use of the phrase *consortium omnis vitae* by the Defender of Marriage and reiterated in the definitive sentence pertaining to marriage; (2) the statement that the contractants did not need to know all the obligations which marriage entailed; and (3) the presumption that the couple married the way all other couples do, which fundamentally meant they intended to have children.

It is, however, the 1888 case, *Ventimiglia*, which declared a marriage invalid due to defective consent because a twelve year, nine month old girl lacked sufficient discretion of judgment; i.e., she was ignorant of the sexual act. The conclusions were insightful because from them we learned that knowledge was equated with discretion of judgment, that puberty was the legitimate age for contracting marriage, and that the necessary knowledge was presumed after puberty. This was why the case was so concerned with the age of the girl, Catherina, who was just beyond the age of puberty. Two other important lessons derived from this case were that the necessary knowledge which came after puberty was a presumption which could be overturned if enough evidence to the contrary was shown and, more importantly, that the presumption cannot be so strongly held that the truth of the matter may be compromised.

These observations show that the focus of knowledge concerning marriage was the *ius in corpus* for acts which in themselves were apt for the procreation of children. Since this was considered at the time to be the primary end of marriage, the knowledge needed for marriage concerned the fact that it was a society for the procreation of children and knowledge was gauged by how much or how little the person knew about the actual sexual copulation. This was a deficiency in the wording of canon 1082 and the debate that ensued relating to knowledge or lack thereof demonstrated this.

Remembering that marriage was viewed as a society and that two of the primary functions of a society were preservation and generation, then it stands to reason why so much discussion centered on the act of copulation and the procreation of children. In one sense, from a canonical perspective, marriage was seen merely as a means to an end: procreation. As one canonist observes:

> It is clear...that marriage was considered a contract whose goal was reproduction, and which centered the rights and obligations of the spouses around making the structural conditions of marriage suitable for achieving that goal. These included above all the stability of the family unit which was safeguarded through the prohibition of divorce (*indissolubilitatis*) and the duty to protect the partner from the temptation of adultery (*remedium concupiscentiæ*), as well as to provide him or her with mutual assistance (*mutuum adiutorium*).[330]

There was little if any discussion on the "mutual help" which was the secondary end of marriage (together with the allaying of concupiscence), since this was not even mentioned in the canon.[331] However, it was still an end. The knowledge that was presumed after puberty was knowledge about sex and procreation; nothing more and nothing less. This, too, was a deficiency in canon 1082. It seems almost ludicrous today to debate that a person has enough knowledge to influence the will for matrimonial consent when the person has no understanding, let alone knowledge, about the sexual act. Yet this was debated and, until rather recently in our history, was held by some to be sufficient for a valid marriage. With the coming of Vatican

[330]K. LÜDICKE, "Matrimonial Consent in Light of a Personalist Concept of Marriage: On the Council's New Way of Thinking about Marriage", in *Studia canonica*, 33 (1999), p. 476.

[331]These were to be found in canon 1013, §1: "Matrimonii finis primarius est procreatio atque educatio prolis; secundarius mutuum adiutorium et remedium concupiscentiæ."

II and the revision of the *Code of Canon Law*, a new age dawned for the richness of marriage. But, even then, did the newly revised canon 1096 go far enough? This shall be discussed in Chapter Three.

CHAPTER THREE

IGNORANCE ACCORDING TO CANON 1096 OF THE 1983 *CIC*

INTRODUCTION

On 25 January 1983, Pope John Paul II signed the Apostolic Constitution *Sacrae disciplinae leges*, officially promulgating the new *Code of Canon Law*, which put into law the reforms of the Second Vatican Council (1962-1965). On 3 February 1983, when the Holy Father officially presented the new Code to the Church, Archbishop Rosalio Castillo Lara, then Pro-President of the Council for the Revision of the Code, stated that the new Code would guarantee the correct and effective application of the reforms of Vatican II to the life of the whole Church following the two fundamental criteria which guided the reform: fidelity to the teachings of Vatican II and fidelity to the legislative-judicial tradition of the Church. This meant that in order to understand and interpret the 1983 *CIC* correctly, there was to be recourse both to Vatican II and to the Pio-Benedictine Code of 1917.[332]

In this chapter we shall begin with a study of the concept of marriage according to Vatican II, concentrating on the "Pastoral Constitution on the Church in the Modern World", *Gaudium et spes*; then, we shall proceed to discuss its implications as they pertain to ignorance. Once this groundwork has been laid, we shall concentrate on the development of canon 1096 through the revision process leading up to delineating the specific elements of the canon itself and those of its counterpart, canon 819 of the *Code of Canons of the Eastern Churches* (*CCEO*). A comparison between canon 1096 and canon 1082 of the 1917 *CIC* shall be made in order to try to understand better the specific reasons why changes were made. Finally, in conclusion, an attempt shall be made to point out for tribunals the ramifications of this canon as presently understood.

I. VATICAN II

It is from Vatican II, specifically the "Pastoral Constitution on the Church in the Modern World", *Gaudium et spes* (7 December 1965), that the fundamental doctrinal principles and the inspiration underlying the revision of matrimonial legislation are drawn.[333] However, we must not overlook the fact that the Council Fathers, in several other documents, established the foundation for these principles and addressed the subject of marriage.

---

[332]CASTILLO LARA, "Discourse of the Pro-President Archbishop", in PONTIFICIA COMMISSIO CODICI IURIS CANONICI RECOGNOSCENDO, *Promulgation and Official Presentation of the Code of Canon Law*, Vatican City, Vatican Polyglott Press, 1983, pp. 13, 19-20.

[333]A. MENDONÇA, "The Theological and Juridical Aspects of Marriage", in *Studia canonica*, 22 (1988), pp. 265-266. For other references pertaining to *Gaudium et spes* and its influence on marriage, see L. DE LUCA, "La Chiesa e la società coniugale", in *Atti del Congresso internazionale di diritto canonico: la Chiesa dopo il Concilio*, vol. 1, Roma, 14-19 gennaio 1970, Milano, A. Giuffrè Editore, 1972, pp. 473-495; E. GRAZIANI, "La Chiesa e il matrimonio", *ibid.*, pp. 455-471; O. FUMAGALLI CARULLI, *Il matrimonio canonico dopo il concilio: capacità e consenso*, Milano, A. Giuffrè Editore, 1978, pp. 3-95; B. HÄRING, "Fostering the Nobility of Marriage and the Family", in *Commentary on the Documents of Vatican II*, vol. 5, H. VORGRIMLER, gen. ed., Freiburg, Herder and Herder, 1969, pp. 225-245.

The importance of this particular document is clearly seen since it is listed in the *fontes* for canons 1055, §1; 1056; 1057, §1 and 1061, §1, of the 1983 *CIC*.

68

a. Council documents in general pertaining to marriage

In the Council's very first document, the "Constitution on the Sacred Liturgy", *Sacrosanctum concilium* (4 December 1963), number 77, the Fathers called for revising and enriching the Roman Ritual so that it would more clearly signify the grace of the sacrament of matrimony and emphasize the spouses' duties.[334]

The "Dogmatic Constitution on the Church", *Lumen gentium* (21 November 1964), number 2, proclaims that God chose to raise up humanity to share in his own divine life and that all the elect were predestined to become conformed to the image of Jesus Christ.[335] In number 5, the people of God are reminded that the Lord poured out his Spirit upon the entire Church, which is the seed and the beginning of the kingdom of God.[336] In number 10, all the baptized are called to holiness.[337] In number 11, matrimony and the call to holiness which is unique to this sacrament as well as the dignity of the family are addressed:

Finally, in virtue of the sacrament of Matrimony by which they signify and share (cf. Eph. 5:32) the mystery of the unity and faithful love between Christ and the Church, Christian married couples help one another to attain holiness in their married life and in the rearing of their children. Hence by reason of their state in life and of their position they have their own gifts in the People of God (cf. 1 Cor. 7:7). From the marriage of Christians there comes the family in which new citizens of human society are born and, by the grace of the Holy Spirit in Baptism, those are made children of God so that the People of God may be perpetuated throughout the centuries. In what may be regarded as the domestic Church, the parents, by word and example, are the first heralds of the faith with regard to their children. They must foster the vocation which is proper to each child, and this with special care if it be to religion.[338]

---

[334]"Ritus celebrandi Matrimonium, qui exstat in Rituali romano, recognoscatur et ditior fiat, quo clarius gratia Sacramenti significetur et munera coniugum inculcentur", in *AAS*, 56 (1964), p. 119.

[335]"Aeternus Pater, liberrimo et arcano sapientiae ac bonitatis suae consilio, mundum universum creavit, homines ad participandam vitam divinam elevare decrevit, eosque lapsus in Adamo non dereliquit, semper eis auxilia ad salutem praebens, intuitu Christi, Redemptoris, «qui est imago Dei invisibilis, primogenitus omnis creaturae» (Col. 1,15). Omnes autem electos Pater ante saecula «praescivit et praedestinavit conformes fieri imaginis Filii sui, ut sit Ipse primogenitus in multis fratribus»", in *AAS*, 57 (1965), pp. 5-6.

[336]"Dominus enim Iesus Ecclesiae suae initium fecit praedicando faustum nuntium, adventum scilicet Regni Dei a saeculis in Scripturis promissi: «Quoniam impletum est tempus, et appropinquavit Regnum Dei» (Marc. 1, 15; cfr. Matth., 4, 17)... Verbum nempe Domini comparatur semini, quod in agro seminatur (Marc. 4, 14): qui illud cum fide audiunt et Christi pusillo gregi (Luc. 12, 32) adnumerantur. Regnum ipsum susceperunt; propria dein virtute semen germinat et increscit usque ad tempus messis (cfr. Marc. 4, 26-29)", *ibid.*, p. 7.

[337]"Baptizati enim, per regenerationem et Spiritus Sancti unctionem consecrantur in domum spiritualem et sacerdotium sanctum, ut per omnia opera hominis christiani spirituales offerant hostias, et virtutes annuntient Eius qui de tenebris eos vocavit in admirabile lumen suum (cfr. 1 Petr. 2, 4-10)", *ibid.*, p. 14.

[338]"Tandem coniuges christiani, virtute matrimonii sacramenti, quo mysterium unitatis et fecundi amoris inter Christum et Ecclesiam significant atque participant (cfr. Eph. 5, 32), se invicem in vita coniugali necnon prolis susceptione et educatione ad sanctitatem adiuvant, adeoque in suo vitae statu et ordine proprium suum in Populo Dei donum habent (cfr. 1 Cor. 7, 7). Ex hoc enim connubio procedit familia, in qua nascuntur novi societatis humanae cives, qui per Spiritus Sancti gratiam, ad Populum Dei saeculorum decursu perpetuandum, baptismo in filios Dei constituuntur. In hac velut Ecclesia domestica parentes verbo et exemplo sint pro filiis suis primi fidei praecones, et vocationem unicuique propriam, sacram vero peculiari cura, foveant oportet".

Thus married couples have the same dignity as anyone else and they are called to the same degree of holiness of life.[339]

In number 11 of the "Decree on the Apostolate of Lay People", *Apostolicam actuositatem* (18 November 1965), the call to holiness and the dignity of the family are further reiterated. These are enhanced by challenging the couple, as well as all people of good will, to be socially involved, in line with the teachings of Popes Pius XI, Pius XII and John XXIII.[340]

In the "Decree on Ecumenism", *Unitatis redintegratio* (21 November 1964), the Council Fathers recognized the work of the Spirit in other ecclesial communities. It followed that the marriage of a Catholic to a Christian of another denomination need not be a source of "perversion" and could indeed be a marriage "in the Lord".[341]

In the "Declaration on Religious Liberty", *Dignitatis humanae* (7 December 1965), especially number 3,[342] the Council Fathers stressed the right of all people to follow their conscience. Örsy states that in light of this teaching the rules for the promises concerning the education of children born from a mixed marriage had to be revised.[343]

Another document which did not refer directly to marriage, but which is nonetheless important to our

---

ibid., pp. 15-16. English translation found in A. FLANNERY, gen. ed., *Vatican Council II; Volume 1: The Conciliar and Post Conciliar Documents* (= FLANNERY, *Vatican II*), rev. ed., Northport, New York, Costello Publishing Co., 1996, pp. 362-363. All English translations of Vatican II texts are from this source. It is to be noted that this passage is listed as one of the *fontes* for canon 1055, §1.

[339]L. ÖRSY, *Marriage in Canon Law*, Wilmington, Delaware, Michael Glazier, Inc., 1986, p. 36.

[340]"Coniugum semper officium fuit, hodie vero maxima apostolatus eorum pars est: indissolubilitatem et sanctitatem vinculi matrimonialis vita sua manifestare et probare; ius et officium prolem christiane educandi, genitoribus et tutoribus inditum, strenue affirmare; dignitatem et legitimam autonomiam familiae defendere. Cooperentur igitur ipsi ceterique christifideles, cum hominibus bonae voluntatis, ut in civili legislatione haec iura sarta serventur; in moderanda societate ratio habeatur necessitatum familiarum quod ad habitationem, educationem puerorum, condicionem laboris, securitatem socialem et tributa pertinet; in migrationibus ordinandis convictus domesticus omnino in tuto ponatur." ("To give clear proof in their own lives of the indissolubility and holiness of the marriage bond; to assert with vigor the right and duty of parents and guardians to give their children a Christian upbringing; to defend the dignity and legitimate autonomy of the family: this has always been the duty of married persons; today, however, it has become the most important aspect of their apostolate. They and all the faithful, therefore, should collaborate with men of good will in seeing that these rights are perfectly safeguarded in civil legislation; that in social administration consideration is given to the requirements of families in the matter of housing, education of children, working conditions, social security and taxes; and that in emigration regulations family life is perfectly safeguarded"), in *AAS*, 58 (1966), p. 848; FLANNERY, *Vatican II*, pp. 778-779. This is also listed as one of the *fontes* for canon 1055, §1.

[341]ÖRSY, *Marriage in Canon Law*, p. 36. Canon 1060 of the 1917 *CIC* most severely prohibited ("severissime prohibet") a Catholic from entering marriage with another baptized person who was a member of a heretical or schismatical sect for fear of the danger of perversion ("perversionis periculum"). Canon 1061, however, allowed for a dispensation from mixed religion if certain conditions were fulfilled.

[342]"Dictamina vero legis divinae homo percipit et agnoscit mediante conscientia sua; quam tenetur fideliter sequi in universa sua activitate, ut ad Deum, finem suum, perveniat. Non est ergo cogendus, ut contra suam conscientiam agat. Sed neque impediendus est, quominus iuxta suam conscientiam operetur, praesertim in re religiosa" ("It is through his conscience that man sees and recognizes the demands of the divine law. He is bound to follow this conscience faithfully in all his activity so that he may come to God, who is his last end. Therefore, he must not be forced to act contrary to his conscience. Nor must he be prevented from acting according to his conscience, especially in religious matters"), in *AAS*, 58 (1966), p. 932; FLANNERY, *Vatican II*, pp. 801-802.

[343]ÖRSY, *Marriage in Canon Law*, p. 36.

70

discussion, is the "Dogmatic Constitution on Divine Revelation", *Dei verbum* (18 November 1965). It is here that the Church affirmed and explained the historical nature of God's revelation to humanity. It followed that marriage, as a saving mystery, can be understood only as embedded in human history as a permanent gift from God which unfolds in our midst.[344]

b. *Gaudium et spes* in particular

It is in *Gaudium et spes*, however, that Vatican II gives its most significant pronouncement on the subject of marriage.[345] In its attempt to address some problems of more special urgency,[346] marriage and family (taken together as one interrelated topic) were viewed as a particular concern which the Council Fathers discussed in numbers 47-52. In number 47, after stating the importance of marriage and family and describing those forces which disrupt this sacred institution, it is pointed out that certain key points will be presented in order to guide and encourage people everywhere to foster the dignity and the supremely sacred value of marriage.[347] It is important to note that the Fathers did not intend to give an exhaustive treatment concerning marriage and family life and avoided using technical and juridical language.[348] However, the pastoral concern expressed and the depth and freshness of the doctrine on marriage presented, did emphasize the fact that the Fathers found the existing concepts and categories inadequate to communicate the richness and complexity of the reality of marriage.[349]

In number 48 of this document, they provide a clear description of Christian marriage when they write in part:

> The intimate partnership of life and the love which constitutes the married state has been established by the creator and endowed by him with its own proper laws: it is rooted in the contract of its partners, that is, in their irrevocable personal consent. It is an institution confirmed by divine law and receiving its stability, even in the eyes of society, from the human act by which the partners mutually surrender themselves to each other; for the good of the partners, of the children, and of society this sacred bond no longer depends on human decision alone.... By its very nature the institution of marriage and married love are ordered to the procreation and education of the offspring and it is in them that it finds its crowning glory. Thus the man and woman, who "are no longer two but one" (Mt. 19:6), help and serve each other by their marriage partnership; they become conscious of their unity and experience it more deeply from day to day. The intimate union of marriage, as a mutual giving of two

---

[344]*Ibid.*

[345] D.E. FELLHAUER, "The *consortium omnis vitae* as a Juridic Element of Marriage", in *Studia canonica*, 13 (1979), p. 108.

[346]"De quibusdam problematibus urgentioribus," in *AAS*, 58 (1966), p. 1066.

[347]"Quapropter Concilium, quaedam doctrinae Ecclesiae capita in clariorem lucem ponendo, christianos hominesque universos illuminare et confortare intendit, qui nativam status matrimonialis dignitatem eiusque eximium valorem sacrum tueri et promovere conantur", *ibid.*, p. 1067.

[348]W.M. ABBOTT, gen. ed., *The Documents of Vatican II*, New York, Guild Press, 1966, p. 250, footnote 153. See also FELLHAUER, "The *consortium omnis vitae* as a Juridic Element of Marriage", p. 108.

[349]A. MENDONÇA, "Antisocial Personality and Nullity of Marriage", in *Studia canonica*, 16 (1982), p. 78.

persons, and the good of the children demand total fidelity from the spouses and require an unbreakable unity between them.[350]

As Örsy points out, the Council recovered the biblical pattern of marriage: first there is the partnership, then the children. This brought to an end the classical presentation of the ends of marriage, for there was no mention of a hierarchy; rather, mutual love was mentioned first.[351] Furthermore, the use of the terms "primary" and "secondary" when referring to the ends of marriage has remained almost totally a thing of the past.[352]

---

[350]"Intima communitas vitae et amoris coniugalis, a Creatore condita suisque legibus instructa, foedere coniugii seu irrevocabili consensu personali instauratur. Ita actu humano, quo coniuges sese mutuo tradunt atque accipiunt, institutum ordinatione divina firmum oritur, etiam coram societate; hoc vinculum sacrum intuitu boni, tum coniugum et prolis tum societatis, non ex humano arbitrio pendet... Indole autem sua naturali, ipsum institutum matrimonii amorque coniugalis ad procreationem et educationem prolis ordinantur iisque veluti suo fastigio coronantur. Vir itaque et mulier, qui foedere coniugali «iam non sunt duo, sed una caro» (Mt. 19, 6), intima personarum atque operum coniunctione mutuum sibi adiutorium et servitium praestant, sensumque suae unitatis experiuntur et plenius in dies adipiscuntur. Quae intima unio, utpote mutua duarum personarum donatio, sicut et bonum liberorum, plenam coniugum fidem exigunt atque indissolubilem eorum unitatem urgent", in *AAS*, 58 (1966), pp. 1067-1068; FLANNERY, *Vatican II*, p. 950.

[351]ÖRSY, *Marriage in Canon Law*, p. 36. See also J.H. PROVOST, "Simulated Consent: A New Way of Looking at an Old Way of Thinking — Part I", in *The Jurist*, 55 (1995), p. 702; M.R. PRIEUR, "The Articulation of the Ends of Marriage in Roman Catholic Teaching: A Brief Commentary", in *Studia canonica*, 33 (1999), p. 530.

[352]PRIEUR, "The Articulation of the Ends of Marriage", p. 531. He writes that the hierarchy of ends "remains conspicuously absent" in various solemn teaching documents such as *Humanae vitae* (1968) and *Matrimonia mixta* (1970); the *Rite of Marriage* (both the 1969 and the 1990 revised editions); *Familiaris consortio* (1981); the *Code of Canon Law* (1983); and the *Catechism of the Catholic Church* (both the 1992 and the 1997 revised editions). He further notes that the only time the traditional ordering of the ends of marriage is referred to by Pope John Paul II is in a general audience on 10 October 1984, without actually mentioning the ends of marriage:
  "According to traditional language, love, as a higher power, coordinates the actions of the persons, the husband and the wife, *in the sphere of the purposes of marriage*. Although neither the conciliar constitution [*Gaudium et spes*] nor the encyclical [*Humanae vitae*], in dealing with the question, use the language at one time customary, they nonetheless deal with what the traditional expressions refer to.
  "Love, as a higher power that the man and woman receive from God along with the particular "consecration" of the Sacrament of Marriage, involves a correct *coordination* of the purposes, according to which — in the traditional teaching of the Church — *there is constituted the moral* (or rather "theological and moral") *order* of the life of the couple.
  "The doctrine of the Constitution *Gaudium et Spes*, as well as that of the Encyclical *Humanae Vitae*, clarifies the same moral order in reference to love, understood as a higher power that confers *adequate content and value* to conjugal acts *according to the truth* of the two meanings, the unitive and the procreative, with respect for their inseparability.
  "In this renewed formulation the traditional teaching on the purposes of marriage (and their hierarchy) is reaffirmed and at the same time deepened from the viewpoint of the interior life of the spouses, that is, of conjugal and family spirituality" (*L'Osservatore Romano*, weekly edition in English, 15 October 1984, p. 8).
  See also E. PFNAUSCH, "The Good of the Spouses in Rotal Jurisprudence: New Horizons", in *The Jurist*, 56 (1996), pp. 527-556; specifically p. 532, footnote 14, where he cites the Pontifical Commission for the Revision of the Code:
  "Following the Constitution (on the Church in the Modern World), the committee decided that this paragraph (i.e. 1917 code canon 1013, §1) the idea of the primary end, that is, the procreation and education of offspring, and the secondary end, namely mutual aid and the remedy of concupiscence, should no longer be employed." The original text reads: "Eandem constitutionem secutus, coetus in hac paragrapho notionem finis primarii, procreationis scilicet atque educationis prolis, et finis secondarii, nimirum mutui adiutorii et remedii concupiscentiae, iam adhibendam non esse censuit", in *Communicationes*, 3 (1971), p. 70.
  He further writes, in the same footnote, "A more forceful expression of that determination is found in response to the request in the final stages that a hierarchy of ends be included: 'The schema does not desire to establish a hierarchy of ends.'" The original text reads: "Schema nullam vult statuere hierarchiam finium", in *Communicationes*, 15 (1983), p. 221.
  There are authors, however, who see the procreative element as fundamental, thus keeping the notion of hierarchy of ends

This was not the first time that the Church focused on mutual cooperation between the spouses.[353] Vatican II was, however, the inspiration and impetus to rethink the juridical problems of marriage[354] as well as to bring into canonical language a more personalist understanding of marriage based on doctrine.[355] The Council gave conjugal love a sustained prominence unprecedented in official Church teachings. For example, in number 48, marriage is referred to in terms of an "intimate partnership of life and the love which constitutes the married state" (*intima communitas vitae et amoris coniugalis*), a "sacred bond" (*vinculum sacrum*), a "marriage partnership" (*coniunctione mutuum*), an "intimate union" (*intima unio*) as seen above.[356] Later, in number 50, it is described as "an indissoluble union between two persons" (*foederis inter personas indissolubilis*) and "a whole manner and community of life" (*totius vitae consuetudo et communio*).[357] The word "contract" is not used when describing marriage.[358] In fact, when speaking of marriage, *Gaudium et spes* consistently uses terminology which is closer to both Roman and medieval language and concepts than to the more juridical expressions characteristic of the period from the mid-nineteenth century until, and including, the 1917 *CIC* and the papacy of Pius XII.[359] Some elements which reflect this renewal of the doctrine of marriage are: the notion of a covenant replaces the contractual view of marriage; marriage is a sharing of the whole of life; it is ordained for the good of the spouses as well as for the procreation and education of

---

alive. For example, see C. BURKE, "Procreativity and the Conjugal Self-Gift", in *Studia canonica*, 24 (1990), pp. 43-49, specifically p. 45: "It is true that the *Code of Canon Law* does not indicate any hierarchy in the ends of marriage, as did the 1917 Code (c. 1013, §1). But the 1983 Code is substantially in the same line as the old in affirming that marriage is "of its very nature ordered to procreation (c. 1055).""

[353] See MENDONÇA, "The Theological and Juridical Aspects of Marriage", pp. 266-267, specifically footnote 3 on page 266.

[354] *Ibid.*, p. 267.

[355] See R.J. SANSON, "Jurisprudence for Marriage: Based on Doctrine", in *Studia canonica*, 10 (1976), pp. 5-36. On p. 5 Sanson writes that Vatican II, in *Gaudium et spes*, not only radically changed the direction of theology but also gave rise to new jurisprudence both in the Roman Rota and in local tribunals. See also J. BERNHARD, "From Life to Law: Matrimonial Law and Jurisprudence", in *Concilium*, 1996/5, pp. 101-102; C. BURKE, "Personalism and the Essential Obligations of Marriage", in *Angelicum*, 74 (1997), pp. 81-94; C. GALLAGHER, "Marriage and the Family in the New Code", in *Studia canonica*, 17 (1983), pp. 151-152; K. LÜDICKE, "Matrimonial Consent in Light of a Personalist Concept of Marriage: On the Council's New Way of Thinking about Marriage", in *Studia canonica*, 33 (1999), pp. 473-503.

[356] It is important to see the original Latin with the English translation in order to notice the different nuances (e.g., both *communitas* and *coniunctio* are interpreted as "partnership" while the term *consortium* which is more often rendered as "partnership" is not used). Be that as it may, the use of the terms illustrates the effort to highlight the personalist dimension of marriage. The translation of all these terms are from FLANNERY, *Vatican II*, p. 950.

[357] FELLHAUER, "The *consortium omnis vitae* as a Juridic Element of Marriage", p. 109.

[358] P.F. PALMER, "Christian Marriage: Contract or Covenant?", in *Theological Studies*, 33 (1972), pp. 617-618. The word under discussion is the Latin *contractus*. It is important to understand that in the original text of *Gaudium et spes*, this particular word is not used. Rather, the word *foedus*, meaning covenant, is used. See HÄRING, "Fostering the Nobility of Marriage and the Family", pp. 232-233. Here the author points out that this non-use of the word *contractus* was intentional. In fact, the word *contractus* was repeatedly requested in the drafting of *Gaudium et spes*, but the commission ultimately rejected it, focusing on the interpersonal dimension of marriage as well as attempting to refrain from the use of a more juridical term.

[359] FELLHAUER, "The *consortium omnis vitae* as a Juridic Element of Marriage", p. 113. For a more complete discussion of the history of the development of the wording in *Gaudium et spes*, concerning this text, see pp. 101-114; and HÄRING, "Fostering the Nobility of Marriage and the Family", pp. 225-245.

children. In short, according to Vatican II, marriage is an interpersonal relationship[360] which consists in the intimate community of life and conjugal love[361] established by the Creator (*GS*, 48); its purposes are the good of the spouses and the procreation and education of children (*GS*, 48, 49); its properties total fidelity and unbreakable unity between the spouses (*GS*, 48).[362]

Probably one of the most significant contributions of Vatican II to the understanding of marriage which led to the development of new thinking in matrimonial jurisprudence was this characterization of marriage from a personalist perspective[363] because it focused on the mutual good derived from the union, and the personal mutual perfection which can be achieved in marriage by husband and wife. The emphasis is on mutual self-giving, companionship in all aspects of life, sexual fulfillment and other goals.[364] Marriage is now to be viewed as an "intimate community of life and conjugal love" (*GS*, 48), referred to in the 1983 *CIC* as *foedus* (covenant) when speaking of *matrimonium in fieri* and as *consortium* (partnership) when speaking of *matrimonium in facto esse*, and not simply as a "contract"[365] as was stated in canon 1012, §1, of the 1917 *CIC*. This is not to say that the 1983 *CIC* rejects the term contract. Indeed, after describing marriage as *foedus* in canon 1055, §1, for example, the term *contractus* is used in the second paragraph.[366] It is also used in canon 1097, §2. Likewise, the verb *contrahere* (to contract), in various forms, appears to be the preferred verb by the redactors[367] when it pertains to entering marriage, as it is used at least 29 times in the canons *De Matrimonio* (canons 1055-1165). Furthermore, when referring to those about to enter marriage, the term preferred is *contrahentes* (contracting parties), which is used 11 times in this section.[368]

---

[360]BERNHARD, "From Life to Law", p. 101.

[361]Here we are literally translating the Latin text "intima communitas vitae et amoris coniugalis".

[362]J. HADLEY, "Note on the 'bonum coniugum'", in Canon Law Society of Great Britain and Ireland *Newsletter*, No. 110, June 1997, p. 77.

[363]T.P. DOYLE, "Marriage", in J.A. CORIDEN, T.J. GREEN, D.E. HEINTSCHEL, eds., *The Code of Canon Law: A Text and Commentary* (= *CLSA Commentary*), commissioned by the Canon Law Society of America, New York, Paulist Press, 1985, p. 738. FELLHAUER, "The *consortium omnis vitae* as a Juridic Element of Marriage", p. 116, comments that this is one of the two noteworthy aspects of the matrimonial teachings of *Gaudium et spes*. The other, he notes, is the silence on a hierarchy of the ends of marriage.

[364]V.J. POSPISHIL, *Eastern Catholic Church Law*, 2nd rev. ed., Staten Island, New York, St. Maron Publications, 1996, pp. 436-437.

[365]For a more in-depth presentation on this topic, see J.F. CASTAÑO, "Natura del 'foedus' matrimoniale alla luce dell'attuale legislazione", in *Questioni canoniche, miscellanea in onore del professore P. Esteban Gomez, o.p., a cura della Pontificia Università S. Tommaso d'Aquino, Roma*, Milano, 1984, Studia Universitatis S. Thomae in Urbe, 22, pp. 214-250, especially pp. 222-226, where he treats the inadequacies of the term *contractus*; G. LO CASTRO, "Il *foedus* matrimoniale come *consortium totius vitae*", in *Il matrimonio sacramento nell'ordinamento canonico vigente*, Studi Giuridici 31, Città del Vaticano, Libreria editrice Vaticana, 1993, pp. 69-90.

For the significance of the term *foedus* and its use, see G. CAPUTO, *Introduzione allo studio del diritto canonico moderno*, vol. 2, Padova, CEDAM, 1987, p. 249; J.J. O'ROURKE, "Thoughts on Marriage", in *Studia canonica*, 22 (1988), pp. 187-188.

[366]CAPUTO, *Introduzione allo studio del diritto canonico moderno*, p. 248.

[367]*Ibid.*, pp. 248-249.

[368]X. OCHOA, *Index verborum ac locutionum Codicis iuris canonici*, 2nd ed., Città del Vaticano, Libreria editrice Lateranese, 1984, p. 112.

While Vatican II offered a richer understanding of marriage, it is important to note that the Council also reiterated the traditional teachings of the Church that marriage is constituted by consent (*GS*, 48),[369] that the couple form an indissoluble bond between themselves (*GS*, 50; *AA*, 11), and that marriage by its nature is ordered to the procreation and education of children (*LG*, 11; *AA*, 11; *GS*, 48, 50, 51). Thus, the Council, while taking into consideration the vision of Church as depicted in *Lumen gentium*, 2, drawing new and old from the treasury of tradition, also followed the legislative tradition of the Church.[370]

At the beginning there was reluctance on the part of some church officials, however, to apply the teachings of Vatican II concerning marriage to the canon law on marriage.[371] For instance, in his decision of 30 November 1968, Fiore writes:

> Although today there are many who believe that in light of the Constitution *Gaudium et Spes* (n. 48) the "intima communitas vitæ et amoris coniugalis" is of the essence of the matrimonial contract, the Fathers [of the Rotal *turnus*] are of the opinion that this is to be completely denied; the reason is that the communion of habitation, bed, and table belongs to the essence and integrity of the *individua vita* rather as an effect of validly-given consent.[372]

This initial reluctance has now given way to the awareness of marriage as a *consortium totius vitae*, and more than merely a contract, as the basis for jurisprudence.[373] Furthermore, the *Coetus* responsible for drafting the new canons on marriage, having met since 1966, published its deliberations concerning two of Vatican II's teachings on marriage and how they were to be incorporated into the new Code:

> On the question of how the personal relationship of the spouses, together with the ordering of marriage and procreation, such as is described in the Pastoral Constitution of Vatican II on the Church in the Modern World, *Gaudium et Spes*, should be expressed in can. 1013 §1, the majority of the committee members finally agreed to affirm the nature of

---

[369]Pope Paul VI in his 9 February 1976 allocution to the Roman Rota. See *AAS*, 68 (1976), p. 206; English translation in W.H. WOESTMAN, ed., *Papal Allocutions to the Roman Rota 1939-1994*, (= WOESTMAN, *Papal Allocutions*), Ottawa, Saint Paul University, 1994, p. 135. See also R.A. KENYON, "The Nature and Nullity of Matrimonial Consent: Arguments Based upon Primary Sources", in *Studia canonica*, 14 (1980), pp. 107-108.

[370]See the Apostolic Constitution *Sacrae disciplinae leges* of 25 January 1983, in *AAS*, 75, part 2 (1983), p. xii; English translation in the *Code of Canon Law, Latin-English Edition*, New English translation, prepared under the auspices of the Canon Law Society of America, Washington, DC, Canon Law Society of America, 1999, p. xxx.

[371]L.G. WRENN, *The Invalid Marriage*, Canon Law Society of America, Washington, DC, 1998, p. 195.

[372]FELLHAUER, "The *Consortium omnis vitae* as a Juridic Element of Marriage", p. 126. The author incorrectly cites the reference for this passage as *RDC*, 19 (1969), pp. 198-199; it is found, however, in "Casalen. seu Taurinen., Nullit. matrim., 30 novembris 1968, *coram* E. Fiore", in *Ephemerides iuris canonici*, 26 (1970), p. 198:
"... quamvis hodie plures censeant, attenta Const. *Gaudium et spes* (n. 48), quod «intima communitas vitae et amoris coniugalis» sit de essentia matrimonialis contractus, hoc pernegandum esse Patres censuerunt, quia communio habitationis, thori et mensae ad essentiam et integritatem individuae vitae poitus pertinent ut effectus consensus vere praestiti."

[373]The earliest confirmation of this in Rotal jurisprudence is the oft-cited decision *coram* ANNÉ of 25 February 1969, in *SRR Dec*, 61 (1969), pp. 174-192, rendered less than a year after the above-cited *coram* FIORE. See also MENDONÇA, "The Theological and Juridical Aspects of Marriage", p. 275; D.E. FELLHAUER, "Psychological Incapacity for Marriage", in *Proceedings of the 5th International Congress of Canon Law*, vol. 2, M. THÉRIAULT and J. THORN, eds., Ottawa, Faculty of Canon Law, Saint Paul University, 1986, p. 1023; WRENN, *The Invalid Marriage*, p. 196.

marriage as an *intima totius vitae coniunctio* between man and woman which, of its very nature, is ordered to the procreation and education of children. Following the Constitution, the committee decided that in this paragraph [i.e., paragraph one of canon 1013] the idea of the primary end, that is, the procreation and education of offspring, and the secondary end, namely mutual aid and the remedy for concupiscence; should no longer be employed. The second paragraph of the canon which deals with the essential properties of marriage, should, it seemed, remain unchanged.[374]

The fact that the teachings of *Gaudium et spes*, although pastoral in nature, were to have juridic relevance was clarified by Pope Paul VI in his allocution to the Roman Rota on 9 February 1976. He effectively put an end to the controversy on the juridic value of conjugal love when he stated, in part:

> We are glad, of course, that the concern of the Second Vatican Council to foster the spiritual side of marriage and to open new doors for the pastoral action of the Church has been echoed by this tribunal. The tribunal has become more aware of its serious obligations and has come to understand the full importance of the personalist approach which the Council emphasizes in its teaching and which consists in rightly esteeming conjugal love and the mutual perfection of the spouses. But this emphasis cannot be allowed to lessen the dignity and stability of the family or to detract from the excellence of the conjugal duty of procreation arising from it (see *GS*, nos. 47-48). The extensive and varied experience of your tribunal enables you, today as in the past, to provide very useful and, indeed, unparalleled material for the new canonical legislation now being drawn up.... Despite its pastoral character, the constitution *Gaudium et spes* clearly teaches the doctrine We have just summarized.[375]

The theology and teachings of Vatican II would, therefore, have a profound impact, not only on the canons that were almost completely reworked from the 1917 *CIC*, e.g., canon 1055,[376] but also, and just as

---

[374]"De quaestione, qua ratione relatio personalis coniugum, simul cum ordinatione matrimonii ad procreationem, prout in constitutione pastorali Concilii Vaticani II De Ecclesia in mundo huius temporis «Gaudium et spes» describitur, in can. 1013 § 1 exprimenda sit, maior pars coetus tandem convenit in affirmanda naturam matrimonii ut intimam totius vitae coniunctionem inter virum et mulierem, quae, indole sua naturali, ad prolis procreationem et educationem ordinatur. Eandem constitutionem secutus, coetus in hac paragrapho notionem finis primarii, procreationis scilicet atque educationis prolis, et finis secundarii, nimirum mutui adiutorii et remedii concupiscentiae, iam adhibendam non esse censuit. Paragraphus autem altera eiusdem canonis, quae agit de proprietatibus essentialibus matrimonii, immutata remanere debere videbatur", in *Communicationes* 3, (1971), p. 70; English translation based on FELLHAUER, "The *Consortium omnis vitae* as a Juridic Element of Marriage", p. 117. It is to be noted that this was a majority, not a unanimous, opinion; the debate continued.

[375]"Gaudemus profecto quod sollicitudo Concilii Vaticani secundi de promovenda indole spirituali matrimonii et de novis aperiendis viis, quas actio pastoralis Ecclesiae percurrat, serium officium istius Tribunalis excitavit idque induxit, ut plenam perciperet significationem rationis magis personalis, quam magisterium Concilii proposuit quaequae in aequa aestimatione amoris coniugalis et in mutua perfectione coniugum nititur. Quibus tamen rebus nihil prorsus detrahi licet de dignitate ac stabilitate instituti familiaris, neque imminui excellentiam et munus coniugale procreationis, inde exorientia. Itaque multiplex experientia, quam Tribunal vestrum hausit, facultatem vobis praebet, nunc — ut ante actis temporibus — materiam perutilem et praestantissimam afferendi novae legislationi canonicae, quae in praesenti apparatur.... Hanc doctrinam Constitutio «Gaudium et spes», licet sit pastoralis indolis, aperte docuit...", in *AAS*, 68 (1976), pp. 205-206; English translation in WOESTMAN, *Papal Allocutions*, p. 134. See also M. THOMAS, "The Consortium Vitae Coniugalis", in *The Jurist*, 38 (1978), pp. 171-172.

[376]Among the *fontes* for canon 1055 are canons 1012, §1, and canon 1013, §1, of the 1917 *CIC*. However, it is evident that the theology of this canon arises from Vatican II, found specifically in *Gaudium et spes*.

76

importantly, for the interpretation of those canons which were almost identical in wording, e.g., canon 1096.[377]

c. Vatican II and Rotal jurisprudence on ignorance

Since the promulgation of *Gaudium et spes* on 7 December 1965, there have been twenty-two referenced Rotal sentences pertaining to ignorance[378] (some listed other grounds as well), seven of which are unpublished.[379] However, it is interesting to note that at the time of this writing there does not seem to be any published cases adjudicated by the Roman Rota on ignorance since the promulgation of the 1983 *CIC*. Of these earlier sentences, eleven were *pro nullitate* and seven *pro vinculo* on the ground of ignorance.[380] To analyze each of them is beyond the scope of this study.[381] For our purposes, however, a brief description of the published cases is in order:

— Canals (15 March 1967): a woman who was molested as a girl and had an aversion to men.[382]

---

[377]The sole *fons* listed for canon 1096 is canon 1082 of the 1917 *CIC*.

[378]R. ZERA, *De ignorantia in re matrimoniali; eius natura iuridica et ambitus quoad consensus validitatem deque eiusdem probatione in iudicio*, Romae, Ancora, 1978, p. 11 lists *coram* LEFEBVRE, 7 December 1968, in *SRR Dec*, 60 (1968), pp. 823-830, as one such sentence. However, it does not concern ignorance, but rather the grounds of defect of discretion of judgment and condition. Pertaining to discretion of judgment, the sentence states that the contractants are to know about the nature of marriage as noted in canon 1082, but it is not required that they use perfect soundness of body or perfect mental discretion when doing so ("Ut autem recte apprehendantur ea quae nupturiens cognoscere debet de natura matrimonii ad mentem can. 1082, non requiritur ut aliquis utatur perfecta corporis valetudine perfectaque mentis discretione"), in *SRR Dec*, 60 (1968), p. 827. Concerning the ground of condition, the sentence states that the petitioner was unable to place any conditions because he was ignorant of their existence ("Patet exinde illum omnino nequivisse apponere conditionem propter motiva quorum exsistentiam ipse ignorabat"), *ibid.*, p. 830.

[379]These are: *coram* CANALS, 15 March 1967, in *SRR Dec* , 59 (1967), pp. 149-153; *coram* LEFEBVRE, 6 July 1967, *ibid.*, pp. 553-561; *coram* ANNÉ, 25 February 1969 (unpublished); *coram* PALAZZINI, 4 February 1970, in *SRR Dec*, 62 (1970), pp. 118-126; *coram* FAGIOLO, 28 May 1971, in *SRR Dec*, 63 (1971), pp. 460-466; *coram* FIORE, 21 March 1972 (unpublished); *coram* LEFEBVRE, 8 July 1972, in *SRR Dec*, 64 (1972), pp. 422-428; *coram* CANALS, 25 October 1972, *ibid.*, pp. 620-627; *coram* DAVINO, 27 October 1972, *ibid.*, pp. 649-655; *coram* Di FELICE, 25 July 1973, in *SRR Dec*, 65 (1973), pp. 619-625; *coram* ANNÉ, 23 October 1973 (unpublished); *coram* ANNÉ, 14 November 1973, *SRR Dec*, 65 (1973), pp. 756-762; *coram* De JORIO, 8 January 1975 (unpublished); *coram* PINTO, 13 January 1975 (unpublished); *coram* EWERS, 1 February 1975, in *SRR Dec*, 67 (1975), pp. 27-33; *coram* SERRANO, 25 April 1975, *ibid.*, pp. 368-375; *coram* EWERS, 13 December 1975, *ibid.*, pp. 724-730; *coram* MASALA, 30 March 1977, in *SRR Dec*, 69 (1977), pp. 157-171; *coram* De JORIO, 6 July 1977 (unpublished); *coram* Di FELICE, 14 December 1977, *ibid.*, pp. 505-508; *coram* POMPEDDA, 29 October 1979, in *SRR Dec*, 71 (1979). pp. 460-467; and *coram* HUOT, 26 February 1981 (unpublished).

[380]Two decisions, *coram* FIORE, 21 March 1972, and *coram* POMPEDDA, 29 October 1979, were declared *pro vinculo* on ignorance but, in both cases, affirmative in forwarding the marriages to the Holy Father as *ratum et non-consummatum* cases.

[381]For more information about these cases, see A. MENDONÇA, comp., *Rotal Anthology: An Annotated Index of Rotal Decisions from 1971 to 1988*, Washington, DC, Canon Law Society of America, 1992, pp. 111-113. This source was used for this section.
See also F. GONZÁLEZ Y GONZÁLEZ, *Ignorancia y consentimiento matrimonial*, León, Colegio Universitario de León, Unidad de Investigación, 24, 1982, pp. 136-142

[382]"«Non mi piaceva stare con Juan perché era un uomo; sarei stata male vicino a qualsiasi altro uomo»", *SRR Dec*, 59 (1967), p. 150.

However, there was no evidence that she was ignorant of the nature of marriage;[383]
— Lefebvre (6 July 1967): if a person thinks that marriage is simply a natural union and considers the marital act horrifying and cannot become accustomed to it, this cannot be explained except by ignorance;[384]
— Palazzini (4 February 1970): a person invalidly contracts marriage if he or she believes it is merely a friendly, economic alliance or a sharing of property. However, it is sufficient to know that marriage is a stable state between a man and a woman for the procreation of children with the necessary, appropriate joining together of bodies; on that account it entails, within the marital union, handing over the right of the body for procreation, but the parties need not know the mode and proper form;[385]
— Fagiolo (28 May 1971): proofs needed in verifying ignorance concerning physical joining, fertility and procreation[386] since ignorance is not presumed after puberty;
— Lefebvre (8 July 1972): the amount of knowledge needed about the mode of procreation;
— Canals (25 October 1972): ignorance of the nature of marriage and its rights and obligations, especially pertaining to the procreation of children. In this case, ignorance is linked with lack of discretion;
— Davino (27 October 1972): ignorance of intercourse and the amount of knowledge needed for valid consent (which may even be confused[387]) of the physical cooperation between a man and a woman;
— Di Felice (25 July 1973): the parties need not know all the rights and obligations of marriage; however, they are essentially to know the object and nature of the martial contract, i.e., the handing over of the body for acts proper for the procreation of offspring;[388]
— Anné (14 November 1973): for valid matrimonial consent, there is to be knowledge of the formal object of the contract, i.e., "a permanent society between a man and a woman for the procreation of children"

[383]"Improbandus utique absonus agendi modus talis patris, lugenda quoque sors infelicis puellae, sed ex allatis factis nullo modo argui potest puellam ignorasse matrimonii naturam...", ibid.

[384]"Ad istam probationem magni momenti est conditio assertae ignorantis tum tempore consummationis matrimonii, tum postea: ita enim ostenditur quasi inaequivocabiliter contrahentem revera penitus ignorare praefatum commercium functionale, ideoque naturam coniugii, si manifestet horrorem actus, nec ipsa possit illum consuetum habere: quae explicari nequeunt nisi ignorantia", ibid., p. 558.

[385]"Quapropter invalide quis contraheret, si putaret matrimonium esse societatem mere amicalem, oeconomicam aut operae locationem in rem familiarem; sed sufficit ut sciat matrimonium esse societatem stabilem inter virum et mulierem ad filios procreandos cum necessario concursu proprii corporis, et idcirco, se in sociando coniugio, tradere alteri parti ius in corpus in ordine ad generationem, licet ea quae ad generationis modum et formam propriam spectant ignoret", SRR Dec, 62 (1970), p. 120.

[386]"...circa agglutinationis, foecundationis et generationis...", SRR Dec, 63 (1971), p. 461.

[387]"...confusa quidem...", SRR Dec, 64 (1972), p. 652.

[388]"Etsi ad validitatem contractus necessarium non est contrahentes consectaria omnia iurium et obligationum eiusdem contractus cognoscere debere, essentialia tamen de obiecto et causa negotii ignorare ipsi non possunt. Legislator ergo in can. 1082 minimam scientiam necessariam pro matrimonio contrahendo determinat ideoque non requirit scientificam notionem a can. 1081, §2. traditam, sed exigit essentialem saltem cognitionem iuris, quod contrahens tradere alteri debet parti. Ignorantia iuris tradendi cum relativa obligatione utendi corpore alterius in ordine ad actus per se aptos ad prolis generationem prohibet scientiam de essentia matrimonii, ideoque impedit consensum matrimonialem, necessarium ad contractum perficiendum", SRR Dec, 65 (1973), p. 621.

78

(can. 1082, §1),[389] but it is sufficient that this knowledge be generic or somewhat confused;[390]

— Ewers (1 February 1975): the parties must be fully ignorant of the object of marriage for it to be invalid.[391] The parties must have knowledge of the diversity of the sexes or are able to designate the difference in the sexual organs, but they need not have distinct or precise acquaintance of their function;[392]

— Serrano (25 April 1975): the *in iure* section concerns the relationship between canons 1081 and 1082, the will and the intellect, citing *Gaudium et spes* and its presentation of marriage as being established by the Creator; as well, it is an intimate union which is constituted by the mutual giving of two people.[393] The understanding of marriage is broader than the knowledge of the *copula*; there is now an interpersonal bond.[394] He is the first Rotal auditor of those published to cite *Gaudium et spes*;

— Ewers (13 December 1975): the grounds of ignorance and the incapacity to assume the essential obligations of marriage. He states that simply any type of knowledge is not sufficient for valid matrimonial consent; rather, there is to be proportionate mental discretion or more mature judgment or critical ability, which is more serious than the ability to know.[395] It is through this critical faculty that the parties are able to undertake the grave obligations of marriage by considering the total way of life and the perpetual community of marriage.[396] Therefore, it sometimes happens that the parties appear to have knowledge of the object of marriage, yet have not acquired the sufficient discretion on the part of the will to make what is called a truly human act;[397]

---

[389]"Validus itaque consensus matrimonialis requirit cognitionem contractus matrimonialis obiecti formalis, quod est, uti refert can. 1082, §1: «societas permanens inter virum et mulierem ad filios procreandos»", *ibid.*, p. 757.

[390]"Sufficit autem huiusmodi cognitio «generica seu in confuso», ut obiectum specificum consensus matrimonialis percipiatur", *ibid.*, p. 758.

[391]"Consensus validus ad negotium iuridicum perficiendum non exstat, si ex parte subiecti adest plena ignorantia circa obiectum ipsius negotii", *SRR Dec*, 67 (1975), p. 28.

[392]"Re quidem vera, in nupturientibus requiritur cognitio diversitatis sexuum seu differentiae organorum quae sexualia dicuntur, at non distincta seu praecisa notitia functionis uniuscuiusque organi", *ibid.*

[393]"...matrimonium sit societas naturalis ab Ipsomet naturae Auctore suis legibus praedita (cfr. Conc. Vat. II, Const. Past. *Gaudium et spes*, n. 48),... in matrimonio, sive ex eiusdem obligationis sensu, sive etiam ex amore et mutua fiducia quibus ordinarie appetitur, prasens sit vel intendatur illa intima unio, quae duarum personarum donationem constituit (cfr. Conc. Vat. II, *ibidem*),..." *ibid.*, p. 371.

[394]"...obligatus ex interpersonali vinculo demonstraretur...", *ibid.*, p. 372.

[395]Ewers makes the distinction between the definition of ignorance as found in a dictionary, i.e., lack of knowledge, and the definition given by Thomas Aquinas, i.e., lack of due knowledge.

[396]"Non quaelibet cognitio sufficit ad validum matrimonialem consensum praestandum, sed postulatur proportionata mentis discretio et maturius iudicium seu critica facultas, quae serius apparet quam facultas cognoscitiva.... Eiusmodi facultas critica, ut iudicium validum de gravi obligatione suscipienda sibimet efformare possit, requirit tantam cognitionem aestimativam ut nubens scientiam theoreticam sibi aptare aliquomodo valeat. Utcumque iudicii maturitas seu discretio ad nuptias valide ineundas debet esse proportionata negotio tam gravi quod ad totius vitae consuetudinem et communionem nubentium perpetuam spectat", *ibid.*, p. 725.

[397]"Pariter nonnumque accidere potest in nupturientibus quod, etiamsi sufficiens adsit cognitio actus qui peragitur ideoque consensus obiecti, tamen ipsi non potiuntur sufficienti animi discretione ex parte voluntatis, ut actus vere humanus dici queat in specie", *ibid.*, p. 726.

It is to be noted that canon 1082 of the 1917 *CIC* did not did not give any indication as to the cause of this lack of

— Masala (30 March 1977): radical ignorance, i.e., having no knowledge of the physical cooperation needed for the procreational aspect of marriage, invalidates;[398]
— Di Felice (14 December 1977): ignorance of the object of marriage not only as a biological union, but also as a psychological and spiritual union which is also perpetual;[399]
— Pompedda (29 October 1979): the necessity of juridical proof of ignorance of marriage, since the norm of paragraph 2 of canon 1082 is not sufficient to resolve the issue.[400] Pompedda refers to the permanent society of marriage as a perpetual communion of life with an obvious, but unstated, reference to *Gaudium et spes*.

As can be seen from the précis of the above cases, until Serrano's sentence in 1975, the basic focus of the decisions was the evaluation of the knowledge of the person(s) pertaining to the procreation of children — whether he or she knew that procreation was part of the nature of marriage or, more often, how much knowledge of the physical *copula* was necessary, taking into consideration the presumption in paragraph two that the person is presumed to have such knowledge after having reached puberty. All of the Rotal auditors, with the exception of Masala (30 March 1977), demonstrate that there is more to the knowledge of marriage than the physical joining of bodies.

While many of these decisions cited Thomas Aquinas, Sanchez, Gasparri, other canonists or a combination thereof, it is worth noting that three previous Rotal decisions were often either quoted or referenced, even in those cases adjudicated after Vatican II. These three decisions are representative of the tendency to concentrate on the procreational aspect of marriage as the primary indication of whether a person was ignorant or not. The first is *coram* CANESTRI, 16 July 1943[401] which states, in part:

It is clear that in any contract the consent must be directed towards its object; therefore, in marriage those who contract ought to be aware of the conjugal rights and duties. But to what degree? It is certain that a spouse who thinks that marriage is merely a friendly association, consents invalidly. Similarly, one who thinks that some unsuitable union of bodies, for example, through kisses, is necessary for the generation of offspring, and consents exclusively to this union, certainly contracts invalidly. On this matter, there are many, who both in jurisprudence and among the doctors, absolutely contend that in the intention of obliging oneself to an association for the purpose of procreating offspring, is implicitly contained also the consent to the means which consists in intercourse. But the concepts still remain undefined. For, the right to the body, which constitutes the object of the matrimonial contract, is specifically directed to the sexes which are the organs of generation, and certainly not to other members which could also be conducive to fostering concupiscence, through embraces, kisses, etc. Hence, as has been said, if a woman is so naive as to think that she can

---

knowledge, this defect of cognition. Thus, the lack of due knowledge was understood to be equivalent to the lack of due discretion.

[398]...ob radicatam ignorantiam neque confuso modo cogitavisse de cooperatione physica corporis viri et muleris, per organa specifica soboli gignendae necessaria...", *SRR Dec.* 69 (1977), p. 171.

[399]...quod obiectum secumfert, praeter unionem biologicam etiam unionem psychicam et spiritualem, eamque perpetuam...", *ibid.*, p. 508.

[400]"Denique tandem superest gravior quaestio de probatione iudiciali eiusmodi ignorantiae naturae matrimonii, neque tamen sufficit §2 citati canonis ad rem satis dirimendam", *SRR Dec.* 71 (1979), p. 462.

[401]*SRR Dec.* 35 (1943), pp. 594-612.

consent to an association for procreating children solely through embraces or kisses, positively excluding whatever she vaguely thinks to be possibly impure, in the sexual arousal, contracts invalidly. It is said: '*positively excluding*', for through an interpretative intention, namely - had I known the necessity of intercourse, I would not have consented - , which does not exist, nothing happens; and then the will, which the contractant had of consenting to marriage just like others do and as it has been established by divine Providence, prevails; once the end is intended, so also are the means. Therefore, it is possible for a person to intend not only an association understood as different from a domestic one, but also some unsuitable giving of bodies which does not establish the matrimonial covenant.[402]

As can be seen in this passage, there must be some knowledge of the *copula* in order for the marriage to be valid, since marriage is a union of two distinct sexual persons.

The second reference is to the often quoted decision *coram* SABATTANI, 22 March 1963,[403] which states, in part, that the difference in opinions of various canonists arises

> from an incorrect understanding of the nature of the defect, which derives more from error than from ignorance...; consequently, in correctly judging cases of this kind, one must proceed only by way of the doctrine on error...; because "the investigation about error is easier and more objective than about ignorance, especially if one attempts to inquire into that which a person might have known from knowledge which is 'vague and confused', and also because ignorance operates only through error concerning the acts to be placed ... Therefore, those persons contract invalidly who consider the society of marriage merely as a friendly one, or a place of service for property or for carrying out business, or as a commercial association, or as a union for maintaining merely platonic love (as it is called) or for offering only mutual assistance, or any other type of association, in which this most special right to the body is given over ... Similarly marriage is null when a contractant thinks that children are given solely 'through heavenly grace', or through the nuptial blessing, or are dropped by God directly into his wife's lap, or generated from the warmth of the marriage-bed in which the spouses sleep.

---

[402]*Ibid.*, pp. 607-608: "Patet in quolibet contractu, consensum in ipsius obiectum esse dirigendum; ideoque, in matrimonio, contrahentes nosse debere iura et officia coniugalia. Sed usque ad quem gradum? Certum est sponsum, qui arbitratur matrimonium esse meram societatem amicalem, invalide consentire. Pariter qui putaret ad generationem prolis aliquam ineptam corporum coniunctionem requiri, v.g. per oscula, *in eaque exclusive consentiret*, certe invalide contraheret. Non desunt hac de re, tum in iurisprudentia, tum inter doctores, qui absolute contendunt in intentione sese obligandi in societatem cum fine procreandi prolem, implicite contineri consensum in medium quod consistit in coitu. Sed conceptus adhuc indeterminati manent. Nam ius in corpus, quod constituit obiectum contractus matrimonialis, specifice dirigitur in sexus, qui sunt organa generationis, minime vero in alia membra quae etiam ad fovendam ordinatam concupiscentiam convenire possunt, per amplexus, oscula etc. Unde, ut dictum est, si qua mulier tam ingenua esset, ut putaret se consentire posse in societatem ad procreandam prolem per solos amplexus vel oscula, *excludens positive*, quidquid ipsa confuse forsan impurum aestimavit in sexuali commotione, invalide contrahit. *«positive excludens»*, nam per intentionem interpretativam, scilicet: «si novissem coitus necessitatem, non consensissem», quae non exsistit, nihil efficitur; et tunc praevalet voluntas quam contrahens habuit *consentiendi in matrimonium sicut et ceteri ac sicut a divina Providentia constitutum est*; atque intento fine, intendendi etiam media. Potest itaque haberi in voluntate contrahendi non solum conceptus societatis diversae a domestica, sed et quaedam inepta traditio corporum qua foedus matrimoniale non constituitur." English translation based on A. MENDONÇA, *Marriage Consent - III (cc. 1096-1107)*, (pro manuscripto). Ottawa, Faculty of Canon Law, Saint Paul University, 1998-1999, p. 15.
This decision was cited in five cases: *coram* LEFEBVRE (8 July 1972), *coram* DAVINO (27 October 1972), *coram* Di FELICE (25 July 1973), *coram* ANNÉ (14 November 1973) and *coram* MASALA (30 March 1977).

[403]*SRR Dec*, 55 (1963), pp. 196-221.

All these erroneous ideas, insofar as they do not take into consideration the right to the body and do not foresee any bodily cooperation on the part of the spouses for procreating children, are contrary to the substance of the cause of marriage. A correct judgment about the diversity of sexes is not sufficient, when the thinking is that there is no functional relationship between that diversity and the ordering of the conjugal association towards the procreation of offspring.[404]

According to this often cited decision, the contracting parties must know that marriage is ordered for the procreation of children and that sexual cooperation is specifically involved.

The third decision is *coram* MATTIOLI, 25 November 1964,[405] which states, in part:

> Now to the matter at hand: in regard to marrying, there are a man and a woman, that is, male and female, who must constitute this special society. Each one must know from these that there is a difference in the nature of the sexes, which however is not based on those which externally appear.... but properly in the difference of the organs...because they constitute and determine the sex. Once this knowledge is acquired, which — we wish to emphasize — does not necessarily imply a precise knowledge of the form and function of each organ, in view of the text of c. 1082, it is furthermore necessary that each contractant know that what one gives of him/herself, in constituting this conjugal society, consists in the cooperation of his/her body with the body of the partner. However, it does not consist in effecting a cooperation of any respective organs of the body, but specifically through those which constitute the sex, whose difference in the male and female is ordered precisely toward intercourse, that is, toward harmonious mutual cooperation in generating children.[406]

---

[404]*Ibid.*, 199-206: "*Varietas et discrepantia opinionum et decisionum provenit ex non plene perspecta natura defectus, qui potius ex errore quam ex ignorantia corrivari debet.... Per unicam viam doctrinae de errore est incedendum in huiusmodi casibus rite diiudicandis....* Facilior dein et magis obiectiva est indagatio de errore, quam de ignorantia, praesertim si quis inquirere satagit de eo quod quis sciverit ex scientia quam dicunt «vagam et confusam».... *Ignorantia non operatur nisi per errorem, relate ad actus ponendos....* Igitur nupturiens, qui iudicet matrimonium societatem mere amicalem, vel operae locationem in rem familiarem aut ad alia negotia gerenda, vel societatem commercialem, vel unionem ad fovendum amorem mere platonicum (quem dicunt) aut ad praestandum tantummodo mutuum adiutorium, vel quamcumque aliam associationem, in qua non tradatur huiusmodi specialissimum ius in corpus, invalide contrahit.... Similiter nullum est matrimonium, quando contrahens opinatur filios dilargiri «*ex gratia coelesti*» tantummodo, vel ex benedictione nuptiali, aut *a Deo directe immitti in sinum uxoris,* aut *progigni ex calore genialis lecti,* in quo coniuges simul cubantur. Haec omnia erronea iudicia, eo quod haud considerent ius in corpus et nullam praevideant cooperationem corporalem coniugum ad filios procreandos, non servant substantiam causae matrimonii. *Non sufficit rectum indicium de diversitate sexuum,* quando aestimatur *nullum adesse nexum functionale* inter illam diversitatem et ordinationem societatis coniugalis ad procreationem prolis.*" English translation based on MENDONÇA, *Marriage Consent - III,* pp. 16, 18.
This was cited in nine Rotal decisions: all of the cases which referenced the Canestri decision, plus *coram* CANALS (15 March 1967), *coram* LEFEBVRE (6 July 1967), *coram* PALAZZINI (4 February 1970) and *coram* SERRANO (25 April 1975).

[405]*SRR Dec.* 56 (1964), pp. 867-883.

[406]*Ibid.*, p. 869: "Age nunc: in connubio sunt vir et mulier, idest mas ac foemina, qui hanc peculiarem societatem constituere debent. Igitur, debet unusquisque ex ipsis cognoscere quod datur in natura sexuum diversitas, non quidem fundata in iis quae externe apparent... sed proprie in differentia organorum, quae ideo sexualia dicuntur, quia sexum constituunt ac determinant. Posita hac cognitione, quae — velimus ne excidat — necessario non implicat praecisam uniuscuiusque organi formae ac functionis notitiam, ulterius, vi verborum can. 1082, necessarium est quod contrahens sciat illud, *quod de suo dat,* in hac constituenda coniugali societate, consistere in cooperatione sui corporis cum corpore consortis: non, autem, in cooperatione efficienda per quaecumque respectivi corporis membra, sed per ea quae sexum constituunt, quorum profecto diversitas, in mare

82

With reference to this decision, those contracting marriage are to know that marriage is a conjugal union, specifically with regard to the respective sex organs of the male and female, which is ordered toward procreation through the use of these organs.

As Rotal decisions were beginning to incorporate the teachings of *Gaudium et spes*, the process of revision was being initiated. We now focus our attention on the deliberations of the process and its impact on Rotal jurisprudence.

II. THE REVISION PROCESS

In 1975, the schema on the sacraments was published[407] which was then sent to the Roman Curia, conferences of bishops and other interested bodies and persons in March 1975. The purpose of the process was to allow for study, critique and suggestions concerning the proposed revision.[408]

a. 1975 *Schema*

In this schema, canon 1082 of the 1917 *CIC* appeared as canon 298:[409]

canon 1082	canon 298
§1. Ut matrimonialis consensus haberi possit, necesse est ut contrahentes saltem non ignorent matrimonium esse societatem permanentem inter virum et mulierem ad filios procreandos	Ut consensus matrimonialis haberi possit, necesse est ut contrahentes saltem non ignorent matrimonium esse consortium permanens inter virum et mulierem ordinatum ad prolem, cooperatione aliqua corporali procreandam.
§2. Haec ignorantia post pubertatem non praesumitur.[410]	Haec ignorantia post pubertatem non praesumitur.

---

et in foemina, praecise ordinatur ad concursum, seu ad concordem mutuam operam dandam pro filiorum procreatione." English translation based on MENDONÇA, *Marriage Consent - III*, p. 34.
    This was cited in six Rotal cases: the five decisions which referenced Canestri plus *coram* FAGIOLO (28 May 1971).

[407]PONTIFICIA COMMISIO CODICI IURIS CANONICI RECOGNOSCENDO, *Schema documenti pontificii quo disciplina canonica de sacramentis recognoscitur* (= 1975 *Schema*), Romae, Typis polyglottis Vaticanis, 1975.

[408]DOYLE, "Marriage" p. 738. See also "Preface to the Latin Edition", in *Code of Canon Law, Latin-English Edition*, New English translation, pp. xl-xli.

[409] 1975 *Schema*, p. 82.

[410]§1: "In order that matrimonial consent may be possible it is necessary that the contracting parties be at least not ignorant that marriage is a permanent society between a man and a woman for the procreation of children.
    §2: "This ignorance is not presumed after puberty", translation found in T.L. BOUSCAREN, A.C. ELLIS, F.N. KORTH, eds., *Canon Law: A Text and Commentary*, 4th revised ed., Milwaukee, Bruce Publishing Company, 1966, pp. 566-567.

Noteworthy are the changes in paragraph one from *societas* to *consortium* and the adaptation of the 1917 phrase *ad filios procreandos* to have it read *ordinatum ad prolem. cooperatione aliqua corporali.* *procreandum.*

As can be seen, no changes were proposed for paragraph two. While this paragraph was not debated nor the wording changed in any way, its importance as a presumption of law was demonstrated in the debates concerning the drafting of what was to become canon 1095 of the 1983 *CIC*, distinguishing *defectu discretionis iudicii* ("lack of discretion of judgment") from ignorance as ordinarily understood to be present in those who had not yet reached puberty;[411] however, once puberty was attained, a person was presumed to be capable of entering marriage. But with the ever increasing influence of the social sciences, the "puberty norm" was no longer considered to be an adequate test for matrimonial capacity.[412] Our discussion here shall focus on the proposed emendations to paragraph one. However, both the ramifications of these changes within the canon in regard to ignorance and the development of jurisprudence will be discussed later in the chapter when canon 1096 of the 1983 *CIC* is analyzed.

1. From "*societas*" to "*consortium*"

From the reports published thus far in *Communicationes* concerning the wording of this canon, there does not appear to have been much discussion on the use of *consortium*. In fact, reference is made to it only four times.[413] The debate concerning marriage as a *consortium* took place earlier within the *Coetus*.[414] Thus, by the time the 1975 *Schema* was distributed to the various consultative bodies, the teachings of *Gaudium et spes* were already incorporated into the proposed canonical language.[415] However, this *Schema* laid the groundwork for further input and, therefore, was subject to more discussion and debate by the Commission once the various bodies returned their observations and comments and noted their concerns. It is not in the purview of this paper to go into detail concerning these debates and discussions. Rather, an overview shall be presented pertinent to the term *consortium*, since this is the specific word used in what would become canon 1096 of the 1983 *CIC*.

---

[411] See *Communicationes*, 7 (1975), p. 42. Also see R.L. BURKE, "Canon 1095, 1° and 2°: Presentation I: Canonical Doctrine", in *Incapacity for Marriage: Jurisprudence and Interpretation: Acts of the III Gregorian Colloquium, 1-6 September 1986* (= *Gregorian Colloquium*), R. SABLE, ed., Rome, Pontificia Universitas Gregoriana, 1987, pp. 114, 122-124.

[412] FELLHAUER, "Psychological Incapacity for Marriage in the Revised *Code of Canon Law*", p. 1021. For a more comprehensive discussion and critique of the "puberty norm", see J.R. KEATING, *The Bearing of Mental Impairment on the Validity of Marriage: An Analysis of Rotal Jurisprudence*, Analecta Gregoriana, 136, Roma, Gregorian University Press, 1964, pp.144-154; I. GRAMUNT and L.A. WAUCK, "Capacity and Incapacity to Contract Marriage", in *Studia canonica*, 22 (1988), pp. 154-159, especially noting the cultural and educational influences upon the development of perceptions and critical judgment upon the maturing person; WRENN, *The Invalid Marriage*, pp 192-194.

[413] See *Communicationes*, 7 (1975), pp. 42, 43, 46, 47, which refers to the work of the *Coetus* preparing the 1975 *Schema*; it is addressed as canon 1082. In *Communicationes*, 8 (1976), p. 212, it is again cited as canon 1082. However, the citation in a speech delivered by Cardinal Felici at the beginning of the academic year at the Lateran University is actually from canon 1081, §2. In *Communicationes*, 9 (1977), p. 371, which refers to a vote within the *Coetus*, it is referred to as "Can. 298 (CIC 1082)". In *Communicationes*, 15 (1983), pp. 231-232, which pertains to the 20-28 October 1981 meeting of the Revision Commission, the canon is cited as "Can. 1050", its ranking in the 1980 *Schema*.

[414] FELLHAUER, "The *consortium omnis vitae* as a Juridic Element of Marriage", p. 116-117. For the report of this *Coetus*, see *Communicationes*, 3 (1971), pp. 69-81.

[415] FELLHAUER, "The *consortium omnis vitae* as a Juridic Element of Marriage", p. 118.

84

Gaudium et spes, 48, as noted above, used the phrase *intima communitas vitae et amoris coniugalis* when it described marriage. The 1975 *Schema*, however, used various phrases to convey that marriage was now viewed as more than simply a contract. For example, canon 1013, §1, which concerned the primary and secondary ends of marriage, was formulated as canon 243, §1, in part to read, "*Matrimonium... est (intima) totius vitae coniunctio* ";[416] canon 1081, §2, which spoke of marriage consent, was revised as canon 295, §2, in part to say, "*Consensus matrimonialis est actus voluntatis quo vir et mulier foedere inter se constituunt consortium vitae coniugalis...*";[417] and canon 1086, §2, which concerned simulation, was amended as canon 303, §2, in part to read, "*... excludat matrimonium ipsum aut ius ad vitae communionem...*"[418] The words *coniunctio, consortium* and *communio* in these various canons seem to convey the same meaning.[419] At the beginning of its work, the *Coetus* determined that the three terms were equivalent.[420] However, as its task progressed, the *Coetus*, after carefully assessing all the suggestions which were offered, preferred the word *consortium* and rejected the other two terms.[421] Thus the Commission, upon the recommendation of the *Coetus*, employed the word *consortium* in a specific and determined sense which clearly conveyed the Vatican II doctrine concerning marriage.[422] Indeed, the word itself was used only in reference to marriage. Therefore, in the revision process, marriage was now to be recognized as a partnership and not merely as a contract, which had been the prevalent understanding in the 1917 *CIC*.[423] As one canonist insightfully states:

> In brief, the theological description of marriage is beautifully expressed in *Gaudium et spes* as an "intimate community of conjugal life and love", and is juridically presented in the new Code as a "partnership of the whole of life". In juridical language it stands for all rights and obligations essential to matrimonial institution (*matrimonium in facto esse*). Whereas, "communion of life" understood in the profound biblical sense, that is, "an intimate relationship between two sexually distinct persons" is an essential element of the *consortium*

---

[416]"Canon 243 (CIC 1013). §1. Matrimonium, quod fit mutuo consensu de quo in cann. 295 ss., est (intima) totius vitae coniunctio inter virum et mulierem, quae, indole sua naturali, ad prolis procreationem et educationem ordinatur", in 1975 *Schema*, p. 72.

[417]"Canon 295 (CIC 1081). §2. Consensus matrimonialis est actus voluntatis quo vir et mulier foedere inter se constituunt consortium vitae coniugalis, perpetuum et exclusivum, indole sua naturali ad prolem generandam et educandam ordinatum", *ibid.*, p. 82.

[418]"Canon 303 (CIC 1086). §2. At si alterutra vel utraque pars positivo voluntatis actu excludat matrimonium ipsum aut ius ad vitae communionem, aut ius ad coniugalem actum, vel essentialem aliquam matrimonii proprietatem, invalide contrahit", *ibid.*, p. 83.

[419]FELLHAUER, "The *consortium omnis vitae* as a Juridic Element of Marriage", p. 120. For more discussion on the history and use of these three terms, see J. HUBER, "Coniunctio, communio, consortium: observationes ad terminologiam notionis matrimonii", in *Periodica*, 75 (1986), pp. 393-408.

[420]*Communicationes*, 9 (1977), pp. 79-80; p. 212. See also HUBER, "Coniunctio, communio, consortium", pp. 396, 408.

[421]HUBER, "Coniunctio, communio, consortium", p. 408.

[422]*Ibid.* See also MENDONÇA, "The Theological and Juridic Aspects of Marriage", pp. 270-273; and U. NAVARRETE, "De iure ad vitae communionem: observationes ad novum schema canonis 1086 § 2", in *Periodica*, 66 (1977), pp. 249-270.

[423]According to the 1917 *CIC*, marriage is referred to as a contract ("contractus") in canons 1012 (in both paragraphs); 1015, §1; 1083, §2; 1084; 1087, §2. It is only in canon 1082, §1, where marriage is described as a "societas".

totius vitae.[424]

2. "*Ad filios procreandos*" to "*ordinatum ad prolem, cooperatione aliqua corporali, procreandum*"

Given the discussion concerning the amount of knowledge that a party must have when entering marriage, it is of no surprise that the debates in the *Coetus* focused upon this particular phrase. The fact that the canon was written in the negative, "the parties be at least not ignorant" implied that there must be some knowledge. The canon, like its predecessor canon 1082, however, did not specify how much knowledge was necessary and thus the debates among canonists, particularly among the auditors of the Roman Rota, regarding the level of knowledge required to enter a valid marriage. Therefore, in order to clarify the issue that there was to be some sort of bodily joining, the phrase *cooperatione aliqua corporali* ("by means of some bodily cooperation") was added to the canon. Since it was presumed that anyone who had reached puberty would have sufficient knowledge concerning copulation, the Commission considered the phrase to be sufficient as explaining what was to be the minimal knowledge necessary for a couple to enter into a valid marriage.[425]

At the 18 May 1977 meeting of the *Coetus*, canon 298 of the 1975 *Schema* was again discussed and a number of further changes proposed. These included changing *saltem non ignorent* to *sciant*, which was not accepted; changing *consortium* back to *societas*, which was not accepted; adding *vitae et amoris* to *consortium*, which was likewise not accepted; and, finally, replacing *sexuali* for *corporali*. This last proposed change ended in a tie vote and the decision was made to keep the text as it was.[426] However, as the revision process progressed, this last change was indeed made; the discussions pertaining to the reasons for it have not yet been published.

b. 1980 *Schema*

In the 1980 *Schema*, canon 298 became canon 1050.[427]

canon 298	canon 1050
§1. Ut consensus matrimonialis haberi possit	Ut consensus matrimonialis haberi valeat,
necesse est ut contrahentes	necesse est ut contrahentes
saltem non ignorent matrimonium esse	saltem non ignorent matrimonium esse
consortium permanens	consortium permanens
inter virum et mulierem	inter virum et mulierem
ordinatum ad prolem	ordinatum ad prolem,
cooperatione aliqua corporali,	cooperatione aliqua corporali,
procreandam	procreandam.

---

[424]MENDONÇA, "The Theological and Juridic Aspects of Marriage", p. 276.

[425]See L. CHIAPPETTA, *Il matrimonio nella nuova legislazione canonica e concordataria: manuale giuridico-pastorale*, Roma, Edizioni Dehoniane, 1990, pp. 212-213.

[426]*Communicationes*, 9 (1977), p. 371.

[427]PONTIFICIA COMMISIO CODICI IURIS CANONICI RECOGNOSCENDO, *Codex iuris canonici: schema Patribus Commisionis reservatum* (= 1980 *Schema*), Città del Vaticano, Libreria editrice Vaticana, 1980, p. 240.

86

§2. Haec ignorantia post pubertatem non praesumitur.	Haec ignorantia post pubertatem non praesumitur.

According to the *Relatio* prepared for the 20-28 October 1981 meeting of the entire Commission,[428] three proposals for changes were presented. The first was to add *ad mutuum amorem complendum* to *ordinatum* and *et educandam* to *procreandam*. These additions were not viewed as clarifying the minimal knowledge required. The second was to place canon 1050 with canon 1048 (which pertained to those incapable of contracting marriage). But, it was decided to keep the order as is. The third recommendation was to replace the word *aliqua* with *quadam* ("some" with "certain"), the reason being that *saltem non ignorent* was indeed imprecise and the required minimal knowledge needed a clearer explanation. The response was that the phrase was not ambiguous because it denotes the required minimal knowledge and its object is expressed by the words that follow. However, at this time it was decided to replace the word *corporali* by *sexuali*.[429]

Nothing was stated in this *Relatio* concerning the change of *possit* ("possible"), which was in both canons 1082, §1, of the 1917 *CIC* and 298, §1, in the 1975 *Schema*, to *valeat* ("prevail"). The records concerning the reasons for this change have not yet been published. For the moment, it can be presumed that this was simply a stylistic change.

c. 1982 *Schema*

In the 1982 *Schema*, canon 1050 became canon 1096.[430]

canon 1050	canon 1096
§1. Ut consensus matrimonialis haberi valeat, necesse est ut contrahentes saltem non ignorent matrimonium esse consortium permanens inter virum et mulierem ordinatum ad prolem, cooperatione aliqua corporali, procreandam.	Ut consensus matrimonialis haberi possit, necesse est ut contrahentes saltem non ignorent matrimonium esse consortium permanens inter virum et mulierem ordinatum ad prolem, cooperatione aliqua sexuali, procreadam.
§2. Haec ignorantia post pubertatem non praesumitur.	Haec ignorantia post pubertatem non praesumitur.

In this final draft of the canon, we can see that *corporali* has been replaced by *sexuali*, as the Commission had directed, thus explaining what "minimal knowledge" of procreation implies. The new canon answers this question by stating it is by *cooperatione aliqua sexuali* ("by means of some sexual cooperation"), which will be discussed later in this chapter. Also, *valeat* was replaced with *possit*, returning to the wording

---

[428]*Communicationes*, 15 (1983), pp. 231-232.

[429]*Ibid.*

[430]PONTIFICIA COMMISSIO CODICI IURIS CANONICI RECOGNOSCENDO, *Codex iuris canonici: schema novissimum*, in Civitate Vaticana, Typis polyglottis Vaticanis, 1982, p. 195.

of the 1975 *Schema* and of canon 1082, §1, of the 1917 *CIC*. Canon 1096 in the 1982 *Schema* became canon 1096 of the 1983 *CIC* without any changes. With the revision process completed, we may now proceed to examine the canon itself following the methodology used in Chapter Two when discussing canon 1082 of the 1917 *CIC*, i.e., analyzing the canon within both its context and its text. Following this, we shall compare canon 1096 with canon 819 of the *CCEO*.

III. Canon 1096 of the 1983 *CIC*

To understand the text of canon 1096,[431] we must first place the canon in its proper context, as directed by canon 17.[432]

a. Context of canon 1096

Title VII in Book IV on the Office of Sanctifying is entitled "Marriage". This title gathers together those canons which frame a juridic-matrimonial system assembled from anthropological truths which constitute marriage as a relation, that of being spouses.[433] Chapter IV, Matrimonial Consent, clarifies the

---

[431]For commentaries on canon 1096, see T.P. DOYLE, "Marriage", p. 779; D. KELLY, "Cann. 1008-1165", in *The Canon Law: Letter & Spirit*, G. SHEEHY et al., eds., Collegeville, Minnesota, Liturgical Press, 1995, p. 613; P.J. VILADRICH, "Commentario c. 1096", in A.J. MARZOA, J. MIRAS, R. RODRIGUEZ-OCANA, eds., *Comentario exegético al Código de derecho canónico*, 2nd ed., vol. 3, Pamplona, Ediciones Universidad de Navarra, 1997, pp. 1260-1270; P.J. VILADRICH, "Commentary on *De consensu matrimoniali*", in E. CAPARROS, M. THÉRIAULT, J. THORN, eds., *Code of Canon Law Annotated*, Latin-English edition of the *Code of Canon Law* and English-language translation of the 5th Spanish-language edition of the commentary prepared under the responsibility of the Instituto Martin de Azpilcueta, Montréal, Wilson & Lafleur Limitée, 1993, pp. 687-688.
See also commentaries specifically on the marriage canons, especially L. CHIAPPETTA, *Il Codice di diritto canonico: commento giuridico-pastorale*, 2nd rev. ed., vol. 2, Roma, Edizioni Dehoniane, 1996, pp. 340-341; I. GRAMUNT, J. HERVADA and L.A. WAUCK, *Canons and Commentaries on Marriage*, Collegeville, Minnesota, The Liturgical Press, 1987, pp. 40-41; ÖRSY, *Marriage in Canon Law*, pp. 132-134; M. LÓPEZ ALARCÓN and R. NAVARRO-VALLS, *Curso de derecho matrimonial canónico y concordado*, Madrid, Tecnos, 1984, pp. 183-187; B.A. SIEGLE, *Marriage: According to the New Code of Canon Law*, New York, Alba House, 1986, pp. 100-101.
See also specialized studies on ignorance itself, especially J.I. BAÑARES, "La relación intelecto-voluntad en el consentimiento matrimonial: notas sobre los cc. 1096-1102 del CIC de 1983", in *Ius canonicum*, 33 (1993), pp. 553-606; P.A. BONNET, "L'errore (can. 1096-1100 CIC)", in *Introduzione al consenso matrimoniale canonico*, Milano, A. Giuffrè Editore, 1985, pp. 37-59; C.E. OLIVIERI, "A ignorância no matrimônio (c. 1096). Origem histórica, desenvolvimento doutrinal e jurisprudencial", in *Cuadernos doctorales*, 12 (1994), pp. 13-84; I. PARISELLA, "L'ignoranza «in re matrimonali»", in *Il consenso matrimoniale canonico: dallo conditium allo jus condendum*, Roma, Officium Libri Catholici, 1988, pp. 11-26; P. PELLEGRINO, "L'errore di diritto nel matrimonio canonico (cann. 1096 - 1099)", in *Il diritto ecclesiastico*, 108, 2 (1997), pp. 363-404; M.F. POMPEDDA, "Maturità psichica e matrimonio nei canoni 1095, 1096", in *Apollinaris*, 57 (1984), pp. 131-150; E. TEJERO, "La ignorancia y el error sobre la identidad del matrimonio", in *Ius canonicum*, 33 (1995), pp. 13-101.

[432]Canon 17: "Leges ecclesiasticae intellegendae sunt secundum propriam verborum significationem in textu et contextu consideratam;...." ("Ecclesiastical laws must be understood in accord with the proper meaning of the words considered in their text and context"). English translation of the 1983 Code in *Code of Canon Law; Latin-English Edition*, New English translation, Canon Law Society of America, Washington, DC, 1999, p. 9. All translations of the 1983 *CIC* are taken from this edition unless otherwise noted.

[433]J.I. BAÑARES, "De matrimonio", in A.J. MARZOA, J. MIRAS, R. RODRIGUEZ-OCANA, eds., *Comentario exegético*, vol. 3, p. 1019.

88

definition presented in canon 1057, §2,[434] by listing the canons which deal with factors rendering consent invalid.[435]

In the Code there are three major sources of nullity of marriage: defect (or absence) of form, impediments and defective consent. Our focus here is on consent. Consent itself can be defective because one or both of the parties were incapable of consenting (canon 1095); or, if they were capable of consenting, the consent was defective because of defects in the intellect (canons 1096-1099) or in the will (canons 1101-1103) of at least one of the parties.[436] Thus, after stating how one or both of the contracting parties may be incapable of marriage, the Code then presents the canons pertaining to those who are capable of consenting but who, for some reason or another, choose not to do so.

As Örsy points out, the value this chapter intends to uphold and safeguard is the integrity of human persons in the act of choosing marriage.[437] Since the issue of consent occupies a central position in the canonical doctrine of marriage,[438] the canons in the chapter point out, in a negative way, those factors which would invalidate consent. Conversely, in a positive way, they paint a picture of what is necessary for true matrimonial consent to occur: the parties are to know the ramifications of the matrimonial covenant into which they are about to enter; they are likewise to know with whom they are entering it; they are to will to do so freely, without force or fear, without reservations or conditions; they are to mean what they say and say what they mean.

The placement of canon 1096 in the Code is identical to that of its predecessor canon 1082 of the 1917 CIC, i.e., the second canon under matrimonial consent. While the 1917 CIC in the corresponding chapter first described marriage (canon 1081, §1) and then defined consent (canon 1081, §2), the 1983 CIC places its counterpart, canon 1057, in the general introductory canons, situating it logically after the Vatican II-oriented definition of marriage (canon 1055) and its essential properties (canon 1056), giving a full portrait of the fundamental nature of marriage, its properties and how it is brought into existence through the consent of the parties.

Canon 1096 begins with the basic premise that those who are about to enter into marriage are capable of doing so, which is fundamental for the canons which follow in this section. Strategically as well as philosophically, canon 1096 is basic, since *Nil enim volitum quin praecognitum* ("Nothing is willed unless it is known beforehand").

b. Text of canon 1096

Our examination of the text begins with a comparison of canon 1096 with its predecessor canon 1082 of the 1917 CIC:

---

[434]Canon 1057, §2: "Consensus matrimonialis est actus voluntatis, quo vir et mulier foedere irrevocabili sese mutuo tradunt et accipiunt ad constituendum matrimonium" ("Matrimonial consent is an act of the will by which a man and a woman mutually give and accept each other through an irrevocable covenant in order to establish marriage").

[435]DOYLE, "Marriage", p. 774.

[436]J.H. PROVOST, "Canon 1095: Past, Present, Future", in *The Jurist*, 54 (1994), p. 92. See also I. GRAMUNT and L.A. WAUCK, "«Lack of Due Discretion»: Incapacity or Error?", in *Ius canonicum*, 32 (1992), pp. 534-535.

[437]ÖRSY, *Marriage in Canon Law*, p. 129.

[438]*Ibid.*, p. 126.

1917 canon 1082	1983 canon 1096
§1. Ut matrimonialis consensus haberi possit, necesse est ut contrahentes saltem non ignorent matrimonium esse societatem permanentem inter virum et mulierem ad filios procreandos.	Ut consensus matrimonialis haberi possit, necesse est ut contrahentes saltem non ignorent matrimonium esse consortium permanens inter virum et mulierem ordinatum ad prolem, cooperatione aliqua sexuali, procreandam.
§2. Haec ignorantia post pubertatem non praesumitur.[439]	Haec ignorantia post pubertatem non praesumitur.[440]

When the texts are placed parallel to each other, the striking similarity between the canons can readily be seen. Just as easily, the two major differences noted above can be observed. The implications of these changes will be addressed when the text of the canon is discussed.[441] But, to understand the meaning of the canon, many times reference must be made to the text and context of canon 1082 of the 1917 *CIC*, always remembering the teachings and theology of Vatican II, which are the two fundamental criteria which guided the reform. Let us begin by reiterating the philosophical/canonical principle stated in canon 1082 of the 1917 *CIC*, i.e., there can be no act of the will to establish consent without the interaction of the intellect; it flows from the very nature of marriage. The will cannot act because the due knowledge concerning marriage on the part of the contractant(s) is lacking.

1. *Ut matrimonialis consensus haberi possit necesse est ut contrahentes saltem non ignorent matrimonium esse...*

The first phrase is identical to that found in the 1917 *CIC*: if the conditions which are to be delineated are fulfilled, the marriage consent will be presumed to be valid.[442] The wording denotes, in the negative, that the parties are to have at least minimal knowledge of what marriage is, i.e., of the substance of marriage. In

---

[439]§1: "In order that matrimonial consent may be possible it is necessary that the contracting parties be at least not ignorant that marriage is a permanent society between man and woman for the procreation of children". §2: "This ignorance is not presumed after puberty", translation as found in BOUSCAREN, *Canon Law: A Text and Commentary*, pp. 566-567.

[440]§1: "For matrimonial consent to exist, the contracting parties must be at least not ignorant that marriage is a permanent partnership between a man and a woman ordered to the procreation of offspring by means of some sexual cooperation. §2: "This ignorance is not presumed after puberty."

[441]For a complete discussion of the changes within the Latin text of the canon, see R. ZERA, *De ignorantia in re matrimoniali; eius natura iuridica et ambitus quoad consensus validitatem deque eiusdem probatione in iudicio*, Romae, Ancora, 1978, pp. 95-100. Although he discusses the changes that occur between canon 1082 of the 1917 *CIC* and canon 298 of the 1975 *Schema*, these were identical to the wording of the present canon 1096.

[442]Where this presumption was upheld by canon 1014 of the 1917 *CIC*, the 1983 *CIC* has the same in canon 1060. "Matrimonium gaudet favore iuris; quare in dubio standum est pro valore matrimonii, donec contrarium probetur" ("Marriage possesses the favor of the law; therefore, in a case of doubt, the validity of a marriage must be upheld until the contrary is proven"), which is taken verbatim from the first part of canon 1014. The second part of canon 1014, "salvo praescripto can. 1127", has been dropped.

90

other words, this is a negative way of expressing what is required.[443] A person is not able to be ignorant of the substance of marriage and, at the same time, contract it.[444] Otherwise, it would be invalid since marriage, as a juridic act, although *sui generis*, is governed by canon 124 in the 1983 *CIC* and by its counterpart canon 931 of the *CCEO* concerning such acts.[445] In this canon, the components necessary for validity are addressed: the person placing the act must be capable of doing so; the act must include all of the essential elements; and the formalities and requirements imposed by law for validity must be observed. Canon 126 stipulates that an act placed out of ignorance (or error) can be, under specific conditions, invalid.[446] Taking into consideration the conditions specified in canons 124 and 126, ignorance as it pertains to marriage consent means that if one or both parties do not have the minimal knowledge necessary about consent itself or about an essential element of marriage, then the act would be invalid.[447] In other words, since a person cannot will that which is not already known, and since matrimonial consent is an act of the will (canon 1057, §2), in such a case it is invalid. Canon 1096 sets forth that which is minimally necessary for the will to act in order for a person

---

[443]*Coram* CACHIA, [Maltese Ecclesiastical Tribunal], 12 June 1985, in *Forum*, 1 (1990) 1, p. 107.

[444]F. BERSINI, *Il nuovo diritto canonico matrimoniale: commento giuridico, teologico, pastorale*, 4th ed., Leumann, Torino, Editrice Elle Di Ci, 1994, p. 101.

[445]Canon 124, §1: "Ad validitatem actus iuridici requiritur ut a persona habili sit positus, atque in eodem adsint quae actum ipsum essentialiter constituunt, necnon sollemnia et requisita iure ad validitatem actus imposita.
§2: "Actus iuridicus quoad sua elementa externa rite positus praesumitur validus."
Canon 124, §1: "For the validity of a juridic act it is required that the act is placed by a qualified person and includes those things which essentially constitute the act as well as the formalities and requirements imposed by law for the validity of the act.
§2: "A juridic act placed correctly with respect to its external elements is presumed valid."
CCEO canon 931, §1: "Ad validitatem actus iuridici requiritur, ut a persona habili et competenti sit positus atque in eodem assint, quae actum ipsum essentialiter constituunt, necnon sollemnia et requisita iure ad validitatem actus imposita.
§2: "Actus iuridicus circa sua elementa externa ad normam iuris positus praesumitur validus."
Canon 931, §1: "For the validity of a juridic act it is required that it be placed by a person able and competent to place it, and that it include those elements which essentially constitute it as well as the formalities and requisites imposed by law for the validity of the act.
§2: "A juridic act correctly placed with respect to its external elements is presumed to be valid."
It is beyond the purview of this study to discuss the subtle differences between the texts. Suffice it to say that they are substantially identical.

[446]Canon 126: "Actus positus ex ignorantia aut ex errore, qui versetur circa id quod eius substantiam constituit, aut qui recidit in condicionem *sine qua non*, irritus est; secus valet, nisi aliud caveatur, sed actus ex ignorantia aut ex errore initus locum dare potest actioni rescissoriae ad normam iuris" ("An act placed out of ignorance or out of error concerning something which constitutes its substance or which amounts to a condition *sine qua non* is invalid. Otherwise it is valid unless the law makes other provision. An act entered into out of ignorance or error, however, can give rise to a rescissory action according to the norm of law").
CCEO canon 933: "Actus iuridicus positus ex ignorantia aut ex errore, qui versatur circa id, quod eius substantiam constituit, aut qui recidit in condicionem sine qua non, nullus est; secus valet, nisi aliter iure cavetur, sed actus iuridicus ex ignorantia aut errore positus locum dare potest actioni rescissoriae ad normam iuris " ("A juridic act placed because of ignorance or error concerning an element which constitutes its substance or which amounts to a condition *sine qua non* is invalid; otherwise it is valid, unless the law makes some other provision. However, a juridic act placed out of ignorance or error can be the occasion for a rescissory action in accordance with the norm of law)".

[447]See VILADRICH, "Commentario c. 1096", p. 1267: "Ello significa que faltando este mínimo conocimiento del matrimonio, más que vicio o anomalía lo que se produce, en rigor, es la imposibilidad misma de existencia del consentimiento, por ausencia completa de su objeto matrimonial. Este es el concreto significado del tenor literal del canon: «Para que pueda haber consentimiento matrimonial, es necesario que los contrayentes no ignoren...»".

to give valid consent.[448] It must be noted, however, that the knowledge required for the juridical validity of marriage may not necessarily be sufficient for personal relationship in the marital union.[449] The canon lists the five characteristics of which the parties "at least not be ignorant"; that marriage is a (1) permanent, (2) partnership (*consortium*), (3) between a man and a woman, (4) ordered to the procreation of offspring, (5) by means of some of sexual cooperation.[450] These elements constitute the substance of the act of marriage consent.[451] This substance of the act, «*substantiam actus*» according to Michiels,[452] refers not to all the constitutive elements of something but only to the constitutive elements that must be explicitly intended by a human agent, since a person cannot explicitly intend something of which he or she is ignorant.[453] Thus these elements which constitute the substance of the act, must be known or, otherwise, according to canon 126, the act is invalid. We shall now discuss each of these elements.

2. ...*Consortium*...

As already seen, the introduction of the term *consortium* into the canons on marriage was a conscious decision on the part of the Commission. It was decided that the term best described, in canonical language, the theological reality as envisioned in *Gaudium et spes*, 48. Although some authors indicate that this particular word is not that important to the meaning of the canon,[454] it appears that the discussions and debates demonstrate otherwise. Furthermore, the specific use of the term in this context directly relates it to canon 1055, § 1,[455] which established the foundation for acknowledging and understanding marriage from the vantage point of Vatican II. The *consortium*, therefore, of which parties are to be "at least not ignorant" is an interpersonal relationship between two people who are equal in dignity, as much in one's bodily aspect as in

[448]CHIAPPETTA, *Il Codice di diritto canonico*, vol. 2, p. 341.

[449]C. ALUEDE OJEMEN, *Psychological Factors in Matrimonial Consent in the Light of Canonical Legislation*, Roma, Pontificia Universitas Urbaniana, 1986, p. 109.

[450]See WRENN, *The Invalid Marriage*, p. 93; R. LLANO CIFUENTES, *Novo direito matrimonial canônico: o matrimônio no Codigo e direito canônico de 1983, estudo comparado com a legislacão Brasileira*, Rio de Janeiro, M. Saraiva, 1988, pp. 341-343; A. MOLINA MELIÁ and E. OLMOS ORTEGA, *Derecho matrimonial canônico: sustantivo y procesal*, Madrid, Editorial Civitas, 1985, p. 200. Other authors, while listing four, still include these five elements. For example, see F.R. AZNAR GIL, *El nuevo derecho matrimonial canônico*, 2nd rev. ed., Salamanca, Universidad Pontificia de Salamanca, 1985, pp. 334; J.F. CASTAÑO, *Il sacramento del matrimonio*, 2nd ed., Roma, Tipolitografia Pioda Gianfranco, 1992, pp. 331-332; CHIAPPETTA, *Il Codice di diritto canonico*, vol. 2, pp. 341.

[451]WRENN, *The Invalid Marriage*, p. 93.

[452]G. MICHIELS, *Principia generalia de personis in Ecclesia: commentarius Libri II Codicis juris canonici, canones praeliminares 87-106*, editio altera penitus retractata et notabiliter aucta, Tornaci, Desclée, 1955, p. 657.

[453]WRENN, *The Invalid Marriage*, p. 93.

[454]For example, see ZERA, *De ignorantia in re matrimoniali*, pp. 96-97. Here the author, citing various magisterial documents, writes that this substitution does not make any substantial difference because the term "society" connotes the same meaning as is implied in "partnership". See also PELLEGRINO, "L'errore di diritto nel matrimonio canonico", p. 382, specifically footnote 61 where the author cites O. FUMAGALLI CARULLI, *Intelletto e volontà nel consenso matrimoniale in diritto canonico*, 2nd ed., Milano, Vita e Pensiero, 1981, p. 161; PARISELLA, "L'ignoranza «in re matrimonial»", p. 13.

[455]TEJERO, "La ignorancia y el error", p. 79.

the spiritual, constituting a community of life,[456] one that is sexual in nature, ordered for the procreation of children. There is now emphasis, from the personalist perspective, on a communal lot, on co-participation in the same life and in the same destiny, both in good times and in bad.[457] The term *consortium* denotes communion of goods, of life and of fortune to be maintained perpetually.[458]

This understanding has a different nuance than the term "society" had in the 1917 *CIC*. There, although it was considered as a companionship, a commonality of interests,[459] a "state" or even as a relationship of equal rights-obligations and responsibility,[460] it was not referred to as an "interpersonal" one. Rather, its primary definition was always viewed as related to the intention of having children. Whereas *consortium* is ordered toward the rights and obligations of the party to each other, i.e., the good of the spouses (*bonum coniugum*) and the procreation and education of children (*bonum prolis*) as seen in canon 1055, §1, without reference to a hierarchy of ends, the rights and obligations which arose from the *societas* of marriage primarily centered on the generation and upbringing of children.

Therefore, when we now speak of the *consortium*, we must always take into consideration the teachings of Vatican II, specifically in *Gaudium et spes*, in order to appreciate fully this term and its implications for this canon as well as for marriage in general.[461] It is important to realize that no definition of marital *consortium* is given, either in Roman law or in canon law. The meaning of *consortium* must be understood and interpreted according to the culture and the customs within which we live, since marriage is a natural, human reality. The meaning of *consortium* thus remains open-ended so doctrine and jurisprudence will be able to gradually identify its constitutive elements.[462] This prudence is best explained by Örsy:

> This wisdom of the ancient Roman *jurisprudentes* may come to our help. They were reluctant to define foundational concepts because once their meaning was fixed they would have lost their flexibility. So the lawyers, prudent as they were, left ample room for life to shape the law. For the future, it seems that this problem [of non definition of the term *consortium*] can be solved better by judicial decisions on the concrete level where life meets the law than by abstract definitions which may be too narrow to include all the variations that life can

---

[456]LÓPEZ ALARCÓN and NAVARRO-VALLS, *Curso de derecho matrimonial canónico*, pp. 185-186. See also L. DE LUCA, "La Chiesa e la società coniugale", in *Atti del Congresso internazionale di diritto canonico: la Chiesa dopo il Concilio*, vol. 1, Roma, 14-19 gennaio 1970, Milano, A. Giuffrè Editore, 1972, p. 492. See also ÖRSY, *Marriage in Canon Law*, p. 264, footnote 3.

[457]PELLEGRINO, "L'errore di diritto nel matrimonio canonico ", p. 384.

[458]See HUBER, "Coniunctio, communio, consortium", pp. 403-406. See also MENDONÇA, "The Theological and Juridic Aspects of Marriage", p. 274.

[459]M.F. POMPEDDA, "Incapacity to Assume the Essential Obligations of Marriage: Presentation II: Determining What Are Essential Obligations", in *Gregorian Colloquium*, pp. 190-191.

[460]PELLEGRINO, "L'errore di diritto nel matrimonio canonico ", p. 382; O. FUMAGALLI CARULLI, *Intelletto e volontà nel consenso matrimoniale in diritto canonico*, 2nd ed., Milano, Vita e Pensiero, 1981, p. 161.

[461]For further discussion on the term *consortium*, see A. JOSEPH, «*Consortium vitae*», *the Essence of Marriage: A Study of Can. 1055 with Particular Reference to India*, Romae, Pontificia Universitas Urbaniana, 1990, pp. 8-20.

[462]MENDONÇA, "The Theological and Juridic Aspects of Marriage", p. 274.

produce.[463]

3. ...*Permanens*...

The Latin was changed from *permanentem* as found in canon 1082 to *permanens*,[464] but the meaning remains the same: permanent, which means that the relationship is not merely casual or transient.[465] As in the 1917 *CIC*, permanence (stability) is differentiated from perpetuity (indissolubility); both are constitutive elements of marriage. Permanence, different from perpetuity, denotes a certain stability of the matrimonial bond, excluding occasional and transitory unions.[466]

Permanence is part of the "substance of the act" of marriage, i.e., it is one of those constitutive elements which must be explicitly intended by the person.[467] Perpetuity, while it does not belong to the substance of marriage, is one of the essential properties of marriage along with unity (canon 1056). Both perpetuity and unity automatically and necessarily flow from the nature of marriage itself and without these qualities marriage cannot exist nor can it be conceived as existing.[468] Permanence refers to the intellect; perpetuity, on the other hand, refers to the will through which marriage comes into being (canon 1057, §1). To the commentators of the 1917 *CIC*, both terms referred to the characterization of the marriage bond.[469]

Regarding necessary knowledge, the parties are to know that marriage is a stable union, i.e.,

[463]ÖRSY, *Marriage in Canon Law*, p. 264.

[464]ZERA, *De ignorantia in re matrimoniali*, pp. 96-97, points out that it certainly is better Latin, but is less "tasteful" juridically.

[465]GRAMUNT, HERVADA and WAUCK, *Canons and Commentaries on Marriage*, p. 41; A.B. CANTÓN, *Compendio de derecho matrimonial canónico*, 7th ed., Madrid, Tecnos, 1991, p. 139. This was also the understanding of permanence in canon 1082, §1, of the 1917 *CIC*. See BOUSCAREN, *Canon Law: A Text and Commentary*, p. 567. WRENN, *The Invalid Marriage*, on p. 137, makes a further distinction: "Something is permanent when it is lasting or non-temporary. It is perpetual when it is everlasting or non-terminable.... Permanence is a divisible notion.... Perpetuity, on the other hand, is an indivisible notion."

In C.T. LEWIS and C. SHORT, eds., *A Latin Dictionary*, Oxford, Oxford University Press, 1984, *permaneo*, on p. 1347, is defined as "to stay to the end; to hold out, last, continue, endure, remain; to persist, to persevere"; *perpetuo*, on p. 1351, is defined as "to continue uninterruptedly, to proceed with continually"; *perpetuus* (as the adjective form) is further defined as "continuing throughout, continuous, unbroken, uninterrupted". One can discern the subtle difference between the terms: permanent has the sense of lasting, remaining; something that is stable. Perpetual has the sense of something that is not ending nor interrupted, which continues endlessly.

[466]PELLEGRINO, "L'errore di diritto nel matrimonio canonico ", pp. 400-401.

[467]WRENN, *The Invalid Marriage*, p. 93. This is specifying the general rule set in canon 126. See pp. 92-93 for more information.

[468]D.J. BURNS, *Matrimonial Indissolubility: Contrary Conditions; A Historical Synopsis and a Commentary*, Canon Law Studies, 377, Washington, DC, The Catholic University of America, 1963, p. 47. See also F.M. CAPPELLO, *Summa iuris canonici*, vol. 2, 4th ed., Romae, apud aedes Universitatis Gregorianae, 1945, p. 287 (n. 298): "Unitas et indissolubilitas dicuntur proprietates *essentiales* matrimonii, quia sponte ac necessario ita profluunt ex ipsa coniugii natura, ut sine iisdem matrimonium nec subsistere neque concipi possit"

[469]This understanding is clearer when one remembers the 1917 *CIC*, when canon 1082, §1, was seen in relation to consent as defined in canon 1081, §2. Canon 1134 of the 1983 *CIC* speaks of the marriage bond as "by its nature is perpetual and exclusive" ("natura sua perpetuum et exclusivum").

94

permanent, although they do not need to know that it is indissoluble.[470] It must be remembered that the canon speaks of the *minimum* of knowledge that is needed for the mind to motivate the will in order to establish marriage. Since the will requires the illumination of the intellect in order to act,[471] all that is required by this phrase in this particular canon is that the person knows — and thus intends — a permanent union, i.e., one that is not sporadic or fleeting. Thus, a person is to know that marriage is permanent but not necessarily that it is perpetual, i.e., indissoluble.[472] The understanding (or misunderstanding) of indissolubility, an essential property of marriage, is one of the concerns specifically listed in canon 1099.[473]

In *Gaudium et spes*, 48, marriage "is rooted in the contract of its partners, that is, in their irrevocable personal consent"[474] which has been codified in canon 1057, §2, replacing canon 1081, §2, of the 1917 *CIC*, which was referring implicitly to *matrimonium in fieri*. Canon 1096, §1, on the other hand, refers to *matrimonium in facto esse*.[475] If we take these two canons together (as were canons 1081, §2 and 1082, §1 of the 1917 *CIC*), the essence (canon 1096, §1) and essential properties (canon 1057, §2) of marriage must be integrally considered to be within everyone's reach as *matrimonium in fieri* constitutes *matrimonium in facto esse*.[476] In other words, a person, when giving consent to marriage, is to know that marriage is permanent, so that an indissoluble union may be implicitly willed.[477]

---

[470]AZNAR GIL, *El nuevo derecho matrimonial canónico*, p. 334; CANTÓN, *Compendio de derecho matrimonial canónico*, p. 139; GRAMUNT, HERVADA and WAUCK, *Canons and Commentaries on Marriage*, p. 41; VILADRICH, "Commentary on *De consensu matrimoniali*", p. 688. This is identical to the understanding of permanence in the 1917 *CIC*, since perpetuity was discussed in canon 1084 (error).
  For an opposing view, see S. VILLEGGIANTE, "Errore e voluntà simulatoria nel consenso matrimoniale in diritto canonico", in *Monitor ecclesiasticus*, 109 (1984), p. 490, where the author states that in his opinion, since the parties are not to be ignorant that marriage is a *totius vitae consortium* (canon 1055, §1), this includes the concepts of unity and indissolubility.
  C. BURKE, "Canon 1057 and the Object of Matrimonial Consent", in *Forum*, 3 (1992) 1, pp. 29-43, seems to interchange the terms permanence and indissolubility (perpetuity). He writes: "The logic of the permanence or indissolubility of marriage corresponds to the aspirations of human love itself: 'I love you for ever. I love you always.'... There is in fact no middle term between permanent and transient. There is no middle choice between the lasting and unbreakable relationship of marriage, and what is no more than a temporary sexual liaison: between a spouse, to whom one gives oneself for life, and a sexual partner, changeable at will", pp. 35-36.

[471]BURNS, *Matrimonial Indissolubility*, p. 53.

[472]This understanding is demonstrated in the Rotal decision *coram* POMPEDDA, 29 October 1979, in *SRR Dec*, 71 (1979), p. 461: "Verum imprimis societas permanens dicit communionem vitae quidem perpetuam, quamvis formalis notio indissolubilitatis non requiratur in contrahente (cfr. can. 1084), atque ideo saltem exigit cognitionem stabilitatis connubii..." ("In truth, in the first place, permanent society certainly asserts perpetual communion of life, although the formal notion of indissolubility is not required of the contractant (see can. 1084), and, therefore, at least demands a knowledge of stability of marriage...").

[473]Canon 1099: "Error circa matrimonii unitatem vel indissolubilitatem aut sacramentalem dignitatem, dummodo non determinet voluntatem, non vitiat consensum matrimonialem" ("Error concerning the unity or indissolubility or sacramental dignity of marriage does not vitiate matrimonial consent provided that it does not determine the will").

[474]FLANNERY, *Vatican II; Volume 1*, p. 950.

[475]PELLEGRINO, "L'errore di diritto nel matrimonio canonico", p. 380; P.A. BONNET, "L'errore di diritto giuridicamente rilevante nel consenso matrimoniale canonico", in *Studi in memoria di Pietro Gismondi*, vol.1, Pubblicazioni della Facoltà di Giurisprudenza, Università degli studi di Roma, Milano, A. Giuffrè Editore, 1987-1988, p. 154.

[476]PELLEGRINO, "L'errore di diritto nel matrimonio canonico", p. 381.

[477]It is our opinion that permanence can — and indeed many times does — lead to perpetuity. However, a person's idea of permanence may vary.

4. ...*Inter virum et mulier*...

As in the 1917 *CIC*, the canon reiterates the basic fact that marriage is between persons of opposite sex, since the *consortium* is directed toward the procreation of children. It is this particularly unique characteristic of the matrimonial *consortium* that distinguishes it from other partnerships and thus makes it exclusively heterosexual in nature.[478] The conjugal union can be established only between persons of different sexes.[479] A person is to know of the heterosexual nature of marriage.[480] This is becoming more of an issue today since some civil legislationa admit "marriages" between persons of the same sex.[481]

Taking this phrase (*inter virum et mulier*) together with the preceding phrase *consortium permanens*, the canon speaks of the exclusive nature of the heterosexual relationship. There is a special character to the partnership between the man and the woman: given the stable basis of the relationship, it is an exclusive union between one man and one woman, as was evidenced by the commentators on the 1917 *CIC* and discussed in Chapter Two.

5. ...*Ordinatum ad prolem...procreandum*...

It is the ordering of the marital *consortium* for the procreation of children which differentiates it from other relationships. Marriage is more than a partnership of friendship, service, economics, etc.[482] When a person decides to marry, he or she is to know that the generation of children is the result of the physical, genital union of their bodies. This, of course, pertains to those who are of child-bearing age.[483] Thus marriage is a conjugal relationship which calls for another specific element, i.e., sexuality, which in turn finds its fullness in procreation. As C. Burke notes:

> If the argument is legitimate that there can be a true marital relationship between a man and a woman without any necessary reference to the procreative aspect of their sexual complementarity, it is hard to see what cogent objections can be offered to the argument that an active relationship between two persons of the same sex can be established on a valid

[478]See PELLEGRINO, "L'errore di diritto nel matrimonio canonico", pp. 401-402. See also A. ABATE, *Il matrimonio nell'attuale legislazione canonica*, 2nd rev. ed., Brescia, Paideia Editrice, 1982, p. 52; *Communicationes*, 7 (1975), p. 54.

[479]VILADRICH, "Commentary on *De consensu matrimoniali*", p. 688.

[480]WRENN, *The Invalid Marriage*, p. 93.

[481]CASTAÑO, *Il sacramento del matrimonio*, p. 331. While he states further, "...questa è solo una farsa", it is becoming more of an issue. As a recent example in the popular Catholic press, the April 2000 edition of *Columbia*, 80 (2000), has a banner headline on the cover, "Stopping Same-Sex Marriage Initiative" with the article "Marriage in the Balance", pp. 12-14, by M. DANIELS. The author writes on pp. 12-13: "Homosexual activists are out to redefine marriage and the family. They will stop at nothing to overturn accepted religious and moral teaching.... At stake is nothing less than the future of marriage."
For more information regarding "same sex marriages" or "domestic partnerships", see "Domestic Partnership Listings", 10/25/1999, <http://www.lambdalegal.com> (1 March 2000). Here, for example, there are 18 pages of state, provincial, local and municipal governments as well as international businesses that recognize same sex unions for the purpose of health care and other non-health care benefits.

[482]AZNAR GIL, *El nuevo derecho matrimonial canónico*, p. 334.

[483]For example, the Rite of Marriage makes provision for those who are older.

96

"marital" basis of similar self-giving.[484]

This conjugal relationship, which specifies the procreational aspect of marriage,[485] is the reason why a person must know that marriage is between a man and a woman.

6. ...Cooperatione aliqua sexuali

Given the debates and discussions through the centuries concerning the amount of knowledge necessary for marriage, the addition of the words *cooperatione aliqua sexuali* was one of the significant changes made to canon 1082 of the 1917 *CIC*. The 1983 *CIC*, while explicitly stating that the procreation of children is by means of some sexual cooperation, implies that it is not the result of kissing, of love, of the reciprocal gazing of the eyes, of the heat of the nuptial bed, or of manifestations of affection.[486] While the couple need not have complete knowledge of the details of sexual copulation,[487] they are to know specifically that it is sexual, i.e., genital, and not merely something physical in a generic kind of way.[488] Those contracting marriage are to know that there is a connection between the interaction of their sexual organs and the conception of a child.[489] While this may seem elementary, one canonist states that this knowledge should be verified especially when marriages took place between youth who were mentally challenged or who grew up in institutions, in closed environments or in families which were morally rigid or sexually reserved.[490]

7. Haec ignorantia post pubertatem non praesumitur

The 1983 *CIC* maintains the presumption of law found in canon 1082, §2, of the 1917 *CIC*, i.e., after puberty (twelve for girls, fourteen for boys), knowledge of marriage is presumed. Before puberty, ignorance

---

[484]C. BURKE, "The Object of the Marital Self-Gift as Presented in Canon 1057, § 2", in *Studia canonica*, 31 (1997), p. 412.

[485]For a more detailed study, see J. GAUDEMET, "Mariage et procréation: les aspects historiques", in *Revue de droit canonique*, 45 (1995), pp. 245-256.

[486]BERSINI, *Il nuovo diritto canonico matrimoniale*, p. 102: "...la generazione sia effetto dei bacci, dell'amore, del reciproco fissarsi negli occhi, del calore del talamo coniugale, delle manifestazioni di affetto..." The author further states that such manifestations could be between persons of the same sex and therefore the canon speaks expressly of the partnership between a man and a woman.

[487]J.-P. SCHOUPPE, *Le droit canonique: introduction générale et droit matrimonial*, Bruxelles, E. Story-Scientia, 1991, p. 177; AZNAR GIL, *El nuevo derecho matrimonial canónico*, pp. 334-335; VILADRICH, "Commentary on *De consensu matrimoniali*", p. 688. This conclusion was also seen in the various Rotal decisions concerning ignorance which were discussed earlier in this chapter.

[488]G. GHIRLANDA, *Il diritto nella Chiesa mistero di communione: compendio di diritto ecclesiale*, Milano, Edizioni Paoline, 1990, p. 354.

[489]J. McAREAVY, *The Canon Law of Marriage and the Family*, Dublin, Colour Books Ltd, 1997, p. 110.

[490]BERSINI, *Il nuovo diritto canonico matrimoniale*, p. 101-102.

97

is presumed.[491] Since this is a presumption of law,[492] it can yield to contrary proof. In his 22 March 1963 landmark decision, Sabattani listed four criteria to utilize when weighing proofs in order to establish whether ignorance is verified or not: the psycho-physical, the educational, the prenuptial and the postnuptial[493] which are as important today and can be readily applied to the 1983 CIC just as it was to the 1917 CIC.

Given the history of the development of ignorance and its effect upon matrimonial consent, the reason for the inclusion of this paragraph in canon 1082 of the 1917 CIC was to codify the long held understanding that a person who reached puberty was ready for marriage.[494] Since this presumption has a long history in jurisprudence, it made sense to include it in the first Code. Likewise, since canon 1096 is an update of canon 1082,[495] it should be understood in the same light, i.e., once a person reaches puberty, he or she has attained the knowledge which normally occurs through natural development and is sufficient for marriage.[496] Most canonists seem to agree.[497] The question is, should it be so? Interestingly, this question was already posed in 1964 by Keating in The Bearing of Mental Impairment,[498] who concludes:

> Summing up, we might say that the puberty norm seems to gain no support either from common human estimation, from the mind of the canonical Legislator, from Rotal jurisprudence, or from the authority of Cardinal Gasparri. In fact, it seems that common human estimation, the canonical Legislator, Rotal jurisprudence, and Cardinal Gasparri are all clearly contrary to the puberty norm.[499]

As already noted, the fundamental assessment of ignorance centered on one or both of the contractants' knowledge of sexual intercourse; specifically, whether it was part of the nature of marriage, i.e., essential for

---

[491]Ibid., p. 102.

[492]Canon 1584: "Presumptio est rei incertae probabilis coniectura; eaque alia est iuris, quae ab ipsa lege statuitur; alia hominis, quae a iudice conicitur" ("A presumption is a probable conjecture about an uncertain matter; a presumption of law is one which the law itself establishes; a human presumption is one which a judge formulates"). In canon 1826 of the 1917 CIC, two types of presumptions of law were listed: simple (iuris simpliciter) which yields to contrary proof and absolute (iuris et de iure) which did not. Since the 1983 CIC dropped this distinction, canonists are of the mind that the presumptions in the 1983 CIC can be overturned, since they are stated in positive ecclesiastical law.

[493]"Criterium psyco-physicum; criterium educationis; criterium praenuptiale; criterium postnuptiale" in SRR Dec, 55 (1963), pp. 209-210. More will be said about these criteria in Chapter Four.

[494]For more on this topic, see V.M. SMITH, Ignorance Affecting Matrimonial Consent, Washington, DC, The Catholic University of America, Canon Law Studies, 245, 1950, pp. 6-10, 72-75.

[495]See PELLEGRINO, "L'errore di diritto nel matrimonio canonico", p. 404; P.A. BONNET, "Errore di diritto e necessità della coscienza dell'importanza vitale dell'opzione matrimoniale", in Il diritto ecclesiastico, 94 (1983), pp. 466-467.

[496]J.T. MARTÍN DE AGAR, A Handbook on Canon Law, Montréal, Wilson & Lafleur Limitée, 1999, p. 160.

[497]For example, see AZNAR GIL, El nuevo derecho matrimonial canónico, p. 335; DOYLE, "Marriage", p. 779; GHIRLANDA, Il diritto nella Chiesa mistero di communione, p. 354; McAREAVY, The Canon Law of Marriage and the Family, p. 110; SCHOUPPE, Le droit canonique, p. 177; VILADRICH, "Commentary on De consensu matrimoniali", p. 688.

[498]See KEATING, The Bearing of Mental Impairment, pp. 144-154. For further discussion, see ALUEDE OJEMEN, Psychological Factors in Matrimonial Consent in the Light of Canonical Legislation, pp. 85-88.

[499]KEATING, The Bearing of Mental Impairment, p. 154.

98

the procreation of children, or if they knew how to perform it, i.e., through some means of physical joining of the genitalia. With the addition of the phrase *cooperatione aliqua sexuali* this second concern has been addressed. While the procreational aspect specifies the understanding of the *consortium* — marriage is more than a friendly or social union of two people — it is necessary that the contractants know that the marital *consortium* has a broader meaning, with responsibilities and obligations. One author goes so far as to list fifteen examples of concrete elements, derived from existing jurisprudence, which are essential to a *consortium* and to which the marriage partner has a right.[500] He concludes by stating:

> If one of the spouses, then, were radically unable to meet these requirements for establishing a community of conjugal life in a satisfactory way, he would deprive his partner of an essential right of Christian marriage. Thus, if at the time consent was given, he was not master over what he promised to give for the rest of his common life, the contract was invalid.[501]

While this can be used as a rule of thumb for both canonists and pastoral ministers, it is not formally sanctioned by canon law or Rotal jurisprudence although it has led to various discussions.[502] While the Code speaks of *consortium*,[503] it does not offer a definition, just as Roman law did not.[504] Rather, its understanding has been conditioned by the culture of the age and by the customs of the people.[505] Therefore, the concept of *consortium* remains open-ended so doctrine and jurisprudence will have ample scope gradually to identify its constitutive elements.[506] As both of these develop through the living experience of the post-Vatican II Church, that which characterizes the *consortium* will become more evident.

However, the basic understanding of *consortium* has already been posited by the Code Commission and gives us direction for understanding it: *consortium* stands for marriage itself or for the totality of the rights and obligations of marriage.[507] Therefore, in relation to the canon under discussion, a person is to have

---

[500]G. LESAGE, "The *Consortium vitæ conjugalis*: Nature and Applications", in *Studia canonica*, 6 (1972), pp.103-104. In his article, "Évolution récente de la jurisprudence matrimoniale", in *Le divorce: l'Eglise catholique ne devrait-elle pas modifier son attitude séculaire à l'égard de l'indissolubilité du mariage?*, Travaux du Congrès de la Société canadienne de Théologie tenu à Montréal du 21 au 24 août 1972, Montréal, Fides, 1973, pp. 13-57, this same author regrouped these examples under five general headings; see pp. 47-48.

[501]LESAGE, "The *Consortium vitæ conjugalis*", p. 104.

[502]See W.A. SCHUMACHER, "The Importance of Interpersonal Relations in Marriage", in *Studia canonica*, 10 (1976), pp. 75-112; G.F. READ, "*Totius vitae consortium*: The Implications for Jurisprudence", in *Studia canonica*, 20 (1986), pp. 123-146; JOSEPH, «*Consortium vitae*», *the Essence of Marriage*, pp. 13-18.

[503]The 1983 *CIC* uses the term *consortium* only four times and only in reference to marriage: canons 1055, §1; 1096, §1; 1098; and 1135. The 1917 *CIC*, on the other hand, also used *consortium* in canons 1130 and 1699, §3, both referring, in essence, to cohabitation.

[504]ÖRSY, *Marriage in Canon Law*, p. 264.

[505]*Ibid.*

[506]MENDONÇA, "The Theological and Juridical Aspects of Marriage", p. 274.

[507]NAVARRETE, "De iure ad vitæ communionem", p. 269. It is to be noted that his preference is to the use of *communio vitae* vel termini aequivalentes «*consortium*», «*consuetudo*», «*coniunctio*», «*consociatio*»... designant matrimonium ipsum seu totalitatem iurium et officiorum matrimonii. Sic in Const. «Gaudium et spes», no. 48, atque in ipso Schemate a Commissione

minimal knowledge of marriage, i.e., of the totality of its rights and obligations. This observation, if utilized by canonists, broadens not only the possibilities of what a person may not know about marriage, but also can make the presumption in paragraph two more difficult to uphold and easier to overturn by means of supporting evidence to the contrary. There is certainly room for discussion. This shall be addressed in greater detail in Chapter Four.

c. Canon 819 of the *CCEO*

It seems useful to our study to examine briefly the difference between canon 1096 of the 1983 *CIC* and canon 819 of the *CCEO*:

canon 1096	canon 819
§1 Ut consensus matrimonialis haberi possit, necesse est ut contrahentes	Ut consensus matrimonialis haberi possit, necesse est, ut matrimonium celebrantes
saltem non ignorent matrimonium esse consortium permanens inter virum et mulierem ordinatum ad prolem, cooperatione aliqua sexuali, procreandum	saltem non ignorent matrimonium esse consortium permanens inter virum et mulierem ordinatum ad filios cooperatione aliqua sexuali procreandos.[508]

§2. Haec ignorantia post pubertatem non praesumitur.

The *fons* for canon 819 is found in the 22 February 1949 *Motu proprio* of Pope Pius XII, *Crebrae allatae*,[509] canon 73:[510]

§1. Ut matrimonialis consensus haberi possit, necesse est ut contrahentes saltem non ignorent matrimonium esse societatem permanentem inter virum et mulierem ad filios procreandos.
§2. Haec ignorantia post pubertatem non praesumitur.

As can be seen, the wording is identical to the text of canon 1082 of the 1917 *CIC*. In this original text, as

---

parato....", *ibid*. However, the truth of his statement is without doubt.

[508]"For matrimonial consent to be valid it is necessary that the contracting parties at least not be ignorant that marriage is a permanent consortium between a man and a woman which is ordered toward the procreation of offspring by means of some sexual cooperation", *Code of Canons of the Eastern Churches, Latin-English Edition*, translation prepared under the auspices of the Canon Law Society of America, Washington, DC, Canon Law Society of America, 1992, pp. 400-401. It is to be noted that this translation is identical to that of canon 1096 found in the *Code of Canon Law, Latin-English Edition*, translation prepared under the auspices of the Canon Law Society of America, Washington, DC, Canon Law Society of America, 1983. The differences, as can be noticed in the Latin text will be discussed. A new translation of the *CCEO* is currently being prepared by the Canon Law Society of America which will, most probably, render the Latin differently.

[509]*AAS*, 41 (1949), pp. 89-117.

[510]*AAS*, 41 (1949), p. 105.

100

there was in the proposed revision, canon 43,[511] there is a second paragraph. It remained as such both in the proposed *Schema canonum de cultu divino*, published in 1977[512] and in the second *Schema* of 1980. Concern was raised that the canon should be similar to that published in the 1983 Latin *CIC*, but if possible to avoid the uncertainty that was noted in the jurisprudence concerning puberty. It was decided that the second paragraph remain as written.[513]

When the *Schema Codicis iuris canonici orientalis* was later published in 1987,[514] the second paragraph was omitted. Three reasons are given in the 1988 draft edition for this omission: (1) puberty was not defined in the *CICO* (*Codicis iuris canonci orientalis*) and therefore, juridically, it is not possible to establish from which time the prohibition begins; (2) to formulate the paragraph in the sense of "after 14 years of age" for "boys" and "after 12 years of age" for "girls", today is no longer possible; (3) to say "before the year NN his ignorance is presumed" is not in the law in force ("legge vigente"). The report also noted that canon 88, §3, of the 1917 *CIC*, which fixes the presumed onset of puberty for legal purposes (as well as canon 17, §2, of the *Motu proprio*, «Cleri sanctitati») has been omitted in the 1983 *CIC*. Where it occurs in the *CICO*, canon 13, §1, pertaining to penal law, there is no mention of "puberty" but simply "no one who has not completed fourteen years".[515] These reasons were reiterated in 1989, when one member asked to have the second paragraph reinstated.[516]

The other two differences in this canon as compared to canon 1096 of the 1983 *CIC* are *celebrantes* instead of *contrahentes* and *filios* instead of *prolem*. The former difference reflects the fact that in the Eastern Churches, the couple celebrate the sacrament of marriage rather than contract it.[517] The Eastern law is less "contractualistic" than the Latin law, placing more emphasis on the spiritual, sacramental and mystical aspects of Christian marriage.[518] The latter change gives a more personal aspect to marriage, since *prolem* is generic and denotes offspring, while *filios* means children.

As the canons are almost identical, the jurisprudence that will evolve concerning canon 1096 of the 1983 *CIC* would also pertain to this canon. The difference will be, however, that the presumption in paragraph two will not need to be invoked as a starting point, which was the case in the Rotal cases previously cited. Thus, for Eastern canonists, there will be a freedom to develop the cases from the standpoint of each person's life experience, without presuming that, because of his or her age, he or she already has the necessary knowledge.

---

[511] *Nuntia*, Città del Vaticano, PONTIFICIA COMMISSIO CODICI IURIS CANONCI ORIENTALIS RECOGNOSCENDO, 8 (1979), p. 17.

[512] *Ibid.*, 15 (1977), p. 77.

[513] *Ibid.*

[514] *Ibid.*, 26 (1987), p. 148.

[515] *Ibid.*, 27 (1988), p. 8.

[516] *Ibid.*, 28 (1989), p. 112.

[517] POSPISHIL, *Eastern Catholic Church Law*, 2nd rev. ed., Staten Island, New York, St. Maron Publications, 1996, p. 552, writes: "those celebrating the marriage".

[518] C. GALLAGHER, "Marriage in the Revised Canon Law for the Eastern Catholic Churches", in *Studia canonica*, 24 (1990), p. 84. See also J. VADAKUMCHERRY, "Marriage Laws in the *Code of Canon Law* and the *Code of Canons of the Eastern Churches*", in *Studia canonica*, 26 (1992), pp. 452-453.

CONCLUSION

In this chapter we began with an overview of the theology and teachings of Vatican II as they pertained to marriage. The Council had a profound influence on the revision of canon law which resulted in the 1983 *CIC* and the 1990 *CCEO*. One of the greatest contributions is that of presenting marriage from a personalist perspective as an "intimate partnership of life and conjugal love" in *Gaudium et spes*, 48, which became translated as *consortium totius vitae* in both Codes. Although the term was found in Roman law (within the context of the law of obligations resulting from contracts) as well as in the 1917 *CIC* (referring to cohabitation), a renewed understanding of its richness has come to light through its nuanced use in *Gaudium et spes*. As our research has demonstrated, the term is pregnant with meaning which will only more fully come to light as the years progress, although the jurisprudence will be based on negative factors, i.e., from adjudicating cases of marriage nullity. In one sense this is unfortunate because what should be viewed as a profound insight into the nature of marriage, undoubtably influenced by the grace of the Holy Spirit upon the Council Fathers, will be utilized primarily to establish reasons why a marriage failed. In another sense, however, by appealing to the Council teachings as written in Church law, canonists are in the unique position not only to give guidance to those who are about to enter into the sacramental reality we call marriage, but also to affirm those who are already living it.

While it is important to have a sense of our canonical tradition, it must be balanced by our openness to the teachings of Vatican II, something that may sound easy but, in reality, is not always that simple. Specifically, a better use of the fullness of the notion of *consortium* in our application of canons 1096 and 819 would allow canonists to have a better sense of whether those who entered marriage had, at the time of consent, an understanding not only of what marriage was, but also of what was expected of them. Rather than quickly assuming that a person is incapable of marriage, as evidenced by the way some tribunals use canon 1095, starting from the perspective that the person is capable but for some reason, maybe yet uncovered, the consent was defective, would open the door not only to the use of canons 1096 and 819, but would also have ramifications for the other canons under matrimonial consent as well.

The question that needs to be posed is: can a person, who for all intents and purposes is capable, actually attempt to enter marriage and not have the degree of knowledge that is required by canon law? The simple answer is "yes". We contend that most who enter marriage are capable of doing so. Should their marriage fail, and the basis for this failure is ignorance, then it must be demonstrated that it was because one or both parties were capable of entering marriage, but lacked the knowledge which was necessary, i.e., a person may truly be ignorant that marriage is permanent, that it is a *consortium*, that it is exclusively between a man and a woman, that it is ordered to the procreation of children and that procreation is through some means of sexual cooperation. While all these are true, it is our contention that the key word is *consortium*, which needs to be better understood and utilized by canonists. How these issues can be appropriately addressed shall be discussed in Chapter Four.

In regard to canon 1096, §2, the presumption stated here was taken verbatim from canon 1082, §2, of the 1917 *CIC*. From the jurisprudence of this paragraph based upon the 1917 *CIC*, as well as that for centuries before the actual writing of it, it is clearly demonstrated that it pertained primarily to knowledge of the act of sexual copulation rather than to knowledge about the permanent society between a man and a woman which is established through marriage. As shown in the Rotal cases concerning ignorance, even when basing the decision upon ignorance about the nature of marriage, the focus was on the *copula*.

Taking into consideration canon 17[519] and Vatican II's theology of marriage from a personalist perspective, this presumption is now broadened to include the fact that marriage is a permanent *consortium* between a man and a woman. We can understand why the presumption was included, since it has been the jurisprudential presumption pertaining to marriage for centuries and thus has its rightful place in the Latin Code. However, it is our opinion that the drafters of the 1983 *CIC* should also have modified it, as they did paragraph one, to reflect the changes brought about by Vatican II, or simply dropped it, since canon 1060 already presumes the validity of marriage.

---

[519]"Leges ecclesiasticae intelligendae sunt secundum propriam verborum in textu et contextu consideratam..." ("Ecclesiastical laws must be understood in accord with the proper meaning of the words considered in their text and context...").

CHAPTER FOUR

APPLICABILITY OF CANON 1096

INTRODUCTION

Canon 1096 succinctly states that a person must at least not be ignorant that marriage is a (1) permanent, (2) *consortium*[520] (3) between a man and a woman (4) ordered for the procreation of offspring (5) by means of some sexual cooperation. If a person is found to be ignorant, i.e., lacking this fundamental knowledge pertaining to marriage, in any one or more of these facets,[521] then the union he or she entered could be declared invalid based on canon 1096. While this canon is for the most part identical to its predecessor canon 1082 of the 1917 *CIC*, the doctrinal and jurisprudential focus at that time was almost exclusively on the knowledge of the sexual and procreational aspect of marriage as was discussed in Chapter Two. In Chapter Three, as we analyzed this canon, we illustrated the shift which was taking place in Rotal jurisprudence, after the promulgation of *Gaudium et spes*, which spoke of marriage in a more personalist way. Thus, while the understanding of marriage remained that of a partnership through which the generation of children is of utmost importance, there began a broadening of the appreciation of the *consortium*, the interpersonal relationship between the man and the woman from which offspring arise. Since there have been no published Rotal cases on the ground of ignorance since 1979, we still remain in the realm of speculation where the jurisprudence will lead us concerning this ground. This, however, does not prevent us from striving to understand canon 1096 more thoroughly and propose a usage that would represent its authentic juridical meaning and applicability.

It is our contention that, for various reasons, the ground of ignorance is not as widely used as it could be, whether because of the emphasis on the use of the psychological titles of canon 1095 or the lack of understanding of canon 1096 itself. As Tribunals "wean" themselves away from canon 1095 at the encouragement of the Apostolic Signatura, with the Rota providing continuing jurisprudence on other grounds of invalidity, it will be important to discern the differences, at times subtle, among the various grounds. While it is beyond the scope of this study to do so in general, it is, however, important to distinguish ignorance from the other grounds; this in turn would aid in its use in the ecclesiastical courts. It is important to note that while reference is made to parallel canons in the Oriental Code where applicable, this dissertation is primarily

---

[520] All English translations of canon 1096, i.e., the American version of the English-language translation: *Code of Canon Law, Latin-English Edition*, New English Translation, prepared under the auspices of the Canon Law Society of America, Washington, DC, Canon Law Society of America, 1999; *The Code of Canon Law*, New revised English Translation, prepared by the Canon Law Society of Great Britain and Ireland in association with The Canon Law Society of Australia and New Zealand and The Canadian Canon Law Society, London, HarperCollins Publishers, 1997 [as well as the 1983 version] use the word "partnership" for *consortium*. However, the 1983 American version of the English language translation of the 1983 Code by the Canon Law Society of America and the 1992 American version of the English-language translation: *Code of Canons of the Eastern Churches, Latin-English Edition*, translation prepared under the auspices of the Canon Law Society of America, Washington, DC, Canon Law Society of America, 1992, kept the Latin term *consortium* in canon 1096 and its parallel canon 816.

It is to be noted that in the other canons which contain the term *consortium* (1055, §1; 1098 and 1135), the *CCEO* parallel canons (776, §1; 821 and 777) are translated as "partnership".

While the term consortium can be translated as "partnership" in classical Latin dictionaries, it is our contention that the meaning and import of the canon is better served by keeping the term in the original Latin.

[521] See J. KOWAL, "L'errore circa le proprietà essenziali o la dignità sacramentale del matrimonio (c. 1099)", in *Periodica*, 87 (1998), pp. 295: "...se i contraenti ignorano alcuno di tali elementi, non possono formare un atto di volontà che sia vero consenso matrimoniale."

concerned with, and our attention is focused on, the Latin Code.

Once these distinctions are understood, we shall then progress to a two-pronged application of our findings concerning ignorance. First, how this knowledge may be utilized by tribunals in cases of marriage nullity: what specifically to look for in cases to determine whether the ground of ignorance may be retained and, by means of a sample law section in an appendix, show how canon 1096 may be effectively implemented. Second, how marriage preparation programs may benefit from a renewed understanding so that ignorance, as understood by canon 1096, may possibly be avoided in the first place.

I. DISTINGUISHING IGNORANCE FROM OTHER GROUNDS OF NULLITY

When considering cases of marriage nullity, it is important for the judge to understand the differences between the various grounds, since the judge is responsible for the *contestatio litis*, the joinder of issues.[522] Once the ground(s) of the controversy are set, the case proceeds with the gathering of evidence which would either substantiate the ground(s) upon which it is based or uphold the presumption of validity. It is crucial that the correct basis be established, so that when the evidence is forthcoming, the judge (or judges) will have the necessary information from which to arrive at moral certitude that the marriage is indeed invalid as alleged in the petition or, failing to do so, to uphold the presumption that the marriage is valid, and thus render a negative decision in response to the doubt formulated by the *contestatio litis*. Thus, it is important that the Presiding Judge not only know the various grounds of nullity but also understand the differences between them. Sometimes distinctions between the grounds are subtle; other times the differences are quite clear. It is hoped that the following will be beneficial in more thoroughly understanding the ground of ignorance.

As we have stated throughout this study, ignorance is best understood in the Thomistic sense as the lack of due knowledge, i.e., the absence of knowledge which a person ought to have.[523] This description presupposes that the person is capable of, but for some reason does not possess, the knowledge he or she is expected to have. Thus, there is no overriding organic or psychic anomaly which prevents the person from having the due knowledge; rather, the opportunity for the experience from which such knowledge would have been gained has been wanting. With this understanding in mind, it is evident that ignorance must first be distinguished from the causes of marriage nullity listed in canon 1095.[524]

---

[522]Canon 1513, §1. "Contestatio litis habetur cum per iudicis decretum controversiae termini, ex partium petitionibus et responsionibus desumpti, definiuntur" ("The joinder of the issue (*contestatio litis*) occurs when the terms of the controversy, derived from the petitions and responses of the parties, are defined through a decree of the judge"). English translation of the 1983 *CIC* in the *Code of Canon Law; Latin-English Edition*, New English translation, Washington, DC, Canon Law Society of America, 1999, p. 471. All translations of the 1983 *CIC* are taken from this edition unless otherwise noted. This is paralleled in the *CCEO*, canon 1195, §1.

[523]*Summa theologiae*, IaIIae, q. 76, 2: "Ignorantia vero importat scientiae privationem, dum scilicet alicui deest scientia eorum quae aptus natus est scire", ("Ignorance denotes a privation of knowledge, i.e., lack of knowledge of those things that one has a natural aptitude to know"), THOMAS AQUINAS, *Summa theologiae*, vol. 2, Prima Secundae, Ottawa, Impensis Studii Generalis O. Pr., 1941, p. 1131 b; English translation in *The "Summa Theologica" of St. Thomas Aquinas*, 2nd ed., vol. 7, Fathers of the English Dominican Province, London, Burns, Oates & Washborne Ltd., 1927, p. 350. All citations of the *Summa theologiae* of Thomas Aquinas will be taken from these editions.

[524]C. ALUEDE OJEMEN, *Psychological Factors in Matrimonial Consent in the Light of Canonical Legislation*, Roma, Pontificia Universitas Urbaniana, 1986, p. 140.

a. Ignorance and canon 1095 (*CCEO* c. 818)

Canon 1095 — The following are incapable of contracting marriage:
1° those who lack the sufficient use of reason;
2° those who suffer from a grave defect of discretion of judgment concerning the essential matrimonial rights and duties mutually to be handed over and accepted;
3° those who are not able to assume the essential obligations of marriage for causes of a psychic nature.[525]

Canon 1095 deals with the incapacity to consent.[526] While the 1917 *CIC* had no substantive norm concerning capacity for marriage,[527] the Roman Rota was already adjudicating cases on various titles such as *amentia*, insanity and lack of discretion of judgment, often making reference to canons 1081, §1;[528] 1089,

---

[525]Canon 1095. "Sunt incapaces matrimonii contrahendi:
1° qui sufficienti rationis usu carent;
2° qui laborant gravi defectu discretionis iudicii circa iura et officia matrimonialia essentialia mutuo tradenda et acceptanda;
3° qui ob causas naturae psychicae obligationes matrimonii essentiales assumere non valent."

[526]For in-depth studies on canon 1095, see, among others, L. ANNÉ, "Le consentement matrimonial et l'incapacité psychique", in *Ephemerides iuris canonici*, 44 (1988), pp. 7-15; C. BURKE, "Reflexiones en tornos al canon 1095", in *Ius canonicum*, 31 (1991), pp. 85-105; R.L. BURKE and D.E. FELLHAUER, "Canon 1095: Canonical Doctrine and Jurisprudence", in *CLSA Proceedings*, 48 (1986), pp. 94-117; D.E. FELLHAUER, "Psychological Incapacity for Marriage in the Revised Code of Canon Law", in *Proceedings of the 5ᵗʰ International Congress of Canon Law*, vol. 2, M. THÉRIAULT and J. THORN, eds., Ottawa, Faculty of Canon Law, Saint Paul University, 1986, pp. 1019-1040; A. MENDONÇA, "Incapacity to Contract Marriage", in *Studia canonica*, 19 (1985), pp. 259-325; "Consensual Incapacity for Marriage", in *The Jurist*, 54 (1994), pp. 477-559; J.H. PROVOST, "Canon 1095: Past, Present, Future", *ibid.*, pp. 81-112.

[527]J.M. SERRANO RUIZ, "Let Us Talk about Incapacity", in *A Swing of the Pendulum: Canon Law in Modern Society*, Monsignor W. Onclin Chair Addendum, Leuven, Katholieke Universiteit, Uitgeveru Peeters, 1996, p. 14.

[528]"Matrimonium facit partium consensus inter personas iure habiles legitime manifestatus; qui nulla humana potestate suppleri valet" ("Marriage is effected by the consent of the parties lawfully expressed between persons who are capable according to law; and this consent no human power can supply"), translation as in T.L. BOUSCAREN, A.C. ELLIS, F.N. KORTH, eds., *Canon Law: A Text and Commentary*, 4ᵗʰ revised ed., Milwaukee, Bruce Publishing Company, 1966, p. 565.

106

§3,[529] and 1982[530] as well as to canon 1082, on ignorance.[531] One distinction to keep in mind, especially when considering numbers 1 and 2 of canon 1095, is that ignorance is the defect of due knowledge while incapacity to consent is the impossibility of reaching this knowledge.[532]

1. Lack of sufficient reason (1°)

Within the context of matrimonial consent, a person who lacks sufficient use of reason[533] is understood to be one who is incapable of performing a human act.[534] This incapacity may be due to something disrupting his or her nature , i.e., by disease (any number of illnesses that attack or affect the mind) or by a condition (such as severe mental retardation). It can also be the result of some disturbing circumstance, i.e., some type of trauma, abuse of alcohol or mind altering drugs, etc.[535] Since the canon does not indicate whether this lack of sufficient reason needs to be permanent or temporary, it is held that if the person was affected at the time of consent,[536] he or she was incapable of taking personal responsibility for the action.[537]

The person who lacks sufficient use of reason is incapable of entering marriage since such a person is incapable of performing a human act. This incapacity is differentiated from ignorance, first of all, because

---

[529]Concerning marriages contracted by proxy: "Si, antequam procurator nomine mandantis contraxerit, hic mandatum revocaverit aut in amentiam inciderit, invalidum est matrimonium, licet sive procurator sive alia pars contrahens haec ignoraverint" ("If, before the proxy has contracted in the name of the principal, the latter has revoked the mandate or become insane, the marriage is invalid, even though these facts were unknown to the proxy or to the other contracting party"), translation from *ibid.*, p. 578.

[530]"Etiam in causis defectus consensus ob amentiam, requiratur suffragium peritorum, qui infirmum, si casus ferat, eiusve acta quae amentiae suspicionem ingerunt, examinent secundum artis praecepta; insuper uti testes audiri debent periti qui infirmum antea visitaverint" ("In cases of lack of consent for reason of insanity, the opinion of experts is also required. These shall, if the case demands it, examine the insane person and the actions which arouse suspicion of insanity according to the rules of science. Moreover, the experts who formerly visited the patient must be heard as witnesses"), translation as in S. WOYWOD, *A Practical Commentary on the Code of Canon Law*, vol. II, rev. and enlarged ed. by C. SMITH, New York, Joseph F. Wagner, Inc., 1957, p. 381.

[531]As a good example, see *coram* WYNEN of 1 March 1930, in *SRR Dec*, 22 (1930), pp. 125-153, which discusses these three titles while quoting canons 1081, §1; 1082, §1, and 1982 as part of the *in iure* section.

[532]J.M. SERRANO RUIZ, "Can a Personal Vision of Marriage Be Supported by the Notions of Ignorance, Error, Deceit, Condition ...Such as They Are Given in cc. 1096ff.?", in *A Swing of the Pendulum: Canon Law in Modern Society*, Monsignor W. Onclin Chair Addendum, Leuven, Katholieke Universiteit, Uitgeveru Peeters, 1996, p. 31.

[533]For more in-depth analyses of this title, see H.M. NAYAKAM, *"Use of Reason" in Marriage: Doctrine and Jurisprudence Based on Canon 1095 — 1°*, Extractum ex Dissertatione ad Doctoratum in Facultate Iuris Canonici, Romae, Pontificia Universitas Urbaniana, 1995, especially pp. 11-29, as well as citations listed for canon 1095, 2°.

[534]MENDONÇA, "Consensual Incapacity for Marriage", pp. 489-490. See also K. RAYAPPEN, *Discretion in Marriage, Doctrine and Jurisprudence: A Study of Canon 1095 — 2° with Special Reference to the Indian Context*, Extractum ex Disseratione ad Doctoratum in Facultate Iuris Canonici, Roma, Pontificia Universitas Urbaniana, 1993, pp. 9-14.

[535]MENDONÇA, "Consensual Incapacity for Marriage", p. 490. See also PROVOST, "Canon 1095: Past, Present, Future", pp. 93-94. For a concise study on this topic, see J.R. KEATING, "The Legal Test of Marital Insanity", in *Studia canonica*, 1 (1967), pp. 21-36.

[536]MENDONÇA, "Consensual Incapacity for Marriage", pp. 491-492.

[537]F.G. MORRISEY, "The Incapacity of Entering into Marriage", in *Studia canonica*, 8 (1974), p. 13.

the presumption of canon 1096 is that the person who is ignorant is capable of making a decision concerning marriage.[538] and secondly, although the person has sufficient use of reason, because of circumstances up to this moment in time, he or she lacks the knowledge necessary to make the informed decision to enter marriage.

This is an important distinction to make since the majority of Rotal sentences, which are cited as *fontes* for canon 1095, 1°,[539] referred to canon 1082 as a basis for *amentia*. One, *coram* CANESTRI of 16 July 1943, was actually based on both incapacity to give consent (*amentia*) and ignorance. For the most part, though, the sentences cited as *fontes* for canon 1095, 1°, involved *amentia*.[540] *Amentia* was the general juridical term for a psychological condition which rendered the act of marriage consent null.[541] In the 1917 *CIC*, *amentia* was considered, as it were, as a species of ignorance, i.e., an insane person was one who had insufficient intellectual insight or lacked deliberation in the will.[542] While the roots of canon 1095, 1°, are found in cases pertaining to *amentia* and ignorance, the actual wording of this number has greater ramifications. Specifically, at the time of consent, a person would have to lack that use of reason which is necessary and sufficient to know what marriage is as described in canon 1096.[543]

2. Grave defect of discretion of judgment (2°)

Myriads of research and writing have been done concerning discretion of judgment.[544] It is beyond

---

[538]Whereas canon 1095 begins with a negative proposition, "Sunt incapaces matrimonii contrahendi" ("The following are incapable of contracting marriage"), canon 1096 begins with the statement, "Ut consensus matrimonialis haberi possit, necesse est ut..." ("For matrimonial consent to exist, it is necessary that..."), indicating that those entering marriage are able to give valid consent but something, i.e., knowledge, may be lacking in one or both.

[539]See *Codex iuris canonici; fontium annotatione et indice analytico-alphabetico auctus*, auctoritate Ioannis Pauli PP. II promulgatus, Vatican City, Libreria editrice Vaticana, 1989, p. 301.

[540]Of the eleven Rotal decisions listed in the *fontes*, all concerned *amentia* with the exceptions of *coram* WYNEN, 13 April 1943, in *SRR Dec.* 35 (1943), pp. 270-281, which dealt with the trauma of falling out of an airplane (temporary insanity); *coram* CANESTRI, 16 July 1943, *ibid.*, pp. 594-612, which was based on ignorance; and *coram* POMPEDDA, 3 July 1979, in *SRR Dec.* 71 (1979), pp. 379-399, which involved psychoses. Two cases, *coram* SABATTANI, 24 February 1961, in *SRR Dec.* 53 (1961), pp. 116-132, and *coram* FELICI, 22 May 1956, in *SRR Dec.* 48 (1956), pp. 467-475, while dealing with *amentia*, were also concerned with chronic alcoholism and fear, respectively.

[541]R.L. BURKE, "Canon 1095, 1° and 2°: Presentation I: Canonical Doctrine", in *Incapacity for Marriage; Jurisprudence and Interpretation: Acts of the III Gregorian Colloquium, 1-6 September 1986*, R. SABLE, ed., Rome, Pontificia Universitas Gregoriana, 1987, p. 89.

[542]*Ibid.*, pp. 113-115. See also SERRANO, "Can a Personal Vision of Marriage Be Supported by the Notions of Ignorance, Error, Deceit, Condition ...", p. 31.

[543]PROVOST, "Canon 1095: Past, Present, Future", p. 93.

[544]For examples, see ALUEDE OJEMEN, *Psychological Factors in Matrimonial Consent in the Light of Canonical Legislation*; C. BURKE, "Some Reflections on Canon 1095", in *Monitor ecclesiasticus*, 117 (1992), pp. 133-150; "The Distinction between 2° and 3° of Canon 1095", in *The Jurist*, 54 (1995), pp. 228-233; R.L. BURKE, "Lack of Discretion of Judgment: Canonical Doctrine and Legislation", in *The Jurist*, 45 (1985), pp. 171-209; "Canon 1095, 1° and 2°: Presentation I: Canonical Doctrine", in *Incapacity for Marriage*, pp. 81-108; "Canon 1095, 1° and 2°: Presentation II: Canonical Legislation", *ibid.*, pp. 109-128; "Canon 1095, 1° and 2°: Presentation III: Jurisprudence", *ibid.*, pp. 129-155; "Grave difetto di discrezione di giudizio: fonte di nullità del consenso matrimoniale", in *Ius canonicum*, 31 (1991), pp. 139-154; E.M. EGAN, "The Nullity of Marriage for Reason of Insanity or Lack of Due Discretion of Judgment", in *Ephemerides iuris canonici*, 39 (1983), pp. 9-54; D.E. FELLHAUER,

108

the scope of this study to enter into that discussion. For our purposes, however, we shall endeavor to present a definition of this term and show how it relates to ignorance. The commentators of the 1917 *CIC* considered *amentia* as a species of ignorance, for "ignorance of the substance of marriage" was sometimes used as a parameter in cases of incapacity to measure the use of reason or "due discretion" without realizing that ignorance was precisely the defect of possible knowledge, while incapacity was the impossibility of reaching this knowledge.[545]

Discretion of judgment is defined as the ability or power to discern particular goods and make particular judgments by differentiating and assessing those goods.[546] Pertaining to marriage, this discretion is related to the maturity of judgment a person acquires after puberty, which allows him or her to enter into a valid union.[547] It is more than simply the use of reason; rather a maturity or discretion of judgment is to be required that is proportionate to the contract. Thus the contractant is to be able to understand the nature and force of the marital contract; otherwise he or she is not able to consent to it.[548] This understanding of discretion of judgment was further clarified in the often cited *coram* SABATTANI sentence of 24 February 1961 when he writes, "The only measure of sufficient consent is the discretion of judgment proportionate to marriage."[549]

Discretion of judgment is the ability to understand and assess, in a critical manner, the rights and obligations which would result from the decision to marry, and understanding these, the person proceeds with the decision. It takes more than mere knowledge to make such an assessment. Thomas Aquinas points this out when he states, "greater discretion of reason is required for looking to the future than for consenting to one present act."[550] As Keating points out:

---

[545]"Psychological Incapacity for Marriage in the Revised *Code of Canon Law*", pp. 1019-1040; J.A. FUENTES, ed., *Incapacidad consensual para las obligaciones matrimoniales*, Pamplona, Ediciones Universidad de Navarra, 1991; L. GUTIÉRREZ MARTÍN, *La incapacidad para contraer matrimonio: Comentarios al c. 1095 del Código de derecho canónico para uso de los profesionales del foro*, Estudios 88, Salamanca, Universidad Pontificia de Salamanca, 1987; MENDONÇA, "The Incapacity to Contract Marriage: Canon 1095", pp. 259-325; M.F. POMPEDDA, "Maturità psichica e matrimonio nei canoni 1095, 1096", in *Apollinaris*, 57 (1984), pp. 131-150; "Incapacity to Assume the Essential Obligations of Marriage: Presentation I: General Overview and Exegesis of Key Terms", in *Incapacity for Marriage: Jurisprudence and Interpretation: Acts of the III Gregorian Colloquium, 1-6 September 1986*, R. SABLE, ed., Rome, Pontificia Universitas Gregoriana, 1987, pp. 157-178; J.H. PROVOST, "Canon 1095: Past, Present, Future", pp. 81-112; "Canon 1095, 2° Seen from Its Sources", *The Jurist*, 56 (1996), pp. 824-874.
For examples of recent Rotal jurisprudence, see *coram* TURNATURI, 22 April 1998, in *Monitor ecclesiasticus*, 124 (1999), pp. 292-333; *coram* De LANVERSIN, 15 May 1997, *ibid.*, pp. 458-489; and *coram* STANKIEWICZ, 24 July 1997, *ibid.*, pp. 614-669.

[545]SERRANO, "Can a Personal Vision of Marriage Be Supported by the Notions of Ignorance, Error, Deceit, Condition...", p. 31.

[546]I. GRAMUNT and L.A. WAUCK, "«Lack of Due Discretion»: Incapacity or Error?", in *Ius canonicum*, 32 (1992), p. 537.

[547]*Ibid.*, p. 536.

[548]See *coram* GRAZIOLI, 1 July 1933, in *SRR Dec*, 25 (1933), p. 407: "At non sufficit usus rationis simpliciter, sed requiritur discretio seu maturitas iudicii contractui proportionata; ita ut contrahens naturam et vim contractus intelligere possit; secus in eumdem consentire nequit."

[549]"Unica mensura sufficientis consensus est discretio iudicii matrimonio proportionata", (*SRR Dec*, 53 [1961], p. 118).

[550]*Summa theologiae, Suppl.*, q. 43, 2: "Major autem discretio rationis requiritur ad providendum in futurum, quam ad consentiendum in actum unum praesentem", THOMAS AQUINAS, *Summa theologiae, Supplementum tertiae partis* (= FRETTÉ), from S.E. FRETTÉ and P. MARÉ, eds., *Opera omnia Thomae Aquinatis*, vol. 6, Parisiis, L. Vivès, 1874, p. 63; English translation

Due discretion for valid marriage does not mean merely the relative aptitude of the psychic powers which is necessary and sufficient to elicit naturally sufficient consent. It is rather the minimum relative aptitude, maturity, integrity of the psychic powers which is necessary that a person, by dint of the natural law, can effectively oblige himself by the marriage contract.[551]

Ignorance, on the other hand, is the absence of due knowledge, i.e., that degree of knowledge which a person within a given situation is expected to have concerning a particular object. While a person may have due knowledge of an object, he or she may lack the ability to make a critical assessment of that object in a given situation.

Sabattani, in the above cited decision, makes this same assessment and further states the difference between lack of discretion of judgment and ignorance:

5. The inability to exercise discretionary judgment is not reducible to a mere question of ignorance.

It is necessary to establish this in order to give a correct decision in the case we are addressing. Both defects are considered consensual defects, since in reality they both lessen the action of the intellect. But — as Lorenc notes so well — «essentially each of these seems to have characteristics distinct from the other: the use of reason and the element of mature discretion are so radically proper to the subject, that they should apparently be considered under the category of the capacity of the persons; on the other hand, necessary knowledge and the apprehension of truth pertain directly rather to a defect in the act of giving consent» ("De ignorantiae influxu in matrimoniali consensu", in *Apollinaris*, 1953, pp. 348-349).

Hence, it is possible that a sufficient knowledge of matrimonial matters can exist simultaneously with a defect in judgmental discretion. This latter defect is attributed more to internal distortions of the development and activation of deliberation than to an inadequate or false understanding of the contract's object.[552]

In other words, the discretion of judgment necessary for marriage means there is the capacity to know,

---

from *The "Summa Theologica" of St. Thomas Aquinas, (Supplement)*, vol. 19, literally translated by the Fathers of the English Dominican Province, London, Burns Oates & Washburn Ltd, 1932, p. 101. For more on discretion of judgment in Thomas Aquinas, see R.L. BURKE, "Canon 1095, 1° and 2°", pp. 96-99.

[551]J.R. KEATING, *The Bearing of Mental Impairment on the Validity of Marriage: An Analysis of Rotal Jurisprudence*, Analecta Gregoriana, 136, Roma, Gregorian University Press, 1964, p. 170.

[552]"5. —*Quaestio defectus discretionis iudicii non reducitur ad meram quaestionem ignorantiae*. Hoc necesse est statuere in recte diiudicanda causa, quae Nos intentos tenet.
Uterque defectus venit nomine vitii consensus, cum reapse aliquid detrahat intellectui. Sed — ut merito notat Lorenc — «in se unum caput ad altero distinctum characterem videtur praebere: nam usus rationis et maturae discretionis elementum ita radicaliter proprium subiecti est, ut sub consideratione *capacitatis personarum* tractandum videatur; e contra, scientia debita et apprehensio veritatis potius ad defectum *ipsius actus* emissionis consensus directe pertinent» (*De ignorantiae influxu in matrimoniali consensu*, in «Apollinaris», 1953, pp. 348-349).
"Componi ideo potest cognitio sat plena de re matrimoniali cum defectu discretionis iudicii, qui defectus magis attingit intimas distorsiones efformationis et excitationis deliberationis quam inadaequatam vel falsam apprehensionem obiecti contractus", *SRR Dec.* 53 (1961), p. 118. English translation from J.H. PROVOST, "Cases; Sources for Canon 1095, 1°, Part Two", in *The Jurist*, 54 (1994), pp. 672-673. It is to be noted that this Rotal decision is listed as one of the *fontes* for both 1° and 2° of canon 1095.

to estimate and to choose. Knowledge means an abstract apprehension of the object under the heading of what is true. Estimation introduces a critical capacity about the object. Choice involves the possibility of bringing the intended object together with various motives in order to choose.[553] As Mendonça points out:

> Choice of any state in life in the Church presupposes sufficient human maturity proportionate to that state. ... In order to contract marriage, therefore, sufficient psychological maturity which enables a person to perceive critically and freely to choose marriage with all its rights and obligations is essential. This "psychological maturity" which enables a person to form a valid consent is expressed in law in terms of "discretion of judgment."[554]

3. Inability to assume essential obligations (3°)

Numbers 1 and 2 of canon 1095 concern the capacity of the individual to form and give valid consent. In number 3,[555] however, the act of consent is presumed to be sufficient but the person has been so affected in some manner ("due to causes of a psychic nature") that he or she is unable to assume those obligations which were promised.[556] Thus, the formal elements of the act of consent may not necessarily be affected; rather it is the formal object of consent.[557] Stankiewicz clearly points this out:

> Incapacity to assume the duties, as prevalent jurisprudence of the Rota contends, does not affect the "formal elements of consent," namely "estimative knowledge and will eliciting consent in the aspect of its operation"; it concerns the "object of consent".... For, incapacity consists in the defect of matrimonial consent "insofar as the person contracting is unable to give and accept the right to the body which has been anticipated by natural law."[558]

---

[553]"...discretionem matrimonio proportionatam inducere capacitatem cognoscendi, aestimandi atque seligendi. Cognitio dicit abstractam apprehensionem obiecti sub specie veri, aestimatio inducit capacitatem criticam circa idem obiectum, selectio secumfert possibilitatem conferendi intentum obiectum cum variis motivis ad electionem faciendam", *coram* FIORE, 30 May 1987, in *SRR Dec*, 79 (1987). p. 337; English translation in J.A. ALESANDRO, ed., *Marriage Studies IV*, Washington, DC, Canon Law Society of America, 1990, pp. 17-18.

[554]MENDONÇA, "Consensual Incapacity for Marriage", pp. 492-493.

[555]For more in-depth analysis of this title, see citations for canon 1095, 2°, as well as P.G. BIANCHI, *Incapacitas assumendi obligationes essentiales matrimonii; analisi della giurisprudenza rotale, particolarmente degli anni 1970-1982*, Roma, Pubblicazioni del Pontificio Seminario Lombardo di Roma, 1992, specifically pp. 159-273; L. RUANO ESPINA, *La incapacidad para asumir las obligaciones escenciales del matrimonio por causas psiquicas, como capitulo de nulidad*, Barcelona, Libreria Bosch, 1989, specifically pp. 53-252.

[556]BURKE, "Canon 1095, 1° and 2°; Presentation I: Canonical Doctrine", p. 85.

[557]MENDONÇA, "Consensual Incapacity for Marriage", p. 506.

[558]"Incapacitas assumendi onera, sicut contendit praevalens Jurisprudentia Nostri Fori, non inficit «elementa formalia consensus», id est «cognitionem aestimativam et voluntatem consensum elicientem sub ratione operationis», tangit autem «obiectum consensus» (decis. *coram* ANNÉ, d. 17 januarii a. 1967, n. 11; *SRR Dec*, vol. LIX, pp. 28-29). Incapacitas enim consistit *in defectu obiecti* consensus matrimonialis «in quantum contrahens incapax sit tradere — acceptare ius in corpus quale a iure naturae praevideatur» (decis. *coram* LEFEBVRE, d. 2 decembris a. 1967, n. 10; vol. LIX, p. 804; — cf. decis. coram BONET, d. 12 decembris a. 1955, n. 2; vol. XLVII, p. 842)", *coram* STANKIEWICZ, 16 December 1982, in *Ephemerides iuris canonici*, 39 (1983). pp. 255-256; English translation from MENDONÇA, "Consensual Incapacity for Marriage", pp. 506-507.

Whereas numbers 1 and 2 of this canon concern directly the act of consent, and knowledge could have ramifications upon the decision to marry, ignorance — as a ground for marriage nullity — needs to be distinguished from the incapacity as delineated in these two titles. However, in number 3, the consent could be intact; there is sufficient use of reason, estimative knowledge and sufficient discretion of judgment.[559] The incapacity lies in the inability of the contractant to assume the essential obligations which he or she is pledging in marriage. In other words, while due knowledge is presumed in the person, it is the will which is lacking.[560] The reasons for this inadequacy in the will must specifically be due to causes of a psychic nature (*ob causas naturae psychicae*).[561] As Mendonça points out:

> The incapacity to assume the essential obligations of marriage causes the nullity of marriage by the fact it affects the will in the very act of election or decision. The election, which is formally an act of the will, of an impossible obligation is empty and inefficacious, nor can it by its very nature produce juridic effects. The will that chooses such an impossible obligation lacks power over what is willed; it lacks the faculty to dispose that object which it cannot retain constantly. For, if the will is inefficient in marriage, it does not produce the effects, namely it cannot establish the conjugal state.[562]

Since it is not a question of knowledge but rather one of inability to assume, i.e., the contractant knows, at least to some extent, what the essential obligations are but is incapable to assume them, we may conclude that there should be little, if any, confusion between the ground of ignorance and the incapacity listed in canon 1095, 3°.

b. Ignorance and error (cc. 1097, 1098, 1099; *CCEO* cc. 820, 821, 822)

There has been a great deal written in canon law concerning the concept of error[563] and its relationship

---

[559]POMPEDDA, "Incapacity to Assume the Essential Obligations of Marriage", p. 171.

[560]See MENDONÇA, "Consensual Incapacity for Marriage", p. 508.

[561]See MENDONÇA, "Incapacity to Contract Marriage: Canon 1095", pp. 295-297; POMPEDDA, "Incapacity to Assume the Essential Obligations of Marriage", pp. 165-167; PROVOST, "Canon 1095: Past, Present, Future", pp. 101-102.
  L. ÖRSY, "Matrimonial Consent in the New Code: *Glossae* on Canons 1057, 1095-1103, 1107", in *The Jurist*, 43 (1983), p. 43, writes concerning the translation of the phrase *ob causas naturae psychicae*:
  "Is it 'for causes of *psychic* nature,' or 'for causes of *psychological* nature'? *Psychic* in English implies some disposition in the *psyche* which is out of the ordinary although not necessarily abnormal. *Psychological* indicates no special disposition, just a movement in the *psyche*, a rather ordinary event which may interfere with the act of consenting. Subtle as this distinction is, it has down-to-earth practical consequences. If 'causes of *psychic* nature' are required to impede consent, the judge may well start searching for out-of-the-ordinary dispositions, such as obsession, narcissism, etc.; if 'causes of *psychological* nature' are enough he may take into account rather ordinary events, e.g., transient emotional disturbances, stresses and tensions originating within a physical illness, etc."

[562]MENDONÇA, "Consensual Incapacity for Marriage", p. 508.

[563]For in-depth works pertaining to error, see the articles in issue I-II of *Monitor ecclesiasticus*, "Errore e dolo nel consenso matrimoniale canonico", 120 (1995), pp. 5-158; and number 69 of *Ius canonicum*, "Estudios sobre el error y el dolo en el matrimonial canónico", 35 (1995), pp. 13-198. See also C. BURKE, "The Effect of Fraud, Condition and Error in Marital Consent: Some Personalist Considerations", in *Monitor ecclesiasticus*, 122 (1997), pp. 295-310, 513-519; E. COLAGIOVANNI, "New (Hot) Grounds of Nullity in Marriage Cases", in *ibid.*, pp. 521-552.

112

to ignorance.[564] As was discussed earlier in this work, canonists, especially those in Europe, referred to ignorance as "error of substance", "substantial error" or "error of law",[565] thus equating ignorance with error.[566] Both concepts deal with the intellect[567] and are understood as defects of knowledge concerning juridic acts. Both are also classified as sources of marriage nullity (*capita nullitatis*) under lack of valid consent, defects of knowledge.[568]

The 1983 *CIC* contains three canons which pertain to error and its effect on marriage: 1097[569] (error of person and error of quality of a person, also known as error of fact), 1098[570] (*dolus* or imposed error), and

---

[564]For examples, see P.A. BONNET, "L'errore nel matrimonio canonico", in *Studi in onore di Pietro Agostino d'Avack*, vol. 1, Pubblicazioni della Facultà di Giurisprudenza dell'Università di Roma, Milano, A. Giuffrè Editore, 1976, pp. 367-376; "Errore di diritto e necessità della coscienza dell'importanza vitale dell'opzione matrimoniale", in *Il diritto ecclesiastico*, 94 (1983) 2, pp. 462-481; "L'errore di diritto giuridicamente rilevante nel consenso matrimoniale canonico", in *Studi in memoria di Pietro Gismondi*, vol. I, Pubblicazioni della Facultà di Giurisprudenza, Università degli studi di Roma, Milano, A. Giuffrè Editore, 1987-1988, pp. 137-172; GRAMUNT and WAUCK, "«Lack of Due Discretion»: Incapacity or Error", pp. 543-546; J.A. MÖHLER, "De errore in qualitate communi ad nuptias quaesita", in *Apollinaris*, 34 (1961), pp. 371-372, 385-387; P. PELLEGRINO, "L'errore di diritto nel matrimonio canonico (cann. 1096 - 1099)", in *Il diritto ecclesiastico*, 108, (1997) 1, pp. 363-404; I.M. SÁNCHEZ, "Causa, error y simulación en el matrimonio canónico", in *Studi in onore di Pietro Agostino d'Avack*, vol. 3, Pubblicazioni della Facultà di Giurisprudenza dell'Università di Roma, Milano, A. Giuffrè Editore, 1976, pp. 53-122; A. STANKIEWICZ, "L'errore di diritto nel consenso matrimoniale e la sua autonomia giuridica", in *Periodica*, 83 (1994), pp. 635-668; E. TEJERO, "La ignorancia y el error sobre la identidad del matrimonio", in *Ius canonicum*, 35 (1995), pp. 13-101; S. VILLEGGIANTE, "Errore e voluntà simulatoria nel consenso matrimoniale in diritto canonico", in *Monitor ecclesiasticus*, 109 (1984), pp. 487-516.

[565]See O. GIACCHI, *Il consenso nel matrimonio canonico*, 3rd ed., Milano, A. Giuffrè Editore, 1968, pp. 56-59. See also G. CARNERO, "Nulidad por error acerca de persona o de sus cualidades", in *Las causas matrimoniales: trabajos de la cuarta semana de derecho canónico celebrada en el monasterio Na. Sa. de Montserrat*, Salamanca, Tipografía FLO-REZ, 1953, p. 205. The author states here that the effect of ignorance is the same as that of error "...claramente que el efecto psicológico del error y de ignorancia sobre el acto voluntario son idénticos." O. FUMAGALLI CARULLI, "La relazione dinamica tra il can. 1082 e il can. 1081 *Cod. Iur. Can.*", in *Ephemerides iuris canonici*, 34 (1978), pp. 247-279, interchanges ignorance and error. Likewise, E. GRAZIANI, *Volontà attuale e volontà precettiva nel negotio matrimoniale canonico*, Pubblicazioni dell'Istituto di scienze giuridiche, economiche, politiche e sociali della Università di Messina, 34, Milano, A. Giuffrè Editore, 1956, p. 98, calls error "a subspecies of ignorance". See also J.M. MANS PUIGARNAU, *El consentimiento matrimonial: defecto y vicios del mismo como causas de nulidad de las nupcias*, Barcelona, Bosch, 1956, pp. 21, 108-115. WERNZ-VIDAL, *Ius canonicum*, vol. 5, *Ius matrimoniale*, pp. 596-623, lists canon 1082 under error.

[566]PELLEGRINO, "L'errore di diritto nel matrimonio canonico (cann. 1096 - 1099)", p. 364: "...alcuni autori parlano di *ignorantia in re matrimoniali*, altri parlano invece di *error iuris* (errore ostativo di diritto)."

[567]Specifically pertaining to error as existing in the intellect, see P. HENNESSEY, "Canon 1097: A Requiem for *Error Redundans*?", in *The Jurist*, 49 (1989), p. 160 and footnote 32 on the same page.

[568]GRAMUNT and WAUCK, "«Lack of Due Discretion»: Incapacity or Error?", p. 534.

[569]Canon 1097, §1: "Error in persona invalidum reddit matrimonium.
§2: "Error in qualitate personae, etsi det causam contractui, matrimonium irritum non reddit, nisi haec qualitas directe et principaliter intendatur."
Canon 1097, §1: "Error concerning the person renders a marriage invalid.
§2: "Error concerning a quality of the person does not render a marriage invalid even if it is the cause of the contract, unless this quality is directly and principally intended."

[570]Canon 1098: "Qui matrimonium init deceptus dolo, ad obtinendum consensum patrato, circa aliquam alterius partis qualitatem, quae suapte natura consortium vitae coniugalis graviter perturbare potest, invalide contrahit" ("A person contracts invalidly who enters into a marriage deceived by malice, perpetrated to obtain consent, concerning some quality of the other partner

1099[571] (error of law). Whereas we define ignorance as a lack of due knowledge, error is wrong, or false, knowledge.[572] People who are in error know something, and they know that they know something, but what they know is not correct.[573] Error can be seen from two perspectives: on the one hand, it can refer to the state of mind of the parties, and on the other hand the content of their mistake.[574] It is beyond the scope of this study to give an exhaustive commentary on the specific contents of each canon relating to error. The purpose of this section is simply to differentiate ignorance from error.

As to canon 1097, §1, error of person, ignorance would not enter into the discussion: the person simply marries the wrong person. This error about the physical identity of the other spouse substantially destroys the act of marital consent because such an error totally vitiates the object of the will act, i.e., the intended exchange of marital rights with this other definite person.[575] This is a case of mistaken identity, not one of ignorance.

In §2, however, whether the person is ignorant or is in error of a specific quality, the juridic effect is the same and therefore the two need not be distinguished[576] as we find in Thomas Aquinas:

> Speaking simply, ignorance differs from error, because ignorance does not of its very nature imply an act of knowledge, while error supposes a wrong judgment of reason about something. However, as regards being an impediment to the voluntary, it differs not whether we call it ignorance or error, since no ignorance can be an impediment to the voluntary, unless it have error in conjunction with it, because the will's act presupposes an estimate or judgment about something which is the object of the will. Wherefore if there be ignorance there must needs be error; and for this reason error is set down as being the proximate cause.[577]

---

which by its very nature can gravely disturb the partnership of conjugal life").

[571]Canon 1099: "Error circa matrimonii unitatem vel indissolubilitatem aut sacramentalem dignitatem, dummodo non determinet voluntatem, non vitiat consensum matrimonialem" ("Error concerning the unity, indissolubility or sacramental dignity of marriage does not vitiate matrimonial consent provided that it does not determine the will").

[572]See also THOMAS AQUINAS, *Summa theologiae, Suppl.*, q. 51, art. 1, 1; PROVOST, "Error as a Ground in Marriage Nullity Cases", p. 308; L.G. WRENN, *The Invalid Marriage*, Washington, DC, Canon Law Society of America, 1998, pp. 92, 96.

[573]PROVOST, "Error as a Ground in Marriage Nullity Cases", p. 308.

[574]See P. VIDAL, *Institutiones iuris civilis romani*, Prati, ex officina Libraria Giachetti, 1915, p. 87: "[E]rrore...est falsa apprehensio rei sive falsa unius pro alio aestimatio seu iudicium positivum falsum de obiecto." English translation in P. HENNESSY, *A Canonical-Historical Study of Error of Person in Marriage*, Roma, Pontificia Studiorum Universitas a S. Thoma Aq. in Urbe, 1978, p. 35.

[575]K. BOCCAFOLA, "Deceit and induced error about a personal quality", in *Monitor ecclesiasticus*, 124 (1999), p. 697.

[576]WRENN, *The Invalid Marriage*, p. 96.

[577]*Summa theologiae, Suppl.*, q. 51, art. 1, 1: "Ad primum ergo dicendum quod ignorantia differt, simpliciter loquendo, ab errore, quia ignorantia de sui ratione non importat aliquem cognitionis actum; sed error ponit iudicium rationis perversum de aliquo. Tamen quantum ad hoc quod est impedire voluntarium, non differt utrum dicatur ignorantia vel error. Quia nulla ignorantia potest impedire voluntarium nisi quae habet errorem adiunctum, eo quod actus voluntatis praesupponit aestimationem sive iudicium de aliquo in quod fertur; unde si est ibi ignorantia, oportet ibi esse errorem. Et ideo etiam ponitur error, quasi causa proxima", FRETTÉ, vol. 6, p. 91; English translation from *The "Summa Theologica" of St. Thomas Aquinas*, (Supplement), vol. 19, 1932, pp. 166-167.

The lack of due knowledge mentioned in canon 1096 concerns specifically marriage as a (1) permanent (2) *consortium* (3) between a man and a woman (4) ordered to the procreation of offspring (5) by means of some sexual cooperation. Therefore, while the juridic effect may be the same, none of the elements listed in canon 1096 are found in canon 1097. Furthermore, this error of quality does not render consent invalid unless it is "directly and principally intended"[578] by the other person, a phrase specifically used by the Code Commission so new and abusive interpretations would be curbed.[579] With the addition of this particular phrase, ignorance cannot be applied not only because the criteria listed in canon 1096 are not present but also because one must know, i.e., be conscious, of the quality which he or she is "directly and principally" intending. Thus there is knowledge, albeit false, which would preclude ignorance. For the sake of argument, it can be maintained that the person in error was ignorant of the fact that the other party did not possess that quality which he or she directly and principally intended, and thus ignorance was the cause of the error. Ignorance, however, cannot be utilized as the ground for nullity in this case because the specificity of what one at least must not be ignorant of, which is delineated in canon 1096, is not present.

In canon 1098, while there is also a quality of the other party which is "unknown" to the other, thus likening it to canon 1097, §2, the differences are that the "unknowing" party was deceived by *dolus*, perpetrated specifically to obtain consent, and this quality, by its very nature, can seriously disturb the *consortium* of conjugal life. *Dolus* is a deliberate act of deception involving forethought (*astutia*) on the part of the deceiver. It is perpetrated to effect an error in another party which will cause that party to act in accordance with the will of the deceiver.[580] The *dolus* must be fraudulently and deliberately committed by someone in order to induce one of the parties to consent to marriage. There must be a connection first between the *dolus* and the error and then between the error and the consent.[581] It does not matter who did the actual deceiving; rather, the purpose was precisely to obtain matrimonial consent.[582] Furthermore, the deception concerned a quality which, by its very nature,
can gravely disturb the *consortium*. While the canon gives an objective criterion, i.e., the quality can gravely disturb marital life,[583] there is openness to subjective criteria which would vary from person to person,

---

[578]Following the third rule of St. Alphonsus Liguori concerning *error redundans*: "si *consensus fertur directe et principaliter in qualitatem*, et minus principaliter in personam" ("if consent is made directly and principally in the quality and less principally in the person") from A. DE LIGUORI, *Theologia moralis*, L. GAUDÉ, ed., Romae. ex Typographia Vaticana, 1905, vol. 4, lib. 6, n. 1016, p. 179; English translation in HENNESSEY, "Canon 1097: A Requiem for *Error Redundans*?", p. 168.

[579]See U. NAVARRETE, "Error in persona (c. 1097 §1)", in *Periodica*, 87 (1998), pp. 392-393: "La volontà della *Commissione di Revisione*...di presentare un testo che esprimesse la stessa dottrina e la stessa disciplina, ma fosse più chiaro e quindi fosse più adatto ad arginare le interpretazioni nuove e abusive che si erano manifestate negli ultimi anni. A questo scopo si ritenne opportuno eliminare dal canone il termine «error qualitatis redundans in errorem personae» e fare in esso esplicita menzione dell'«error qualitatis directe et principaliter intentae»."

[580]P.T. SUMNER, "*Dolus* as a Ground for Nullity of Marriage", in *Studia canonica*, 14 (1980), p. 178.

[581]BOCCAFOLA, "Deceit and induced error about a personal quality", p. 704.

[582]J.I. BAÑARES, "La relación intelecto-voluntad en el consentimiento matrimonial: notas sobre los cc. 1096-1102 del CIC de 1983", in *Ius canonicum*, 33 (1993), p. 595: "En cuanto al *sujeto* — o sujetos — causantes, es irrelevante quiénes sean — la comparte, o terceros —, puesto que la manipulacióon, su objecto, y su alcance, resultarían idénticos en cualquier caso, ya que tienen lugar en la *pars decepta*; pero se exige sin embargo la intención de engañar precisamente para obtener el consentimiento matrimonial..."

[583]BOCCAFOLA, "Deceit and induced error about a personal quality", pp. 705-706.

depending upon particular circumstances.[584]

Once again, as in the case of canon 1097, §2, there is knowledge, and again it is erroneous. However, in canon 1098, the false knowledge was purposely caused by *dolus*. It is not so much the *dolus* which affects marital consent but rather the error induced by the *dolus*.[585] Since there is knowledge (erroneous as it may be), then ignorance cannot be used.

In canon 1099, there is a distinctiveness to the error in question, i.e., the error concerns unity, indissolubility or sacramental dignity. It is beyond the scope of this study to enter into the discussion about what quantity or quality of error is needed to determine the will. However, it is important for our understanding to clarify how this particular error differs from ignorance.

The "error" mentioned in canon 1099 implies an incorrect judgment, a wrong conclusion, a false understanding of unity, indissolubility or sacramental dignity which a person has when entering marriage. It is first to be noted that none of these is part of the substance of marriage, as listed in canon 1096. Rather, unity and indissolubility are essential properties of marriage as stated in canon 1056.[586] Thus, according to canon 1099, if one is in error about one of these properties, or the sacramental dignity of marriage, and that error determines the will, that person invalidly contracts marriage. In other words, when there is error, the person has reached a conclusion (about one or more of these attributes) and that conclusion is wrong. The person knows something but does not realize what is known is incorrect. This is different from being ignorant about these characteristics where the person simply does not know about them and thus has no preconceived notions about them. Furthermore, both canons are very explicit: canon 1096 lists what a person must at least not be ignorant of; canon 1099 specifically determines the content of the error. In canon 1099 there are three qualities of which the contracting party is to have knowledge and, although such knowledge may be incorrect, the fact remains that unity, indissolubility and sacramental dignity are known. Therefore, both, in our opinion, are mutually exclusive by virtue of the contents of the canons and what is perceived to be known or not known.

c. Ignorance and Simulation (c. 1101; *CCEO* c. 824)

Canon 1101

§1: The internal consent of the mind is presumed to conform to the words and signs used in celebrating the marriage.

§2: If, however, either or both of the parties by a positive act of the will exclude marriage itself, some essential element of marriage, or some essential property of marriage, the party contracts invalidly.[587]

---

[584]BLANCO, M., "El dolo: requisitos y prueba", in *Ius canonicum*, 35 (1995), pp. 192-193.

[585]BOCCAFOLA, "Deceit and induced error about a personal quality", p. 695.

[586]Canon 1056: "Essentiales matrimonii proprietates sunt unitas et indissolubilitas, quae in matrimonio christiano ratione sacramenti peculiarem obtinent firmitatem" ("The essential properties of marriage are unity and indissolubility, which in Christian marriage obtain a special firmness by reason of the sacrament").

[587]Canon 1101, §1: "Internus animi consensus praesumitur conformis verbis vel signis in celebrando matrimonio adhibitis."
§2: "At si alterutra vel utraque pars positivo voluntatis actu excludat matrimonium ipsum vel matrimonii essentiale aliquod elementum, vel essentialem aliquam proprietatem, invalide contrahit."

116

Traditionally, simulation [588] can be either total or partial, as has been the common and consistent jurisprudence of the Roman Rota.[589] The distinction between each is stated succinctly in *coram* FUNGHINI, 14 October 1992:

It has become customary in both doctrine and jurisprudence to consider the two-fold simulation: total is the marriage itself is excluded, and partial if the essential goods or even any essential element is excluded.[590]

The distinction between total and partial simulation is also clarified in *coram* PALESTRO, 27 May 1992:

Whoever totally simulates has no intention whatsoever of contracting marriage; but whoever excludes some property of marriage wants to contract marriage, but does so as it is conceived by onself, namely its object is something else from that object unto which, by its very nature, matrimonial consent is directed.[591]

Generally speaking, simulation consists in a positive act of the will excluding something essential and the result of this exclusion is that the marriage is contracted invalidly.[592] In other words, simulation consists in a deliberately intended discrepancy between the internal will and its external manifestation.[593] Thus, simulation arises when a person knows what is correct, objectively speaking, but excludes it from the act of

[588]For more in-depth studies on simulation, see C. BURKE, "Simulated Consent", in *Forum*, 9 (1998) 2, pp. 65-82; G. CANDELIER, "La simulation d'après les sentences de Mgr José Maria Serrano Ruiz", in *Studia canonica*, 31 (1997), pp. 373-402; J. FORNÉS, "Simulación y condicio", in *Ius canonicum*, 33 (1993), pp. 295-311; F. GIL DE LAS HERAS, "El concepto canónico de simulación", in *Ius canonicum*, 33 (1993), pp. 229-257; P. KITCHEN, "Matrimonial Intention and Simulation", in *Studia canonica*, 28 (1994), pp. 347-406; A. MENDONÇA, "Exclusion of the Sacramentality of Marriage: Recent Trends in Rotal Jurisprudence", in *Studia canonica*, 31 (1997), pp. 5-48; S. PANIZO, "Exclusión de la indisolubilidad del matrimonio", in *Ius canonicum*, 33 (1993), pp. 259-293; E.G. PFNAUSCH, "Simulated Consent: A New Way of Looking at an Old Way of Thinking, Part II", in *The Jurist*, 55 (1995), pp. 721-739; J.H. PROVOST, "Simulated Consent: A New Way of Looking at an Old Way of Thinking, Part I", *ibid.*, pp. 698-720; "Simulated Consent: A New Way of Looking at an Old Way of Thinking, Part III", *ibid.*, pp. 740-744; ROBITAILLE, "Simulation, Error Determining the Will, or Lack of Due Discretion? A Case Study", pp. 397-432; A. STANKIEWICZ, "De iurisprudentia rotali recentiore circa simulationem totalem et partialem (cc. 1101, §2 CIC; 824, §2 CCEO)", in *Monitor ecclesiasticus*, 122 (1997), pp.189-234; 425-512; "Concretizzazione del fatto simulatorio nel «positivus voluntatis actus»", in *Quaderni studio rotale*, 9 (1998), pp. 34-51.

[589]STANKIEWICZ, "De iurisprudentia rotali recentiore circa simulationem totalem et partialem", p. 203.

[590]*Coram* FUNGHINI, 14 October 1992, in *SRR Dec*, 84 (1992), p. 467: "Usu venit in doctrina et jurisprudentia duplicem considerare simulationem, totalem si matrimonium ipsum excluditur, partialem si bona essentialia vel essentiale quoddam elementum excluditur." See STANKIEWICZ, "De iurisprudentia rotali recentiore circa simulationem totalem et partialem", p. 204.

[591]*Coram* PALESTRO, 27 May 1992, *ibid.*, pp. 281-282: "Qui totaliter simulat nullam habet intentionem contrahendi matrimonium, qui vero aliquod excludit bonum vult, e contra, matrimonium contrahere, sed idem intendit utpote a se conceptum, nempe eius obiectum est aliquid aliud ab obiecto in quod, natura sua, matrimonialis consensus fertur." See STANKIEWICZ, "De iurisprudentia rotali recentiore circa simulationem totalem et partialem", p. 208.

[592]PROVOST, "Simulated Consent, Part I", p. 702.

[593]"Simulatio autem consistit in deliberate intenta a subiecto (simulante) *discrepantia* inter voluntatem internam et externam eius manifestationem seu declarationem", STANKIEWICZ, "De iurisprudentia rotali recentiore circa simulationem totalem et partialem", p. 200.

the will by which marriage is contracted.[504] Simulation, then, occurs when a person says one thing but actually wants something else. There is a divergence or contradiction of wills or intentions:[595] a dichotomy between what is expected and what is actually intended by the simulator. There is conflict between the belief system of the person and the teaching of the Church and the person resolves it in favor of self rather than in favor of the Church. If a person is aware that his or her lifestyle and beliefs are contrary to what the Church understands as marriage and persists in adhering to them at the time of consent, then simulation occurs.[596] The conformity between the mind and what is communicated, as presumed in canon 1101, §1, therefore, does not exist.

Simulation may occur not only because of a conscious exclusion but also because of a conscious inclusion of elements which would contradict the understanding of marriage taught by the Church. In *coram* De LANVERSIN, 31 July 1990, we read:

> Total simulation arises not only by the exclusion of marriage itself, or of the other party, but also by including elements which radically contradict those of the community of life and love established by the Creator's laws.[597]

For the marriage nullity, it is not necessary that both parties simulate consent, but it suffices if at least one of the two parties does, and this is because of the individuality of the marriage contract.[598] Since §1 is a presumption of law, there must be facts to the contrary in order to overturn it and this consists in proving the existence of a contrary "positive act of the will".[599]

Simulation differs from both ignorance and error. There is no conflict or dichotomy between what is externally expressed and what one knows (which would result from error) or does not know (which would be ignorance). In cases of ignorance there is no positive act of the will to exclude something essential or include something contrary to what the Church teaches and understands about marriage.[600]

Simulation is distinct from ignorance. In order to "say one thing and think another", there must already be some kind of knowledge present. Although this knowledge is incorrect or perceived to be incorrect

[504]PROVOST, "Error as a Ground in Marriage Nullity Cases", p. 308.

[595]D.M. CAMPBELL, "Canon 1099: The Emergence of a New Juridic Figure?", in *Quaderni studio rotale*, 5 (1990), p. 57. See also S. VILLEGGIANTE, "Errore e volontà simulatoria nel consenso matrimoniale in diritto canonico", p. 508.

[596]L.A. ROBITAILLE, "Simulation, Error Determining the Will, or Lack of Due Discretion? A Case Study", p. 414.

[597]*Coram* De LANVERSIN, 31 July 1990, in SRR Dec, 82 (1990), p. 678: "Simulatio totalis perficitur etiam non solum per exclusionem ipsius matrimonii, vel istius nupturientis, sed etiam per inclusionem elementorum quae radicitus contradicunt illi communitati vitae et amoris quae firmatur a lege Creatoris (Dec. Coram Collagiovanni, diei 25 maii 1982, ARRT Dec., vol. LXXIV, p. 292)." English translation in PROVOST, "Simulated Consent, Part I", p. 710.

[598]STANKIEWICZ, "De iurisprudentia rotali recentiore circa simulationem totalem et partialem", p. 201, quoting *coram* FALTIN, 18 January 1988, in *SRR Dec*, 80 (1980), p. 5: "[A]d nullitatem matrimonii non requiritur, ut «utraque pars», sed sufficit, ut saltem «alterutra pars» consensum simulat, propter individualitatem contractus matrimonialis."

[599]For a more detailed study on this topic, see J.M. SERRANO RUIZ, "What about that Famous 'Positive' Act of the Will?", in *A Swing of the Pendulum: Canon Law in Modern Society*, Monsignor W. Onclin Chair Addendum, Leuven, Katholieke Universiteit, Uitgeveru Peeters, 1996, pp. 21-30; and L.A. ROBITAILLE, "Proofs in Defect of the Will Cases: Jurisprudence regarding Positive Acts of the Will Contrary to Marriage", in *CLSA Proceedings*, 57 (1995), pp. 337-354.

[600]See PROVOST, "Simulated Consent, Part I", p. 706.

118

on the part of the simulator,[601] it is precisely the fact that the person not only has knowledge but also is aware that this knowledge is in conflict with the Church, which results in simulation. Furthermore, taking into consideration the specific knowledge which a person is at least not to be ignorant of, as listed in canon 1096, it seems quite clear that simulation and ignorance are mutually exclusive of each other.

Another interesting scenario proposed by various authors under the ground of simulation is that of "non-inclusion",[602] i.e., rather than consciously excluding marriage or an essential part or an essential element, the party/parties did not include it. Other versions of non-inclusion have been identified as "inadequate consent" and "lack of commitment". Under these headings, the person entering marriage fails to have the motivation or commitment needed for fulfilling the consent he or she is making.[603] Principally, these headings have been used by tribunals in England, Ireland, Scotland and Wales[604] seeing it as a form of simulation (either total or partial) or lack of due discretion.[605] While these authors hold it is a form of simulation, other authors, including A. Stankiewicz, do not.[606]

Rather than taking sides in this particular issue or proposing another heading for nullity, we wish to introduce another approach. The authors already mentioned state that there is an invalid marriage due to the lack of commitment or non-inclusion because there is an inadequate consent, based on canon 1057:

§1: The consent of the parties, legitimately manifested between persons qualified by law, makes marriage; no human power is able to supply this consent.

§2: Matrimonial consent is an act of the will by which a man and a woman mutually

---

[601]ROBITAILLE, on page 413 of her article, "Simulation, Error Determining the Will, or Lack of Due Discretion? A Case Study", makes a very interesting and insightful observation. She states that while there is the straightforward understanding of ignorance, i.e., a person may be truly unaware of the teachings of the Church, there is also a second possibility: a person may be aware of the Church's teachings in a general way but is not aware that his or her erroneous beliefs are against the Church's teachings. She refers to both of these scenarios as "the issue of ignorance of the Church's teaching of marriage". While the first example is a classic illustration of ignorance, the second one is nuanced and deserving of further consideration.

In regard to this proposal, we could note that canon 1096 does not simply reiterate "the teachings of the Church" but rather states the understanding of marriage founded in the natural law, since we are dealing with the minimum of knowledge necessary to inform the will in order to act so that consent can be made.

[602]See the decision *coram* SHEEHY, in the *Canon Law Society of Great Britain Newsletter*, 6 (1974), Appendix II, pp. 1-21. See also the writings of R. BROWN, specifically "Inadequate Consent or Lack of Commitment: Authentic Grounds for Nullity?", in *Studia canonica*, 9 (1975), pp. 249-265; "Total Simulation — A Second Look", in *Studia canonica*, 10 (1976), pp. 235-249; "Non-Inclusion: A Form of Simulation?", in *CLSA Proceedings*, 71 (1979), pp. 1-11; and "Simulation Versus Lack of Commitment", in *Studia canonica*, 14 (1980), pp. 335-345. See also J. HUMPHREYS, "Lack of Commitment in Consent", in *Studia canonica*, 2 (1976), pp. 345-362.

[603]BROWN, "Inadequate Consent of Lack of Commitment", pp. 251-252.

[604]BROWN, "Total Simulation — A Second Look", p. 235.

[605]BROWN, "Inadequate Consent of Lack of Commitment", pp. 250-253.

[606]See STANKIEWICZ, "De iurisprudentia rotali recentiore circa simulationem totalem et partialem", p. 205. To corroborate his position, he quotes *coram* POMPEDDA, 9 May 1970, in *SRR Dec*, 62 (1970), p. 476: "Ad simulationem matrimonii efficiendam non sufficit simplex *absentia* intentionis contrahendi. Consensus etenim externe manifestatur per actum positivum voluntatis, qui eliditur tantummodo per contrarium actum positivum."

give and accept each other through an irrevocable covenant in order to establish marriage.[607]

Their conclusion, however, was that the party or parties either simulated consent (canon 1101, §2) or lacked the discretion of judgment (canon 1095, §2) necessary to give full consent. Rather than place the titles of non-inclusion, lack of commitment and inadequate consent either under the headings of simulation or grave lack of discretion of judgment, the research and jurisprudence of these titles[608] could be applied to utilize canon 1096 to a much greater extent. Let us explain.

Canon 1057 refers to marriage which is described in canon 1055, §1:

> The matrimonial covenant, by which a man and a woman establish between themselves a partnership of the whole of life and which is ordered by its nature to the good of the spouses and the procreation and education of offspring, has been raised by Christ the Lord to the dignity of a sacrament between the baptized.[609]

Marriage is further described in canon 1056:

> The essential properties of marriage are unity and indissolubility, which in Christian marriage obtain a special firmness by reason of the sacrament.[610]

Thus, according to canon 1057, in order to "make" marriage, the consent of the parties must include that they are establishing a partnership of the whole of life, whose essential properties are unity and indissolubility, which is ordered to the good of the spouses and the procreation and education of offspring. Three similarities between canon 1055, §1, and canon 1096, §1, can be identified: (1) the joining of a man and a woman (2) into a partnership (*consortium*) which (3) is ordered to the procreation of offspring.[611] The most important point for our study is the *consortium*. Given today's society with its many prevalent

---

[607]Canon 1057, §1: "Matrimonium facit partium consensus inter personas iure habiles legitime manifestatus, qui nulla humana potestate suppleri valet."
§2. "Consensus matrimonialis est actus voluntatis, quo vir et mulier foedere irrevocabili sese mutuo tradunt et accipiunt ad constituendum matrimonium." This was also seen in canon 1081 of the 1917 *CIC*, where the wording of §1 is identical and §2 was reformulated in light of Vatican II.

[608]The *Combined Index to the Matrimonial Decisions of England and Wales (1967-1979) and the Matrimonial Decisions of Great Britain and Ireland (1980-1989)*, pp. 57-59, lists 151 descriptions of cases adjudicated under the title of "Inadequate Consent". It is to be noted that not all these cases could be used, since some descriptions (e.g., husband's drinking problem [p. 57]; parents pressurized couple into marriage [p. 58]; husband was narcissistic [p. 59] to name a few) would more fittingly be placed under other headings of nullity.

[609]Canon 1055, §1: "Matrimoniale foedus, quo vir et mulier inter se totius vitae consortium constituunt, indole sua naturali ad bonum coniugum atque ad prolis generationem et educationem ordinatum, a Christo Domino ad sacramenti dignitatem inter baptizatos evectum est."

[610]Canon 1056: "Essentiales matrimonii proprietates sunt unitas et indissolubilitas, quae in matrimonio christiano ratione sacramenti peculiarem obtinent firmitatem."

[611]We have already described in earlier chapters how unity and exclusivity and indissolubility and permanence are similar but not identical.

"mentalities" (e.g., divorce,[612] contraception, infidelity, machismo and feminism to name a few), we propose, for the sake of further study and development, that contractants can be ignorant of what the Church understands marriage to be, especially in regard to the *consortium* according to canon 1055, and thus canon 1057 is not fulfilled and marriage is not established. Because of ignorance of the *consortium*, there is an inadequate consent, a lack of commitment to the marriage or a non-inclusion of good of the spouses or the procreation and education of children and, possibly, the essential properties.

Similarly, the understanding of the *bonum coniugum*[613] might be better served by using it in relation to the non-inclusion title under ignorance rather than under simulation following the criteria mentioned above. This may well allow the *bonum coniugum* to "come of age" so to speak. Rather than debate whether it is one of the *bona* as understood in Augustinan terms[614] and whether it can be included in simulation[615] or psychic incapacity,[616] it can be seen as what it is: an essential element of the *consortium*.[617] If a party is ignorant of the *bonum coniugum*, which is an essential element of the *consortium*, then he or she cannot give full consent to marriage. If full consent is not given, then marriage, according to canon 1057, §1, is not brought into existence. This could certainly be an area where more research and discussion can be done.

d. Ignorance and Condition (c. 1102; *CCEO* c. 826)

Canon 1102
§1: A marriage subject to a condition about the future cannot be contracted validly.
§2: A marriage entered into subject to a condition about the past or the present is valid or not insofar as that which is subject to the condition exists or not.
§3: The condition mentioned in §2, however, cannot be placed licitly without

---

[612]Concerning the divorce mentality, see the Pope's allocution to the Roman Rota, 21 January 2000, "The Ratified and Consummated Sacramental Marriage", in *Origins*, 29 (1999-2000), pp. 553-555.
We can also add an "annulment" mentality; see C.J. VAN DER POEL, "Influences of an 'Annulment Mentality'", in *The Jurist*, 40 (1980), pp. 384-399.

[613]For recent articles concerning this subject, see C. BURKE, "The *Bonum Coniugum* and the *Bonum Prolis*; Ends or Properties of Marriage?", in *The Jurist*, 49 (1989), pp. 704-713; J.A. DEWHIRST, "*Consortium Vitae, Bonum Coniugum*, and Their Relation to Simulation: A Continuing Challenge to Modern Jurisprudence", in *The Jurist*, 55 (1995), pp. 794-812; M.F. POMPEDDA, "Il «bonum coniugum» nella dogmatica matrimoniale canonica", in *Quaderni studio rotale*, 10 (1999), pp. 5-21, and L.A. ROBITAILLE, "Simulation and the *bonum coniugum*; 'In love we choose to live'", in Canon Law Society of Australia and New Zealand, *Proceedings of the Thirty Second Annual Convention*, September 21-25, 1998, pp. 15-23.

[614]For example, see BURKE, "The *Bonum Coniugum* and the *Bonum Prolis*", pp. 705-709.

[615]See ROBITAILLE, "Simulation and the *bonum coniugum*". On p. 17, she writes: "Nonetheless, neither exclusion of the *bonum coniugum* as total or partial simulation has yet been proven at the Roman Rota (although it is being used as a ground of nullity by first instance tribunals). Rather, the Rota has only spoken theoretically, thus far, on the issue and dealt practically with the question of the *bonum coniugum* and incapacity."

[616]See M.F. POMPEDDA, "Il «bonum coniugum» nella dogmatica matrimoniale canonica", p. 6.

[617]DEWHIRST, "*Consortium Vitae, Bonum Coniugum*, and Their Relation to Simulation", p. 799. See also A. MENDONÇA, "The Theological and Juridical Aspects of Marriage", in *Studia canonica*, 22 (1988), pp. 286-287.

the written permission of the local ordinary.[618]

A condition[619] exists when a person makes one thing a prerequisite for another.[620] In other words, a condition is a circumstance attached to the marriage on which the validity of the marriage depends;[621] it is a circumstance to which the consent in the marriage contract is attached in such a way that the validity of the marriage depends on the fulfillment or the non-fulfillment of that circumstance.[622] In the strict sense, conditions are circumstances which refer to the future; in the broad sense, these circumstances can refer to the past or present.[623]

For a clearer understanding of condition, it must be differentiated from other concepts which are similar, but not identical: mode, cause, demonstration, postulate, prerequisite and supposition. In *coram* De LANVERSIN, the following distinctions concerning these terms are made:

> *Condition* is defined as a circumstance which is attached to an act and whose value it suspends for a future and uncertain time. A true condition must not be confused:
> — with a *mode* or burden, with which we want to oblige the contracting party after the fulfilment of the act;
> — with a *cause*, which denotes the "motive for contracting";
> — with a *demonstration*, or quality by which the person with whom one is contracting is determined or described;
> — with a *postulate*, which affects the intention to contract, but not the consent itself;
> — with a *prerequisite*, on which one's will to marry depends;

---

[618]Canon 1102. §1 "Matrimonium sub condicione de futuro valide contrahi nequit."

§2: "Matrimonium sub condicione de praeterito vel de praesenti initum est validum vel non, prout id quod condicioni subest, exsistit vel non."

§3: "Condicio autem, de qua in §2, licite apponi nequit, nisi cum licentia Ordinarii loci scripto data."

In the *CCEO*, canon 826 is much simpler: "Matrimonium sub condicione valide celebrari non potest"("Marriage based on a condition cannot be validly celebrated").

[619]For more in-depth studies on condition, see BURKE, "The Effect of Fraud, Condition and Error in Marital Consent: Some Personalist Considerations", pp. 302-307; P.R. LAGGES, "Conditional Consent to Marriage", in *CLSA Proceedings*, 58 (1996), pp. 237-260; P. LORENZO, "Jurisprudencia rotal sobre el estado de duda en el consentimiento condicionado", in *Ius canonicum*, 33 (1993), pp. 189-225; L.A. ROBITAILLE, "Conditioned Consent: Natural Law and Human Positive Law", in *Studia canonica*, 26 (1992), pp. 75-110; "The Ground of Conditioned Consent", in *Forum*, 8 (1997) 1, pp. 95-127. This latest article lists many resources, both books and articles concerning condition, in footnote 2, p. 95. See also L.G. WRENN, *Law Sections*, Washington, DC, Canon Law Society of America, 1994, pp. 72-81.

For a recent example of Rotal jurisprudence, see *coram* De LANVERSIN of 17 July 1996, in *Forum*, 9 (1998) 1, pp. 227-251.

[620]PROVOST, "Error as a Ground in Marriage Nullity Cases", p. 308.

[621]WRENN, *The Invalid Marriage*, p. 155.

[622]D.J. BURNS, *Matrimonial Indissolubility: Contrary Conditions; A Historical Synopsis and a Commentary*, Canon Law Studies, 377, Washington, DC, The Catholic University of America, 1963, p. 79.

[623]ROBITAILLE, "The Ground of Conditioned Consent", p. 96. See also WRENN, *The Invalid Marriage*, p. 155.

122

— with a *supposition*, by which a determined quality is required in the partner.[624]

It is important to note that when speaking of conditions in relationship to marriage, matrimonial consent is what is conditioned, not the marriage itself. If a condition is placed, marriage itself does not yet exist.[625] According to the 1917 *CIC*, if a future condition were placed, the marriage did not come into existence until the condition was fulfilled. In the 1983 *CIC*, however, the marriage is invalid (canon 1102, §1).[626] If it is a past or present condition, the marriage exists or not at the time of consent (canon 1102, §2), even though the condition may or may not be verified for years.[627] Thus, it is more correct to say that the internal consent, the act of willing, receives the condition rather than the contract.[628] Therefore, we are placing conditions in the category of marriage nullity cases involving intention rather than capacity or knowledge.[629]

A condition has, as its effect, either rendering the action invalid (if the condition is not fulfilled), suspending its efficacy or allowing the action to be rescinded at some later date.[630] It is precisely this understanding of conditional consent which differentiates the *CIC* from the *CCEO*. For where the *CIC* lists past, present and future conditions, the *CCEO* simply states that a marriage based on a condition cannot be celebrated. Pospishil explains the reason:

> Eastern marriage law sees the marriage rite as a religious celebration, culminating in the blessing imparted by the priest. This cannot be reconciled with a marriage of which the validity is not yet known to exist, or not existing at all. Hence a marriage which is claimed and proved to have been entered on condition will be declared invalid due to a defect in the consent: "The blessing of the marriage cannot be realized except if the consent is granted without any condition."[631]

A condition affects the intention and thus the will, but that does not mean that the intellect is not

---

[624]*Coram* De LANVERSIN, 17 July 1996, in Forum, 9 (1998) 1, pp. 233-234. ROBITAILLE, "The Ground of Conditioned Consent", pp. 101-103, distinguishes condition from a presupposition, a postulation, a cause and a mode. Both LAGGES, "Conditional Consent to Marriage", pp. 248-250, and WRENN, *The Invalid Marriage*, pp. 158-159, differentiate condition from a mode, cause, demonstration and postulate. V.J. POSPISHIL, *Eastern Catholic Church Law*, 2nd re. ed., Staten Island, New York, St. Maron Publications, 1996, p. 566, speaks of mode, cause and demonstration.

[625]LAGGES, "Conditional Consent to Marriage", p. 246. See also BURNS, *Matrimonial Indissolubility: Contrary Conditions*, pp. 87-88.

[626]ROBITAILLE, "The Ground of Conditioned Consent", p. 99.

[627]*Ibid.*, p. 100.

[628]B.T. TIMLIN, *Conditional Matrimonial Consent: An Historical Synopsis and Commentary*, Canon Law Studies, 89, Washington, DC, The Catholic University of America, 1934, pp. 132-133.

[629]LAGGES, "Conditional Consent to Marriage", p. 247. Here the author clarifies these categories in footnote 25: lack of capacity (canon 1095), lack of knowledge (ignorance, qualitative error or fraud), or lack of intention (simulation, condition, determinative error, force or fear).

[630]*Ibid.*, p. 246.

[631]POSPISHIL, *Eastern Catholic Church Law*, p. 566. See also WRENN, *The Invalid Marriage*, pp. 161-162.

involved. Rather, the intellect is necessary in order for a condition to be formulated.[632] As Burns points out, quoting Conte a Coronata:

> Both the intellect and the will operate in the conditional consent: the intellect considers the circumstances which are the object of the condition, and presents them to the will; the will gives consent to the contractual obligations only dependently, making the matrimonial consent depend on the fulfillment of the condition. This does not mean, however, that these are two distinct acts; it is one act, but an act which is not simple, but conditional.[633]

Regarding ignorance and condition: while ignorance may sometimes play a part in the placing of a condition, its role is very specified, i.e., the person who is placing the condition may be ignorant about whether the condition itself is invalidating. This is demonstrated in a sentence *coram* PINTO, 26 June 1971:

> Jurisprudence, even Rotal jurisprudence, has sometimes held that a true condition can only be placed by a person who is aware of its invalidating effect. But this is not true. People are generally aware of such legalities and in no way realize that entering marriage conditionally results in invalidity. All they know is that on occasion a particular circumstance is so important to them that they rate it higher than marriage itself and that, if they cannot have the circumstance or quality, they do not want the marriage either. Now everybody agrees that that sort of mentality or intention conditions marital consent. And consequently Rotal jurisprudence, especially as it has evolved in recent years, holds that a true condition can coexist with ignorance of its invalidating effect as long as it is clear that the person would not have consented to marry unless the quality had been present.[634]

It is evident, however, that the person placing the condition is aware of the fact that he or she is actually doing so, whether explicitly or implicitly, because in order for a condition to be formulated there must be a positive act of the will.[635] A positive act of the will presupposes the interaction of an informed intellect so that a condition may be established in the first place. In the case of ignorance, the person lacks the minimal knowledge of certain essential elements and/or characteristics of marriage and because of this, the marriage is invalid. In the case of condition there is not a lack of knowledge, but rather a lack of intention. That is to

---

[632]LAGGES, "Conditional Consent to Marriage", p. 247.

[633]BURNS, *Matrimonial Indissolubility: Contrary Conditions*, p. 84. "Conditio duo importat: respectum intellectus ad circumstantiam illam quae est ipsum conditionis obiectum et actum voluntatis quo negotium iuridicum, matrimonium dependenter ab illa circumstantia initur. Actus tamen voluntatis ad negotium seu matrimonium necessarius et appositio conditionis, ut diximus, non sunt duo actus distincti, sed unicus actus non purus nec simplex sed conditionatus", in M. CONTE A CORONATA, *De sacramentis;tractatus canonicus*, vol. 3, *De matrimonio*, Taurini, Marietti, 1945, p. 665.

[634]"Aliquando iurisprudentia, etiam N. S. T., tenuit veram conditionem tantummodo apponi posse ab illo qui eius effectum dirimentem noverat. Quod quidem nequit admitti. Plerumque fideles, iuris ignari, minime sciunt se matrimonium sub conditione cum effectu dirimenti contrahere valere. Tantummodo sciunt se aliquando circumstantiam quamdam tanti facere ut matrimonio anteponant et, nisi ipsa exsistat, nuptias nolunt. Tunc matrimonialem consensum conditionatum esse nemo negabit. Ideo iurisprudentia N. S. T., praesertim recens, tenet veram conditionem cum ignorantia ipsius effectus dirimentis exstare posse, dummodo constet, illa deficiente, consensum matrimonialem haud datum fore", *SRR Dec*, 63 (1971), p. 560; English translation in WRENN, *The Invalid Marriage*, p. 157.

[635]ROBITAILLE, "The Ground of Conditioned Consent", p. 103.

124

say, the intellect truly grasps what marriage is and would allow the person to enter into a valid marriage; however, at the same time, the intellect also considers specific conditions under which the person will give consent to that marriage, thus placing restrictions on the will and making the marriage invalid if the condition is not fulfilled.

II. CANON 1096 AND THE TRIBUNAL

Having established the distinctions between ignorance and other grounds of marriage nullity, we can now determine how best to proceed in order to utilize the insights gained. First, we shall address possible ways a person who is considering marriage could be ignorant of what marriage is. This will, by no means, be an exhaustive list. It will, however, be a starting point from which other insights and observations may be drawn so that the possibilities of utilizing canon 1096 may be enhanced.

Second, what are the questions to be asked of the person in order to establish whether he or she was truly ignorant, in accord with the norm of canon 1096. The more focused and precise the question, the more valuable the information to be extracted. In other words, what are the "ground specific" issues that need to be raised in order to determine whether or not the person was ignorant of marriage?

Third, once the basic information has been collected from the parties and witnesses and the case moves into the decision phase of the process, how is the data to be applied to the case at hand? Proposed elements of a sample law section concerning ignorance, therefore, is presented in the Appendix, thus complementing this section.

a. The person who is ignorant of marriage

Given the sexual milieu of today's society, especially in North America, where sexual innuendo as well as explicit sexual overtones are commonplace throughout the various forms of the media (radio, television, movies, theater productions and, in an ever increasing way, the internet), the primary question of whether a couple knows how to engage in sexual intercourse, which was the fundamental question upon which the jurists applying canon 1082 concentrated, has almost come to be non existent. While it is true that such a person may come forward (which will be discussed), the question is not so much whether the person knows "how" to do it as much as whether the person knows the context within which intercourse is to occur.

1. In general

Sabattani, in his 22 March 1963 Rotal decision, listed four criteria to use when considering ignorance as a possible invalidating factor in marriage consent:

a) Psycho-physical criterion: Ignorance of sexual things is more likely present in those whose psycho-physical development is imperfect...more frequently the lacking psychic development will be apparent through enfeebled sexual instinct.
b) Educational criterion: It is necessary to consider the location (national, regional, community, district) in which the party lived, the persons with whom he/she lived and formed his/her frame of mind, if the party was shy of friendships and lived a solitary adolescence. Ignorance is more likely in those whose education was rigid and narrow, who received an outdated and constricted moral formation, and whose parents were severe.

c) Prenuptial criterion: which can be considered in two ways — examining the *cause of marriage*, if the party spoke of a wrong estimate of the nature of marriage, astonished at the most intimate sense in marriage; if, on the contrary, the person was forced into the marriage, especially by the mother; examining the *conduct of the party during the engagement*: if the person acted and spoke in childish, uncontrolled, silly and thoughtless ways.

d) Postnuptial criterion: One is most carefully to assess the conduct of the party when he/she perceives the true nature of the conjugal purpose. If this was a reaction of horror and repugnance, or if the party made it clear to the other party that she/he did not know what was expected of her/him, or, even after being instructed by the other party, she/he could not be persuaded to have sexual intercourse, then there is a presumption that the party was truly ignorant about the giving and acceptance of the right [*circa traditionem-acceptationem iuris in corpus*] to acts which of their nature are open to the procreation of children.[636]

While these criteria were developed before the 1983 *CIC*, they are still just as pertinent today, especially if we substitute "procreation of offspring by means of some sexual cooperation", as stated in canon 1096, for the phrase *ius in corpus* in the fourth criterion. Thus, these criteria could, and should, be more widely employed.

2. Influence of culture

In the discussion of the effect of ignorance upon marriage, we must also be aware of the influence of culture. While we may speak of an "American culture", we must also realize that there are subcultures within this context which will affect mentalities, relationships and, of course, marriage.[637] Pope John Paul II

---

[636]*SRR Dec*, 55 (1963), pp. 209-210: "*a) Criterium psyco-physicum*. Ignorantia rerum sexualium (ex qua errores) potest quandoque esse primaria, sed frequentius apparet secundaria evolutioni psycho-physicae [sic] imperfectae... Sed frequentius apparebit deficiens evolutio psychica *per mancum instinctum genesicum... b) Criterium educationis*. Considerare oportet locum (nationem, regionem, civitatem, pagum) in quo degit pars... personas quibuscum vixit earumque formam mentis, si amicitias (et cuius generis) foverit, si adolescentiam solitariam duxerit. Sed praesertim aestimari debet educatio ab illa recepta, si nimis rigida, si angusta, si antiquis omnino moribus constricta; si parentes severiores... *c) Criterium praenuptiale*, quod dupliciter considerari potest: — examinando *causam contrahendi*, si pars quae dicitur falso aestimasse naturam matrimonii, intimo sensu ducta in nuptias inhiabat; si. e contra, uti frequenter in huiusmodi factispeciebus, ad coniugum adigebatur praesertim a matre; — esaminando [sic] *modum se gerendi eiusdem partis in sponsalibus*: si modum gesserit puerilem, si sermones fuderit ingenuos et ridendos; si futiles et improvidas apprehensiones expresserit. *d) Criterium postnuptiale*. Plurimum valet perpendere quomodo se gesserit illa pars, quando percepit suum iudicium de natura coniugii obiectivae veritati haud respondere... [S]i, pars horrorem et repugnantiam expresserit plenam; si alteri parti debitum petenti responderit verbis et magis adhuc gestibus se non intelligere quid quaeratur et expectetur ab ea; si, patienter edocta de coniugali obligatione, sibi intime persuadere non possit matrimonium tale debitum exigere et protestetur tale officium se non esse impleturam; *tunc trahi debet praesumptio partem illam erravisse* circa traditionem-acceptationem iuris in corpus", English translation based on *coram* PAYNE, [Dublin], 29 September 1988, in *Matrimonial Decisions of Great Britain and Ireland*, 24 (1988), p. 37.

[637]For recent articles concerning the influence of culture on marriage, see R.R. CALVO, "The Impact of Culture in Marriage Cases", in *CLSA Proceedings*, 55 (1993), pp. 108-120; A. MENDONÇA, "The Importance of Considering Cultural Contexts in Adjudicating Marriage Nullity Cases with Special Reference to Countries of Southeast Asia", in *CLSA Proceedings*, 57 (1995), pp. 231-292; "Recent Rotal Jurisprudence from a Socio-Cultural Perspective (Part I)", in *Studia canonica*, 29 (1995), pp. 29-84; (Part II), pp. 317-356; "Recent Rotal Jurisprudence from a Socio-Cultural Perspective", in *Canonical studies*, 1995, pp 58-143. While the article in *Canonical studies* is basically the same as found in *Studia canonica*, on pp. 100-108, the author presents Rotal sentences pertaining to simulation, reverential fear and impotence from a cultural perspective. See also J.P. BEAL, "The Substance of Things Hoped For: Proving Simulation of Matrimonial Consent", in *The Jurist*, 55 (1995), pp. 745-793; PROVOST, "Simulated Consent: A New Way of Looking at an Old Way of Thinking, Part III", pp. 740-744; E.G. PFNAUSCH.

126

emphasized this in his Apostolic Exhortation, *Familiaris consortio*, 4:

> Since God's plan for marriage and the family touches men and women in the concreteness of their daily existence in specific social and cultural situations, the Church ought to apply herself to understanding the situations within which marriage and family are lived today, in order to fulfill her task of serving.[638]

Likewise, in his 1991 allocution to the Roman Rota, he continued this theme, dedicating his annual address to the impact of culture on marriage. He stated:

> Precisely because it is a reality that is deeply rooted in human nature itself, marriage is affected by the cultural and historical conditions of every people. They have left their mark upon the institution of marriage. The Church, therefore, cannot prescind from the cultural milieu.[639]

What a person brings to the marriage is a result of his or her family's influence which, in turn, has been affected by the culture and subculture within which that family found itself. While these factors would not necessarily impact upon all five facets of marriage which are stated in canon 1096 concerning ignorance,[640] they can still have ramifications. As it pertains to the topic at hand, because of a person's upbringing and cultural understanding of marriage, one can be ignorant of the fact that marriage is a partnership, a *consortium*, an interpersonal relationship where there is a giving and receiving of each other. Instead, a man can understand marriage as (1) the wife becoming his possession; (2) the state of life where he is head of household and therefore makes all the decisions which his wife is to follow; (3) his wife is simply the caretaker of the house and the bearer of his children. By the same token, a woman, coming from a culture which is predominantly patriarchal, will simply follow the lead of the man and see herself as a spouse, fulfilling her role as noted above.

Another example would be the couple being ignorant of the exclusivity of marriage where polygamy

---

"Simulated Consent: A New Way of Looking at an Old Way of Thinking, Part II", pp. 721-739; L.A. ROBITAILLE, "Consent, Culture and the Code ", in *Studia canonica*, 33 (1999), pp. 125-138.

[638]"Quoniam consilium Dei de matrimonio et familia virum et mulierem respicit in ipso cotidianae vitae usu constitutos ac quidem in certis ac definitis condicionibus socialibus et *culturalibus*, Ecclesia ut ministerium suum adimpleat, studeat oportet cognoscere adiuncta, in quibus matrimonium et familia temporibus nostris efficiuntur". JOHN PAUL II, Apostolic Exhortation, *Familiaris consortio*, 22 November 1981, in *AAS*, 74 (1982), p. 84; English translation in A. FLANNERY, gen. ed., *Vatican II: More Post Conciliar Documents*, Northport, New York, Costello Publishing Company, 1982, p. 817.

[639]"Proprio perché realtà profondamente radicata nella stessa natura umana, il matrimonio è segnato dalle condizioni culturali e storiche di ogni popolo. Esse hanno sempre lasciato una loro traccia nella istituzione matrimoniale. La Chiesa, pertanto, non ne può prescindere", JOHN PAUL II, Allocution to the Roman Rota, 28 January 1991, "Marriage and Culture", in *AAS*, 83 (1991), p. 948; English translation in W.H. WOESTMAN, ed., *Papal Allocutions to the Roman Rota, 1939-1994*, Ottawa, Faculty of Canon Law, Saint Paul University, 1994, p. 214.

[640]Of the five elements specified in canon 1096 in regard to the content of ignorance, the knowledge of the "ordered for the procreation of offspring" would not necessarily be negatively influenced by culture or subculture. It is a universal aspect of marriage, even among primitive cultures, that being fruitful and having children are important. The aspect of "by means of some sexual cooperation" is one that may or may not be negatively influenced, but in a culture or subculture just described where a couple is expected to be fruitful, it would seem likely that the sexual aspect of marriage is explained as part of the ritual, either of engagement or marriage itself.

is cultural. Where the Church teaches the permanent union of one man and one woman, this would not be known to people who are reared in cultures where multiple spouses are the norm. The effect of rampant divorce would be similar.

While such negative influences were articulated by the Holy Father in his 1991 allocution to the Rota, he also stated positive aspects:

> It is in the journey of history and the variety of cultures that God's plan is fulfilled. If, on the one hand culture has sometimes had a negative influence on the institution of matrimony, having effects on it which are contrary to God's plan such as polygamy and divorce, on the other hand in many cases it has been the instrument which God used to prepare the soil for a better and deeper understanding of his original intentions.[641]

Thus, those involved in tribunal ministry must be aware of the impact of culture, both positive and negative, upon the values, understanding and knowledge of marriage which the couple brings to their union. Likewise, the cultural biases that are present within the person, be he or she judge, defender of the bond, auditor, advocate or assessor need to be addressed so that each case may be adjudicated justly and equitably.[642]

3. Specific examples

Keeping in mind that a person who enters marriage must at least not be ignorant that marriage is a (1) permanent (2) *consortium* (3) between a man and a woman (4) for the procreation of offspring (5) by means of some sexual cooperation, the following are some scenarios for the plausible utilization of canon 1096. The purpose of these examples is to show various possibilities to which the ground of ignorance may be pertinent. It is by no means an exhaustive list; rather, it is one intended to help expand the horizons of opportunities available. It should be noted, however, that other grounds, such as error or simulation or condition may be applicable, depending upon the evidence gathered. While these examples are grouped under each of the characteristics as delineated in the canon, there will, at times, be overlapping:

a. permanent

— A person grows up in a family situation where divorce is common. The parents have been married a number of times and, therefore, there is little if any concept of permanence. When things do not work out or when there are problems, the solution is to divorce the spouse and find someone else. This differs from the intention against permanence (simulation) because there is no idea, no knowledge, that marriage is a permanent institution.

641"È nel cammino della storia e nella varietà delle culture che si realizza il progetto di Dio. Se da una parte la cultura ha segnato a volte negativamente l'istituzione matrimoniale, imprimendovi deviazioni contrarie al progetto divino, quali la poligamia e il divorzio, dall'altra in non rari casi essa è stata lo strumento di cui Dio si è servito per preparare il terreno ad una migliore e più profonda comprensione del suo intendimento originario", JOHN PAUL II, Allocution to the Roman Rota, in AAS, 83 (1991), p. 949; English translation in WOESTMAN, *Papal Allocutions to the Roman Rota 1939-1994*, p. 215.

642See MENDONÇA, "The Importance of Considering Cultural Contexts in Adjudicating Marriage Nullity Cases", pp. 291-292.

128

— The man and woman, products of today's "Generation X"[643] society with its "live only for today" mentality, marry. Here we have either no concept of permanence, which would be ignorance, or an understanding of permanence which meant something that will last until it wears out, like the "permanent" shine of a new car or the "permanent" clear sound of a CD (compact disc), which would be error. They soon tire of the other and they divorce. For them, "permanence" either had no bearing on their decision or it could have meant until the experience became "routine" or the "fun" disappeared. So, there was either no knowledge or false assumptions about permanence.

b. *consortium*

— Two people are married but live separate lives: he spends all his time with co-workers or "out with the guys" while she is the "good wife" who takes care of the home. There is no interaction between them on an emotional, spiritual or affective level. There is no understanding of the intimate, interpersonal relationship. There is no knowledge that there should be an interpersonal relationship whereby they share hopes, dreams, aspirations, future.

— The couple gets married because their parents, who are non-emotional, sex-is-taboo Southerners, are married; it is expected of them at a certain age. There is no discussion nor is there evidence of a partnership within the family of origin. They have no idea of the real *consortium* that is marriage.

— The couple marries because it is the only "legitimate" way they are able to have sexual intercourse. They want to have sex and have babies because "that is what marriage is all about." The primary focus of the couple is on the sexual intercourse aspect of marriage. Again, in this scenario, there is no knowledge of the interpersonal relationship that is to be established between them.

— A couple, both coming from broken homes, marry. Within each of their families there was the routine abuse of alcohol. The couple has no concept of love as they had never experienced it themselves in their families of origin. The man was possessive, jealous and prone to physically abuse the woman. Both having lacked this basic knowledge and experience of love, they did not fully enter into a *consortium* with each other.[644]

c. between a man and a woman

— The man's father, although married, has had numerous affairs. The father, when drinking, bragged about them. The mother, being a good Christian woman tolerated it. The son grew up never knowing that marriage was to be an exclusive relationship. This differs from error as found in canon 1099 because here the man had no knowledge that marriage was exclusive, that it was between a man and a woman, specifically one man and one woman. Also, the notion of *consortium* necessarily must be taken into consideration when faced with the circumstances as outlined here.

— A child grows up in a family unit where the "parents" are of the same sex. When "marriage" is discussed, it is within the context that any two people who truly love each other and want to commit themselves to each other are able to marry. The child grows up not knowing that marriage, as taught by the Church (and traditionally by society), is a heterosexual union. While the child may have been instructed (in

---

[643]"Generation X", according to the website www.cc.colorado.edu.generationx96. is that group of people born between 1961 and 1981, thus products of the 1970's, 1980's and 1990's. According to the 29 October 1999 edition of the *National Catholic Reporter*, p. 18: "It [Generation X] has grown up in one of the most conservative and economically divisive times of the 20th century.... This generation has been raised in the wake of Vatican II."

[644]See *coram* HERTEL, [Paterson Diocesan Tribunal], 12 August 1974, in *Studia canonica*, 8 (1974), pp. 441-442.

religious education classes at Church or in sociology classes in school) that marriage is between a man and a woman, his or her own experience, fortified by the relationship of the "parents" in the family unit, however, teaches differently. Thus, the basic value system established by this homosexual family unit is reinforced in the child.

d. ordered for the procreation of offspring

— A couple, who are of age for childbearing, marries not knowing that children are part of marriage. They marry simply for companionship rather than for offspring.

— A couple marries simply because of economic reasons, not knowing that their "partnership" is to bring about children rather than simply being focused on economic gains.

e. by means of some sexual cooperation

— A woman experiences an extremely strict upbringing where neither sex nor its ramifications are explained. She marries and is shocked when the facts of life are described to her.[645]

— A man or a woman grows up in a very sheltered environment as an only child. He or she is told that children are "a gift from God" or that they are "delivered by the stork". The person grows up never realizing that sexual copulation is necessary for the procreation of children.

— In a similar vein, a woman grows up as an only child and thus never has the opportunity to experience first hand the fact that women give birth to children. It was not something that was discussed by her mother or father. She grows up never realizing that the process of sexual intercourse and childbirth are part of marriage.

— A child grows up in a family where there is no physical contact between the parents. The parents are friendly, cordial and loving but are not affectionately demonstrative toward each other when in the company of their children. The children come of age within the context of a family where the parents are seen as friends rather than lovers. When getting married, this is the paradigm which is used to find a spouse. Once married, the person is shocked and horrified to learn that sex is part of marriage.

b. Ground specific questions to ask

In order to prepare a case for adjudication, the right questions need to be asked so that factual information, i.e., proofs, pertinent to the case at hand will be gathered which would support either the presumption of validity or the ground(s) of nullity of the marriage under investigation.[646] Since the tribunal is seeking information on a specific ground (or number of grounds), it stands to reason that generic questions will not always bring the evidence which is being sought. While there is merit to asking questions which will, in a sense, "set the stage" for what is needed, it is important to be able to focus upon areas which are

---

[645]*coram* BROWN, [Westminster Tribunal], 27 July 1972, in *Matrimonial Decisions for England and Wales*, 7 (1972), p. 232. For a similar cases, see *coram* ACTON, [Southwark Tribunal], 17 February 1977, in *Matrimonial Decisions for England and Wales*, 13 (1977), pp. 50-51; and *coram* READ, [Brentwood, England], 7 May 1998, in A. MENDONÇA, *Marriage Consent - III (cc. 1096-1107)*, (pro manuscripto), Ottawa, Faculty of Canon Law, Saint Paul University, 1998-1999, pp. 33-38.

[646]See M.J. ARROBA CONDE, *Diritto processuale canonico*, 2nd ed., Roma, EDIURCLA, 1994, pp. 346-347. For an in-depth presentation concerning proofs, see BEAL, "The Substance of Things Hoped For: Proving Simulation of Matrimonial Consent", pp. 745-793. While the thrust of the article pertains to proving cases of simulation, it offers a very good overview of *De Probationibus* as well as giving concrete examples of what to look for in marriage nullity cases.

130

appropriate to the selected ground(s).

Concerning the ground of ignorance, the following are possible examples of specific questions which may be asked of the parties and, with some variation, asked of the witnesses. This is by no means a definitive list. Rather the questions simply form the basis from which the interviewer, taking the particular circumstances of each case into consideration, can utilize to surface pertinent information. Not all of the questions can, or should, be asked of every party. Some are very basic and, because they are elementary can easily be overlooked, forgotten or taken for granted. A rule of thumb to keep in mind is not to presume anything (e.g., because a party is Catholic he or she knows what the Church teaches about marriage). Instead, a party should be asked a question and have his or her answer for the record. Unless a "yes" or "no" answer is actually sought, preliminary questions which elicit such a response should be followed up immediately with questions which seek specific information.

Ignorance about permanence:

At the time of your marriage, did you know marriage was permanent? At the time of your marriage, did your spouse know marriage was permanent?

At the time of your marriage, what was your understanding of "marital permanence"? At the time of your marriage, what was your former spouse's understanding of "marital permanence"?

Please explain how your upbringing, family background and life experiences influenced your understanding of "marital permanence".

Please explain how your former spouse's upbringing, family background and life experiences influenced his/her understanding of "marital permanence".

Ignorance about the heterosexuality of marriage:

At the time of your marriage, did you know that marriage is only between a man and a woman, i.e., that it cannot be a "same sex union"? If not, what was your understanding of marriage?

At the time of your marriage, did your former spouse know that marriage is only between a man and a woman, i.e., that it cannot be a "same sex union"? If not, what was your former spouse's understanding of marriage?

Please explain how your upbringing, family background and life experiences influenced your understanding of marriage.

Please explain how your former spouse's upbringing, family background and life experiences influenced his/her understanding of marriage.

Ignorance about exclusivity:

At the time of your marriage, did you know that marriage is an exclusive union, i.e., marriage is between one man and one woman, not allowing more than one partner? At the time of your marriage, did your former spouse know that marriage is an exclusive union as described in the previous question?

When you married, what was your understanding of marriage being an "exclusive union"? When you married, what was your spouse's understanding of marriage as an "exclusive union"?

Please explain how your upbringing, family background and life experiences influenced your understanding of marriage as an "exclusive union".

Please explain how your former spouse's upbringing, family background and life experiences influenced his/her understanding of marriage as an "exclusive union".

Ignorance of the *consortium*:

At the time of your marriage did you know marriage was a partnership? At the time of your marriage, did your former spouse know marriage was a partnership?

At the time of your marriage, what was your understanding of marriage being a "partnership"? At the time of your marriage, what was your former spouse's understanding of marriage as a "partnership"?

In what specific ways did you contribute in making your married life a partnership? In what specific ways did your former spouse contribute in making married life a partnership? (E.g., in what ways were you and your spouse able to share hopes, dreams, aspirations, fears, concerns, future plans, etc.?)

How did you and your spouse show respect and appreciation for each other?

In what ways did you and your spouse share marital responsibilities?

During the marriage, did you and your spouse live more as partners or two independent people? Please explain.

During the marriage, did you and your spouse have mutual friends or did you each have your own separate friends? Please explain why this was important to both of you.

Please explain how your upbringing, family background and life experiences influenced your understanding of marriage as a "partnership".

Please explain how your former spouse's upbringing, family background and life experiences influenced his/her understanding of marriage as a "partnership".

How did you and your spouse spend your free time? (E.g., more often doing activities with each other or with mutual friends or more often by yourselves or with your own individual friends?)

Ignorance about children:

At the time of your marriage, did you know that children were an essential part of marriage? At the time of your marriage, did your former spouse know that children were an essential part of marriage?

When you married, what was your understanding of marriage and having children?

When you married, what was your former spouse's understanding of marriage and having children?

Please explain how your upbringing, family background and life experiences influenced your understanding of "children being an essential part of marriage".

Please explain how your former spouse's upbringing, family background and life experiences influenced his/her understanding of "children being an essential part of marriage".

Ignorance about sexual intercourse:

At the time of your marriage, did you know children can result by means of sexual intercourse? If "No", what was your reaction to this fact?

Please explain how your upbringing, family background and life experiences influenced your lack of understanding of the means by which children are procreated.

At the time of your marriage, did your former spouse know children can result by means of sexual intercourse? If "No", what was his/her reaction to this fact?

Please explain how your former spouse's upbringing, family background and life experiences influenced his/her lack of understanding of the means by which children are procreated.

If you were unaware that children came from sexual intercourse, did you have sexual intercourse with your former spouse? If this did not occur during the honeymoon, when did it occur?

If your former spouse was unaware that children came from sexual intercourse, did he/she have sexual intercourse with you?

What was your former spouse's reaction to having sexual intercourse? Was sexual intercourse a part of your relationship? Please explain.

132

c. Application of what we know

Once the forthcoming evidence has been collected, following the norms and procedures set forth in the law the judge, or in the case of a collegiate tribunal the judges, render a definitive sentence concerning the validity or invalidity of the marriage in question.[647] To help settle the controversy arising from the use of the ground of ignorance, the Appendix contains elements of a general law section which could be used as appropriate, choosing those portions of the law section which are pertinent to the particular case under investigation.

III. CANON 1096 AND PREPARATION FOR MARRIAGE

As stated in canon 1063[648] and further developed in Pope John Paul II's 1981 Apostolic exhortation *Familiaris consortio* (65-69),[649] in the American Bishop's 1989 *Faithful to Each Other Forever: A Catholic Handbook of Pastoral Help for Marriage Preparation,*[650] and in the Pontifical Council for the Family's 1996 document *Preparation for the Sacrament of Marriage,*[651] there is obviously an on-going need for marriage

---

[647]As was pointed out in Chapter Three, it appears that no cases have been adjudicated at the Rota on the ground of ignorance since the promulgation of the 1983 *CIC*. However, four decisions from tribunals of first instance that have been published which have been on canon 1096 are *coram* CACHIA, [Maltese Ecclesiastical Tribunal], 12 June 1985, in *Forum*, 1 (1990) 1, pp. 106-115; *coram* PAYNE, [Dublin], 29 September 1988, in *Matrimonial Decisions of Great Britain and Ireland*, 24 (1988), pp. 34-42; *coram* RAMOS, [Tribunal Ecclesiastico de Mallorca], 23 December 1986, in *Revista española de derecho canónico*, 45 (1988), pp. 403-409; *coram* DALEY, [Liverpool], 14 May 1997, in *Matrimonial Decisions of Great Britain and Ireland*, 33 (1997), pp. 75-78. A fifth case, *coram* READ, [Brentwood, England], 7 May 1998, has not been published but is mentioned in A. MENDONÇA, *Marriage Consent - III (cc. 1096-1107)*, (pro manuscripto), Ottawa, Faculty of Canon Law, Saint Paul University, 1998-1999, pp. 33-38.

[648]Canon 1063: "Pastors of souls are obliged to take care that their ecclesiastical community offers the Christian faithful the assistance by which the matrimonial state is preserved in a Christian spirit and advances in perfection. This assistance must be offered especially by:
1° preaching, catechesis adapted to minors, youth and adults, and even the use of instruments of social communication, by which the Christian faithful are instructed about the meaning of Christian marriage and about the function of Christian spouses and parents;
2° personal preparation to enter marriage, which disposes the spouses to the holiness and duties of their new state;
3° a fruitful liturgical celebration of marriage which is to show that the spouses signify and share in the mystery of the unity and fruitful love between Christ and the Church;
4° help offered to those who are married, so that faithfully preserving and protecting the conjugal covenant, they daily come to lead holier and fuller lives in their family."

[649]JOHN PAUL II, Apostolic exhortation, *Familiaris consortio*, 22 November 1981, in *AAS*, 74 (1982), pp. 81-191, specifically pp. 158-167; English translation in A. FLANNERY, gen. ed., *Vatican II: More Post Conciliar Documents*, Northport, New York, Costello Publishing Company, 1982, pp. 815-893, specifically pp. 868-874.

[650]NATIONAL CONFERENCE OF CATHOLIC BISHOPS, BISHOPS' COMMITTEE FOR PASTORAL RESEARCH AND PRACTICE, *Faithful to Each Other Forever: A Catholic Handbook of Pastoral Help for Marriage Preparation*, Washington, DC, United States Catholic Conference, 1989.

[651]PONTIFICAL COUNCIL FOR THE FAMILY, *Preparation for the Sacrament of Marriage*, Città del Vaticano, Libreria Editrice Vaticana, 1996.

preparation programs. In 1995, Creighton University of Omaha, Nebraska, published its report[652] concerning Marriage Preparation Programs in the United States. The publication was the result of a proportional random sampling from among 72, 725 couples who, in the seven years between 1987 and 1993 had used the FOCCUS (Facilitating Open Couple Communication Understanding and Study) inventory as part of the marriage preparation program of the Catholic Church and had it scored at Creighton University.[653] Of these 72,725 couples, 30,025 (41.3%) had given written permission to be contacted for future research, of which 3,195 couples were specially selected. Of the 3,195 couples selected, 400 were chosen from each of the seven years the study covered, 1987-1993, yielding 2,800 couples. The couples selected were such that they represented each region of the United States on a proportional basis. This initial sample of 2,800 couples was further supplemented with couples from special subpopulations so the final sample would adequately represent these subpopulations (e.g., couples who were pregnant during the marriage preparation program, couples in inter-church marriages, couples with children, couples who were either under 21 or over 31 years of age).[654]

Ten general conclusions resulting from this study have been reached:

1. The vast majority of individuals who have participated in marriage preparation programs view the experience as valuable early in their marriage.[655]
2. The perceived value of marriage preparation declines significantly over time.[656]
3. The mandatory nature of marriage preparation in the Catholic Church does not appear to get in the way of participants finding value in it.[657]
4. Marriage preparation is perceived most valuable when it is presented by a team.[658]
5. The intensity of a marriage preparation program contributes importantly to its perceived value.[659]
6. The topics addressed in marriage preparation that were perceived as most helpful were the five Cs: communication, commitment, conflict resolution, children and church (values and sacramental activity).[660]
7. Religious education in high school and ongoing religious education in adulthood is the best long range formal education the Church can offer.[661]
8. Individuals who were more active in Church life and/or who had a greater sense of

[652]D.T. VAN DYKE, Project Director, *Marriage Preparation in the Catholic Church: Getting it Right: Report of a Study on the Value of Marriage Preparation in the Catholic Church for Couples Married One through Eight Years*, Omaha, Center for Marriage and Family, Creighton University, 1995.

[653]*Ibid.*, p. 11

[654]*Ibid.*, p. 12.

[655]*Ibid.*, p. 19.

[656]*Ibid.*, p. 21.

[657]*Ibid.*

[658]*Ibid.*, p. 26.

[659]*Ibid.*, p. 23.

[660]*Ibid.*, p. 28.

[661]*Ibid.*, p. 37.

belonging to the Church perceived a greater value in marriage preparation.[662]
9. Inter-church couples, who comprised 39% of respondents in the present study, are most at risk for drift from church belonging and practice.[663]
10. Those who come to marriage preparation with high expectations derive more benefit from it than those who come with low expectations.[664]

At the end of the presentation of these conclusions, the study gives the implications and challenges of these conclusions to Church leaders and people involved in marriage preparation.[665] While the study was quite thorough in its methodology, presentation and conclusions, it was not intended to present a specific "one size fits all" kind of marriage preparation program. Rather, it gives its readers a basis from which to start: what is good, what works, what is perceived as not being beneficial, what needs to be included or improved. Thus, the readers do not know what the exact content of the presentations was, but rather the content areas.[666]

In considering each of these ten conclusions and its implications, since the specific information presented in each area is not known, we shall point out which ones are important from our perspective and recommend how these may be improved. There are four conclusions, in our opinion, which could have bearing on helping prevent ignorance in couples preparing for marriage: conclusions one, six, seven and eight.

1. The vast majority of individuals who have participated in marriage preparation programs view the experience as valuable early in their marriage.

93.8% agreed that marriage preparation was important in the first year of marriage; 78.4% in the second year. The implication is that marriage preparation serves a useful purpose in preparing couples for marriage.[667] From our perspective, part of a marriage preparation program would be not only a presentation of the theological and practical aspects of marriage, as can be seen from the areas of topics already listed, but also of the canonical understanding of marriage,[668] using canons 1055-1057 as a basis.

As part of the program, reference, in a positive way, could be made to the canons pertaining to the specific diriment impediments (canons 1083-1094) and most of those concerning matrimonial consent (canons 1095-1103). For example, canon 1083 gives the age at which a valid marriage can take place. Presenting this canon, one would address why those of a younger age are not allowed to marry (using canon 1055, §1, for

---

[662]*Ibid.*, p. 34.

[663]*Ibid.*, p. 35.

[664]*Ibid.*, p. 33.

[665]*Ibid.*, pp. 45-48.

[666]*Ibid.*, Table 18, p. 31, lists the following areas: dual career marriage, leisure activities, balancing home and career, commitment, personality issues, communications, conflict resolution, sex and intimacy, extended family issues (in-laws), roles in marriage, finances, family planning, role of religion and values in your life, marriage sacraments, friends, children, compatibility of background and drugs-alcohol.

[667]*Ibid.*, p. 45.

[668]Concerns for those preparing for marriage are noted in canons 1063-1072, "Pastoral Care and Those Things Which Must Precede the Celebration of Marriage" ("De Cura pastorali et de iis quae matrimonii celebrationi praemitti debent"). The first canon, 1063, specifically addresses "pastors of souls" (*pastores animarum*) and obliges them to prepare the Christian faithful for marriage. While listing specific areas to be covered, the Code remains general in its approach.

example, as a basis for the psychological maturity needed to enter into a life-long relationship and understanding the concept of partnership; and canon 1057, §2, for the consciousness of implications of the giving and receiving of each other). Another example would be using canon 1096 in a positive light: what each person who marries is to know about marriage (that it is a permanent *consortium* [partnership] between a man and a woman for the procreation of offspring by means of some sexual cooperation). Thus, the couples preparing for marriage will have a better understanding and be more aware of what the Church expects of its members who are entering marriage.

6. **The topics addressed in marriage preparation that were perceived as most helpful were the five Cs: communication, commitment, conflict resolution, children and church (values and sacramental activity).**

One of the implications concerning this conclusion was that there needs to be an enhancement of these areas since all of them are crucial in the early developmental stage of marriage.[669] The five "Cs", as they were called in the study, are all clearly related to the *consortium*, the partnership. Thus, concentrating on these particular topics would help the contractants understand more fully what the Church, in its canon law and its teachings, means by the *consortium*. Since the partnership, the *consortium*, is marriage, assisting couples in knowing, appreciating and living it will hopefully serve to strengthen their commitment to each other, to their marriage and to the Church.

7. **Religious education in high school and ongoing religious education in adulthood is the best long range formal education the Church can offer.**

This study validated the importance of both high school and ongoing adult religious education.[670] The study also showed that the least correlation between religious education and marriage preparation was that on the grammar school level.[671] In one sense, this is not surprising, given the age and perceived distance between children and marriage. Once again, it would be important for high school religious education programs as well as ongoing adult religious education programs to have, as part of their curricula, marriage from a canonical perspective as discussed above. From a high school religious education perspective, marriage would be presented based on a developmental model, designed according to the psychological needs and awareness of the age group. From an adult religious education perspective, it would be presented as the sacramental, theological, canonical and sociological reality it is.

8. **Individuals who were more active in Church life and/or who had a greater sense of belonging to the Church perceived a greater value in marriage preparation.**

One of the implications of this conclusion was marriage preparation does not and cannot stand alone, meaning there needs to be a pre-marriage preparation as well as a post-marriage preparation.[672] Pre-preparation was also called pre-evangelization: an ongoing adult religious education program where those

---

[669]VAN DYKE, *Marriage Preparation in the Catholic Church*, p. 46.

[670]*Ibid.*

[671]*Ibid.*, p. 39.

[672]*Ibid.*, p. 47.

136

contemplating marriage will benefit from being part of a church community, developing in them a sense of belonging to the Church and practice in its life.[673] Post-marriage preparation is an enrichment program whereby couples would be able to maintain and enhance both their belonging to the Church (more specifically, a parish community) and the practice of their religious education.[674]

From a canonical perspective, the Code briefly addresses, in canon 1063, 4°, pastoral care and what should be done after the celebration of marriage to assist couples. There is much to be said about continuing education and marriage enrichment programs which would not only help pastors of souls but also encourage the couples themselves to live this sacrament. On-going programs which balance theological, sacramental, canonical and sociological perspectives of marriage would serve to strengthen couples in their commitment to marriage and to each other. While these particular programs would not prevent couples from having been ignorant at the time of the marriage, in the long run such efforts could very well be beneficial from the standpoint that as the couple grow in their commitment to their marriage and Church, an awareness of the importance of marriage will be such that their children will also be educated in the practices and laws of the Church. Thus, hopefully, generations will be involved in the Church, becoming more knowledgeable in what the Church teaches about marriage while sharing this learning and understanding with their families.

CONCLUSION

The purpose of this final chapter has been two-fold: first, to illustrate how canon 1096 can be better utilized as a ground for nullity, and secondly, in what ways, having grasped a better understanding of ignorance in relation to marriage, can our knowledge be employed to prevent couples from being ignorant of what the Church teaches about marriage. Some general conclusions can now be drawn.

It goes without saying that canonists need to be aware of the differences between the various grounds for nullity as prescribed in the 1983 *CIC*. While this is certainly true for those working in tribunals who deal directly with marriage nullity cases, it is also true that canonists in general also need to be aware, since many times, if addressing groups about canon law, questions will be posed by people concerning marriage nullity cases (grounds, procedures, cost, etc.) whether the topic under discussion is directly related to nullity or not.

While there are differences and nuances among the various grounds for nullity, it is important to understand these distinctions for two basic reasons: (1) that there are, indeed, variations — sometimes subtle — but it is precisely these characteristics which make each ground specific; and (2) each case of nullity and the evidence given is unique, and in order to render justice to that particular case as well as maintain the integrity of canon law, the correct ground is to be utilized.

Ignorance as a ground of nullity is specific, this is seen in the concise wording of the canon. This means that the use of the ground of ignorance is restricted to what a contractant does not know about marriage. This is important because canon 1096 cannot be used as a basis for nullity if, for example, a contractant did not know that marriage was considered a sacrament.

A better understanding of ignorance as seen in relation to the other grounds of nullity, as well as in contrast to them, will hopefully encourage its more widespread and correct use, drawing from canonical tradition and the theology of Vatican II.

Having a deeper understanding of marriage as seen through canon 1096 will also, on the other hand,

---

[673]*Ibid.*

[674]*Ibid.*

help those involved with pre-marital preparation programs to develop seminars, talks, presentations, etc., on the concept of marriage so that, as more and more people actively participate in these programs, they will come to know what marriage is and thus at least not be ignorant that marriage truly is a permanent *consortium* between a man and a woman ordered for the procreation of offspring by means of some sexual cooperation.

GENERAL CONCLUSION

At the end of our study, it is time to present general conclusions. To facilitate our approach, we shall present these in numbered form.

1. **Ignorance as lack of due knowledge**. Technically, ignorance is not simply the lack of knowledge, but rather the lack of *due* knowledge, i.e., that certain degree of knowledge a person is expected to have in relation to the act to be carried out. We contend this is the more correct understanding of ignorance when relating to marriage.

2. **Ignorance is not incapacity**. Before the 1983 *CIC*, ignorance was often assumed into the phrases "lack of sufficient reason" or "lack of discretion of judgment". Since ignorance was seen as the lack of due knowledge, these grounds were simply other ways of saying that one or both of the contractants were ignorant. However, these grounds are now spelled out separately and distinctly in canon 1095, 1° and 2° of the 1983 *CIC* and in canon 818, 1° and 2° of the 1990 *CCEO*. They are indeed distinct from ignorance. The difference lies in the fact that these canons begin by stating that the parties are incapable of contracting marriage, while the canon pertaining to ignorance begins with the premise that the parties were capable, but did not give consent.

3. **Ignorance influencing the will**. Given the present legislation, we contend that those who enter marriage, for the most part, are capable of doing so. This is an unstated presumption. Canon 1058 states "All persons who are not prohibited by law can contract marriage" (*Omnes possunt matrimonium contrahere, qui iure non prohibentur*), thus presuming capacity. Canon 1095 is the only canon on marriage consent which begins with the phrase "The following are incapable of marriage" (*Sunt incapaces matrimonii contrahendi*), thus limiting consensual incapacity to the three titles within that canon. Should the marriage break down, and the basis for this is ignorance, then the presumption is that one or both parties were capable of entering marriage but lacked the knowledge necessary to do so. Ignorance, understood as lack of due knowledge, can and does move the will for the parties who are consenting to something they think is marriage. Thus, an act of the will is also involved. However, what is lacking is their understanding of what marriage is; they want something different from marriage as understood from natural law and taught by the Church. For example, two people want to marry. They do not know that marriage is ordered to the procreation of offspring. They marry simply to be together. The intellect, flawed as it is, informs the will and the parties consent to marry. Later, when they discover marriage is much more, i.e., ordered for procreation, they part.

4. **Ignorance of marriage as a heterosexual union**. Canon 1096 succinctly states that the essence of marriage includes two elements: the *personalist* element (the "permanent *consortium* between a man and a woman") and the *procreational* element ("ordered to the procreation of offspring by means of some sexual cooperation"). A growing issue of importance today is the sociological "reinterpretation" of marriage as a union between a couple of the same sex and its possible influence upon mentalities. In Canada, the Supreme Court recently ruled same-sex unions have the same status as a heterosexual marriage. In the United States, there is the ongoing controversy of recognizing same sex unions as an acceptable status in life. There is also the ever increasing number of industries as well as various levels of governments that acknowledge the legitimacy of same sex "marriages" for various benefits. Thus, in the future contractants might not really know that marriage is essentially and exclusively heterosexual and, therefore, they can be ignorant of marriage as exclusively a union between a man and a woman.

5. **Importance of the *consortium***. When the couple consent to marry, they have in mind a concept of marriage. Therefore, the intellect does inform the will and there is that act of the will necessary for

matrimonial consent. However, the contractants may truly be ignorant of what a *consortium* is. They may very well have no knowledge that marriage is indeed a partnership between two people, ordained for the procreation of children. They have the natural capacity for such knowledge but, because of upbringing or other reasons, lacked the opportunity to learn it, and thus were ignorant at the time of consent. This, we believe, is where canon 1096 (and canon 819 of the *CCEO*) could be utilized to a greater extent.

6. **The presumption of knowledge.** In regard to canon 1096, §2, it has been shown that the presumption of knowledge related only to the act of procreation, having been taken verbatim from canon 1082, §2, of the 1917 *CIC*. Given the jurisprudence in this area, both before and after the 1917 *CIC*, it is clearly demonstrated that the presumption pertained only to the act of sexual copulation. However, taking into consideration canon 17 and Vatican II's theology of marriage, this presumption is now expanded to include the fact that marriage is a permanent *consortium* between a man and a woman ordered to the procreation of offspring. Therefore, a person is to have minimal knowledge of the nature of marriage, i.e., of its totality of its rights and obligations as understood from the teachings of Vatican II. This broadens not only the possibilities of what a person may not know about marriage, but also can make the presumption in paragraph two more difficult to uphold and easier to overturn by means of supporting evidence to the contrary. We can understand why the paragraph was included; however, in our opinion, the drafters of the 1983 *CIC* might have modified it, as they did paragraph one, to reflect the changes precipitated by Vatican II, or even have simply dropped it, since canon 1060 already presumes the validity of marriage.

7. **The scope of ignorance.** Ignorance of any one or more of the five facets of canon 1096, §1, i.e., that marriage is a (1) permanent, (2) *consortium* (3) between a man and a woman (4) ordered for the procreation of offspring (5) by means of some sexual cooperation renders the marriage invalid. The question raised by the commentators on the 1917 *CIC* — how much knowledge of the actual sexual *copula* is needed — has been remedied by the phrase "by means of some sexual cooperation" to show that there must be a minimal amount of such knowledge in order for the marriage to be valid. Thus, if a person does not even have such minimal knowledge, the marriage is invalid. Such a conclusion was clearly shown by decisions by the Congregation of the Council and the Roman Rota both before and after the 1917 *CIC*. As has been indicated throughout this study, the focus of ignorance was basically on the physical mechanics of sexual intercourse. Then came Vatican II with its emphasis on the personalist element of marriage. We now are to understand marriage from an interpersonal dimension, with an emphasis on the relationship between the man and the woman. Thus, taking this interpersonal-personalist-relational aspect into consideration, as well as the description of marriage from the 1983 *CIC* (and the 1990 *CCEO*), it now sets the stage for a broader understanding of how ignorance can invalidate marriage. For example, it stands to reason that a person who does not know that marriage is permanent cannot enter into a life-long relationship. Given the North American society's high divorce rate, it is very easily conceivable that couples will marry "as long as we both shall love" rather than "as long as we both shall live". Likewise, if a person does not know what a *consortium* is, how can he or she give consent to marriage as we understand it to be? Knowing that marriage is an exclusive union between one man and one woman is a benchmark of marriage and a person must know that it is such in order to enter into the *consortium*. Furthermore, the nuptial union is more than merely a friendly alliance or economic association. It is, by its very nature, ordered to preservation and generation, which, in canonical language means ordered to the procreation of offspring. If a person is ignorant of this, the union entered is invalid.

8. **Using canon 1096 beyond the Tribunal.** As was demonstrated in Chapter Four, in canon 1063, in Pope John Paul II's 1981 Apostolic exhortation *Familiaris consortio* 64-69, in the Pontifical Council for

the Family's 1996 document *Preparation for the Sacrament of Marriage*, and in the American Bishop's 1989 *Faithful to Each Other Forever: A Catholic Handbook of Pastoral Help for Marriage Preparation*, there is the on-going need for marriage preparation programs. The richness of canon 1096 can be utilized not only for marriage nullity cases, but also the elements listed within the canon can be adopted as a basis for such a marriage preparation program. In this way, the possibility of couples being ignorant of the essence of marriage could be addressed in a positive way and thus help them know and understand what marriage is.

9. **Expanding the understanding of canon 1096.** Finally, we propose two new areas for canonical consideration, utilizing canon 1096 in relation to canon 1057: first with the understanding of "non-inclusion", "inadequate consent" and "lack of commitment"; and secondly, in regard to the *bonum coniugum.*

In the years after Vatican II, but before the promulgation of the 1983 *CIC*, canonists were struggling with interpreting the Council's teaching of marriage, especially taking into consideration the "intimate partnership of life and love" of *Gaudium et spes*, 48, and applying it to cases of marriage nullity. Different titles were being proposed and used by tribunals, specifically in English speaking countries. Using the expertise of these canonists and applying it to our research, we propose that if a party is ignorant of the *consortium*, there is an inadequate consent or lack of commitment since the person cannot consent to something that he or she does not know (*nil volitum quin praecognitum*). Furthermore, if there is ignorance of the *consortium*, then there could very well be non-inclusion of the good of the spouses (*bonum coniugum*), the procreation and education of offspring, or both.

Since 1983, the concept of the *bonum coniugum* has been widely discussed. We are of the opinion that if we see it in relation to ignorance, this could help canonists appreciate it for what it is, i.e., an essential element of the *consortium* as can be interpreted from canon 1055, §1. In other words, if a party enters into marriage not knowing what the *bonum coniugum* means, then the notion of the *consortium* would be lacking, indicating consent would be deficient and the marriage could be declared invalid. We look forward to further development, study and discussion concerning the conclusion presented here.

APPENDIX:

ELEMENTS OF A PROPOSED LAW SECTION FOR CANON 1096

A. The canons

Canon 15, §1 [*CCEO* canon 1497, §1]
Ignorance or error about invalidating or disqualifying laws does not impede their effect unless it is expressly established otherwise.

Canon 124 [*CCEO* canon 931]
§ 1: For the validity of a juridic act it is required that the act is placed by a qualified person and includes those things which essentially constitute the act itself as well as the formalities and requirements imposed by law for the validity of the act.
§2: A juridic act placed correctly with respect to its external elements is presumed valid.

Canon 126 [*CCEO* canon 933]
An act placed out of ignorance or error concerning something which constitutes its substance or which amounts to a condition *sine qua non* is invalid. Otherwise it is valid unless the law makes other provision. An act entered into out of ignorance or error, however, can give rise to a recissory action according to the norm of law.

Canon 1096 [*CCEO* canon 819]
§1: For matrimonial consent to exist, the contracting parties must be at least not ignorant that marriage is a permanent consortium between a man and a woman ordered to the procreation of offspring by means of some sexual cooperation.
§2: This ignorance is not presumed after puberty.

Canon 1584
A presumption is a probable conjecture about an uncertain matter; a presumption of law is one which the law itself establishes; a human presumption is one which a judge formulates.

B. Church Teachings

In *Gaudium et spes*, 47-52, we have the articulation of the Church's teaching concerning marriage and family life. Of particular significance is number 48:

> The intimate partnership of life and the love which constitutes the married state has been established by the creator and endowed by him with its own proper laws: it is rooted in the contract of its partners, that is, in their irrevocable personal consent. It is an institution confirmed by divine law and receiving its stability, even in the eyes of society also, from the human act by which the partners mutually surrender themselves to each other; for the good of the partners, of the children, and of society this sacred bond no longer depends on human decision alone... By its very nature the institution of marriage and married love are ordered to the procreation and education of the offspring and it is in them that it finds its crowning glory. Thus the man and woman, who "are no longer two but one" (Mt. 19:6), help and serve each other by their marriage partnership; they become conscious of their unity and experience it

more deeply from day to day. The intimate union of marriage, as a mutual giving of two persons, and the good of the children demand total fidelity from the spouses and require an unbreakable unity between them. [See A. FLANNERY, gen. ed., *Vatican Council II: More Post Conciliar Documents*, vol. 2, Collegeville, Minnesota, The Liturgical Press, 1982, p. 950; *AAS*, 58 (1966), pp. 1067-1068.]

Also of importance for us is the further elucidation of these teachings in the 25 July 1968 encyclical of Pope Paul VI, *Humanae vitae*:

[H]usband and wife, through that mutual gift of themselves [in marriage], which is specific and exclusive to them alone, seek to develop that kind of personal union in which they complement one another in order to co-operate with God in the generation and education of new lives...

[Married] love is above all fully *human* ... It is not, then, merely a question of natural instinct or emotional drive. It is also, and above all, an act of the free will...

Then it is a love which is *total* — that very special form of personal friendship in which the husband and wife generously share everything... content to be able to enrich the other with the gift of himself.

Again, married love is *faithful* and *exclusive* of all other, and this until death. Though this fidelity of husband and wife sometimes presents difficulties, no one can assert that it is impossible...

And finally this love is *creative for life*, for it is not exhausted by the loving interchange of husband and wife, but also contrives to go beyond this to bring new life into being. 'Marriage and married love are by their character ordained to the procreation and bringing up of children. Children are the outstanding gift of marriage'[*Gaudium et spes*, 50; *AAS*, 58 (1966), pp. 1070-1072].

Married love, therefore, requires of husband and wife the full awareness of their obligations in the matter of responsible parenthood... Responsible parenthood, moreover, in the terms in which we use the phrase, retains a further and deeper significance of paramount importance which refers to the objective *moral* order instituted by God, — the order of which a right conscience is the true interpreter. [See FLANNERY, *Vatican II*, pp.400-402; *AAS*, 60 (1968), pp.485-487.]

While *Humanae vitae* speaks of conjugal love rather than *consortium*, the values set forth, i.e., fully human, total, faithful and exclusive, creative for life (fruitful) and moral, are important for our understanding, because conjugal love arises within the context of the *consortium*. These same values were further reiterated by Pope John Paul II in his 22 November 1981 exhortation, *Familiaris consortio*, numbers 18-20:

The family, which is founded and given life by love, is a community of persons: of husband and wife, of parents and children, of relatives. Its first task is to live with fidelity the reality of communion in a constant effort to develop an authentic community of persons.... The love between husband and wife... is given life and sustenance by an unceasing inner dynamism leading the family to ever deeper and more intense *communion*, which is the foundation and soul of the *community* of marriage and the family.... The first communion is the one which is established and which develops between husband and wife: by virtue of the covenant of married life, the man and the woman "are no longer two but one flesh"[Mt 19:6; cf. Gen 2:24] and they are called to grow continually in their communion through day-today fidelity to their marriage promise of total mutual self-giving.... Such a communion is radically contradicted by polygamy: this, in fact, directly negates the plan of God which was revealed from the beginning, because it is contrary to the equal personal dignity of men and women who in matrimony give themselves with a love that is total and therefore unique and exclusive....Conjugal communion is characterized not only by its unity but also by its indissolubility: "As a mutual gift of two persons, this intimate union, as well as the good of children, imposes total fidelity on the spouses and argues for an unbreakable oneness between them" [*Gaudium et spes*, 48]. [See FLANNERY, *Vatican Council II*, pp.828-831; *AAS*, 74 (1982), pp.100-104.]

This teaching was repeated by the Holy Father in his 28 January 1982 address to the Rota:

> The Council saw marriage as a covenant of love (see *GS*, no.48). This covenant is "freely and consciously chosen, whereby man and woman accept the intimate community of life and love willed by God himself" (*Familiaris consortio*, no. 11).... Love is essentially a gift. Speaking of the act of love the Council envisages an act of giving, which is one, decisive, irrevocable because it is a total giving which wants to be and remain mutual and fruitful... Marriage consent is an act of the will which signifies and involves a mutual giving which unites the spouses between themselves and at the same time binds them to the children which they may eventually have, with whom they constitute one family, one single home, a "domestic Church" (*LG*, no. 11). [See WOESTMAN, *Papal Allocutions to the Roman Rota*, p. 172; *AAS*, 74 (1982), pp. 450-451.]

In the 1992 *Catechism of the Catholic Church*, pp. 352-353, concerning the Sacrament of Matrimony, we read:

> **1661** The sacrament of Matrimony signifies the union of Christ and the Church. It gives spouses the grace to love each other with the love with which Christ has loved his Church; the grace of the sacrament thus perfects the human love of the spouses, strengthens their indissoluble unity and sanctifies them on the way to eternal life (cf. Council of Trent: *DS* 1799).
>
> **1664** Unity, indissolubility and openness to fertility are essential to marriage. Polygamy is incompatible with the unity of marriage; divorce separates what God has joined together; the refusal of fertility turns married life away from its "supreme gift", the child (*GS* 50 §1).

Taking into consideration the Church's teaching on marriage as seen in *Gaudium et spes*, the teachings of Popes Paul VI and John Paul II and the *Catechism of the Catholic Church*, we now have laid the foundation for how ignorance may effect matrimonial consent.

C. Jurisprudence

It is to be noted that between *Gaudium et spes* of 7 December 1965 and the 1983 *CIC*, there have been a number of referenced Rotal decisions pertaining to ignorance. In only two cases, *coram* SERRANO of 25 April 1975 and *coram* POMPEDDA of 29 October 1979, is reference made to Vatican II, the latter implicitly. Until Serrano's decision in 1975, the basic focus of the decisions was the evaluation of the knowledge of the

144

person(s) pertaining to the procreation of children — whether he or she knew that procreation was part of the nature of marriage or, more often, how much knowledge of the physical *copula* was necessary, taking into consideration the presumption in paragraph two of canon 1082 that the person is presumed to have such knowledge after having reached puberty. All of the judges, with the exception of Masala (in his 30 March 1970 decision), demonstrate that there is more to the knowledge of marriage than the physical joining of bodies.

Also of note is the fact that there appears to have been no cases adjudicated in the Rota on the ground of ignorance since the promulgation of the 1983 *CIC*.

It is in the 22 March 1963 landmark *coram* SABATTANI decision based on ignorance that we find listed four criteria to utilize when weighing proofs in order to establish whether ignorance is verified or not: the psycho-physical, the educational, the prenuptial and the postnuptial [See *SRR Dec*, 55 (1963), pp. 209-210]. These criteria are as important today and can be readily applied to the 1983 *CIC* just as they were to the 1917 *CIC*:

a) Psycho-physical criterion: Ignorance of sexual things is more likely present in those whose psycho-physical development is imperfect...more frequently the lacking psychic development will be apparent through enfeebled sexual instinct.

b) Educational criterion: It is necessary to consider the location (national, regional, community, district) in which the party lives, the persons with whom he/she lives and forms his/her frame of mind, if then party was shy of friendships and lives a solitary. Ignorance is more likely in those whose education was rigid and narrow, who received an outdated and constricted moral formation, and whose parents were severe.

c) Prenuptial criterion: which can be considered in two ways — examining the *cause of marriage*, if the party spoke of a wrong estimate of the nature of marriage, astonished at the most intimate sense in marriage; if, on the contrary, the person was forced into the marriage, especially by the mother; examining the *conduct of the party during the engagement*: if the person acted and spoke in childish, uncontrolled, silly and thoughtless ways.

d) Postnuptial criterion: One is most carefully to assess the conduct of the party when he/she perceives the true nature of the conjugal purpose. If this was a reaction of horror and repugnance, or if the party made it clear to the other party that she/he did not know what was expected of her/him, or, even after being instructed by the other party, she/he could not be persuaded to have sexual intercourse, then there is a presumption that the party was truly ignorant about the giving and acceptance of the right [*circa traditionem-acceptationem iuris in corpus*] to acts which of their nature are open to the procreation of children.

D. Analysis

Canon 1096 succinctly states that a person must at least not be ignorant that marriage is a (1) permanent, (2) *consortium* (3) between a man and a woman (4) ordered for the procreation of offspring (5) by means of some sexual cooperation. In other words, this canon states that the essence of marriage includes two elements: the *personalist* element (the "permanent *consortium* between a man and a woman") and the *procreational* element ("ordered to the procreation of offspring by means of some sexual cooperation"). [See L.G. WRENN, *Decisions*, 2nd rev. ed., Washington, DC, Canon Law Society, 1983, p. 129.] The canon further indicates that substantial ignorance regarding some portion of either element can invalidate marriage.

The 1983 *CIC* maintains the presumption of law found in canon 1082, §2, of the 1917 *CIC*, i.e., after puberty (twelve for girls, fourteen for boys), knowledge of marriage is presumed. Before puberty, ignorance is presumed. Since this is a presumption of law, it can yield to contrary proof, cf. canon 1584.

It is to be remembered that canon 1096 and its parallel canon 819 in the *CCEO* are examples of areas which determine that ignorance hinders the effectiveness of invalidating or disqualifying laws, which, generally speaking, it does not according to canon 15, §1, and its parallel canon 1497, §1, of the *CCEO*. Two details need to be pointed out concerning these canons: (1) they refer to both ignorance and error, but we are concerned only with ignorance; and (2) generally speaking according to these canons, both ignorance and error do not hinder the effectiveness of invalidating or disqualifying laws unless expressly stated in the law.

Marriage is a juridic act and thus subject to the regulations delineated in the canons pertaining to juridic acts (canons 124-128). First of all, for validity, we follow canon 124 (*CCEO* canon 931). Thus, for a juridic act to be valid, the person must be capable (both naturally and juridically) of placing it; it must include all of its essential elements; and the formalities and requirements imposed by law for validity must be observed. Ignorance is specifically mentioned in canon 126 (and its parallel canon 933 in the *CCEO*).

Ignorance about the essential nature of marriage is best understood in the Thomistic sense. It is not only the privation or lack of knowledge in a person who is naturally capable of such knowledge, but also, more specifically, it is the lack of *due* knowledge, i.e., the degree of knowledge that a person within a given situation is expected to have. Thus, ignorance is distinguished from nescience, which is the total absence of knowledge. A minimal knowledge of the nature of marriage is required by the natural law itself, since one cannot intend or will to enter the marriage covenant without knowing what it is, following the adage *nil volitum nisi praecognitum* ("Nothing is willed unless it is known before").

According to the canon, detailed and sophisticated knowledge of the essence of marriage is not required; in fact, canon 1096 presents the minimum which is needed for a person or persons to enter into marriage by presenting the basic, yet essential, description of marriage: a (1) permanent, (2) *consortium* (partnership) (3) between a man and a woman (4) for the procreation of offspring (5) by means of some sexual cooperation. However, a person should have more than an abstract notion of marital consent: there is to be a realization of the personal implications of that to which he or she is consenting. Thus, according to canon 1096, the spouses must know that marriage is a permanent relationship of a special nature between a man and a woman. They must also know that this relationship is ordered to the generation of children through sexual cooperation.

E. Application

Pope Paul VI set forth five values of conjugal love (total, fully human, exclusive, creative and moral) which, if we take them into consideration in light of the following five elements, respectively, we can see a correspondence between them. Let us describe each of these elements individually:

(1) **permanent**: all that is required is that the parties know that marriage is a stable relationship; one that is not sporadic or fleeting. They must also know, as stated *coram* SERRANO (25 April 1975) that the relationship is, of its nature, permanent and cannot be terminated by the parties themselves. However, a formal understanding of indissolubility is not required in this knowledge.

(2) *consortium* (**partnership**): the *consortium* referred to in the canon is understood not simply as

the context within which procreative sexual acts take place. It is the total self-giving partnership of the spouses which is clearly seen in the Church's teaching (*Gaudium et spes* 47-52; canon 1055). This requires the knowledge that some mutual cooperation, support, and companionship is required. Pompedda, in his 29 October 1979 decision, writes that the minimum knowledge required on the part of the contractants to consent validly concerns marriage as a permanent society, that is, a perpetual communion of life and a communion between two sexually distinct persons and ordered to a specific end.

(3) **between a man and a woman**: this partnership is an exclusive one, not allowing for more than the two spouses. Furthermore, since it is ordered for the procreation of offspring, it is heterosexual; i.e., between a man and a woman. Marriage does not, by its very nature, allow for same sex unions.

(4) **for the procreation of offspring**: it is the ordering of the marital *consortium* for the procreation of children which differentiates it from any other relationship. Marriage is more than a partnership of friendship, service, economics, etc. Marriage is a conjugal relationship which calls for the specific element of sexuality which, in turn, finds its fullness in procreation.

(5) **by means of some sexual cooperation**: here the 1983 *CIC* explicitly states that the procreation of children is by some means of sexual cooperation. While the couple need not have complete knowledge of the details of sexual copulation, they are to know specifically that it is sexual, i.e., genital, and not merely something physical in a generic kind of way. See *coram* EWERS, 1 February 1975 in *SRR Dec*, 67 (1975), pp. 27-33; *coram* MASALA, 30 March 1977, in *SRR Dec*, 69 (1977), 157-171.

Ignorance is more properly ascribed to those who have the basic capacity for knowledge but lacked the opportunity rather than the capacity to learn. Confusing and conflicting social customs and value systems can prevent a person from learning that the notions of permanent commitment and self-sacrifice are acceptable facets of life. Because of these social realities, canonical jurisprudence no longer presumes that all persons marry in the manner intended by God, as stated in *coram* EWERS (16 May 1968).

Consequently, a person could go through a wedding ceremony and yet be ignorant of the fact that the subsequent marriage involves a self-sacrificing community of life ordered to the good of the spouses and the procreation and education of children. Therefore, taking all these factors into consideration, if there is ignorance, i.e., lack of due knowledge, on the part of the contractant(s) in one or more of the five elements we have described in the canon, the marriage is invalid.

BIBLIOGRAPHY

SOURCES

ABBOTT, W.M., gen. ed., *The Documents of Vatican II*. New York, Guild Press, 1966. xxi, 794 p.

Acta Apostolicae Sedis. (= *AAS*). Romae, Typis Polyglottis Vaticanis, 1909-1928; Civitate Vaticana, Typis polyglottis Vaticanis, 1929-.

Acta Sanctae Sedis, (= *ASS*). Romae, Typographia Polyglotta, 1865-1908.

AUGUSTINUS, A., *De libero arbitrio*. [*On free choice of the will*], A.S. BENJAMIN and L.H. HACKSTAFF, trans., Indianapolis, Bobbs-Merril, 1964, xxxii, 162 p.

-----, *De libero arbitrio*, W.M. GREEN, ed., Turnholti, Typographi Brepols, 1968, *Corpus christianorum. Series latina*, vol. 29, viii, 380 p.

-----, *De Trinitate* [The Trinity], S. McKENNA, trans., Washington, DC: Catholic University of America Press, 1963, *The Fathers of the Church*, Vol. 45, *The Writings of Saint Augustine*, xvii, 539 p.

-----, *De Trinitate*, W.J. MOUNTAIN, ed., Turnholti, Typographi Brepols, 1968, *Corpus christianorum. Series latina*, vol. 50, cii, 380 p.

BENEDICTUS XIV, *De synodo dioecesana*, libri tredecim in duos tomos distributi, Romae, ex Typographia Sacrae Congregationis de Propaganda Fide, 1806, 2 vol.

Catechism of the Catholic Church, English translation, Ottawa, Publications Service, Canadian Conference of Catholic Bishops, 1994, 698 p.

Codex canonum Ecclesiarum orientalium, auctoritate Ioannis Pauli P.P. II promulgatus, in *AAS*, 82 (1990), part 2, pp. 1033-1364.

American version of the English-language translation: *Code of Canons of the Eastern Churches. Latin-English Edition*, translation prepared under the auspices of the Canon Law Society of America, Washington, DC, Canon Law Society of America, 1992, xlvii, 785 p.

Codex canonum Ecclesiarum orientalium, fontium annotatione auctus, auctoritate Ioannis Pauli PP. II promulgatus, Vatican City, Libreria editrice Vaticana, 1995, xxx, 617 p.

Codex iuris canonici, Pii X Pontificis Maximi iussu digestus, Benedicti Papae XV promulgatus, in *AAS*, 9 (1917), part 2, 593 p.

Codex iuris canonici, Pii X Pontificis Maximi iussu digestus, Benedicti Papae XV auctoritate promulgatus, Romae, Typis polyglottis Vaticanis, 1917, lii, 916 p.

Codex iuris canonici, auctoritate Ioannis Pauli P.P. II promulgatus, in *AAS*, 73 (1983), part 2, xxx, 317 p.

148

Codex iuris canonici; fontium annotatione et indice analytico-alphabetico auctus, auctoritate Ioannis Pauli PP. II promulgatus, Vatican City, Libreria editrice Vaticana, 1989, xxxii, 669 p.

American version of the English-language translation: *Code of Canon Law, Latin-English Edition*, New English Translation, prepared under the auspices of the Canon Law Society of America, Washington, DC, Canon Law Society of America, 1999, xliii, 751 p.

The Code of Canon Law, New revised English translation, prepared by the Canon Law Society of Great Britain and Ireland in association with The Canon Law Society of Australia and New Zealand and The Canadian Canon Law Society, London, HarperCollins Publishers, 1997, xvi, 509 p.

Communicationes, Roma, PONTIFICIA COMMISSIO CODICI IURIS CANONICI RECOGNOSCENDO, vol. 1(1969) - 15 (1983); PONTIFICIA COMMISSIO AD CODICEM IURIS CANONICI AUTHENTICE INTERPRETANDUM, 16 (1984) - 20 (1988); PONTIFICIUM CONSILIUM DE LEGUM TEXTIBUS INTERPRETANDIS, 21 (1989) - .

CONSILIUM [sic] TRIDENTIUM, 1545-1563, *Diariorum, actorum, epistolarum, tractatuum nova collectio*, Edidit Societas Goerresiana, Friburgi Brisgoviae, Herder, 1901-1938, 13 vol.

CONGREGATION OF THE COUNCIL, *Dispensationis matrimonii, ASS*, Romae, Typogràphia Polyglotta, 5 (1869), pp. 551-554.

-----, *Ventimilien, ASS*, Romae, Typographia Polyglotta, 21 (1888), pp. 162-181.

Corpus iuris canonici, ed. Lipsiensis secunda post A. L. RICHTERI curas ad librorum manu scriptorum et editionis Romanae fidem recognovit et adnotatione critica, instruxit A. FRIEDBERG, Lipsiae, ex officina B. Tauchnitz, 1879-1881, 2 vol.

Corpus iuris civilis, Berolini, Apud Weidmannos, 1928-1929, 3 vol.

FLANNERY, A., gen. ed., *Vatican Council II: More Post Conciliar Documents*, vol. 2, Collegeville, Minnesota, The Liturgical Press, 1982, xxi, 920 p.

-----, *Vatican II. Constitutions, Decrees, Declarations*, rev. ed., Northport, New York, Costello Publishing Co., 1996, xiv, 610 p.

-----, *Vatican Council II: Volume 1: The Conciliar and Post Conciliar Documents*, rev. ed., Northport, New York, Costello Publishing Co., 1996, xvi, 1036 p.

JOHN PAUL II, Apostolic exhortation, *Familiaris consortio*, 22 November 1981, in *AAS*, 74 (1982), pp. 81-191; English translation in A. FLANNERY, gen. ed., *Vatican II: More Post Conciliar Documents*, Northport, New York, Costello Publishing Company, 1982, pp. 815-893.

-----, Allocution to the Roman Rota, 28 January 1982, in *AAS*, 74 (1982), pp. 449-454; English translation in W.H. WOESTMAN, ed., *Papal Allocutions to the Roman Rota 1939-1994*, (= WOESTMAN, *Papal Allocutions*), Ottawa, Saint Paul University, 1994, pp. 171-175.

JOHN PAUL II, Allocution to the Roman Rota, 26 February 1983, in *AAS*, 75 (1983), pp. 554-559; English translation in WOESTMAN, *Papal Allocutions*, pp. 176-180.

-----, Allocution to the Roman Rota, 26 January 1984, in *AAS*, 76 (1984), pp. 643-649; English translation in WOESTMAN, *Papal Allocutions*, pp. 181-186.

-----, Allocution to the Roman Rota, 25 January 1988, in *AAS*, 80 (1988), pp. 1178-1185; English translation in WOESTMAN, *Papal Allocutions*, pp. 197-203.

-----, Allocution to the Roman Rota, 28 January 1991, in *AAS*, 83 (1991), pp. 947-953; English translation in WOESTMAN, *Papal Allocutions*, pp. 214-218.

-----, Allocution to the Roman Rota, 30 January 1993, in *AAS*, 85 (1993), pp. 1256-1260; English translation in WOESTMAN, *Papal Allocutions*, pp. 223-226.

-----, Allocution to the Roman Rota, 21 January 2000, in *Origins*, 29 (1999-2000), pp. 553-555.

LOMBARDUS, P., *Libri IV Sententiarum, studio et curo PP. Collegii S. Bonaventurae in lucem editi*, 2nd ed., prope Florentiam, ex Typograhia Collegii S. Bonaventurae, 1916, 2 vol.

Nuntia, Città del Vaticano, PONTIFICIA COMMISSIO CODICI IURIS CANONCI ORIENTALIS RECOGNOSCENDO, 1975-1990, 31 vols.

PAUL VI, Encyclical letter, *Humanae vitae*, 25 July 1968, in *AAS*, 60 (1968), pp. 481-503; English translation in A. FLANNERY, gen. ed., *Vatican Council II: More Post Conciliar Documents*, vol. 2, Collegeville, Minnesota, The Liturgical Press, 1982, pp. 397-416.

-----, Allocution to the Roman Rota, 9 February 1976, in *AAS*, 68 (1976), pp. 204-208; English translation in WOESTMAN, *Papal Allocutions*, pp. 133-137.

PIUS XI, Encyclical letter, *Casti connubii*, 31 December 1930, in *AAS*, 22 (1930), pp. 539-592; English translation in *Five Great Encyclicals: Labor, Education, Marriage, Restructuring the Social Order, Atheistic Communism*, New York, The Paulist Press, 1959, pp. 77-117.

PIUS XII, Allocution to the Congress of the Italian Catholic Union of Midwives, 29 October 1951, in *AAS*, 43 (1951), pp. 835-854; English translation in V.A. YZERMANS, ed., *The Unwearied Advocate: Public Addresses of Pope Pius XII*, Saint Cloud, Minnesota, Saint Cloud Bookshop, 1956, vol. 2, pp. 117-132.

-----, Address to the Congress of the 'Family Front' and the Federation of Associations of Large Families, 26 November 1951, in *AAS*, 43 (1951), pp. 855-860; English translation in V.A. YZERMANS, ed., *The Unwearied Advocate: Public Addresses of Pope Pius XII*, Saint Cloud, Minnesota, Saint Cloud Bookshop, 1956, vol. 2, pp. 132-136.

PONTIFICIA COMMISSIO CODICI IURIS CANONICI RECOGNOSCENDO, *Schema documenti pontificii quo disciplina canonica de sacramentis recognoscitur*, Romae, Typis polyglottis Vaticanis, 1975, 95

150

p.

PONTIFICIA COMMISSIO CODICI IURIS CANONICI RECOGNOSCENDO, *Codex iuris canonici: schema Patribus Commisionis reservatum*, Città del Vaticano, Libreria editrice Vaticanis, 1980, xxiii, 382 p.

-----, *Codex iuris canonici: schema novissimum*, in Civitate Vaticana, Typis polyglottis Vaticanis, 1982, xviii, 308 p.

ROTAE ROMANAE TRIBUNAL, *Decretâ selecta inter ea quae anno 1987 prodierunt cura apostolici tribunalis edita*, Città del Vaticano, Libreria editrice Vaticana, 1996-1998, 5 vol.

Sacrae Romanae Rotae decisiones seu sententiae quae prodierunt anno [...] cura eiusdem Tribunalis editae, (= *SRR Dec*), vols. 1-40 (1909-1948), Romae, Typis polyglottis Vaticanis, 1912-1958; TRIBUNAL APOSTOLICUM SACRAE ROMANAE ROTAE, vols. 41-58 (1949-1966), Romae, Typis polyglottis Vaticanis, 1959-1975; Vatican City, Libreria Editrice Vaticana, vol. 59-66 (1967-1974), 1977-1983; TRIBUNAL APOSTOLICUM ROTAE ROMANAE, vols. 67-72 (1975-1980), Vatican City, Libreria Editrice Vaticana, 1986-1987; APOSTOLICUM ROTAE ROMANAE TRIBUNAL, vols. 73- (1981 -), Vatican City, Libreria editrice Vaticana, 1987- .

Sacrosanctum Concilium oecumenicum Vaticanum II. constitutiones, decreta, declarationes, Romae, Typis polyglottis Vaticanis, 1967, 2 vol.

SECOND VATICAN COUNCIL, Pastoral Constitution on the Church in the Modern World, *Gaudium et spes*, 7 December 1965, in *AAS*, 58 (1966), pp. 1025-1120; English translation in A. FLANNERY, gen. ed., *Vatican II. Constitutions, Decrees, Declarations*, rev. ed., Northport, New York, Costello Publishing Co., 1996, pp. 163-282.

Thesaurus resolutionum Sacrae Congregationis Concilii, Romae, Typographia Vaticana, 1739-1963, 153 vol.

-----, vol. 145, Romae, Typographia Vaticana, 1885, iv, 683 p.

-----, vol. 147, Romae, Typographia Vaticana, 1888, vi, 876 p.

THOMAS AQUINAS, *Commentum in quattor libros Sententiarum Petri Lombardi*, from S.E. FRETTÉ and P. MARÉ, eds., *Opera Omnia Thomae Aquinatis*, Parisiis, L. Vivès, 1871-1880, 34 vol.

-----, *Quaestiones disputatae*, vol. 3, *De veritate*, 6th ed., Taurini, Marietti, 1931, 333 p.

-----, *Summa theologiae*, Latin text and English translation, introductions, notes, appendices and glossaries, Cambridge, England, Blackfriars in conjunction with Eyre & Spottiswoode, London, 1964-1981, 61 vol.

-----, *Summa theologiae*, vol. 5, *Supplementum tertiae partis*, Ottawa, Impensis Studii Generalis O. Pr., 1945, xliv, 525, 16 p.

THOMAS AQUINAS, *The "Summa Theologica" of St. Thomas Aquinas, Third Part (Supplement)*, literally translated by Fathers of the English Dominican Province, London, Burns, Oates & Washbourne, Ltd., 1932, vi, 376 p.

JURISPRUDENCE

For the sake of consistency and clarity, *SRR Dec* is used in this list denoting the volumes of Rotal decisions.

I. JURISPRUDENCE OF THE ROMAN ROTA

A. PUBLISHED

coram ANNÉ, 25 February 1969, no. 39, in *SRR Dec*, 61 (1969), pp.174-192.

-----, 14 November 1973, no. 190, in *SRR Dec*, 65 (1973), pp. 756-762.

coram BRENNAN, 20 January 1964, no. 5, in *SRR Dec*, 56 (1964), pp. 15-21.

coram BOCCAFOLA, 27 February 1992, no. 16, in *SRR Dec*, 84 (1992), pp. 91-102.

coram CANALS, 9 July 1964, no. 114, in *SRR Dec*, 56 (1964), pp. 593-598.

-----, 15 March 1967, no. 35, in *SRR Dec*, 59 (1967), pp. 149-153.

-----, 25 October 1972, no. 250, in *SRR Dec*, 64 (1972), pp. 620-627.

coram CANESTRI, 16 July 1943, no. 57, in *SRR Dec*, 35 (1943), pp. 594-612.

coram DAVINO, 27 October 1972, no. 255, in *SRR Dec*, 64 (1972), pp. 649-655.

coram De LANVERSIN, 31 July 1990, no. 103, in *SRR Dec*, 82 (1990), pp. 676-684.

-----, 17 July 1996, in *Forum*, 9 (1998) 1, pp. 227-251.

-----, 15 May 1997, in *Monitor ecclesiasticus*, 124 (1999), pp. 458-489.

coram Di FELICE, 25 July 1973, no. 154, in *SRR Dec*, 65 (1973), pp. 619-625.

-----, 14 December 1977, no. 176, in *SRR Dec*, 69 (1977), pp. 505-508.

coram EWERS, 1 February 1975, no. 15, in *SRR Dec*, 67 (1975), pp. 27-33.

-----, 13 December 1975, no. 149, in *SRR Dec*, 67 (1975), pp. 724-730.

152

coram FAGIOLO, 28 May 1971, no. 112, in *SRR Dec*, 63 (1971), pp. 460-466.

coram FALTIN, 18 January 1988, no. 4, in *SRR*, 80 (1988), pp. 1-14.

coram FELICI, 22 May 1956, no. 114, in *SRR Dec*, 48 (1956), pp. 467-476.

coram FUNGHINI, 14 October 1992, no. 75, in *SRR*, 84 (1992), pp. 461-482.

coram GRAZIOLI, 1 July 1933, no. 47, in *SRR Dec*, 25 (1933), pp. 405-419.

-----, 7 August 1936, no. 60, in *SRR Dec*, 28 (1936), pp. 570-582.

-----, 12 January 1942, no. 3, in *SRR Dec*, 34 (1942), pp. 31-41.

coram HEARD, 13 July 1946, no. 36, in *SRR Dec*, 38 (1946), pp. 360-368.

-----, 30 July 1959, no. 139, in *SRR Dec*, 51 (1959), pp. 420-424.

coram JULLIEN, 21 December 1938, no. 77, in *SRR Dec*, 30 (1938), pp. 715-726.

-----, 16 April 1948, no. 21, in *SRR Dec*, 40 (1948), pp. 119-128.

coram LEFEBVRE, 30 October 1965, no. 153, in *SRR Dec*, (1965), pp.769-775.

-----, 6 July 1967, no. 129, in *SRR Dec*, 59 (1967), pp. 553-561.

-----, 7 December 1968, no. 218, in *SRR Dec*, 60 (1968), pp. 823-830.

-----, 8 July 1972, no. 200, in *SRR Dec*, 64 (1972), pp. 422-428.

coram MANNUCCI, 30 July 1927, no. 40, in *SRR Dec*, 19 (1927), pp. 351-356.

-----, 10 November 1930, no. 54, in *SRR Dec*, 22 (1930), pp. 605-612.

coram MASALA, 30 March 1977, no. 41, in *SRR Dec*, 69 (1977), pp. 157-171.

coram MASSIMI, 2 August 1929, no. 43, in *SRR Dec*, 21 (1929), pp. 363-369.

coram MATTIOLI, 25 November 1964, no. 155, in *SRR Dec*, 56 (1964), pp. 867-883.

coram MORI, 17 March 1910, no. 12, in *SRR Dec*, 2 (1910), pp. 112-122.

coram PALAZZINI, 4 February 1970, no. 25, in *SRR Dec*, 62 (1970), pp. 118-126.

coram PALESTRO, 27 May 1992, no. 46, in *SRR Dec*, 84 (1992), pp. 279-305.

coram PARRILLO, 16 February 1928, no. 6, in *SRR Dec*, 20 (1928), pp. 57-81.

-----, 20 July 1929, no. 36, in *SRR Dec* 21 (1929), pp. 306-312.

coram PINNA, 30 October 1958, no. 177, in *SRR Dec*, 50 (1958), pp. 556-564.

coram PINTO, 26 June 1971, no. 138, in *SRR Dec*, 63 (1971), pp. 559-567.

-----, 6 November 1972, no. 257, in *SRR Dec*, 64 (1972), pp. 672-680.

coram POMPEDDA, 9 May 1970, no. 100, in *SRR Dec*, 62 (1970), pp. 475-481.

-----, 23 January 1971, no. 16, in *SRR Dec*, 63 (1971), pp. 53-59.

-----, 3 July 1979, no. 128, in *SRR Dec*, 71 (1979), pp. 379-399.

-----, 29 October 1979, no. 164, in *SRR Dec*, 71 (1979), pp. 460-467.

coram QUATTROCOLO, 7 August 1929, no. 47, in *SRR Dec*, 21 (1929), pp. 392-405.

coram SABATTANI, 24 February 1961, no. 29, in *SRR Dec*, 53 (1961), pp. 116-132.

-----, 22 March 1963, no. 44, in *SRR Dec*, 55 (1963), pp. 196-221.

coram SERRANO RUIZ, 25 April 1975, no. 67, in *SRR Dec*, 67 (1975), pp. 368-375.

coram STAFFA, 17 May 1957, no. 103, in *SRR Dec*, 49 (1957), pp. 426-430.

coram STANKIEWICZ, 16 December 1982, in *Ephemerides iuris canonici*, 39 (1983), pp. 255-265.

-----, 24 July 1997, in *Monitor ecclesiasticus*, 124 (1999), pp. 614-669.

coram TEODORI, 26 May 1948, no. 33, in SRR Dec, 40 (1948), pp. 203-208.

-----, 8 July 1949, no. 62, in *SRR Dec*, 41 (1949), pp. 368-373.

coram TURNATURI, 22 April 1998, in *Monitor ecclesiasticus*, 124 (1999), pp. 292-333.

coram WYNEN, 1 March 1930, no. 12, in *SRR Dec*, 22 (1930), pp. 125-153.

-----, 14 March 1935, no. 16, in *SRR Dec*, 27 (1935), pp. 128-150.

-----, 13 April 1943, no. 29, in *SRR Dec*, 35 (1943), pp. 270-281.

-----, 27 February 1947, no. 15, in *SRR Dec*, 39 (1947), pp. 119-128.

154

B. UNPUBLISHED

coram ANNÉ, 25 February 1969, no. 43, in *SRR Dec*, 61 (1969).

-----, 23 October 1973, no. 164, in *SRR Dec*, 65 (1973).

coram De JORIO, 8 January 1975, no. 1, in *SRR Dec*, 67 (1975).

-----, 6 July 1977, no. 106, in *SRR Dec*, 69 (1977).

coram FIORE, 30 November 1968, no. 215, in *SRR Dec*, 60 (1968).

-----, 21 March 1972, no. 71, in *SRR Dec*, 64 (1972).

coram HUOT, 26 February 1981, no. 34, in *SRR Dec*, 73 (1981).

coram PINTO, 13 January 1975, no. 3, in *SRR Dec*, 67 (1975).

II. JURISPRUDENCE OF OTHER TRIBUNALS

coram ACTON, [Southwark Tribunal], 17 February 1977, in *Matrimonial Decisions for England and Wales*, 13 (1977), pp. 50-51.

coram BROWN, [Westminster Tribunal], 27 July 1972, in *Matrimonial Decisions for England and Wales*, 7 (1972), pp. 232-237.

coram CACHIA, [Maltese Ecclesiastical Tribunal], 12 June 1985, in *Forum*, 1 (1990) 1, pp. 106-115.

coram CUNNINGHAM, [Scottish National Tribunal], 19 May 1992, in *Matrimonial Decisions of Great Britain and Ireland*, 28 (1992), pp.131-133.

coram DALEY, [Liverpool], 14 May 1997, in *Matrimonial Decisions of Great Britain and Ireland*, 33 (1997), pp. 75-78.

coram DUNDERDALE, [Westminster Tribunal], 8 October 1968, in *Matrimonial Decisions for England and Wales*, 2 (1968), pp. 210-213.

coram FARAONE, [Tribunal Ecclesiasticum Regionis Conciliaris Sardiniae], 21 December 1982, in *Il diritto ecclesiastico*, 94 (1983) 2, pp. 462-481.

coram FEDERICI, [Vicariatus Urbis Tribunal Appellationis], 16 March 1961, in *Il diritto ecclesiastico*, 72 (1961) 2, pp. 396-397.

coram FRATTEGIANI, [Tribunale Regionale Umbro], 11 March 1954, in *Il diritto ecclesiastico*, 68 (1957)

2, pp. 31-39.

coram HERTEL, [Paterson Diocesan Tribunal], 12 August 1974, in *Studia canonica*, 8 (1974), pp. 439-443.

coram HUMPHREYS, [Birmingham Tribunal], 29 November 1973, in *Matrimonial Decisions for England and Wales*, 8 (1973), pp. 309-316.

coram LOFTUS, [Leeds], 26 October 1978, in *Matrimonial Decisions for England and Wales*, 14 (1978), pp. 52-54.

coram PAYNE, [Dublin], 29 September 1988, in *Matrimonial Decisions of Great Britain and Ireland*, 24 (1988), pp. 34-42.

coram RAMOS, [Tribunal Ecclesiastico de Mallorca], 23 December 1986, in *Revista española de derecho canónico*, 45 (1988), pp. 403-409.

coram READ, [Brentwood, England], 7 May 1998, in A. MENDONÇA, *Marriage Consent - III (cc. 1096-1107)*, (pro manuscripto), Ottawa, Faculty of Canon Law, Saint Paul University, 1998-1999, pp. 33-38.

coram STENSON, [Dublin], 15 January 1979, in *Matrimonial Decisions for England and Wales*, 15 (1979), pp. 58-63.

-----, [Dublin], 27 March 1981, in *Matrimonial Decisions of Great Britain and Ireland*, 17 (1981), pp. 117-122.

-----, [Dublin], 30 March 1981, *ibid.*, pp. 122-125.

-----, [Dublin], 19 May 1981, *ibid.*, pp. 72-75.

-----, [Dublin], 6 July 1981, *ibid.*, pp. 4-8.

-----, [Dublin], 23 February 1982, in *Matrimonial Decisions of Great Britain and Ireland*, 18 (1982), pp. 85-87.

Tribunal of Barcelona, 11 June 1971, in L. DEL AMO, *Sentencias, casos y cuestiones en la Rota española*, Pamplona, Ediciones Universidad de Navarra, 1977, pp. 749-758.

Tribunal of Granada, 11 May 1957, in L. DEL AMO, *Sentencias, casos y cuestiones en la Rota española*, Pamplona, Ediciones Universidad de Navarra, 1977, pp. 31-39.

156

BOOKS

ABATE, A., *Il matrimonio nell'attuale legislazione canonica*, 2ⁿᵈ rev. ed., Brescia, Paideia Editrice, 1982, 352 p.

ABBO, J.A. and J.D. HANNAN, *The Sacred Canons: a Concise Presentation of the Current Disciplinary Norms of the Church*, rev. ed., St. Louis, Herder, 1957, 2 vol.

ACKERMANN, R.J., *Theories of Knowledge: A Critical Introduction*, New York, McGraw-Hill, 1965, ix, 305 p.

ALUEDE OJEMEN, C., *Psychological Factors in Matrimonial Consent in the Light of Canonical Legislation*, Roma, Pontificia Universitas Urbaniana, 1986, 396 p.

AMOS, S., *The History and Principles of the Civil Law of Rome: An Aid to the Study of Scientific and Comparative Jurisprudence*, London, K. Paul, Trench & Co., 1883, xv, 475 p.

ARROBA CONDE, M.J., *Diritto processuale canonico*, 2ⁿᵈ ed., Roma, EDIURCLA, 1994, iv, 538 p.

AYRINHAC, H.A. and P.J. LYDON, *Marriage Legislation in the New Code of Canon Law*, new rev. ed., New York, Benziger, 1939, xix, 394 p.

AZNAR GIL, F.R., *El nuevo derecho matrimonial canónico*, 2ⁿᵈ rev. ed., Salamanca, Universidad Pontificia de Salamanca, 1985, 543 p.

BACHOFEN, C.A., *A Commentary on the New Code of Canon Law*, 6ᵗʰ rev. ed., St. Louis, Herder, 1925-1936, 8 vol.

BADII, C., *Institutiones iuris canonici ad usum scholarum*, 3ʳᵈ ed., Florentiae, Editrice Fiorentina, 1921-1922, 2 vol.

BAYON, J.G.F., *Tractatus canonico-moralis de sacramento matrimonii*, Madrid, Editorial del C. de Maria, [s.d.], 2 vol. in 1.

BERGER, A., *Encyclopedic Dictionary of Roman Law*, transactions of the American Philosophical Society, new series, vol. 43, part 2, Philadelphia, 1953, 808 p.

BERNÁRDEZ CANTON, A., *Compendio de derecho matrimonial canónico*, 7ᵗʰ ed., Madrid, Tecnos, 1991, 302 p.

BERSINI, F., *Il nuovo diritto canonico matrimoniale: commento giuridico, teologico, pastorale*, 4ᵗʰ ed., Leumann, Torino, Editrice Elle Di Ci, 1994, 275 p.

BESTE, U.C., *Introducio in Codicem quam in usum et utilitatem scholae et cleri ad promptam expeditamque canonum interpretationem*, 4ᵗʰ ed., Neapoli (Italia), M. D'Auria, 1956, 1097 p.

BEYER, J., et al., *Il Nuovo codice di diritto canonico, studi*, Torino, Editrice Elle Di Ci, 1985, 318 p.

BIANCHI, P.G., *Incapacitas assumendi obligationes essentiales matrimonii: analisi della giurisprudenza rotale. particolarmente degli anni 1970-1982*, Roma, Pubblicazioni del Pontificio Seminario Lombardo di Roma, 1992, xi, 349 p.

BLACK, H.C., *Black's Law Dictionary: Definitions of the Terms and Phrases of American and English Jurisprudence, Ancient and Modern*, 6th ed., St. Paul, West Publishing Co., 1990, xiv, 1657 p.

BLANCO NÁJERA, D.F., *El Código de derecho canónico, traducido y comentado*, Cadiz, Establecimientos Cerón, 1942-1945, 2 vol.

BLAT, A., *Commentarium textus Codicis iuris canonici*, Romae, ex Typographia Pontificia in Instituto Pii IX (Iuvenum Opificum a S. Ioseph), 1921-1938, 5 books in 6 vol.

BOLOGNINI, F., *Lineamenti di diritto canonico*, 4th ed., Torino, G. Giappichelli, 1993, 489 p.

BONNET, P.A., *L'essenza del matrimonio canonico: contributo all studio dell'amore coniugale*, Pubblicazioni dell'Istituto di diritto pubblico della Facultà di giurisprudenza, Università degli studi di Roma, series 3, vol. 30, Padova, CEDAM, 1976, 628 p.

-----, *Introduzione al consenso matrimoniale canonico*, Pubblicazioni della Facultà di Giurisprudenza, Dipartimento di scienze giuridiche, Università di Modena, nuova serie, 3, Milano, A. Giuffrè Editore, 1985, xii, 207 p.

BOURKE, V.J., *Wisdom from St. Augustine*, Houston, Texas, Center for Thomistic Studies, University of St.Thomas, 1984, viii, 224 p.

BOUSCAREN, T.L., ed., *The Canon Law Digest*, Milwaukee, Bruce Publishing Com., 1934-1954, volumes 1-3; T.L. BOUSCAREN and J.I. O'CONNOR, eds., Milwaukee, Bruce Publishing Com., 1958-1969, volumes 4-6; J.I. O'CONNOR, ed., Mundelein, Illinois, St. Mary of the Lake Seminary, 1975-1986, volumes 7-10; E.G. PFNAUSCH, ed., Washington, DC, Canon Law Society of America, 1991, volume 11.

BOUSCAREN, T.L., A.C. ELLIS, F.N. KORTH, eds., *Canon Law: A Text and Commentary*, 4th revised ed., Milwaukee, Bruce Publishing Company, 1966, xvi, 1011 p.

BREITENBECK, M.A., *The Role of Experts in Ecclesial Decision-Making in the 1983 Code of Canon Law*, Canon Law Studies, 522, Washington, DC, The Catholic University of America; Ann Arbor, Michigan, UMI, 1988, vi, 345 p.

BRUGGER, W., ed., *Philosophical Dictionary*, K. BAKER, trans. and ed. of the American edition, Spokane, Washington, Gonzaga University Press, 1974, xxiii, 460 p.

BURDICK, W.L., *The Principles of Roman Law and their Relation to Modern Law*, Rochester, Lawyers Co-operative Publishing Co., 1938, xxi, 748 p.

158

BURKE, R.L., *Lack of Discretion of Judgment Because of Schizophrenia: Doctrine and Recent Jurisprudence*, Analecta Gregoriana, 238, Roma, Editrice Pontificia Università Gregoriana, 1986, 254 p.

BURNS, D.J., *Matrimonial Indissolubility: Contrary Conditions: A Historical Synopsis and a Commentary*, Canon Law Studies, 377, Washington, DC, The Catholic University of America, 1963, ix, 158 p.

BURRELL, D.P., *Aquinas: God and Action*, Notre Dame, University of Notre Dame Press, 1979, xiii, 194 p.

CALDERWOOD, H., *Vocabulary of Philosophy*, New Delhi, Akashdeep Publishing House, 1992, vi, 353 p.

CAMMACK, J.S., *Moral Problems of Mental Defect*, London, Burns, Oates & Washbourne, 1938, xi, 200 p.

CANDELA, S., *S. Agostino*, Napoli, Edizioni "Cenacolo serafino", 1966, 211 p.

CAPARROS, E., M. THÉRIAULT, J. THORN, eds., *Code of Canon Law Annotated*, Latin-English edition of the *Code of Canon Law* and English-language translation of the 5th Spanish-language edition of the commentary prepared under the responsibility of the Instituto Martin de Azpilcueta, Montréal, Wilson & Lafleur Limitée, 1993, 1631 p.

CAPPELLO, F.M., *Summa iuris canonici in usum scholarum concinnata*, 4th ed., Romae, apud aedes Universitatis Gregorianae, 1945, 3 vols.

-----, *De matrimonio*, in *Tractatus canonico-moralis de sacramentis*, 7th ed., vol. 5, Romae, Marietti, 1947-1963, xi, 961 p.

CAPPELLINI, E., et al., eds., *La Normativa del nuovo codice*, 2nd ed., Brescia, Queriniana, 1985, 515 p.

CAPUTO, G., *Introduzione allo studio del diritto canonico moderno*, Padova, CEDAM, 1984-1987, 2 vol.

CASTANO, J.F., *Il sacramento del matrimonio*, 2nd ed., Roma, Tipolitografia Pioda Gianfranco, 1992, 530 p.

CHELODI, I., *Ius canonicum de matrimonio et de iudiciis matrimonialibus*, 5th ed., Vicenza, Società Anonima Tipographica Editrice, 1947, xi, 296 p.

CHRÉTIEN, P., *De matrimonio: praelectiones*, 2nd ed., Metis, Journal "le Lorrain", 1937, vii, 491 p.

CHIAPPETTA, L., *Il matrimonio: nella nuova legislazione canonica e concordataria: manuale giuridico-pastorale*, Roma, Dehoniane, 1990, ix, 904 p.

-----, *Il Codice di diritto canonico: commento giuridico-pastorale*, 2nd rev. ed., Roma, Edizioni Denoniane, 1996, 3 vol.

CICOGNANI, A.G., *Canon Law*, 2nd rev. ed., J. O'HARA and F. BRENNAN, trans., Philadelphia. Dolphin Press, 1935, xiv, 892 p.

CLARK, M.T., ed., *An Aquinas Reader: Selections from the Writings of Thomas Aquinas*, 5th ed., New York, Fordham University Press, 1996, 597 p.

COCCHI, G., *Commentarium in Codicem iuris canonici ad usum scholarum*, Taurinorum Augustae, Marietti, 1932-1942, 5 books in 8 vol.

COLLINSON, D., *Fifty Major Philosophers: A Reference Guide*, London and New York, Routledge, 1987, 170 p.

CONNOR, J.E., *The Invalidity of Marriage in the Roman Catholic Church and in the Civil Laws of the United States: A Comparative Study*, Canon Law Studies, 456, Washington, DC, The Catholic University of America; Ann Arbor, Michigan, UMI, 1969, vi, 448 p.

CONTE A CORONATA, M., *De sacramentis: tractatus canonicus*, Taurini, Marietti, 1943-1946, 3 vol.

CORECCO, E., *The Theology of Canon Law: A Methodological Question*, F. TURVASI, trans., Pittsburgh, Duquesne University Press, ix, 159 p.

CORIDEN, J.A., T.J. GREEN, D.E. HEINTSCHEL, eds., *The Code of Canon Law: A Text and Commentary*, commissioned by the Canon Law Society of America, New York, Paulist Press, 1985, xxvi, 1152 p.

CORIDEN, J.A., *An Introduction to Canon Law*, New York, Paulist Press, 1991, xiv, 232 p.

COURTEMANCHE, B.F., *The Total Simulation of Matrimonial Consent*, Canon Law Studies, 270, Washington, DC, The Catholic University of America, 1948, xx, 120 p.

CURRAN, C.E., *Invincible Ignorance of the Natural Law according to St. Alphonsus*, [Doctoral thesis], Romae, Academia Alphonsiana, 1961, 87 p.

D'ANNIBALE, G., *Summula theologiae moralis*, 2nd ed., Mediolani, S. Josephi, 1881, 3 vols in 1.

D'AVACK, P.A., *Cause di nullità e di divorzio nel diritto matrimoniale canonico*, vol. 1, Firenze, Casa Editrice del Dott. Carlo Cya, 1952, xiv, 761 p.

-----, *Corso di diritto canonico: il matrimonio*, Milano, A. Giuffrè Editore, 1959, viii, 274 p.

DE ECHEVERRIA, L., ed., *Código de derecho canónico, edición bilingüe comentada*, Madrid, Biblioteca de Autores Cristianos, La Editorial Catolica, S.A., 1984, lii, 921 p.

DEFARRARI, R.J. and M.I. BARRY, *A Complete Index of the Summa Theologica of St. Thomas Aquinas*, Washington, DC, Catholic University of America Press, 1956, ix, 386 p.

-----, *A Latin-English Dictionary of St. Thomas Aquinas. Based on the Summa Theologica and Selected*

Passages of His Other Works, Boston, St. Paul Editions, 1960, 1115 p.

DELLA ROCCA, F., *Manual of Canon Law*, A. THATCHER, trans., Milwaukee, Bruce, 1959, xx, 624 p.

-----, *Diritto matrimoniale canonico: tavole sinottiche: volume di aggiornamento*, Pavoda, CEDAM, 1982-1995, 4 vol.

DÈ LIGUORI, A.M., *Theologia moralis*, editio nova cum antiquis editionibus diligenter collata in singulis auctorum allegationibus recognita notisque criticis et commentariis illustrata cura et studio L. GAUDÈ, Romae, Typographia Vaticana, 1905-1912, 4 vol.

DE MAURI, L., *Regulae iuris: raccolta di 2000 regole del diritto eseguita sui migliori testi, con l'indicazione delle fonti, schiarimenti, capitoli riassuntivi et la versione italiana riprodotta dai piu celebri commentatori*, 11th ed., Milano, U. Hoepli, 1936, xi, 268 p.

DE SMET, L., *Tractatus theologico-canonicus de sponsalibus et matrimonio*, Brugis, Car. Beyaert, 4th ed., 1927, xiv, 840 p.

DODS, M., ed., *The Works of Aurelius Augustine. a New Translation*, Edinburgh, T&T Clark, 1872-1881, 15 vol.

DOHENY, W.J., *Canonical Procedure in Matrimonial Cases*, vol. 1, Milwaukee, The Bruce Publishing Company, 1948, I, 1277 p.

EDWARDS, P., editor in chief, *The Encyclopedia of Philosophy*, vol. 1, New York, The Macmillan Company and the Free Press, 1967, li, 439 p.

ELMENDORF, J.J., *Elements of Moral Theology Based on the Summa Theologiae of St. Thomas Aquinas*, New York, E. S. Gorham, 1902, xxiv, 655 p.

FARRUGIA, N., *De matrimonio et causis matrimonialibus tractatus canonico-moralis iuxta Codicem iuris canonici*, Taurini-Romae, Marietti, 1924, vii, 564 p.

FAZZARI, G.M., *Valutazione etica e consenso matrimoniale*, Napoli, M. D'Auria, 1951, 81, [1] p.

FEDELE, P., L'"Ordinatio ad prolem" nel matrimonio in diritto canonico, Milano, A. Giuffrè Editore, 1962, 556 p.

FERM, V., ed., *Encyclopedia of Morals*, New York, Greenwood Press, 1969, x, 682 p.

FLEMING, W., *The Vocabulary of Philosophy: Mental, Moral and Metaphysical*, London, R. Griffin, 1857, vi, 560 p.

FLEW, A. ed., *A Dictionary of Philosophy*, New York, St. Martin's Press, 1979, xi, 351 p.

FUENTES, J.A., ed., *Incapacidad consensual para las obligaciones matrimoniales*, Pamplona, Ediciones

Universidad de Navarra, 1991, 384 p.

FUMAGALLI CARULLI, O., *Il matrimonio canonico dopo il concilio: capacità e consenso*, Milano, A. Giuffrè Editore, 1978, xiii, 238 p.

-----, *Intellecto e volontà nel consenso matrimoniale in diritto canonico*, 2ⁿᵈ ed., Milano, Vita e Pensiero, 1981, xxxii, 482 p.

GARCIA GARRIDO, M.J., *Diccionario de jurisprudencia romana*, 3ʳᵈ ed., Madrid, L'Auteur, 1988, ix, 459 p.

GARNER, B.A., ed., *Black's Law Dictionary*, 7ᵗʰ ed., St. Paul, West Group, 1999, xxiii, 1738 p.

GASPARRI, P., *Codex iuris canonici. (Schema Codicis Iuris Canonici: sub secreto pontificio)*, Romae, Typis polyglottis Vaticanis, 1916, vii, 1013 p.

-----, *Tractatus canonicus de matrimonio, ed. nova ad mentem Codicis I. C.*, Città del Vaticano, Typis polyglottis Vaticanis, vol. 2, 1932, 636 p.

GAUTHIER, A., *Roman Law and Its Contribution to the Development of Canon Law*, 2ⁿᵈ ed., Ottawa, Saint Paul University, 1996, vii, 169 p.

GHERRO, S., *Diritto matrimoniale canonico: lezioni: edizione provvisoria e parziale: capp. I-VII*, Padova, CEDAM, 1985, vii, 237 p.

GHIRLANDA, G., *Il diritto nella Chiesa mistero di communione: compendio di diritto ecclesiale*, Milano, Edizioni Paoline, 1990, 711 p.

GIACCHI, O., *Il consenso nel matrimonio canonico*, 3ʳᵈ ed., Milano, A. Giuffrè Editore, 1968, 373 p.

GOFFI, T., ed., *Enciclopedia del matrimonio*, (edited by) P.G. CABRA, Brescia, Queriniana, 1960, xxvi, 957 p.

GONZÁLEZ DEL VALLE, J.M., *Derecho canónico matrimonial: según el Código de 1983*, Pamplona, Ediciones Universidad de Navarra, 1983, 180 p.

GONZÁLEZ Y GONZÁLEZ, F., *Ignorancia y consentimiento matrimonial*, León, Colegio Universitario de León, Unidad de Investigación, 24, 1982, xxviii, 320 p.

GOVE, P.B., editor in chief, *Webster's Third New International Dictionary of the English Language, Unabridged*, Springfield, Massachusetts, G&C Merriam Company, 1981, 102a, 2662 p.

GRAMUNT, I., J. HERVADA, L.A. WAUCK, *Canons and Commentaries on Marriage*, Collegeville, Minnesota, The Liturgical Press, 1987, vii, 198 p.

GRAZIANI, E., *Volontà attuale e volontà precettiva nel negozio matrimoniale canonico*, Pubblicazioni

162

dell'Intituto di scienze giuridiche, economiche, politiche e sociali della Università di Messina, 34, Milano, A. Giuffrè Editore, 1956, 208 p.

GROCHOLEWSKI, Z., *De exclusione indissolubilitatis ex consensu matrimoniali eiusque probatione; considerationes super recentiores sententias rotales*, Bibliotheca "Monitor ecclesiasticus", 43, Napoli, M. D'Auria, 1973, 198 p.

GROCHOLEWSKI, Z., M.F. POMPEDDA, C. ZAGGIA, *Il matrimonio nel nuovo Codice di diritto canonico: annotazioni di diritto sustanziale e processuale*, Padova, Libreria Gregoriana Editrice, 1984, 265 p.

GUTIÉRREZ MARTÍN, L., *La incapacidad para contraer matrimonio: Comentarios al c. 1095 del Código de derecho canónico para uso de los profesionales del foro*, Estudios 88, Salamanca, Universidad Pontificia de Salamanca, 1987, 177 p.

HAMILTON, W., *Lectures on Metaphysics*, H.L. MANSEL and J. VEITCH, eds., Edinburgh, William Blackwood and Sons, 1859-1860, 2 vol.

HENNESSY, P., *A Canonical-Historical Study of Error of Person in Marriage*, Roma, Pontificia Studiorum Universitas a S. Thoma Aq. in Urbe, 1978, xviii, 329 p.

HESTON, E.L., *The Holy See at Work*, Milwaukee, Bruce Publishing Company, 1950, xiv, 188 p.

HUDSON, J.E., *Documentation II on Marriage Nullity Cases*, Ottawa, Saint Paul University, 1979, xvi, 503 p.

-----, *Handbook II for Marriage Nullity Cases*, Ottawa, Faculty of Canon Law, Saint Paul University, 1980, x, 320 p.

HUELS, J.M., *The Pastoral Companion: A Canon Law Handbook for Catholic Ministry*. New Series, 2nd ed., rev., updated and expanded, Quincy, Illinois, Franciscan Press, 1995, xvii, 432 p.

JAFFE, P., *Regesta pontificum romanorum ab condita Ecclesia ad annum post Christum natum MCXCVIII*, 2nd ed., Lipsiae, Viet, 1885-1889, 2 vol.

JEMOLO, A.C., *Il matrimonio nel diritto canonico: dal concilio di Trento al Codice del 1917*, Bologna, Società editrice il Mulino, 1993, 505 p.

JOSEPH, A., *«Consortium vitae», the Essence of Marriage: A Study of Can. 1055 with Particular Reference to India*, Romae, Pontificia Universitas Urbaniana, 1990, xxv, 150 p.

JUGIS, P.J., *A Canonical Analysis of the Meaning of humano modo in Canon 1061.1*, Canon Law Studies, 541, Washington, DC, The Catholic University of America; Ann Arbor, Michigan, UMI, 1992, xi, 393 p.

KEATING, J.R., *The Bearing of Mental Impairment on the Validity of Marriage: An Analysis of Rotal*

Jursiprudence, Analecta Gregoriana, 136, Roma, Gregorian University Press, 1964, vi, 221 p.

KIERNAN, T.P., ed., *Aristotle Dictionary*, New York, Philosophical Library, 1962, 524 p.

KOCH, A. and A. PREUSS, *A Handbook of Moral Theology. Based on the "Lehrbuch der moraltheologie" of the late Antony Koch*, 3rd rev. ed., St. Louis, Herder, 1925-1933, 5 vol.

KUZIONA, J.M., *The Nature and Applicaiton of Juridical Acts according to Canon 124 of the Code of Canon Law*, Ottawa, Saint Paul University, 1998, vii, 243 p.

LAZZARATO, D., *Jurisprudentia pontificia*, Neapoli, M. D'Auria, 1956-1973, 3 vol. in 5 books.

LESAGE, G. and F.G. MORRISEY, *Documentation on Marriage Nullity Cases*, Ottawa, Saint Paul University, 1973, vi, 312 p.

-----, *Selected Texts from Documentation on Marriage Nullity Cases*, J.E. HUDSON, trans., Ottawa, Saint Paul University, 1976, vii, 195 p.

LEWIS, C.T. and C. SHORT, eds., *A Latin Dictionary*, Oxford, Oxford University Press, 1984, xiv, 2019 p.

LLANO CIFUENTES, R., *Novo direito matrimonial canônico: o matrimônio no Codigo e direito canônico de 1983, estudo comparado com a legislacão Brasileira*, Rio de Janeiro, M. Saraiva, 1988, xvii, 505 p.

LOMBARDÍA, P. and J.I. ARRIETA, *Codice di diritto canonico, edizione bilingue commentata*, L. CASTIGLIONE, Italian ed., Roma, Edizioni Logos, 1986, 2 vol.

LONERGAN, B.J.F., *Verbum, Word and Idea in Aquinas*, D.B. BURRELL, ed., Notre Dame, Indiana, University of Notre Dame Press, 1967, xviii, 300 p.

LÓPEZ ALARCÓN, M. and R. NAVARRO-VALLS, *Curso de derecho matrimonial canónico y concordado*, Madrid, Tecnos, 1984, 476 p.

LORENC, F., *De ignorantiae influxu in matrimoniali consensu*, Romae, Pontificium Athenaeum Lateranense, 1955, 43 p.

LYDON, P.J., *Ready Answers in Canon Law: A Practical Summary of the Code for the Parish Clergy*, 2nd rev. ed., New York, Benzinger Brothers, 1939, xvii, 523 p., xxvii.

MACHLUP, F., *Knowledge: Its Creation, Distribution, and Economic Significance*, Princeton, Princeton University Press, 1980-1984, 3 vol. in 1.

MACKIN, T., *Marriage in the Catholic Church*, New York, Paulist Press, 1982-1989, 3 vol.

MANS PUIGARNAU, J.M., *El consentimiento matrimonial: defecto y vicios del mismo como causas de*

164

nulidad de las nupcias, Barcelona, Bosch, 1956, viii, 313 p.

MANS PUIGARNAU, J.M., *Derecho matrimonial canónico*, Barcelona, Bosch, 1959, 2 vol.

MARITAIN, J., *Distinguer pour unir ou. Les degrés du savior*, 6th éd. rev. et augm., Paris, Desclée de Brouwer, 1959, xxii, 941 p.

MARTÍN DE AGAR, J.T., *A Handbook on Canon Law*, Montreal, Wilson & Lafleur Limitée, 1999, xviii, 268 p.

MARTINEZ, H.G., *De scientia debita in matrimonio ineundo: doctrina auctorum et iurisprudentia Sacrae Romanae Rotae*, Roma, Desclée, 1966, 249 p.

MARZOA, A., J. MIRAS, R. RODRIGUEZ-OCANA, eds., *Comentario exegético al código de derecho canónico*, 2nd ed., Pamplona, Ediciones Universidad de Navarra, 1997, 5 vol.

MAYR, R., ed., *Vocabularium codicis Iustiniani*, Hildesheim, G. Olms, 1965, 2 vol.

McAREAVEY, J., *The Canon Law of Marriage and the Family*, Dublin, Colour Books Ltd, 1997, 254 p.

McCLINTOCK, J. and J. STRONG, *Cyclopedia of Biblical and Ecclesiastical Literature*, New York, Harper, 1867-1881, 10 vol.

MENDONÇA, A., comp., *Rotal Anthology: An Annotated Index of Rotal Decisions from 1971 to 1988*, Washington, DC, Canon Law Society of America, 1992, ix, 771 p.

MICHIELS, G., *Normae generales juris canonici: commentarius Libri I Codicis juris canonici. Ed. altera penitus retractata et notabiliter aucta*, Tornaci, Desclée, 1949, 2 vol.

-----, *Principia generalia de personis in Ecclesia: commentarius Libri II Codicis juris canonici. canones praeliminares 87-106*, editio altera penitus retractata et notabiliter aucta, Tornaci, Desclée, 1955, xviii, 708 p.

MOLANO, E., *Contribución al estudio sobre le esencia del matrimonio*, Pamplona, Ediciones Universidad de Navarra, 1977, 265 p.

MOLINA MELIÁ, A. and E. OLMOS ORTEGA, *Derecho matrimonial canónico: sustantivo y procesal*, Madrid, Editorial Civitas, 1985, 399 p.

MONDIN, B., *Il pensiero di Agostino: filosofia, teologia, cultura*, Roma, Città nuova editrice, 1988, 370 p.

MOMMSEN, T., P. KRUEGER, A. WATSON, eds., *The Digest of Justinian*, Philadelphia, University of Pennsylvania Press, 1985, 4 vol.

MONETA, P., *Il matrimonio nel nuovo diritto canonico*, Genova, Edizione Culturali Internationali, 1989, 242 p.

165

MONTERO Y GUTIÉRREZ. E., *El matrimonio y las causas matrimoniales: disciplina de la Iglesia y de los principales estados, especialmente de España y jurisprudencia de la S. Rota romana, con las normas de la S. Congregación de sacramentos regulando la dispensa 'super matrimonio rato et non consummato', y el procedimiento en las causas de nulidad de matrimonio*, 5th rev. ed., Madrid, Sáez, 1950, 576 p.

MONTSERRAT MELIA. V., *Derecho matrimonial canónico: comentario de los canones 1012-1143, jurisprudencia seleccionada de los tribunales de Roma hasta el ano 1960*, Barcelona, Editorial Liturgica Espanola, 1961, viii, 499 p.

MOURANT, J.A., *Introduction to the Philosophy of Saint Augusine. Selected Readings and Commentaries*, University Park, Pennsylvania State University Press, 1964, ix, 366 p.

MUÑOZ SANTOS, M., *La ignorancia del derecho en el Código canónico*, Badajoz, Tipografia Nuevo Diario, 1925, 35 p.

MUSSELLI. L., *Manuale di diritto canonico e matrimoniale*, Bologna, Monduzzi Editore, 1995, xv, 413 p.

NASH. R.H., *The Light of the Mind: St. Augustine's Theory of Knowledge*, Lexington, University of Kentucky Press, 1969, viii, 146 p.

NATIONAL CONFERENCE OF CATHOLIC BISHOPS, BISHOPS' COMMITTEE FOR PASTORAL RESEARCH AND PRACTICE, *Faithful to Each Other Forever: A Catholic Handbook of Pastoral Help for Marriage Preparation*, Washington, DC, United States Catholic Conference, 1989, 154 p.

NAU. L.J., *Manual on the Marriage Laws of the Code of Canon Law*, 2nd rev. ed., New York, Frederick Pustet Co., Inc., 1934, x, 254 p.

NAYAKAM, H.M., *"Use of Reason" in Marriage: Doctrine and Jurisprudence Based on Canon 1095 — 1°*. Extractum ex Dissertatione ad Doctoratum in Facultate Iuris Canonici, Romae, Pontificia Universitas Urbaniana, 1995, viii, 163 p.

NICHOLAS, B., *An Introduction to Roman Law*, Oxford, Clarendon Press, 1962, xiii, 281 p.

NOLDIN. H., *De iure matrimoniali iuxta Codicem iuris canonici*, Lincii, Typis Associationis Catholicae, 1919, 208 p.

OCHOA. X., *Index verborum ac locutionem Codicis iuris canonici, paravit ac digessit*, 2nd ed., Città del Vaticano, Libreria editrice Lateranese, 1984, xvi, 593 p.

OESTERLE, G., *Consultationes de jure matrimoniali*, Romae, Officium Libri Catholici, 1942, 376 p.

ORGAN, T.W., *An Index to Aristotle in English Translation*, Princeton, Princeton University Press, 1949, vi, 181 p.

ORSY, L., *Marriage in Canon Law: Texts and Comments, Reflections and Questions*, Wilmington, Delaware,

166

Michael Glazier, 1986, 328 p.

PALLOTTINI, S., *Collectio omnium conclusionum et resolutionum quae in causis propositis apud S. Congregationem Cardinalium Concilii Tridentini interpretum prodierunt ab eius institutione anno MDLXIV ad annum MDCCCLX, distinctis titulis alphabetico ordine per materias digesta*, Romae, Typis S. Congregationis de Propaganda Fide, 1868-1895, 18 vol.

PAYEN, G., *De matrimonio in missionibus ac potissimum in Sinis*, vol. II, Zi-Ka-Wei, 1936, xxiv, 950 p., 39 p.; vol. III, Zi-Ka-Wei, 1936, xxx, 938 p.

PEGIS, A.C., ed., *Basic Writings of Saint Thomas Aquinas*, New York, Random House, 1945, 2 vol.

POMPEDDA, M.F., *Studi di diritto matrimoniale canonico*, Milano, Giuffrè Editore, 1993, xix, 518 p.

PONTIFICIA COMMISSIO CODICI IURIS CANONICI RECOGNOSCENDO, *Promulgation and Official Presentation of the Code of Canon Law*, Vatican City, Vatican Polyglott Press, 1983, 39 p.

PONTIFICAL COUNCIL FOR THE FAMILY, *Preparation for the Sacrament of Marriage*, Città del Vaticano, Libreria Editrice Vaticana, 1996, 30 p.

PORTALIÉ, E., *A Guide to the Thought of Saint Augustine*, R.J. BASTIAN, trans., Chicago, Henry Regnery Company, 1960, xxxviii, 428 p.

POSPISHIL, V.J., *Eastern Catholic Marriage Law: According to the Code of Canons of the Eastern Churches*, Brooklyn, New York, St. Maron Publications, 1991, 534 p.

-----, *Eastern Catholic Church Law*, 2nd rev. ed., Staten Island, New York, St. Maron Publications, 1996, liv, 938 p.

POTTHAST, A., *Regesta pontificum romanorum inde ab a. post Christum natum MCXCVIII ad a. MCCCIV*, Berolini, 1874-1875, 2 vol.

PRÜMMER, D.M., ed., *Manuale theologiae moralis secundum principia S. Thomae Aquinatis, in usum scholarum*, Friburgi Brisboviae, Herder, 1931-1933, 3 vol.

RAMSTEIN, M., *A Manual of Canon Law*, Hoboken, New Jersey, Terminal Printing & Publishing, 1947, vii, 747, xviii p.

RAYAPPEN, K., *Discretion in Marriage. Doctrine and Jurisprudence: A Study of Canon 1095 — 2° with Special Reference to the Indian Context*, Extractum ex Disseratione ad Doctoratum in Facultate Iuris Canonici, Roma, Pontificia Universitas Urbaniana, 1993, viii, 114 p.

REGATILLO, E.F., ed., *Interpretatio et iurisprudentia Codicis iuris canonici*, Santander, Sal Terrae, 1949, 600 p.

-----, *Ius sacramentarium*, 4th ed., Santander, Sal Terrae, 1964, xi, 998 p.

RÉGIS, L.-M., *Epistemology*, I.C. BYRNE, trans., New York, Macmillan, 1959, 549 p.

REY-MERMET, T., *Moral Choices: The Moral Theology of Saint Alphonsus Liguori*, P. LAVERDURE, trans., Liguori, Missouri, Liguori Publications, 1998, xxv, 180 p.

RI, S.-G., *L'errore nel consenso matrimoniale canonico secundo il canone 1097*, Estratto di Tesi di Dottorato nella Facultà di Diritto Canonico, Pontificia Universitas Urbaniana, Corea, Tae-Gu, 1993, v, 119 p.

RIST, J.M., *Augustine: Ancient Thought Baptized*, Cambridge, Cambridge University Press, 1994, xix, 334 p.

ROMANI, S., *Institutiones juris canonici*, vol. 2, Romae, Editrice 'Iustitia', 1945, ix, 854 p.

ROSS, W.D., ed., *The Works of Aristotle*, Oxford, Clarendon Press, 1908-1952, 12 vol.

RUANO ESPINA, L., *La incapacidad para asumir las obligaciones escenciales del matrimonio por causas psiquicas, como capitulo de nulidad*, Barcelona, Libreria Bosch, 1989, 307 p.

RUNES, D.D., *The Dictionary of Philosophy*, 2nd ed., New York, Philosophical Library, 1942, vii, 342, [1] p.

SANCHEZ, T., *De sancto matrimonii sacramento disputationum tomi tres*, Norimbergae, Sumptibus Jo. C. Lochneri, 1706, 3 vol. in 1.

SCHOUPPE, J-P., *Le droit canonique: introduction générale et droit matrimonial*, Bruxelles, E. Story-Scientia, 1991, xvii, 239 p.

SCHROEDER, H.J., *Canons and Decrees of the Council of Trent: Original Text with English Translation*, St. Louis, B. Herder Book Co., 1941, xxxiii, 608 p.

SCHULZ, F., *Classical Roman Law*, Oxford, Clarendon Press, 1951, xii, 650 p.

-----, *Principles of Roman Law*, Oxford, Clarendon Press, 1936, xvi, 268 p.

SCICLUNA, C.J., *The Essential Definition of Marriage according to the 1917 and 1983 Code of Canon Law: An Exegetical and Comparative Study*, Lanham, Maryland, University Press of America, 1995, xxiv, 380 p.

SCOTT, S.P., trans., *Corpus Iuris Civilis: The Civil Law*, New York, AMS Press, 1973, 17 vol. in 7 books.

SCOTT, T.K., *Augustine: His Thought in Context*, New York, Paulist Press, 1995, iv, 253 p.

SEBOTT, R. and C. MARUCCI, *Il nuovo diritto matrimoniale della Chiesa: commento giuridico e teologico al can. 1055-1165 del nuovo CIC*, Napoli, Edizioni Dehoniane, 1985, 284 p.

SERRANO POSTIGO, C., *La causa típica en el derecho canónico matrimonial: las anomalias del negocio*

168

juridico matrimonial: alternativa "De iure condendo" desde la perspectiva de la causa, Colegio universitario de Leon, Unidad de investigacion, Publicaciones 18, Leon, Colegio universitario de Leon, 1980, 330 p.

SHEEHY, G. et al., eds., *The Canon Law, Letter and Spirit: a Practical Guide to the Code of Canon Law*, prepared by the Canon Law Society of Great Britain and Ireland in association with the Canadian Canon Law Society, Collegeville, The Liturgical Press, 1995, xxv, 1060 p.

SIEGLE, B.A., *Marriage Today: A Commentary on the Code of Canon Law*, 3rd rev. ed., New York, Alba-House, 1979, various pagings.

-----, *Marriage: According to the New Code of Canon Law*, New York, Alba-House, 1986, xv, 297 p.

SIPOS, I., *Enchiridion iuris canonici ad usum scholarum et privatorum*, 6th ed., Romae, Orbis Catholicus, 1954, x, 913 p.

SMITH, V.M., *Ignorance Affecting Matrimonial Consent*, Canon Law Studies, 245, Washington, DC, The Catholic University of America, 1950, viii, 118 p.

STEWART, J.A., *Notes on the Nicomachean Ethics of Aristotle*, Oxford, Clarendon Press, 1892, 2 vol.

SWOBODA, I.R., *Ignorance in Relation to the Imputability of Delicts: An Historical Synopsis and Commentary*, Canon Law Studies, 143, Washington, DC, The Catholic University of America Press, 1941, xii, 271.

THOMAS, J.A.C., *Textbook of Roman Law*, Amsterdam, North-Holland Publishing Co., 1976, xix, 562 p.

THOMSON, J.R. ed., *A Dictionary of Philosophy in the Words of Philosophers*, London, R.D. Dickinson, 1887, xlviii, 479 p.

TIMLIN, B.T., *Conditional Matrimonial Consent: An Historical Synopsis and Commentary*, Canon Law Studies, 89, Washington, DC, The Catholic University of America, 1934, x, 381 p.

TISSOT, P.-A., trans., *Corpus juris civilis: Les douze livres du Code de l'empereur Justinien*, 2nd ed., Aalen, Allemagne, Scientia Verlag, 1979, 14 vol.

TOCANEL, P., *Compendium praelectionum de normis generalibus et de personis in genere*, Romae, Pontificium Institutum utriusque iuris, 1949-1950, 543 p.

URMSON, J.O., ed., *The Concise Encyclopaedia of Western Philosophy and Philosophers*, London, Hutchinson, 1960, 431 p.

VAN DYKE, D.T., Project Director, *Marriage Preparation in the Catholic Church: Getting it Right: Report of a Study on the Value of Marriage Preparation in the Catholic Church for Couples Married One through Eight Years*, Omaha, Center for Marriage and Family, Creighton University, 1995, 118 p.

VAN OMMEREN, W.A., *Mental Illness Affecting Matrimonial Consent*, Canon Law Studies, 415, Washington, DC, The Catholic University of America, 1961, xi, 243 p.

VAN STEENBERGHEN, F., *Épistémologie*, 3rd ed., Louvain, Publications universitaires de Louvain, 1956, 272 p.

VAN VLIET, A.H. and C.G. BREED, *Marriage and Canon Law: A Concise and Complete Account*, London, Burns & Oates, 1964, xii, 308 p.

VERMEERSCH, A., *Theologia moralis principia, responsa, consilia*, 4th ed., v. 3, *De personis, de sacramentis, de legibus Ecclesiae et censuris*, Roma, Pontificia Università Gregoriana, 1948, xv, 590 p.

VERMEERSCH, A. and I. CREUSEN, *Epitome iuris canonici: cum commentariis ad scholas et ad usum privatum*, 7th ed., Mechliniae, H. Dessain, 1949-1956, 3 vol.

VIDAL, P., *Institutiones iuris civilis romani*, Prati, ex officina Libraria Giachetti, 1915, 616 p.

VITALE, E.G., *Corso di diritto matrimoniale canonico: anno accademico 1985-1986*, Milano, A. Giuffrè Editore, 1986, 189 p.

VITALE, E.G. and S. BERLINGÒ, *Il matrimonio canonico*, Milano, A. Giuffrè Editore, 1994, xi, 249 p.

VLAMING, T.M., *Praelectiones iuris matrimonii ad normam Codicis iuris canonici*, 4th ed., Bussum in Hollandia, 1950, xx, 574 p.

WEBER, A., *Histoire de la philosophie européenne*, 7th ed., Paris, Fischbacher, 1905, 631 p.

WERNZ, F.X. and P. VIDAL, *Ius canonicum*, vol. 5, *Ius matrimoniale*, Romae, Apud aedes Universitatis Gregorianae, 1946, xv, 953 p.

WETZEL, J., *Augustine and the Limits of Virtue*, Cambridge, Cambridge University Press, 1992, xv, 246 p.

WOESTMAN, W.H., ed., *Papal Allocutions to the Roman Rota 1939-1994*, Ottawa, Saint Paul University, 1994, ix, 243 p.

WOYWOD, S., *A Practical Commentary on the Code of Canon Law*, rev. and enlarged ed. by C. SMITH, New York, J. F. Wagner, 1957, 2 vol. in 1, xvii, 1762 p.

WRENN, L.G., *Decisions*, 2nd rev. ed., Washington, DC, Canon Law Society, 1983, vi, 199 p.

-----, *Law Sections*, Washington, DC, Canon Law Society of America, 1994, iii, 93 p.

-----, *Annulments*, 6th ed., Washington, DC, Canon Law Society of America, 1996, v, 232 p.

-----, *The Invalid Marriage*, Washington, DC, Canon Law Society of America, 1998, v, 238 p.

170

ZERA, R., *De ignorantia in re-matrimoniali: eius natura iuridica et ambitus quoad consensus validitatem deque eiusdem probatione in iudicio*, Romae, Ancora, 1978, 108 p.

ZETTA, C., *Il matrimonio, contratto naturale, sacramentale, giuridico secondo il nuovo Codice di diritto canonico: trattatello teorico-practico ad uso del giovane clero e dei sacerdoti in cura d'anime*, Torino, P. Marietti, 1920, xv, 226 p.

ARTICLES

ABATE, A.M., "Il consenso matrimoniale nel nuovo Codice di diritto canonico", in *Apollinaris*, 59 (1986), pp. 445-491.

ABBO, I.A., "De quibusdam quaestionibus iuris matrimonialis iuxta rotalem iurisprudentiam", in *Apollinaris*, 40 (1967), pp. 571-590.

ADAMI, F.E., "Contributo alla dottrina canonistica in tema di oggetto del consenso matrimoniale", in *Il diritto ecclesiastico*, 77 (1966) 1, pp. 33-69.

AHERN, M.B., "Psychological Incapacity for Marriage", in *Studia canonica*, 7 (1973), pp. 227-251.

-----, "The Marital Right to Children; a Tentative Re-examination", in *Studia Canonica*, 8 (1974), pp. 91-107.

-----, "Error and Deception as Grounds for Nullity", in *Studia canonica*, 11 (1977), pp. 225-259.

ALVAREZ FERNANDEZ, A., "El tema de la ignorancia en el consentimiento matrimonial", in *El consentimiento matrimonial, hoy: trabajos de la XV Semana de Derecho Canónico*, Barcelona, Banchs, 1976, pp. 31-61.

ANNÉ, L., "Le consentement matrimonial et l'incapacité psychique", in *Ephemerides iuris canonici*, 44 (1988), pp. 7-15.

ARZA, A., "Los 'homosexuales' incapaces para contraer matrimonio?", in *Atti del Congresso internazionale di diritto canonico: la Chiesa dopo il Concilio*, vol. 2, Roma, 14-19 gennaio 1970, Milano, A. Giuffrè Editore, 1972, pp. 27-92.

BAÑARES, J.I., "La relacion intelecto-voluntad en el consentimiento matrimonial: notas sobre los cc. 1096-1102 del CIC de 1983", in *Ius canonicum*, 33 (1993), pp. 553-606.

-----, "Error «causam dans» y error en cualidad directa y principalmente pretendida", in *Ius canonicum*, 35 (1995), pp. 103-115.

BEAL, J.P., "The Substance of Things Hoped For: Proving Simulation of Matrimonial Consent", in *The Jurist*, 55 (1995), pp. 745-793.

BERLINGÒ, S., "Autonomia delle diverse fattispecie normative dell'errore e del dolo previste nei cann.

1097-1099 del Codice di Diritto Canonico", in *Monitor ecclesiasticus*, 120 (1995), pp. 5-38.

BERNHARD, J., "The New Matrimonial Law", in *Concilium*, 185 (1986), pp. 45-53.

-----, "Fidélité et indissolubilité du mariage: questions posées à la doctrine canonique", *Revue de droit canonique*, 44 (1994), pp. 83-99.

-----, "From Life to Law: Matrimonial Law and Jurisprudence", in *Concilium*, 1996/5, pp. 98-104.

BERTOLINO, R., "Gli constitutivi del *bonum coniugum* stato della questione", in *Monitor ecclesiasticus*, 120 (1995), pp. 557-586.

BIDAGOR, R., "Dissertationes et quaesita varia: circa ignorantiam naturae matrimonii", in *Periodica*, 29 (1940), pp. 269-289.

BLANCO, M., "El dolo: requisitos y prueba", in *Ius canonicum*, 35 (1995), pp. 183-198.

BOCCAFOLA, K., "El error acerca de la dignidad sacramental del matrimonio: limites de su objecto y prueba", in *Ius canonicum*, 35 (1995), pp. 143-165.

-----, "Deceit and induced error about a personal quality", in *Monitor ecclesiasticus*, 124 (1999), pp. 692-710.

BONNET, P.A., "L'errore nel matrimonio canonico", in *Studi in onore di Pietro Agostino d'Avack*, vol. 1, Pubblicazioni della Facultà di Giurisprudenza dell'Università di Roma, Milano, A. Giuffrè Editore, 1976, pp. 357-392.

-----, "Errore di diritto e necessità della coscienza dell'importanza vitale dell'opzione matrimoniale", in *Il diritto ecclesiastico*, 94 (1983) 2, pp. 462-481.

-----, "L'errore (can. 1096-1100 CIC)", in *Introduzione al consenso matrimoniale canonico*, Milano, A. Giuffrè Editore, 1985, pp. 37-59.

-----, "L'errore di diritto giuridicamente rilevante nel consenso matrimoniale canonico", in *Studi in memoria di Pietro Gismondi*, vol.1, Pubblicazioni della Facultà di Giurisprudenza, Università degli studi di Roma, Milano, A. Giuffrè Editore, 1987-1988, pp. 137-172.

-----, "Il consenso matrimoniale", in *Matrimonio canonico fra tradizione e rinnovamento*, vol. 7 of *Il Codice del Vaticano II*, A. LONGHITANO et al. eds., Bologna, EDB, 1991, pp. 159-222.

BROWN, R., "Inadequate Consent or Lack of Commitment: Authentic Grounds for Nullity?", in *Studia canonica*, 9 (1975), pp. 249-265.

-----, "Total Simulation — A Second Look", in *Studia canonica*, 10 (1976), pp. 235-249.

-----, "Non-Inclusion: A Form of Simulation?", in *CLSA Proceedings*, 71 (1979), pp. 1-11.

172

BROWN, R., "Simulation Versus Lack of Commitment", in *Studia canonica*, 14 (1980), pp. 335-345.

BURKE, C., "The *Bonum Coniugum* and the *Bonum Prolis*; Ends or Properties of Marriage?", in *The Jurist*, 49 (1989), pp. 704-713.

-----, "Procreativity and the Conjugal Self-Gift", in *Studia canonica*, 24 (1990), pp. 43-49.

-----, "Reflexiones en tornos al canon 1095", in *Ius canonicum*, 31 (1991), pp. 85-105.

-----, "Canon 1057 and the Object of Matrimonial Consent", in *Forum*, 3 (1992) 1, pp. 29-43.

-----, "The Essential Obligations of Matrimony," in *Studia canonica*, 26 (1992), pp. 376-399.

-----, "Some Reflections on Canon 1095", in *Monitor ecclesiasticus*, 117 (1992), pp. 133-150.

-----, "The Distinction between 2° and 3° of Canon 1095", in *The Jurist*, 54 (1995), pp. 228-233.

-----, "Renewal, Personalism and Law", in *Canon Law and Marriage*, Monsignor W. Onclin Chair 1995, Leuven, Katholieke Universiteit, Uitgeveru Peeters, 1995, pp. 11-21.

-----, "Personalism and the Essential Obligations of Matrimony", in *Angelicum*, 74 (1997), pp. 81-94.

-----, "The Effect of Fraud, Condition and Error in Marital Consent: Some Personalist Considerations", in *Monitor ecclesiasticus*, 122 (1997), pp. 295-310, 513-519.

-----, "The Object of the Marital Self-Gift as Presented in Canon 1057, § 2", in *Studia canonica*, 31 (1997), pp. 403-421.

-----, "Simulated Consent", in *Forum*, 9 (1998) 2, pp. 65-82.

BURKE, R.L., "Lack of Discretion of Judgment: Canonical Doctrine and Legislation", in *The Jurist*, 45 (1985), pp. 171-209.

-----, "Canon 1095, 1° and 2°; Presentation I: Canonical Doctrine", in *Incapacity for Marriage: Jurisprudence and Interpretation: Acts of the III Gregorian Colloquium, 1-6 September 1986*, R. SABLE, ed., Rome, Pontificia Universitas Gregoriana, 1987, pp. 81-108.

-----, "Canon 1095, 1° and 2°; Presentation II: Canonical Legislation", in *Incapacity for Marriage: Jurisprudence and Interpretation: Acts of the III Gregorian Colloquium, 1-6 September 1986*, R. SABLE, ed., Rome, Pontificia Universitas Gregoriana, 1987, pp. 109-128.

-----, "Canon 1095, 1° and 2°; Presentation III: Jurisprudence", in *Incapacity for Marriage: Jurisprudence and Interpretation: Acts of the III Gregorian Colloquium, 1-6 September 1986*, R. SABLE, ed., Rome, Pontificia Gregoriana, 1987, pp. 129-155.

-----, "Grave difetto di discrezione di giudizio: fonte di nullità del consenso matrimoniale", in *Jus canonicum*,

173

31 (1991), pp. 139-154.

BURKE, R.L., and D.E. FELLHAUER, "Canon 1095: Canonical Doctrine and Jurisprudence", in *CLSA Proceedings*, 48 (1986), pp. 94-117.

BURNS, D.J., "The Sacrament of Marriage", in *Chicago Studies*, 23 (1984), pp. 63-76.

BUYS, L., "De matrimoniis acatholicorum baptizatorum", in *Periodica*, 37 (1948), pp. 227-241.

CALVO, R.R., "The Impact of Culture in Marriage Cases", in *CLSA Proceedings*, 55 (1993), pp. 108-120.

CAMPBELL, D.M., "Canon 1099: The Emergence of a New Juridic Figure?", *Quaderni studio rotale*, 5 (1990), pp. 35-72.

CANDELIER, G., "La simulation d'après les sentences de Mgr José María Serrano Ruiz", in *Studia canonica*, 31 (1997), pp. 373-402.

CARNERO, G., "Nulidad por error acerca de persona o de sus cualidades", in *Las Causas Matrimoniales: Trabajos de la cuarta semana de derecho canónico celebrada en el monasterio Na. Sa. de Montserrat*, Salamanca, Tipografia FLO-REZ, 1953, pp. 205-232.

CARON, P.G., "L''ignorantia' en droit canonique", in *Ephemerides iuris canonici*, 2 (1946), pp. 5-56, 201-223.

CASTAÑO, J.F., "Natura del 'foedus' matrimoniale alla luce dell'attuale legislazione", in *Questioni canoniche, miscellanea in onore del professore P. Esteban Gomez. o.p., a cura della Pontificia Università S. Tommaso d'Aquino. Roma*, Milano, 1984, Studia Universitatis S. Thomae in Urbe, 22, pp. 214-250.

CONNELL, F.J., "Ligouri, St. Alphonsus and Catholic Moral Theology", in *Encyclopedia of Morals*, New York, Greenwood Press, 1969, pp. 294-302.

CORECCO, E., "Ecclesiological Bases of the Code", in *Concilium*, 185 (1986), pp. 3-13.

CUNNINGHAM, R., "Marriage and the Nescient Catholic", in *Studia canonica*, 15 (1981), pp. 263-283.

DANIELS, M., "Marriage in the Balance", in *Columbia*, 80 (2000), pp. 12-14.

D'AVACK, A., "Le mariage dans le nouveau Code de droit canonique et dans la réforme du droit oriental", in *Studi in memoria di Pietro Gismondi*, vol.1, Pubblicazioni della Facultà di Giurisprudenza, dell'Università degli studi di Roma, Milano, A. Giuffrè Editore, 1987-1988, pp. 525-540.

DE BLAS ARROYO, L.A., "La significación matrimonial en la doctrina de Candido Pumar", in *Excerpta e dissertationibus in iure canonico*, 7 (1989), Facultas Iuris Canonici, Universitas Studiorum Navarrensis, Pamplona, Servicio de Publicaciones, Universidad de Navarra, 1989, pp. 75-131.

174

DE_LA HERA, A., "El supuesto de hecho de c. 1082, §1: 'ignorata natura matrimonii'", in *Ius canonicum*, 4-2 (1964), pp. 533-556.

DE LUCA, L., "La Chiesa e la società coniugale", in *Atti del Congresso internazionale di diritto canonico: la Chiesa dopo il Concilio*, vol. 1, Roma, 14-19 gennaio 1970, Milano, A. Giuffrè Editore, 1972, pp. 475-495.

-----, "The New Law on Marriage", in *Proceedings of the 5th International Congress of Canon Law*, 2 vol., M. THÉRIAULT and J. THORN, eds., Ottawa, Faculty of Canon Law, Saint Paul University, 1986, pp. 827-851.

DI FELICE, A., "Le innovazioni normative del diritto matrimoniale del nuovo 'Codex iuris canonici'", in *Monitor ecclesiasticus*, 108 (1983), pp. 168-195.

DEWHIRST, J.A., "*Consortium Vitae, Bonum Coniugum*, and Their Relation to Simulation: A Continuing Challenge to Modern Jurisprudence", in *The Jurist*, 55 (1995), pp. 794-812.

DI JORIO, O., "Causae nullitatis matrimonii secundum novissimam iurisprudentiam rotalem", in *L'amore coniugale: annali di dottrina e giurisprudenza canonica*, Città del Vaticano, Libreria Editrice Vaticana, 1971, pp. 159-173.

DOYLE, T.P., "The Moral Inseparability of the Unitive and Procreative Aspects of Human Sexual Intercourse", in *Monitor ecclesiasticus*, 109 (1984), pp. 447-469.

-----, "Marriage", in *The Code of Canon Law: A Text and Commentary*, J.A. CORIDEN, T.J. GREEN, D.E. HEINTSCHEL, eds., commissioned by the Canon Law Society of America, New York, Paulist Press, 1985, pp. 737-833.

EGAN, E.M., "The Nullity of Marriage for Reason of Insanity or Lack of Due Discretion of Judgment", in *Ephemerides iuris canoni*, 39 (1983), pp. 9-54.

FALTIN, D., "The Exclusion of the Sacramentality of Marriage with Particular Reference to the Marriage of Baptized Non Believers", E.G. Pfnausch and W.A. Varvaro, trans., in *Marriage Studies: Reflections in Canon Law and Theology, IV*, J.A. ALESANDRO, ed., Washington, DC, Canon Law Society of America, 1990, pp. 66-104.

FEDELE, P., "La definizione del matrimonio in diritto canonico", in *Ephemerides iuris canonici*, 1 (1945), pp. 41-52.

-----, "Error qualitatis e dolo nel matrimonio in diritto canonico", in *Monitor ecclesiasticus*, 120 (1995), pp. 149-158.

FELLHAUER, D.E., "The Exclusion of Indissolubility: Old Principles and New Jurisprudence", in *Studia canonica*, 9 (1975), pp. 105-133.

-----, "The *consortium omnis vitae* as a Juridic Element of Marriage", in *Studia canonica*, 13 (1979), pp. 7-

171.

FELLHAUER, D.E., "Psychological Incapacity for Marriage in the Revised *Code of Canon Law*", in *Proceedings of the 5th International Congress of Canon Law*, vol. 2, M. THÉRIAULT and J. THORN, eds., Ottawa, Faculty of Canon Law, Saint Paul University, 1986, pp. 1019-1040.

FIORE, E., "Casalen. seu Taurinen., Nullit. matrim., 30 novembris 1968, *coram* E. Fiore", in *Ephemerides iuris canonici*, 26 (1970), pp. 197-208.

FINNEGAN, J.T., "The Capacity to Marry", in *The Jurist*, 29 (1969), pp. 141-156.

FORNÉS, J., "Simulación y condicio", in *Ius canonicum*, 33 (1993), pp. 295-311.

-----, "Error y dolo: fundamentos y diferencias", in *Ius canonicum*, 35 (1995), pp. 165-181.

FUMAGALLI CARULLI, O., "L''errore redundans' nel quadro della identificazione della persona nel matrimonio canonico", in *Studi in onore di Pietro Agostino d'Avack*, vol. 2, Pubblicazioni della Facultà di Giurisprudenza dell'Università di Roma, Milano, A. Giuffrè Editore, 1976, pp. 543-578.

-----, "La relazione dinamica tra il can. 1082 e il can. 1981 *Cod. Iur. Can.*", in *Ephemerides iuris canonici*, 33 (1977), pp. 247-279.

FUNGHINI, R., "L'errore sulla qualità della persona direttamente e principalmente intesa", in *Monitor ecclesiasticus*, 120 (1995), pp. 39-68.

GALLAGHER, C., "Marriage and the Family in the New Code", in *Studia canonica*, 17 (1983), pp. 149-170.

-----, "Marriage in the Revised Canon Law for the Eastern Catholic Churches", in *Studia canonica*, 24 (1990), pp. 69-90.

GANGOITI, B., "Error, nullatenus dolus, est causa directa nullitatis matrimonii", in *Quaestiones de matrimonio hisce diebus controversae*. Studia Universitatis S. Thomae in Urbe, 5, Roma, Herder, 1974, pp. 5-60.

GARCIA, E., "Matrimonial Consent", in *Philippiniana sacra*, 21 (1986), pp. 84-100.

GAUDEMET, J., "Mariage et procréation: les aspects historiques", in *Revue de droit canonique*, 45 (1995), pp. 245-256.

GIL DE LAS HERAS, F., "El concepto canónico de simulación", in *Ius canonicum*, 33 (1993), pp. 259-293.

GRAMUNT, I., "The Essence of Marriage and the *Code of Canon Law*", in *Studia canonica*, 25 (1991), pp. 365-383.

GRAMUNT, I. and L.A. WAUCK, "Moral Certitude and the Collaboration of the Court Expert in Cases of Consensual Incapacity", in *Studia canonica*, 20 (1986), pp. 69-84.

176

GRAMUNT, I. and L.A. WAUCK, "Capacity and Incapacity to Contract Marriage", in *Studia canonica*, 22 (1988), pp. 147-168.

-----, "«Lack of Due Discretion»: Incapacity or Error?", in *Ius canonicum*, 32 (1992), pp. 533-558.

GRAZIANI, E., "L'ignoranza circa la natura del matrimonio", in *Il diritto ecclesiastico*, 75 (1964) 2, pp. 3-23.

-----, "La Chiesa e il matrimonio", in *Atti del Congresso internazionale di diritto canonico: la Chiesa dopo il Concilio*, vol. 1, Roma, 14-19 gennaio 1970, Milano, A. Giuffrè Editore, 1972, pp. 457-471.

-----, "Riflessioni sul can. 1082 del Codex", in *Ius populi Dei: miscellanea in honorem Raymundi Bidagor*, III, Roma, Università Gregoriana Editrice, 1972, pp. 493-510.

GRESSIER, J., "L'inexistence du consentement", in *Studia canonica*, 32 (1998), pp. 371-395.

GROCHOLEWSKI, Z., "De 'communione vitae' in novo schemate 'de matrimonio' et de momento iuridico amoris coniugalis", in *Periodica*, 68 (1979), pp. 439-480.

-----, "Relatio inter errorem et positivam indissolubilitatis exclusionem in nuptiis contrahendis", in *Periodica*, 69 (1980), pp. 569-601.

-----, "Positivo l'atto di volontà come causa di nullità del matrimonio secondo il can. 1101 par. 2 del nuovo Codice", in *Questioni canoniche. miscellanea in onore del professore P. Esteban Gomez. o.p.. a cura della Pontificia Università S. Tommaso d'Aquino. Roma*, Milano, 1984, Studia Universitatis S. Thomae in Urbe, 22, pp. 251-270.

GUTIÉRREZ, A., "Matrimonii essentia, finis, amor coniugalis", in *Apollinaris*, 46 (1973), pp. 97-147.

HADLEY, J., "Note on the 'bonum coniugum'", in Canon Law Society of Great Britain and Ireland *Newsletter*, No. 110, June 1997, pp. 76-77.

HARMAN, F., "Lack of Due Discretion, Part 1", in H.F. DOOGAN, ed., *Catholic Tribunals: Marriage. Annulment, Dissolution*, Newtown, E.J. Dwyer, 1990, pp. 71-81.

HEINTSCHEL, D.E., "'...A New Way of Thinking'", in *The Jurist*, 44 (1984), pp. 41-47.

HENNESSEY, P., "Canon 1097: A Requiem for *Error Redundans*?", in *The Jurist*, 49 (1989), pp. 146-181.

HILL, R.A., "General Norms: Canons 124-114", *The Code of Canon Law: A Text and Commentary*, J.A. CORIDEN, T.J. GREEN, D.E. HEINTSCHEL, eds., commissioned by the Canon Law Society of America, New York, Paulist Press, 1985, pp. 88-114.

HUBER, J., "Coniunctio, communio, consortium: observationes ad terminologiam notionis matrimonii", in *Periodica*, 75 (1986), pp. 393-408.

HUMPHREYS, J., "Lack of Commitment in Consent", in *Studia canonica*, 2 (1976), pp. 345-362.

HÜRTH, F., "Defectus consensus in matrimoniis acatholicorum", in *Periodica*, 37 (1948), pp. 209-226.

KEATING, J.R., "The Legal Test of Marital Insanity", in *Studia canonica*, 1 (1967), pp. 21-36.

KELLY, D., "Canon 1096", in G. SHEEHY et al., eds., *The Canon Law, Letter and Spirit: a Practical Guide to the Code of Canon Law*, prepared by the Canon Law Society of Great Britain and Ireland in association with the Canadian Canon Law Society, Collegeville, The Liturgical Press, 1995, pp. 612-613.

KENYON, R.A., "The Nature and Nullity of Matrimonial Consent: Arguments Based upon Primary Sources", in *Studia canonica*, 14 (1980), pp. 107-154.

KITCHEN, P., "Matrimonial Intention and Simulation", in *Studia canonica*, 28 (1994), pp. 347-406.

KOWAL, J., "L'errore circa le proprietà essenziali o la dignità sacramentale del matrimonio (c. 1099)", in *Periodica*, 87 (1998), pp. 287-327.

LAGGES, P.R., "Conditional Consent to Marriage", in *CLSA Proceedings*, 58 (1996), pp. 237-260.

LEFEBVRE, C., "De defectu discretionis iudicii in rotali iurisprudentia", in *Periodica*, 69 (1980), pp. 555-567.

LESAGE, G., "The *Consortium vitae conjugalis*: Nature and Applications", in *Studia canonica*, 6 (1972), pp. 99-113.

-----, "Évolution récente de la jurisprudence matrimoniale", in *Le divorce: l'Eglise catholique ne devrait-elle pas modifier son attitude séculaire à l'égard de l'indissolubilité du mariage?*, Travaux du Congrès de la Société canadienne de Théologie tenu à Montréal du 21 au 24 août 1972, Montréal, Fides, 1973, pp. 13-57.

-----, "Relative Incapacity and Invalidity of Marriage", in *CLSA Proceedings*, 41 (1979), pp. 76-82.

LO CASTRO, G., "Il *foedus* matrimoniale come *consortium totius vitae*", in *Monitor ecclesiasticus*, 118 (1993), pp. 69-90; also in *Il matrimonio sacramento nell'ordinamento canonico vigente*, Studi Giuridici 31, Città del Vaticano, Libreria editrice Vaticana, 1993, pp. 69-90.

LORENZO, P., "Jurisprudencia rotal sobre el estado de duda en el consentimiento condicionado", in *Ius canonicum*, 33 (1993), pp. 189-225.

LÜDICKE, K., "Matrimonial Consent in Light of a Personalist Concept of Marriage: On the Council's New Way of Thinking about Marriage", in *Studia canonica*, 33 (1999), pp. 473-503.

MAJER, P., "El error determinante de la voluntad (can. 1099 del CIC 83): naturaleza y tipificación jurídica", in *Cuadernos doctorales*, 13 (1995), pp. 13-81.

MANTUANO, G., "*Elementum amoris* e matrimonio canonico", in *Proceedings of the 5th International*

178

Congress of Canon Law, vol. 2, M. THÉRIAULT and J. THORN, eds., Ottawa, Faculty of Canon Law, Saint Paul University, 1986, pp. 989-1001.

MARTÍN DE AGAR, J.T., "El error sobre las propiedades esenciales del matrimonio", in *Ius canonicum*, 35 (1995), pp. 117-141.

MENDONÇA, A., "The Theological and Juridical Aspects of Marriage", in *Studia canonica*, 22 (1988), pp. 265-304.

-----, "The Incapacity to Contract Marriage: Canon 1095", in *Studia canonica*, 19 (1985), pp. 259-325.

-----, "Recent Developments in Matrimonial Jurisprudence", in *Canonical studies*, 1990, pp. 3-24.

-----, "Consensual Incapacity for Marriage", in *The Jurist*, 54 (1994), pp. 477-559.

-----, "The Importance of Considering Cultural Contexts in Adjudicating Marriage Nullity Cases with Special Reference to Countries of Southeast Asia", in *CLSA Proceedings*, 57 (1995), pp. 231-292.

-----, "Recent Rotal Jurisprudence from a Socio-Cultural Perspective (Part I)", in *Studia canonica*, 29 (1995), pp. 29-84.

-----, "Recent Rotal Jurisprudence from a Socio-Cultural Perspective (Part II)", in *Studia canonica*, 29 (1995), pp. 317-356.

-----, "Recent Rotal Jurisprudence from a Socio-Cultural Perspective", in *Canonical studies*, 1995, pp. 58-143.

-----, "Exclusion of the Sacramentality of Marriage: Recent Trends in Rotal Jurisprudence", in *Studia canonica*, 31 (1997), pp. 5-48.

MÖHLER, J.A., "De errore in qualitate communi ad nuptias quaesita", in *Apollinaris*, 34 (1961), pp. 369-404.

MOLINA MELIA, A., "La 'communitas vitae et amoris' en el Concilio Vaticano II," in *El "consortium totius vitae": curso de derecho matrimonial y procesal canónico para profesionales del foro*, 7, Salamanca, Universidad pontificia de Salamanca, 1986, Bibliotheca salmanticensis Estudios, 83, pp. 37-68.

MONETA, P., "La qualità che per sua natura può gravemente turbare il consorzio della vita coniugale", in *Monitor ecclesiasticus*, 120 (1995), pp. 123-143.

MONTAGNA, E., "Considerazationi in tema di *bonum coniugum* nel diritto matrimoniale canonico", in *Il diritto ecclesiastico*, 104, 1 (1993) 1, pp. 663-703.

MORLOT, F., "Vices du consentement matrimonial relatifs à l'indissolubilité", in *Revue de droit canonique*, 43 (1993), pp. 43-97.

MORRISEY, F.G., "Preparing Ourselves for the New Marriage Legislation", in *The Jurist*, 33 (1973), pp.

343-357.

MORRISEY, F.G., "The Incapacity of Entering into Marriage", in *Studia canonica*, 8 (1974), pp. 5-21.

MOSTAZA RODRIGUEZ, A., "El 'consortium totius vitae' en el nuevo Código de derecho canónico" in *El "consortium totius vitae": curso de derecho matrimonial y procesal canónico para profesionales del foro*, 7, Salamanca, Universidad Pontificia de Salamanca, 1986, Bibliotheca salmanticensis Estudios, 83, pp. 69-107.

MURTAGH, C., "The Judicial Importance of 'amor conjugalis'", in *Studia canonica*, 7 (1973), pp. 49-57.

NAVARRETE, U., "De iure ad vitae communionem: observationes ad novum schema canonis 1086 § 2 ", in *Periodica*, 66 (1977), pp. 249-270.

-----, "Error circa personam et error circa qualitates communes seu non identificantes personam (c. 1097)", in *Periodica*, 82 (1993), pp. 637-667.

-----, "Attuali problematiche in dottrina e giurisprudenza circa il can. 1097", in *Quaderni studio rotale*, 8 (1994), pp. 71-84.

-----, "Error in persona (c. 1097 §1)", in *Periodica*, 87 (1998), pp. 351-401.

OESTERLE, G., "Nullitas matrimonii ex capite ignorantiae (*can. 1082*)", in *Ephemerides theologicae lovanienses*, 15 (1938), pp. 647-673.

-----, "Consentement matrimonial", in *Dictionnaire de Droit canonique*, vol. 4, R. NAZ, ed., Paris, Letouzey et Ané, 1949, 1528 col.

OGORZALY, S.J., "The Law in Psychological Inability Cases", in *The Jurist*, 30 (1970), pp. 103-106.

OLIVIERI, C. E., "A ignorância no matrimônio (c. 1096). Origem histórica, desenvolvimento doutrinal e jurisprudencial", in *Cuadernos doctorales*, 12 (1994), pp. 13-84.

OLMOS ORTEGA, M.E., "La definición del matrimonio y su objeto esencial: 1917-1960", in *El "consortium totius vitae": curso de derecho matrimonial y procesal canónico para profesionales del foro*, 7, Salamanca, Universidad pontificia de Salamanca, 1986, Bibliotheca salmanticensis Estudios, 83, pp. 11-35.

O'ROURKE, J.J., "Thoughts on Marriage", in *Studia canonica*, 22 (1988), pp. 187-191.

ÖRSY, L., "Matrimonial Consent in the New Code: *Glossae* on Canons 1057, 1095-1103, 1107", in *The Jurist*, 43 (1983), pp. 29-68.

-----, "General Norms: Canons 1-28", in *The Code of Canon Law: A Text and Commentary*, J.A. CORIDEN, T.J. GREEN, D.E. HEINTSCHEL, eds., commissioned by the Canon Law Society of America, New York, Paulist Press, 1985, pp. 23-45.

180

ÖRSY, L., "*Novus Habitus Mentis*: New Attitude of Mind", in *The Jurist*, 45 (1985), pp. 251-258.

-----, "The Meaning of *Novus Habitus Mentis*: The Search for New Horizons", in *The Jurist*, 48 (1988), pp. 429-447.

PALMER, P.F., "Christian Marriage: Contract or Covenant?", in *Theological Studies*, 33 (1972), pp. 617-665.

PANIZO, S., "Exclusión de la indisolubilidad del matrimonio", in *Ius canonicum*, 33 (1993), pp. 259-293.

PARISELLA, I., "L'ignoranza 'in re matrimoniali'", in *Il consenso matrimoniale canonico: dallo jus conditum allo jus condendum*, Studia et documenta iuris canonici, 13, Annali di dottrina e giurisprudenza canonica, 7, Roma, Officium Libri Catholici, 1988, pp. 11-26.

PARLATO, V., "Osservazioni sul significato del can. 1.082", in *Ius canonicum*, 12 (1972), pp. 333-342.

PELLEGRINO, P., "Il *bonum coniugum*: essenza e fine del matrimonio canonico", in *Il diritto ecclesiastico*, 107, 3-4 (1996) 1, pp. 804-835.

-----, "L'errore di diritto nel matrimonio canonico (cann. 1096 - 1099)", in *Il diritto ecclesiastico*, 108 (1997) 1, pp. 363-404.

PFNAUSCH, E.G., "Simulated Consent: A New Way of Looking at an Old Way of Thinking, Part II", in *The Jurist*, 55 (1995), pp. 721-739.

-----, "The Good of the Spouses in Rotal Jurisprudence: New Horizons", in *The Jurist*, 56 (1996), pp. 527-556.

POMPEDDA, M.F., "Il consenso matrimoniale", in Z. GROCHOLEWSKI, M.F. POMPEDDA, C. ZAGGIA, *Il matrimonio nel nuovo codice di diritto canonico: annotazioni di diritto sustanziale e processuale*, Padova, Libreria Gregoriana Editrice, 1984, pp. 25-138.

-----, "Maturità psichica e matrimonio nei canoni 1095, 1096", in *Apollinaris*, 57 (1984), pp. 131-150.

-----, "Incapacity to Assume the Essential Obligations of Marriage: Presentation I: General Overview and Exegesis of Key Terms", in *Incapacity for Marriage: Jurisprudence and Interpretation: Acts of the III Gregorian Colloquium, 1-6 September 1986*, R. SABLE, ed., Rome, Pontificia Universitas Gregoriana, 1987, pp. 157-178.

-----, "Incapacity to Assume the Essential Obligations of Marriage: Presentation II: Determining What Are Essential Obligations", in *Incapacity for Marriage: Jurisprudence and Interpretation: Acts of the III Gregorian Colloquium, 1-6 September 1986*, R. SABLE, ed., Rome, Pontificia Universitas Gregoriana, 1987, pp. 179-198.

-----, "Incapacity to Assume the Essential Obligations of Marriage: Presentation III: What Is Meant by the Term 'Incapacity'?", in *Incapacity for Marriage: Jurisprudence and Interpretation: Acts of the III Gregorian Colloquium, 1-6 September 1986*, R. SABLE, ed., Rome, Pontificia Universitas

181

Gregoriana, 1987, pp. 199-217.

POMPEDDA, M.F., "Fede e sacramento del matrimonio - mancanza di fede e consenso matrimoniale: aspetti giuridici", in *Studio rotale*, 2 (1987), pp. 41-71; English translation, "Faith and the Sacrament of Marriage - Lack of Faith and Matrimonial Consent: Juridic Aspects", by T. Doran, in *Marriage Studies: Reflections in Canon Law and Theology, IV*, J.A. ALESANDRO, ed., Washington, DC, Canon Law Society of America, Catholic University of America, 1990, pp. 33-65.

-----, "Jurisprudence as a Source of Law in the Canonical System of Marriage Legislation", K.E. Boccafola, trans, in *Marriage Studies: Reflections in Canon Law and Theology, IV*, J.A. ALESANDRO, ed., Washington, DC, Canon Law Society of America, Catholic University of America, 1990, pp. 105-131.

-----. "Il «bonum coniugum» nella dogmatica matrimoniale canonica", in *Quaderni studio rotale*, 10 (1999), pp. 5-21.

PRIEUR, M.R., "The Articulation of the Ends of Marriage in Roman Catholic Teaching: A Brief Commentary", in *Studia canonica*, 33 (1999), pp. 527-535.

PROVOST, J.H., "Canon 1095: Past, Present, Future", in *The Jurist*, 54 (1994), pp. 81-112.

-----, "Error as a Ground in Marriage Nullity Cases," in *CLSA Proceedings*, 57 (1995), pp. 306-324.

-----, "Simulated Consent: A New Way of Looking at an Old Way of Thinking, Part I", in *The Jurist*, 55 (1995), pp. 698-720.

-----. "Simulated Consent: A New Way of Looking at an Old Way of Thinking, Part III", in *The Jurist*, 55 (1995), pp. 740-744.

-----, "Canon 1095, 2° Seen from Its Sources", in *The Jurist*, 56 (1996), pp. 824-874.

PUNZI NICOLÓ, A.M., "Problematica attuale dell'errore e del dolo nel matrimonio canonico", in *Diritto, persona e vita sociale: scritti in memoria di Orio Giacchi*, vol. 1, Milano, Vita e Pensiero, 1984, pp. 538-558.

RAVÀ, A., "Il 'defectus discretionis iudicii' come causa di nullità del matrimonio nella giurisprudenza Rotale", in *Il diritto ecclesiastico*, 68, 3 (1957) 2, pp. 345-486.

READ, G.F., "Totius vitae consortium: The Implications for Jurisprudence", in *Studia canonica*, 20 (1986), pp. 123-146.

REGATILLO, E.F., "Ignorancia de la naturaleza del matrimonio", in *Sal terre*, 10 (1959), pp. 571-572.

ROBITAILLE, L.A., "Conditioned Consent: Natural Law and Human Positive Law", in *Studia canonica*, 26 (1992), pp. 75-110.

-----, "Proofs in Defect of the Will Cases: Jurisprudence regarding Positive Acts of the Will Contrary to

182

Marriage", in *CLSA Proceedings*, 57 (1995), pp. 337-354.

ROBITAILLE, L.A., "Simulation, Error Determining the Will, or Lack of Due Discretion? A Case Study", in *Studia canonica*, 29 (1995), pp. 397-432.

-----, "The Ground of Conditioned Consent", in *Forum*, 8 (1997) 1, pp. 95-127.

-----, "Consent, Culture and the Code ", in *Studia canonica*, 33 (1999), pp. 125-138.

-----, "Simulation and the *bonum coniugum*", Canon Law Society of Australia and New Zealand, *Proceedings of the Thirty Second Annual Convention*, September 21-25, 1998, pp. 15-23.

ROBLEDA, O., "Dissertationes et quaesita varia: "De conceptu actus iuridici", in *Periodica*, 51 (1962), pp. 413-446.

ROCHE, G.J., "Consent Is a Union of Wills: A Study of the Bilateral Dimension of Matrimonial Consent", in *Studia canonica*, 18 (1984), pp. 415-437.

SÁNCHEZ, I.M., "Causa, error y simulación en el matrimonio canónico", in *Studi in onore di Pietro Agostino d'Avack*, vol. 3, Pubblicazioni della Facultà di Giurisprudenza dell'Università di Roma, Milano, A. Giuffrè Editore, 1976, pp. 53-122.

SANSON, R.J., "Jurisprudence for Marriage: Based on Doctrine", in *Studia canonica*, 10 (1976), pp. 5-36.

SCHMIDT, K.W., "*Educatio prolis* and the Validity of Marriage", in *The Jurist*, 55 (1995), pp. 243-280.

-----, "The 'Raising of Children' as an Essential Element of Marriage", in *CLSA Proceedings*, 59 (1997), pp. 223-266.

SCHUMACHER, W.A., "The Importance of Interpersonal Relations in Marriage", in *Studia canonica*, 10 (1976), pp. 75-112.

SERRANO RUIZ, J.M., "Sobre el conocimiento que se requiere para la validez del matrimonio (can. 1082)", in *Angelicum*, 50 (1973), pp. 357-375.

-----, "La consideración existencial del matrimonio en las Causas canónicas de nulidad por incapacidad psíquica", in *Angelicum*, 68 (1991), pp. 33-63, 173-230.

-----, "Acerca del caracter personal del matrimonio: digresiones y retornos", in *A Swing of the Pendulum: Canon Law in Modern Society*, Monsignor W. Onclin Chair, Leuven, Katholieke Universiteit, Uitgeveru Peeters, 1996, pp. 19-31.

-----, "The Personal Character of Marriage, a Swing of the Pendulum", in *A Swing of the Pendulum: Canon Law in Modern Society*, Monsignor W. Onclin Chair, Leuven, Katholieke Universiteit, Uitgeveru Peeters, 1996, pp. 33-45.

183

SERRANO RUIZ, J.M., "The End of Distinctions and Analogies: Towards a Greater Autonomy of Language and Concepts in Matrimonial Canon Law", in *A Swing of the Pendulum: Canon Law in Modern Society*, Monsignor W. Onclin Chair Addendum, Leuven, Katholieke Universiteit, Uitgeveru Peeters, 1996, pp. 5-12.

-----, "Let Us Talk about Incapacity", in *A Swing of the Pendulum: Canon Law in Modern Society*, Monsignor W. Onclin Chair Addendum, Leuven, Katholieke Universiteit, Uitgeveru Peeters, 1996, pp. 13-19.

-----, "What about that Famous 'Positive' Act of the Will?", in *A Swing of the Pendulum: Canon Law in Modern Society*, Monsignor W. Onclin Chair Addendum, Leuven, Katholieke Universiteit, Uitgeveru Peeters, 1996, pp. 21-30.

-----, "Can a Personal Vision of Marriage Be Supported by the Notions of Ignorance, Error, Deceit, Condition ...Such as They Are Given in cc. 1096ff.?", in *A Swing of the Pendulum: Canon Law in Modern Society*, Monsignor W. Onclin Chair Addendum, Leuven, Katholieke Universiteit, Uitgeveru Peeters, 1996, pp. 31-37.

-----, "Diferencias entre incapacidad y exclusión (cc. 1095-1101) en las causas de nulidad de matrimonio", in *A Swing of the Pendulum: Canon Law in Modern Society*, Monsignor W. Onclin Chair Addendum, Leuven, Katholieke Universiteit, Uitgeveru Peeters, 1996, pp. 39-49.

SHERBA, J.M., "Canon 1096: Ignorance as a Ground for Nullity", in *CLSA Proceedings*, 59 (1997), pp. 282-299.

SOBRINO VILA, B., "Esquizofrenia y nulidad del matrimonio", in *Excerpta e dissertationibus in iure canonico*, 1 (1983), Facultas Iuris Canonici, Universitas Studiorum Navarrensis, Pamplona, Ediciones Universidad de Navarra, 1983, pp. 219-274.

SPINELLI, L., "Intorno all'"error in qualitate personae" quale capo di nullità del vincolo matrimoniale", in *Quaderni studio rotale*, 8 (1994), pp. 85-92.

STANKIEWICZ, A., "De causa iuridica foederis matrimonialis", in *Periodica*, 73 (1984), pp. 203-234.

-----, "L'errore di diritto nel consenso matrimoniale e la sua autonomia giuridica", in *Periodica*, 83 (1994), pp. 635-668.

-----, "De iurisprudentia rotali recentiore circa simulationem totalem et partialem (cc. 1101, §2 CIC; 824, §2 CCEO)", in *Monitor ecclesiasticus*, 122 (1997), pp. 189-234, 425-512.

-----, "Concretizzazione del fatto simulatorio nel «positivus voluntatis actus»", in *Quaderni studio rotale*, 9 (1998), pp. 34-51.

SUMNER, P.T., "*Dolus* as a Ground for Nullity of Marriage", in *Studia canonica*, 14 (1980), pp. 171-194.

TEJERO, E., "La ignorancia y el error sobre la identidad del matrimonio", in *Ius canonicum*, 35 (1995), pp. 13-101.

TESTERA, F., "The Nature of Christian Marriage", in *Philippiniana sacra*, 21 (1986), pp. 54-83.

THOMAS, M., "The Consortium Vitae Coniugalis", in *The Jurist*, 38 (1978), pp. 171-179.

VADAKUMCHERRY, J., "Marriage Laws in the *Code of Canon Law* and the *Code of Canons of the Eastern Churches*", in *Studia canonica*, 26 (1992), pp. 437-460.

VAN DER POEL, C.J., "Influences of an 'Annulment Mentality'", in *The Jurist*, 40 (1980), pp. 384-399.

VIGLINO, C., "Oggetto e fine primario del matrimonio" in *Diritto ecclesiastico italiano*, 35 (1929), pp. 142-149.

VILADRICH, P.J., "Marriage and the Matrimonial System of the Church: Reflections on the Mission of Matrimonial Canon Law in Contemporary Society", in *Marriage Studies: Reflections in Canon Law and Theology, IV*, J.A. ALESANDRO, ed., Washington, DC, Canon Law Society of America, Catholic University of America, 1990, pp. 132-157.

VILLEGGIANTE, S., "Errore e voluntà simulatoria nel consenso matrimoniale in diritto canonico", in *Monitor ecclesiasticus*, 109 (1984), pp. 487-516.

-----, "L'amore coniugale e il consenso matrimoniale canonico", in *Ephemerides iuris canonici*, 46 (1990), pp. 87-109.

-----, "L'esclusione del 'bonum sacramenti'", in *Monitor ecclesiasticus*, 115 (1990), pp. 349-385.

-----, "Il 'bonum coniugum' e l'oggetto del consenso matrimoniale in diritto canonico", in *Monitor ecclesiasticus*, 120 (1995), pp. 289-323.

WALF, K., "La fidélité conjugale: droit canonique et traditions", in *Revue de droit canonique*, 44 (1994), pp. 35-46.

ZUSY, J.B., "Matrimonial Consent and Immaturity", in *Studia canonica*, 15 (1981), pp. 199-239.

ABSTRACT

Before Vatican II, marriage was often considered, or at least popularly expressed, as a union of bodies; that is to say, marriage was an exclusive contract by which a man and a woman mutually handed over their bodies for the purpose of acts which led to the procreation of children. Matrimonial jurisprudence was primarily focused on this marital contract. With the advent of Vatican II and its emphasis on the personalist notion of marriage, a new age dawned whereby canonists, especially auditors of the Roman Rota, were henceforth to view marriage as a union of persons. "Person" is more than a "body"; rather, a person is an individual consisting of wants, needs, desires, impulses, hopes and dreams, whose life experience has been shaped by the milieu — cultural, familial, religious — from which he or she comes. "Union" is not only simply understood as a "contract", but also is now once again recognized as a "covenant", a concept which, at least in the Latin Church, was prevalent until the 12th century.

One of the canons of the 1983 *CIC*, although almost identical in wording to its predecessor in the 1917 *CIC*, but which now must be understood and interpreted in light of the teachings of Vatican II, is canon 1096 which pertains to the effect of ignorance on matrimonial consent. Given the current appreciation of marriage founded in the teachings of Vatican II, especially in *Gaudium et spes*, reiterated by Popes Paul VI and John Paul II and described in the *Catechism of the Catholic Church*, complicated by today's western society's stress on individualism and permeated by a divorce mentality, what is the impact of this canon on matrimonial consent? How can its meaning, once understood as being wider than merely the sexual act itself, be better utilized by those in tribunal ministry? This is the major thrust of the present work.

The research of the history and development of the concept of ignorance in canonical writings, how its understanding broadened especially after Vatican II and our conclusions on how to apply its richness to marriage nullity led us to expand the use of this canon: how it can aid in the development of pre-marital preparation programs which would not only possibly help prevent couples from being ignorant of the essence of marriage but also help them to appreciate this richness more deeply in their own lives so that marriage truly can become, as we read in canon 1055, "a partnership of the whole of life which is ordered by its nature to the good of the spouses and the procreation and education of offspring". It is our sincere hope that this study, with its extensive footnotes and up-to-date bibliography will not only be of benefit to all who read it but also will serve as a spring board for further discussion and use of this canon as a ground for nullity and other pastoral uses.

186

Girard Michael Sherba was born 6 June 1952. He received an AB in education from Marywood College (now University), Scranton, Pennsylvania, in 1974. He received a MDiv from Saint Meinrad School of Theology in 1979 and was ordained a priest for the Diocese of Raleigh, North Carolina, on 9 March 1979. He received his JCL from Saint Thomas University (the Angelicum), Rome, in 1987. He has had various pastoral assignments in the Diocese of Raleigh since ordination. Currently he is the Rector of Sacred Heart Cathedral, Vicar Judicial and Vice Chancellor for the Diocese of Raleigh.

Printed in the United States
1843